WEARING THE ROBE

THE ART AND RESPONSIBILITIES OF JUDGING IN TODAY'S COURTS

Paul,
We have a cherished
profession!
Jim Gray

JUDGE JAMES P. GRAY

SQUAREONE
PUBLISHERS

EDITOR: Helene Ciaravino
COVER DESIGNER: Jeannie Tudor
TYPESETTER: Gary A. Rosenberg

Square One Publishers
115 Herricks Road
Garden City Park, NY 11040
(516) 535–2010 • (877) 900–BOOK
www.squareonepublishers.com

Library of Congress Cataloging-in-Publication Data

Gray, James P., 1945–
  Wearing the robe : the art and responsibilities of judging in today's courts :
a guide to the principles and practices of being a judge / By James P. Gray.
      p. cm.
  Includes index.
  ISBN 978-0-7570-0242-7
  1. Judges—United States. 2. Judicial process—United States. I. Title.
  KF8775.G73 2008
  347.73'14—dc22
                        2008012504

Copyright © 2009 by James P. Gray

Printed in the United States of America

10   9   8   7   6   5   4   3   2   1

Contents

*Dedicated with love
to my wonderful wife
Grace Walker Gray.*

Preface

The best decision I have ever made was in choosing my parents. I was blessed to be raised by a supportive and loving mother and father, and I had a stable environment in which to grow up and progress. During my childhood my father was an attorney who had his own law firm in Los Angeles. And while I was in law school and an attorney, he was a judge of the United States District Court for the Central District of California.

I passed the bar in 1971. During my time as an attorney I appeared in numbers of different types of jurisdictions and practiced in criminal, civil, and military courts. At the end of 1983 I was appointed to the bench in Orange County, California, by Governor George Deukmejian. Since that time I have presided over many different judicial calendars and have had occasion to learn from a wide range of different attorneys, judges, and legal seminars. As such, I have been in a position throughout my lifetime to observe and learn from many legal professionals.

But one thing I have not been able to do is to read a book about judging and what it is like to be a judge. So I have taken the opportunity to write this one and to share with you what I have learned about judging in numbers of different circumstances. In doing this I offer you the knowledge I have gained on how to be an effective and artful judge. The job of a judge is difficult and a lot more complicated, diversified, and filled with potential pitfalls than most people think. But it can be done, and done effectively.

Writing this book has also provided me with an opportunity to convey a bit of my own judicial philosophy and to make some suggestions for specific improvements to our great System of Justice. The goal of these recommendations is to make the justice system even more fair, less time consuming, less costly, and more available to all. Over the years, I have seen some things that are not being done well and must, in my view, be changed. So in some way I hope that these pages will help to bring about constructive changes both in judicial approaches and in judicial and non-judicial attitudes.

I acknowledge that the book is longer than I anticipated it would be, but there really is a lot of ground to cover. So if you really do not want to read anything about, for example, traffic calendars, civil cases, or court administration, you have my complete "permission" to skip those sections and go on to trial tips, settlement skills, and judicial ethics. Nevertheless, one way or the other, after concentrating on whatever pages interest you the most, I believe you will be quite a bit more appreciative of the positive contributions of the Judicial Branch of Government to our lives. In fact, once you are exposed to what it is like to be a judge, it would not surprise me if many of you who are not already judges will seek to be blessed enough, like I have been, to become one.

Before proceeding further I must give a disclaimer that as a judge I am prohibited from practicing law. As such, it is not my intent to give any legal advice in any fashion in these pages. Instead, I simply intend to raise issues and stimulate a discussion. In addition, laws and ethical standards can be different in each jurisdiction, of course. So if you have a specific judicial concern, you must research the issues, laws, and ethical standards with reference to your own location.

Whatever judicial wisdom and insights I have learned I gladly pass along to you. No matter if you are a new or more experienced judge, an attorney or other person who might some day like to become a judge, or a member of the general public who would like to learn more about the Third Branch of Government, we all have a vested interest in enforcing our laws in a reasonable, responsible, fair, and equitable manner. And one way or the other, every one of us can achieve a large amount of gratification by learning about and joining in our own way the noble pursuit of "Justice for All."

There can be no peace
in a land without justice

Introduction

"Injustice anywhere is a threat to justice everywhere."[1]
—DR. MARTIN LUTHER KING, JR.

Judges are in the service business. And like other businesspeople, judges have clients—the parties involved in courtroom cases and, to a lesser extent, the attorneys who represent those parties. From the start, these clients present challenges. First, most of them are under considerable stress when they come through the courtroom doors. Judges must be those "quieter voices" that create an atmosphere of clarity and fairness. Second, the number of clients and cases that judges deal with each day is frequently large. So judges must maintain focused energy and responsible calm throughout the day. Yet because judges are service-oriented, they must embrace and effectively meet these challenges. After all, it is a judge's responsibility to resolve cases as best as possible under the facts and the applicable law, and to leave those involved with two well-founded beliefs: that they had a fair hearing, and that they have received justice. Another way of saying this is that justice is a process as well as a result.

Judges are the ultimate generalists. Disputes and the laws applied to resolving them are amazingly varied, but judges are called upon to address each situation knowledgeably, effectively, and promptly. Of course, it is simply not possible for any judge to know all of the law, to be familiar with the inner workings of all segments of society, or even to be able to make the "right" decision immediately every time. But someone must address and attempt to resolve various failed relationships and problems among human beings, corporations, institutions, political bodies, etc., and no one is in a better position to do that than a well-trained, ethical, and dedicated judge.

There are additional challenges to being a judge. Consider that judges really do live in fishbowls. Their finances and personal lives, and those of their spouses, are subject to public disclosure and scrutiny. A judge's effectiveness and even career can be directly, publicly, and permanently threatened by actions and reactions for which others might never be so harshly scrutinized: a loss of patience, much less a display of temper; a misdeed in one's public or personal life; an inappropriate or off-color remark; overuse of alcohol or, worse yet, an illicit substance; or a transgression of just one of the many ethical obligations.

Nevertheless, even though the impact and importance of judges' decisions continue to increase, in some ways judges are decreasingly appreciated. While the decisions judges are called upon to make are getting more complicated and more highly litigated, resources continue to decrease for an expanding population, and judicial positions are becoming ever more politicized. As a result, judges are on the "line of scrimmage" in addressing disputes in our society—and just like in a game of football, the line of scrimmage can be a vicious place. So when litigants emerge from our courts with what they see as an unfavorable outcome, the judge is the most convenient target for their bitterness and wrath. Threats to the physical safety of judges and their families—and occasions in which these threats are actually carried out—are alarmingly on the rise, in spite of increasing efforts to protect judges and their staffs, as well as the litigants and their counsel.

So it seems a legitimate question to ask, "Why would someone want to be a judge?" In my view, the short answer to the question is that it can be an immensely gratifying and interesting job. In fact, I remember a few years ago waking up on a Saturday morning and thinking to myself, "Oh, nuts, I don't get to go to work today." Then I smiled and figured that I could somehow make it through the weekend. But I knew then—and I know now—that being a judge is a great and important opportunity. In fact, for most of my time as a judge I have kept a hand-printed sign on my bench that reads, "There Can Be No Peace in a Land without Justice." This serves to remind me that every decision I make is important to someone, and that it can contribute to or detract from the reservoir of good will that people have for their government. Therefore, every decision should be made with as much care, concern, and wisdom as I am able to offer.

As Chief Justice John Roberts once confided to a friend, judging is "much harder than I thought it would be. The questions are much harder and closer than I thought."[2] Yes, the job can be difficult, but the gratification of being a judge can be enormous. To quote a hackneyed phrase, you really can "make a difference" in almost countless ways to many people throughout the spectrum of life. As a judge you are in a position visibly to eschew mediocrity and pursue excellence in yourself and in others. You can help to mentor our nation's children and many other people in need. You can use your wisdom and experience in helping to determine what is—and what is not—a just result under the facts and the law. You can speak for society in holding people rightly accountable for their actions, but you can also be understanding, patient, and helpful to people at times when they are most vulnerable. You can be an artist and apply the law not only fairly but also with passion and compassion. In other words, you can be a person who helps to bring justice to our land, and thereby you will be a force for peace in the world. It is hard to ask for more than that.

What is it like to be a judge? What do judges actually do? What are the benefits and the drawbacks? How does one obtain the position? *Wearing the Robe* will answer these questions. Part I of this book will provide the background you need to understand more deeply the processes of the judicial world: how our independent judiciary developed and is continuing to evolve in order to make proceedings fairer, more understandable, and less costly; how various courts are organized and administered; how trials are managed; and what settlement strategies are effective. To say that there is a broad lack of understanding in our country about the makeup and functions of our courts would be misleading because, for the most part, there is no understanding at all. Therefore, Part I includes a comprehensive discussion of judicial "calendars" or assignments. When many people think of our courts, they think only of criminal trials and criminal sentencing. However, there are many other types of calendars or assignments, including Civil, Juvenile, Family, Probate, Mental Health, and Adoptions. And there are many subdivisions thereunder. So Part I offers a wealth of information about these judicial roles, and it also gives me an opportunity to offer my professional advice and opinions about them along the way.

Part II provides a study of the benefits and drawbacks of being a judge and the necessary steps in making that career move if you decide to try to do so. It also tackles judicial ethics and even gives numbers of pointers on how to handle the basic difficulties that come along with the position. There is a chapter that studies the acknowledged responsibilities, winning attributes, and productive professional habits of effective judges so that you can learn what makes the best judges *be* the best judges. Part II also addresses such challenging subjects as how judges can use their free time optimally to contribute to the betterment of the community, and how judges should deal with the media. Therefore, it not only teaches you how to become a judge, but also how to be an *effective* judge! Finally, the Conclusion details my own visions for improvements in the judicial system.

Throughout the book you will find my own "pearls of wisdom" that I have gathered after serving as a judge for many years. The audience for whom I intend these helpful hints is varied. I believe *Wearing the Robe* will be valuable to those who are considering becoming a judge and those who are new judges just "learning the ropes." It will help the reader to focus more fully upon what the profession is, what the public expects of us, and how we judges can live up to their expectations and trust by carrying out our obligations more effectively. Yet *Wearing the Robe* is also appropriate for veteran judges, because the book exposes them to some different approaches. One of the problems with the job is that judges are mostly sheltered from the opportunity to see how someone else acts upon the bench. I hope these pages will help to break down that barrier, at least to some degree.

This book is further intended to assist attorneys in understanding and appreciating what judges do, or at least what they should be doing, for two separate and distinct reasons.[3] First, maybe it will spur their interest in someday becoming a judge. Second, although it sounds counterintuitive, one really must learn to be a judge before one can learn to be an effective trial attorney. It is the goal of attorneys either to persuade judges (if the attorneys are in litigation for their clients) or to predict how judges will rule (if the attorneys are advising their clients about what actions to take in certain situations). The best way both can be done is to understand how judges go about making decisions.[4] And finally, *Wearing the Robe* will be equally helpful for those who simply would like to learn more about the judicial system itself.

After reading *Wearing the Robe,* I believe that you—as a judge, future judge, attorney, or general member of society—will be even more impressed with our judicial system and understand more fully how it functions and has progressed. So thank you for joining me in this study of the Third Branch of Government, because this branch affects society just as much as the other two branches—the Legislative and Executive Branches. As George Washington once said, "The administration of justice is the firmest pillar of Government,"[5] and I welcome you in learning about it, discussing it, and participating in it.

PART I

Getting to Know a Judge's World

From Our Founding Fathers to Our Current Court Systems

We are about to begin a journey through many facets of our great System of Justice. Over the next couple of chapters, *Wearing the Robe* will walk you through a number of the options and responsibilities presented in the life of a judge. Part I studies the various calendars in which you will have the opportunity to be involved, and it will help you to identify the calendars that may best match your personality, talents, and interests. It will also provide tips and insights about how to preside over each of these calendars more creatively and effectively. In addition, this part of the book explores the different stages of the trial and settlement processes, while offering pertinent advice on how creatively and effectively to manage them as well.

As we start our journey, it is important to keep an open mind. Perhaps you have always pictured yourself sitting on high-profile criminal cases. But are you prepared for the steady diet of psychological stress that they can trigger? Did you instead ever consider shaping much of the public's perspective of the judiciary by serving as a Small Claims Court judge? Or maybe you might discover that your personal calling involves presiding over probate issues that are splintering families. Of course, you might also gravitate toward directly enhancing your fellow citizens' family lives on an Adoptions Court calendar. These are just a few of the possibilities that will be presented to you as you read through Part I. But first let us start with a firm foundation—the history of the judiciary. That way, we can all gain a larger appreciation for the wheres and whys behind how our System of Justice developed.

Chapter 1

The History and Continuing Evolution of Our Judicial System

*"No freeman shall be taken, or imprisoned, or outlawed,
or exiled, or in any way harmed, nor will we go upon
him nor will we send upon him, except by the legal
judgment of his peers or by the law of the land."*

—FROM THE *MAGNA CARTA*, CLAUSE 39

If you think about it, there are many ways to make decisions and resolve disputes other than to take them to courts of law as we know them. Throughout the history of the world, many, if not most, critically important disputes were resolved unilaterally by individual people such as monarchs, chieftains, or family patriarchs. Disputes have also been decided by wars, gunfights, brawls, duels, and other forms of violence; by chance, such as by a flip of a coin, the drawing of lots, the cutting of cards, or the roll of the dice; or by hiring a surrogate so that whoever's knights or thugs or "boys from the ranch" joust or fight successfully against their opponents win the dispute.

Yet leaving the settlement of disputes up to the leader, luck, or local hero of the day has resulted in many disputes' being resolved in an extremely arbitrary manner. At least those approaches provided the benefit of deciding the issues quickly, decisively, and in most cases finally. Still, it is hard to argue that "justice for all" was served very often.

Our system of dispute-resolution—which applies neutral judicial rules and procedures that are administered by impartial and independent judges and juries—has taken a long time to develop. But as a direct result of this development, the Rule of Law has become the foundation of the modern social order and has materially lessened the rule of force and despotic whim.[1]

9

HISTORIC BENCHMARKS BUILD A FRAMEWORK

In order truly to appreciate our present judicial system, it is important to look at some of the historical steps that led up to its existence. The seeds of our system date back to the early Hebrews, the ancient Romans, and the Medieval British. And from those heritages the modern concept of judge, jury, and the fair and impartial administration of justice emerged.

The Early Hebrew References to Judges

A judge is commonly defined today as a public administrator, elected or appointed, who has the authority to decide the outcome of cases in a court of law. But the earliest uses of the term were not necessarily parallel to today's accepted definition. One of the first mentions of "judges" in history is in the *Book of Judges* in the Hebrew Scriptures, which are also referred to as the Old Testament of the Christian Bible. The judges referenced in that book were not the ones we think of today. They were instead the governing leaders of the Israelites at the beginning of the Iron Age. For those who are history buffs, that would be after Joshua and before the time of the Kings, around 1200 to 1000 BCE. These judges were revered by the Israelites as direct servants of God, and it was their task to deliver the Israelites to the Promised Land.

In contrast with our concept of what a judge is today, the Hebrew judges were as much military leaders as they were judicial authorities. Hebrew scriptures explain that the Israelites were not having any particular success in defending themselves against attackers. But every once in a while, God would extend help by sending a special figure—a judge—to lead the people and increase their chances of being triumphant over their enemies. Unfortunately, the judges' words and ways were not always heeded, and after a judge's death, the people usually went back to the former ways that were ineffective. Although this role of the judge is not exactly parallel to modern notions, the idea of a judge as a wise instructor certainly carries through. The position of judge therefore began as one of considerable respect.

The Roman Roots of Our Judicial System

The concept of judge is not the only aspect of the legal world that slowly developed over time. What we today refer to as an *independent judiciary* has also evolved over many centuries. This concept has come to mean that we can count upon the fact that judicial decisions are made by judges who have no vested interest in the outcome, except to do what is right and appropriate under the facts and the law of the cases. Of course, their judgments must also be grounded in common sense. But the benefits of an independent judiciary are enormous.

As a result, we can trust that people will be held accountable for their actions, and that our contracts will be enforced regardless of which judge is making the decision or which political party may be in power at the time. Among other things, that figuratively means that we will have to prepare and keep only one set of books. And not only will we not have to make any "under the table" payments to influence the outcome of a dispute, but we can also be assured that our opponent will not be doing so either.

There have been countless general *observations* about the principles of justice throughout history. For example, the Code of Hammurabi in Babylonia in 1760 BCE set forth a list of crimes and their various punishments, as well as guidelines for appropriate conduct of its citizens and settlements of common disputes. Another significant historical event regarding the principles of justice was the balanced constitution instituted by Solon in Ancient Athens, around 600 BCE. It included provisions for social equality, economic opportunity, and a citizen jury system to protect some of the rights of its citizens. But the strongest roots of our independent judiciary are found in Ancient Rome.

It was the Romans who were the first to *codify* practical principles of jurisprudence. They did so through the *Twelve Tables of Roman Law,* which were meant to apply to both the upper and the lower classes—also referred to as patricians and plebeians, respectively—and were unveiled to the people of the Roman Republic in about 451 BCE. The *Twelve Tables* covered all areas of the law, actually differentiated between intentional and accidental crimes, and even provided for different degrees of murder and assault. Even though they were intentionally drafted in ambiguous language so that the patrician judges could interpret them in a manner that best served their interests, the *Twelve Tables* are widely considered to be the beginning of codified law for the Western world. As a result of the *Twelve Tables,* courts were established and trial jurors for civil disputes were selected from the middle class as well as the upper class. In addition, appeals were allowed to be taken from the local court systems to the Roman Assembly, the latter of which was a legislative group of elected plebeians.

By the time of Hadrian's rule in the second century CE, the Roman Empire had become extremely large. Therefore, numbers of court jurisdictions were established in different geographical areas around Europe. In addition, specific procedures for appeals were set forth, and judges were authorized to publish their opinions.

In another major development, the *Perpetual Edict* was written by Roman jurist Salvius Julianus. It was codified into laws that set forth regulations for legal procedures, property rights, and commerce. Among other things, these laws required sellers of goods to disclose hidden defects and also imposed liability for the intentional destruction of the property of another.

By the time of the rule of Justinian in the middle of the sixth century CE, the Roman laws had been scattered into numbers of diverse manuscripts and scrolls throughout the Empire. So in one of Western Civilization's most pivotal deeds, Justinian had all of these laws brought together into a three-volume document, issued from 529 to 534 CE, that came to be known as *Corpus Juris Civilis.* This work enabled the laws and traditions of the Roman Empire to be preserved for centuries in many areas of the Western World. The impact of this preservation was most significant when William the Conqueror triumphed over England in 1066, because he and his sons subsequently imposed a new court system that was based upon Roman Law as set forth in surviving copies of the *Corpus Juris Civilis*.[2] For more on England's hand in shaping American justice, see the next section.

As a result, most of our basic legal doctrines have their roots buried deeply in Roman Law, including most of our laws that govern wills, successions, contracts, easements, liens, mortgages, adverse possession, evidence, and judgments. In addition, today's concepts of "every man's home is his castle," the right of ownership of physical objects, the legal concept of a corporation, and our fundamental doctrine of *habeas corpus* (which prevents people from being deprived of their liberty without the due process of law) have been inherited from ancient Roman law.

The British Background of Our Judicial System

As mentioned above, William the Conqueror and his familial successors worked to revise England's court system. But England in the Middle Ages was still a far cry from having the same system of justice that is present today in the United States. For example, it was not at all uncommon for the king or queen to lock judges or jurors up in the Tower of London until they agreed to return with a decision on a case that was more to the monarch's liking. But this situation changed radically when the barons of Medieval England forced King John to sign the *Magna Carta* on the fields of Runnymeade, near Windsor Castle, in the year 1215. This "Great Charter" was the first formal modern restriction upon the ability of monarchs to impose their authoritarian will upon their subjects. Moreover, a trial by a jury of one's peers in criminal matters was guaranteed for the first time in modern history. These limitations on absolute royal power were confirmed by King Edward I in 1297, when he signed a translation of the *Magna Carta*.

The protections provided by the *Magna Carta* against arbitrary executive rule—including the right to a trial by jury, "equal protection under the law," "due process of law," "law of the land," the doctrine of being a "free man," and many other fundamental concepts—were all brought over to the American colonies from England by the early settlers. The settlers relied upon these concepts when establishing American "common law." In fact, the *Magna Carta* not only served as a basis for the United States Constitution and many state constitutions, but it also served as one of the foundations for our Revolution. You might recall from history class that the Stamp Act and similar legislation shifted the jurisdiction of the failure to pay the taxes to the Admiralty Courts, where the defendants were tried without a jury. The colonists argued that the rights of "no taxation without representation" and the right of trial by a jury of one's peers were guaranteed by the *Magna Carta*.

The pivotal points of history discussed above show that America's judicial system inherited numbers of features from past cultures. The Founding Fathers of the United States of America had a wealth of judicial history to look back upon and study, and they had the intelligence and insight to pick and choose the elements of judicial history that would work for a new democracy that prioritized the power of "We the People." And all of these were merged into the glories of the Constitution of the United States of America.

AMERICA CUSTOMIZES ITS OWN SYSTEM OF JUSTICE

Our nation is known for its rugged independence and success in its entrepreneurship. But it is equally known for the liberties it guarantees its people. As previously mentioned, the United States cannot claim to have started from scratch when shaping its judicial system, but it *can* claim to have sculpted a unique and respected system that has thereafter been admired, emulated, and imitated. Not only does the United States Constitution provide for a critical system of checks and balances in the exercise of governmental power, but it also promotes the concept of *federalism*, which basically provides that the most local government that has the ability to address and control a particular course of conduct is the government that has jurisdiction to do so. In addition, and most famously, it includes a specified list of rights that the government will not transgress. In effect, the United States Constitution is the culmination of all of the pivotal legal treatises and doctrines in the Western World. So it is rightly seen as the most important product of the Enlightenment, if not the most important document ever written by the hand of Mankind.

The Judiciary as an Equal Partner

In 1789, during the early days of an independent America, Article 3 of the United States Constitution put into place the formal framework of our independent judicial system. According to Alexander Hamilton in *Federalist Papers No. 78*, this was the best way to guarantee "a steady, upright, and impartial administration of the laws," and to safeguard against "injury of the private rights of particular classes of citizens, by unjust and partial laws." But through the *Marbury v. Madison* case, discussed below, that judicial power was brilliantly tempered and restricted by a system of checks and balances among our three branches of government: Judicial, Legislative, and Executive. Yes the judges in our court system can have a great deal of power in making decisions that affect us all, but judges are restrained in exercising that power in numbers of different ways.

To begin with, judges in our country can decide only matters that are brought to them by others, which is to say that judges cannot stake out an agenda and bring in selected cases so that they can carry out that agenda. Further, judges can decide only what is known as an actual "case or controversy," which means that judges are not authorized to give advisory opinions about things that have not yet happened, or to rule on disputes that have not yet arisen. Judges also have no "power of the purse," so they must rely upon the Legislative Branch of Government for funding. Additionally, judges do not have a police force or army to enforce their decisions. So, as a practical matter, judges must stay within the realm of reason or they will have no way of getting their orders and judgments enforced. And judges either must be appointed by the Executive Department or run for (re)election, which requires them, to some degree, to be aware of the practical world around them and to keep these limitations in mind.

Another protection for litigants is the doctrine of Stare Decisis, which encourages past legal decisions or legal precedents to be followed as much as possible. That provides more foreseeability in the law so the people can govern their conduct and their business transactions accordingly. But the implementation of all of these doctrines can be threatened if judges are not trained in the law. That is why most jurisdictions have legal requirements that must be satisfied in order for a person to become a judge. For a comment on a related issue, see the inset "Are Non-Judges Doing the Judging?" below.

Establishing the *framework* for an independent judiciary in our young country was one thing, but it was another for the judiciary to be shaped into the role of an equal *partner* as one of three branches of the federal government. Basically, that status was defined by the Great Chief Justice John Marshall in the case of *Marbury v. Madison* in 1803. In that case, Marshall established the doctrine of judicial review by the courts over the laws of the United States. That doctrine author-

ARE NON-JUDGES DOING THE JUDGING?

It is true that throughout history our states and territories have empowered some people who did not have legal training to serve as judges—and not all of these people were out in the Wild West. In fact, some states like New York and Arizona still have non-legally-trained Justices of the Peace who simply have to be elected in order to obtain the office. Unfortunately, some of them have been quoted as saying alarming things such as, "I just follow my own common sense; the hell with the law," and "Every woman needs a good pounding every now and then." Commonsense justice is fine, but it is easy to understand that decisions are best rendered when based upon the law. In that way, there is less risk that someone's personal views and/or prejudices will become the prime factor in a court decision.

izes judges to verify that the laws are within the holdings of the United States Constitution, which is, of course, the supreme law of the land.

The genius of our system was well placed into context by my friend Judge Andrew J. Guilford of the U.S. District Court for the Central District of California. He aptly said:

> The greatest achievement of the last millennium was the precocious experiment in democracy resulting in our Constitution, finally ratified in 1789. The Constitution has been an extraordinary success because it balances powers among three branches. The most important branch is the one most responsible for enforcing the balance of powers: The Judicial Branch. Thus, American judges serve the most important institution in the greatest achievement of humanity over the last thousand years. In the process, judges punish our criminals, resolve our disputes, and protect our rights. The job should indeed be taken seriously.
>
> But, just as the balance of powers is important, so judges should act responsibly with the powers they are given. Judges can best act responsibly if they are humble in pursuing their duties, and this occurs by not taking themselves too seriously.

Yet even to this day many people in our country, including many legislators, do not understand that the judiciary is a separate and independent branch of our government. As an example, consider a quote from Chief Justice Ronald M. George of the California Supreme Court: "Sometimes, out of frustration, I have to proclaim we are not like the Department of Fish and Game or the Board of Cosmetology; we are a separate co-equal branch of government."[3] This makes one wonder if there is something fundamentally wrong with a county agency having the power to decide on such things as the size of the court staff, or the Sheriff's Office having administrative control of the court's bailiffs. I believe that control over the court's personnel should be with the courts.

The Two Systems of the Courts

While the judiciary in the United States is one branch of the government, it involves two principal systems of courts. These are the federal and the state systems. Each one will be discussed below, as will smaller, additional court systems that have been formed over the years for various purposes.

The federal court system has jurisdiction to try disputes involving federal issues, conflicts between or among the various states, and matters among citizens of different states in which the amount at issue exceeds $75,000. The trial court level in federal courts is the United States District Courts. Each state is guaranteed to have at least one judicial district, and most states have more. For example, California has four districts. This trial level includes Magistrate Judges, Bankruptcy Judges, and District Judges. The Magistrates mostly try misdemeanors and oversee various preliminary matters; the Bankruptcy Judges obviously handle bankruptcy cases; and the District Judges supervise the Magistrate and Bankruptcy Courts as well as handle the trials of everything else.

Appeals from the United States District Courts, with only a few exceptions, go to one of eleven United States Circuit Courts, plus one for the District of Columbia and one for the Federal Circuit. The Federal Circuit Court handles appeals for customs and patents and appeals from the United States Court of Claims, which is a special court that adjudicates claims against the United States Government. Appeals from the United States Circuit Courts go to the United States Supreme Court, but the Supreme Court for the most part is able to choose which cases it wishes to hear and decide. Of course, legal appeals must end somewhere, and the United States Supreme Court is the final arbiter of the interpretation of the laws of our country. Justice Robert H. Jackson of the U.S. Supreme Court recognized that fact when he stated, "We are not unaware that we are not final because we are infallible; we know that we are infallible only because we are final."[4] For a chuckle on the "supremacy" of federal judges, see the inset "What Do You Call a Group of Federal Judges?" below.

Now let us cover the state level. All of our fifty states and the District of Columbia have their own judicial system, although the D.C. courts have federal judges and staff. The titles of the various courts often vary, but each state uses the same basic type of system: trial courts, appellate courts, and a supreme court. Cases in the state courts that involve federal constitutional issues can often be appealed to the federal system. Chapters 2 through 5 will go more fully into the breakdown of the various court calendars.

There are also numbers of other courts in our country, such as courts for military justice, workers' compensation courts, immigration courts, and tax courts. Moreover, there are numbers of administrative courts, such as those for departments of motor vehicles, Social Security, the Occupational Safety and Health Administration (OSHA), and the enforcement of ethical standards of behavior in our professions. Most of these administrative courts are much less formal in their

WHAT DO YOU CALL A GROUP OF FEDERAL JUDGES?

As a true sidelight of the legal fact that federal law is often supreme to state laws, many federal judges request a certain title when it comes to their gatherings. They would have us believe that, just as when a group of the same species congregates and is given a particular term—like a "gaggle" of geese or a "pride" of lions—when they gather in a group they should be known as a "supremacy" of federal judges. To me, though, it is more like a gaggle.

procedures and in the taking of evidence than the state and federal judicial systems, but under many circumstances the litigants may appeal the administrative decisions to judicial courts.

In addition, in today's world there are an increasing number of civil contracts that provide for disputes among the parties to be heard exclusively by private professional judges, with only restricted rights of appeal from the arbitrator's decisions to either the state or federal judicial systems. Those who can afford the expense can get a private retired judge or other experienced litigator to help resolve cases by either mediation or binding arbitration. *Mediation* is the effort to settle the case by negotiation. *Binding arbitration* is actually a condensed trial that is tried to one or more legal professionals who then will make a decision that can be taken to the court system to become an enforceable judgment without virtually any appeal from the decision.

Why do people pay extra money to obtain the services of a private professional judge? This approach results in a more expeditious and speedy resolution of a dispute, and hearing dates that can almost always be counted upon. These systems are increasingly being utilized by the "rich and famous" in order to get their cases heard promptly and out of the public hearing so that they can avoid public scrutiny.[5]

To be honest, and notwithstanding my own libertarian principles, I feel embarrassed that the industry of private judging continues to grow. I believe that all people in our country should be confident and able to come to the *public* courts to receive a full, fair, and prompt adjudication of their disputes. But it appears that private judging is here to stay, and I guess that my working ever harder on my cases is not likely to change that reality.

It is amazing to think about the way our judicial system has developed into an independent branch of the government that holds equal weight when compared with the Legislative and Executive Branches. The noble desires of our Founding Fathers become evident when we grasp how very diligent they were in ensuring our system of checks and balances. This in and of itself should make those who partake in the judiciary's work quite proud. It is also heartening to see how our judicial system has organized itself into a rather consistent, accessible pathway to justice at both the federal and the state levels. But the work continues, as described in the next section on the continuing evolution of the Third Branch of Government.

THE JUDICIAL SYSTEM CONTINUES TO EVOLVE

As transportation, business and commerce, education, technology, medicine, travel, and many other fields continue to evolve, so too must the judicial system. The following paragraphs comment on some of the changes that have been made and that are currently being implemented. These changes are done not only so that all people and entities in our country may have access to justice, but also so that they may understand and be appreciative of that fact.

A Steady Increase in Litigation

People in our country have always tended to bring their disputes, real or imagined, to court. But overall the types of cases being submitted to our nation's courts continue to rise in number. This increase in litigation ratifies Alexis de Tocqueville's observations in the early 1800s that "There is hardly a political question in the United States which does not sooner or later turn into a judicial one."[6]

The swelling numbers of court cases can only partially be explained by the increase in our population and by the increasing complexity of our lives. A further reason for the increase in litigation is that two of the institutions that historically have resolved disputes in our society, namely the family and our religious organizations, have been breaking down, which often leaves the courts as the only effective institution that remains for dispute resolution.

Yet another reason for the increase in litigation is that our courts have, over the years, continually agreed to expand their jurisdiction to oversee and address more types of issues. In that regard, courts have accepted and decided appeals from decisions by school boards, administrative agencies, religious groups, athletic conferences, and other organizations whose cases they previously did not adjudicate. And courts in our country have also agreed to hear and resolve disputes that have been generated on the high seas—even those that occurred long ago in other countries, such as theft claims against the Nazis in Germany in the 1930s and 1940s, and similar claims against people like Ferdinand Marcos in the Republic of the Philippines and Salvador Allende in Chile.

Further Tangible Changes in the Judicial System

We continue to see further substantial changes in our country's courts. For example, in small claims cases in which litigants must represent themselves and where the rules of evidence barely apply, some states have raised the jurisdictional limit to allow plaintiffs to be awarded up to $7,500. This would have been unthinkable even ten years ago.

There are large numbers of other examples of fairly recent changes in the judicial system, and it is helpful to mention just a few. Since the *Gideon v. Wainwright* case in 1963, the U.S. Supreme Court has ordered that defendants in criminal trials be provided with an attorney to represent them if they do not have the financial ability to obtain one on their own. The case of *Miranda v. Arizona* is yet another sign of judicial evolution. That 1966 case decided that police are required to warn criminal suspects who are under arrest that they are not required to talk to the police and that they are entitled to have an attorney present during the questioning if they wish. Consider, as a final example, that the prosecutors now pretty much are required to "open their files" to the defense attorneys and provide them with statements of witnesses and all other materials that might tend to reflect upon the defendant's guilt *or* innocence. That was not always the case, and the concept did not really gain impetus until the decision in *Brady v. Maryland* was handed down in 1963.

The Promotion of "Access to Justice"

Issues of justice for all are seen as so critical that now virtually all of the courts in our land are promoting programs under a movement called "Access to Justice." In many ways throughout the history of the world, justice has been looked upon as a benefit mainly for the rich. Obviously it has always been true that the wealthy could afford better legal representation, and it probably always will be so. But most courts are genuinely trying to make their services more available and more "user friendly" to everyone. Some of the innovations in this pursuit are discussed below.

Promulgation of Information to All Cultures

Programs are increasingly being implemented throughout our country's courts to provide information about how our judicial system works. The intention is to reach people in culturally appropriate ways and in numbers of different languages, and also to provide legal information in simple, clear terms, frequently using the help of volunteers from local law schools. The purpose of these efforts is to connect better with our constituencies, and thereby to reduce to zero the number of people who are abused, ignored, marginalized, or alienated by the court system.

These programs are being created in various ways, the most prevalent of which are as follows: establishing informational clinics and workshops in courthouses and community centers; broadcasting bimonthly informational radio programs in different languages; creating programs like American Indian Storytelling about the courts; setting up computer kiosks in courthouses and elsewhere to answer questions in numbers of different languages about how to prepare and file legal forms, serve legal documents, prepare for court appearances, locate court facilities, present a case, and even find parking; and collaborating with various community boards and non-profit mediation agencies to offer dispute-resolution services, with a special emphasis upon small claims. In addition, there is a movement to set up Self-Help Centers for "Self-Represented Litigants" at each courthouse in the nation. These centers are to be staffed by paralegals and attorneys who will provide information and assistance for small claims, domestic violence situations, landlord/tenant issues, family law and guardianship matters, and much more. The programs are based upon the understanding that "procedural fairness"—having a sense that court decisions are made through processes that are fair—is the strongest predictor or public approval and confidence in our courts.

Elimination of Bias in the Courts

Naturally people will not have faith in the judicial system or the judicial process itself if they feel that it is overseen by other people who are biased against their race, gender, natural origin, religion, language, disability, or other identifying factor. Therefore, our nation's courts are increasingly focusing upon the elimination of bias in their entire operations. They are also attempting to make this fact known to their communities, so that literally everyone may meaningfully turn to the courts to have their rights vindicated.

This is being accomplished in many ways. One way involves outreach programs through which judges speak to chambers of commerce, religious groups, service clubs, and similar organizations that mostly comprise minority groups. Another involves making judges available for interviews on minority group radio and television shows or through other minority media venues. An increasing number of jurisdictions have also made political decisions that the diversity of the state's residents will be reflected in the appointment of judges.

Publication of "How To" Manuals

Since the cost for professional legal representation continues to increase, more litigants are being forced to represent themselves. As a result, many courts are attempting to assist these litigants by publishing step-by-step procedural manuals in the areas of small claims, name changes, landlord/tenant relations, guardianships, restraining orders, family law, and traffic matters for the Self-Represented Litigant at both the trial and the appellate levels. These manuals are also being used by legal secretaries and attorneys who are not familiar with appellate practices as a guide for their appeals, so that they can avoid procedural mistakes that can be fatal to their lawsuits. Additional how-to manuals address issues of gender fairness, people with disabilities, childcare, and sexual orientation fairness.[7]

Information on Courts as Curriculum

Some educational programs have been adopted that enable large numbers of high school students to observe real legal appeals in action, with contemporary explanations about the process from legal experts. Not only do students come away from the experience with a greater understanding of and appreciation for our legal system, but they also better comprehend the "concept of complexity." Knowledge of that concept will carry over to their voting practices and general understanding of the way life happens.

Education of Teachers

Many high school seniors around the country are now required to take a class in government and learn about the scope and operation of their state courts. Unfortunately, many of their teachers are not formally educated about these subjects.

So programs to educate teachers have been established. These programs not only provide instruction to teachers, but they also often provide a CD or DVD of materials that the teachers can take back with them to their classrooms to help them teach their students about the justice system.

Guardianship Facilitation and Outreach Programs

These programs attempt to de-mystify the child guardianship process. They also try to locate and provide information to people like grandparents and other potential caregivers who could become guardians of children who might otherwise be removed from their families. The value of programs like these can be enormous, since if they contribute in even a small way to enabling a family unit to remain intact, that will probably influence the people of that family for generations to come.

Protection of Elders

With the increase of the elderly population comes an increase in their physical, emotional, and financial abuse. Often these abuses are not easily detectable. Courts aim to be in the forefront of that detection and protection by instituting educational programs for law enforcement agencies and the public in general, as well as by providing assistance about and prosecution of elder abuse. More on efforts to stop elder abuse can be found in Chapter 4, beginning on page 107.

Modernization of the Courts

Many courts are using new technology to manage the heavy workloads that they continue to face. This modernization includes the equipping of the courts and the public in general with automated records management. It also involves the standardization and easier filing of legal forms, which in many cases are available online. Finally, it promotes availability of legal information, status of different cases, and even pleadings in individual case files through court websites (except for unduly sensitive cases like in the Juvenile or Mental Health Courts).

In addition, more courts around the nation are adding Evidence Presentation Technologies to their courtrooms, so that evidence may be presented electronically to the courts and juries during trials. And they are expanding the use of telephone and video conferencing capabilities, so that counsel may appear electronically for trial setting conferences and Law and Motion matters. Yet the changes do not stop there. The courts are also attempting to make all filing fees for civil cases uniform throughout their respective states, allow the payment of traffic citations to be made online, put their jury instructions into "plain English," and streamline appellate rules. Finally, jurors are increasingly able to pick the dates for their service, or at least obtain deferrals, by use of the Internet. All of this is being done in an attempt to make our courts and the judicial system more "user friendly."

Reduction of Confusion and Intrusion for Jurors

More and more jurisdictions are allowing jurors to be "on call" for duty, instead of waiting at the courthouses to be called. As mentioned above, many are able to select their time of service on the Internet. In addition, many jurisdictions have changed their programs so that if jurors are not put on a jury panel after one day, they are excused from further service for a year.

Establishment of Night Courts

Understanding that it is often more than inconvenient for people to take time off work during the day to appear in court, many more night courts are being implemented for traffic, small claims, and child support calendars. Unfortunately night courts are expensive because they require the courts to be open for extended hours, which means increased costs for staffing, security, maintenance, and utilities. But realizing how helpful this can be to the litigants, most courts are really extending themselves to keep this service available.

Creation of "Day on the Bench" Programs for Legislators

Many courts have established "Day on the Bench" programs. These give legislators a chance to spend a day at a court in their district. The goal is to provide the legislators with a better understanding about the challenges faced by the Judicial Branch.

Development of Court Resource and Complaints Departments

Without giving legal advice, many courts have established Information Desks in their lobbies. At these desks, people can find answers to "Where do I go?" and "How do I?" questions. In addition, the staffs at the desks are instructed on how to handle complaints and refer them to the appropriate official. These programs to provide practical and procedural advice are seen as having a key part in the "Access to Justice" efforts.

Formation of New Judge Orientation Programs

Educational programs are increasingly providing newly appointed or elected judges with "nitty-gritty" information they will need to make the transition more effectively from being an attorney to being a judicial officer. Realizing that judges are the ultimate generalists, that most of them will be called upon to serve in areas in which they have little background, and that they will often be confronted with delicate and emotional situations, most courts are expending serious efforts to train judges in the art and responsibilities of judging. This is accomplished both through traditional lecture and classroom instruction as well as online.

The great energy, intelligence, and number of resources being put into the continuing positive evolution of our judicial system is quite extraordinary. In fact, it could be deemed unprecedented. And the fact that the judicial system is so dynamic and committed to serving the population as a whole better is a direct testament to its strength and dedication.

CONCLUSION

I believe most people will agree with me that formulating a just set of laws and making them available to all people are the ultimate of human endeavors—more important than bridges and more important than computers. Unlike us, many other countries of the world do not have the tradition of an independent judiciary to fall back upon in addressing and balancing security against civil liberty interests. In this way, the former Soviet Union and other countries with similar authoritarian governments were not unlike Medieval England, where *dependent* judges simply did the bidding of the authoritarians. But fortunately within the recent past many of these countries have experienced their own revolutions and have begun to follow our example, putting them on a track toward a more democratic form of government with an independent judiciary. This is an exciting and gratifying development, and most of these countries have looked to our institutions and our balanced form of government as the models to which they aspire.

Yet we must understand that there is nothing that will ensure the perpetuation of even our own cherished form of government, so brilliantly created and installed for us by our Founding Fathers, except our own continued vigilance. That vigilance starts with the recognition of and education about our system of justice. I hope this book will help, in its own way, to ignite or at least retain some of that vigilance.

From what I have seen, virtually without exception my fellow judicial officers realize the important contributions we are called upon to make in a free, equal, and competitive society, and they undertake their duties with a reverence. Probably only some of them are aware of the roots of our system of an independent judiciary that upholds the law and protects the rights of all people no matter who they are or where they come from. But I believe that whether they are aware of the derivations of our great system of justice or not, all of our country's judges should be proud of the role that they play in bringing peace to our land by promoting justice. Of course, we must continue to be diligent in our efforts to improve and refine our judicial system. But we do have a right to be proud of what we are doing, and I believe the rest of our nation should be proud of us as well.

Chapter 2

The Criminal Court System

"Crime is violation of people and relationships. It creates obligations to make things right. Justice involves the victim, the offender, and the community in a search for solutions which promote repair, reconciliation, and reassurance."[1]

—HOWARD ZEHR

The purpose of the criminal justice system is straightforward: to reduce crime and all of the harm and misery that accompanies it. In my view, this can best be accomplished by enforcing the following mandate: there must be negative consequences for criminal acts. And the more promptly those consequences are imposed, the more effective they will be. Of course, we also want to keep in mind the timeless wisdom of Benjamin Franklin, as published in *Poor Richard's Almanac*: "Laws too gentle are seldom obeyed; too severe, seldom executed."[2]

But in this regard, we must also keep in mind that one of the best ways of reducing crime and its accompanying misery is to assist the offenders to grapple with their problems and to help them to find the tools to overcome them. As a result, the enforcement of the mandate set forth above can be complicated and even sometimes subtle. In reality, the criminal laws use a combination of the threat of punishment, punishment itself, and the threat of additional punishment in trying to deter people from crime. But in most cases I believe the laws can best be met by also using the concept of *Restorative Justice* in addition to the deterrence of punishment. As we will see, this includes rehabilitation for the offenders, restitution by the offenders to the victims of their offenses, and community healing. Restorative Justice will be discussed more completely in the Conclusion of this book, when I make recommendations about improvements in our System of Justice. But we will begin to explore the concept in this chapter.

Criminal Court cases are those brought by governmental prosecutorial agencies against individuals and other entities such as partnerships and various types of corporations. If convicted beyond a reasonable doubt by a judge or a jury, a defendant can be punished by imprisonment and/or a fine. The federal courts are designed to address more complicated or sophisticated interstate criminal acts, while the state courts are intended to address the much larger volume of the more local and "everyday" street crimes.

When most people think of a court system, they usually think of criminal trials and criminal sentencing. But just as most attorneys in our country never actually appear in court at all, most judicial calendars (or judicial assignments) are not in the area of criminal cases. And even the calendars that *are* Criminal Court assignments are often broken up into many specialized sections.

In larger jurisdictions, state Criminal calendars are usually divided into three areas: *felonies,* which are crimes punishable by being placed in state prison for more than a year; *misdemeanors,* which are crimes punishable by up to a year in a local jail; and *infractions,* which are crimes punishable only by the imposition of a fine. These Criminal Court calendars are some of the most vibrant and technical areas in the field of judicial service. After all, matters governing criminal searches, detentions, arrests, admissibility of statements and other evidence, as well as sentencing have become quite complex. Keeping up on the changing law is almost a full-time job in and of itself.

In addition to the above-mentioned calendars, many jurisdictions include so-called *Specialty calendars,* such as Traffic Court, which deals with infractions regarding the use of a vehicle. Another example of a Specialty calendar is Drug Court, in which judges and their staffs utilize drug testing, counseling, health awareness, employment training, and anger management classes to monitor and guide drug users. There are additional Specialty calendars as well. If you are curious about how often a judge's judicial calendar typically changes, see the inset "How Often Do Judicial Calendars Change?" on page 27.

The type of calendar to which a Criminal Court judge is assigned is one piece of the story. Then there are several more matters that Criminal Court judges handle, such as arrest warrants and search warrants. Before an *arrest* warrant can be issued, a sworn police officer must file an affidavit or sworn declaration with the court. This document must set forth sufficient facts to find probable cause that a particular offense has been committed, and that the named subject is the one who committed it. Before a *search* warrant can be issued, judges must receive a similar document that swears that a specific offense has been committed and that there is probable cause to believe that evidence that would identify the offenders or lead to their conviction would *at that time* be found in a specified location. "Probable cause" means that it is more likely than not that this will be the result.

Most Criminal Court judges also contend with bail issues. One of the critical protections that is overseen by the judiciary is the principle that people should

How Often Do Judicial Calendars Change?

In a majority of the large urban areas judges are most often assigned to a particular "judicial calendar," such as misdemeanor arraignments, felony trials, or unlimited civil trials, just to offer a few examples. Those judicial assignments can be rotated whenever the Presiding Judge wishes, but that usually is not more often than every six months, and it most commonly occurs once a year. So judges in a large urban area could be assigned to a Family Law Court panel for one year and then rotated to a Small Claims Court assignment. With that rotation, they would be changing their "judicial calendars."

In smaller or more rural state courts most judges handle whatever comes through the door, which can be highly varied. Similarly, in most federal courts judges handle whatever cases come through the door, which can be civil, criminal, patents, anti-trust, and the list goes on.

not be punished for an offense before they are actually convicted. These issues frequently arise in decisions involving the posting of bail pending trial. Basically, only two questions are relevant on issues of bail: Will the defendants make all of their appearances in court throughout the trial process, and will the defendants be a threat to society if they are released pending that trial?

Therefore, in addressing the issues of bail, it is important to determine what ties a defendant has to the community. If a criminal defendant has a steady job, a spouse at home and children in school, owns a home, has no prior failures to appear in court, and is a citizen of this country, the odds are good that the defendant will appear at trial. But that does not end the inquiry. Obviously, the nature of the alleged offense is important in determining bail as well. The odds are far greater that a person will flee the jurisdiction before trial if he is charged with a serious offense that could result in being imprisoned for thirty years than if he is charged with an offense that could result in only ninety days in jail and a $1,000 fine. Also, the existence of a criminal record of prior *convictions* is relevant. In my view, it is not appropriate even to consider charges for which there was no conviction. Other issues are considered as well with regard to bail: the presence or absence of any prior failures to appear in court; the presence or absence of violence in the charged offense; the amount of danger posed by the subject to the community; and whether the defendant has made any threats upon the life or safety of any witnesses or anyone else.

It quickly becomes evident how many significant issues Criminal Court judges manage. This chapter will take a close look at Felony, Misdemeanor, and Specialty Court calendars so you can gain a solid understanding of judicial assignments in the Criminal Court system. For each type of calendar, I offer tech-

nical information and then my own tips for effectively presiding over that particular calendar. Toward the end of the chapter, I have a detailed section on the
process of criminal sentencing, which offers further general information on the
challenges of being a judge on a criminal assignment.

FELONY COURTS

As defined on page 26, felonies are crimes that are severe enough to be punishable by a state prison sentence of more than a year. The heavy-duty felony cases
usually are handled by highly experienced and skilled attorneys, which is a professional treat for the judges sitting on such trials. Still, you would not want to
go into a felony calendar unless you are prepared to see some of the truly tragic
and often senseless things that happen somewhat routinely in many of our communities.

The Basics of Felony Calendars

As a fact of life, many judges who were former prosecutors want to be assigned
to a Felony calendar and never leave. Similarly, judges who do not have a background in felony trials frequently try to avoid them. But the laws and rules of
evidence are the same for felonies as they are for any other criminal trials, and in
many ways the felony cases are not as complicated as the misdemeanors or even
the infractions. For example, it is much harder to determine if a defendant
intended to sell half of an ounce of marijuana than it is to determine if a defendant intended to sell half of a ton of marijuana. In addition, in most murders
the fact that there was a crime can be fairly straightforward, but sometimes
whether an alleged simple assault was actually committed can be more difficult
to determine.

Like anything else, some felony trials can be interesting and unique, and
some can be run-of-the-mill and tedious. Occasionally some of them can be sensational and grab headlines, but so can misdemeanors, depending upon who the
defendant is or what the circumstances happen to be. Most felony trials involve
assaults and batteries that result in some form of severe injury to the victim;
thefts, criminal mischief or criminal frauds that result in a loss of an amount of
money greater than a statutory minimum; or various statutory violations, such
as elections violations, pollution of the environment, securities transactions, or
almost countless other things.

The novelty and complexity of certain felony cases can be amazing. Some of
these felony offenses can result in untold damage to individuals or society in
general (see the inset "Gang Culture Increasingly Infests the Criminal Court System" on page 29 for an applicable comment), and some of them cause us to wonder why the action under discussion is considered an offense at all. But in the
end, judges must deal with all of them.

GANG CULTURE INCREASINGLY INFESTS THE CRIMINAL COURT SYSTEM

Most sociologists would agree with me that the volume of criminal cases generally goes up and down over time. But the number of really serious, if not gruesome, cases seems to be increasing. Unfortunately, the amount of callousness demonstrated in the committing of these crimes is also increasing. In fact, many of the cases that really leave me scratching my head involve gangs. The lowering of the value of human life can be appalling. In some gang cultures, young people shoot and kill other "rival" gang members as a part of initiation requirements. Other murders are perpetrated simply as a reaction to some sort of "disrespect"—or, better said, a lack of the showing of fear—real or imagined, that one gang member receives from another. As a result of the large numbers of crimes and the wantonness of the behavior, many city police departments have formed specialized units to monitor and keep track of the gang activities within their communities. It is common for judges to feel deeply discouraged by what they see and hear in matters of this kind.

Here is an almost incredible example of the depth of the problems we are facing. I once heard about a fourteen-year-old gang member who was shot in the leg. Unfortunately in today's gang culture that is not a particularly unusual occurrence. But what got my attention was that this youngster was completely shocked and surprised that it *hurt* to get shot in the leg. The fact that this missile tearing through his flesh could cause pain was totally outside his experience level. Yet if you think about it from his perspective, how many video games had he played in which people or alien beings were killed? How many movies or television shows had he watched in which killing was common but did not appear painful? So this is what we are increasingly facing in the criminal justice system—cases involving people who have no respect for or understanding of life or the infliction of pain.

Advice for the Felony Court Judge

From the information given on page 28 on Felony calendars, it is clear that this type of judicial service can be both intellectually fascinating and emotionally draining, and the cases can be both intriguing and horrifying. One thing is for sure: a Felony Court judge has the power to put people in prison for a long time. Maybe this will make America's streets safer, or maybe it will not. But the following are some suggestions on how to handle the stressful yet gratifying job of being a judge on a Felony calendar.

Keep an Emotional Distance

The pathos of some criminal cases can be so consuming that I want to pass along to you a story I often tell attorneys who specialize in this type of litigation. There was a criminal defense attorney whose client was close to being indicted for a number of felony charges. The attorney did everything she could to keep that from occurring, but eventually the indictment came down. So the attorney planned her trial strategy and continued to work tirelessly for her client. Soon enough the matter went to trial, where again the attorney did everything she could within the standards of ethics to defend her client. But the jury found the defendant guilty, and the judge sentenced him to prison. The same attorney represented her client on appeal and worked diligently to get the guilty verdict reversed, all to no avail.

Finally, the attorney was standing in court as her client was just about to be taken into custody, when the client asked her, "Well, what do we do now?"

The attorney replied, "Well, you're going to jail, and I'm going to dinner."

Retelling this story is my way of saying that professionals in the Felony Court system simply cannot allow themselves to get too close to the matters upon which they work. The attorneys and the judge did not create the facts, and they are not the responsible parties. Therefore, although they always should do everything they reasonably can to work for the right result within the ethics of the profession, they also must keep their distance and realize that the ultimate responsibility belongs to the parties who committed the offenses. Professionals who serve the Criminal Courts cannot allow their own personal health and lives to suffer.

Deal "Judiciously" with Motions to Suppress Evidence

Something else that often comes up on Felony (and other criminal) calendars are motions to suppress evidence due to alleged violations of statutes, procedures, or the state or federal constitutions by one or more law enforcement officers. Critically, in this area as in all others, it should not make any difference whether judges agree with the laws governing police behavior or not. It is the judges' job to decide what the facts of the case are and then apply the laws as best as they can with the appropriate standard of proof. They must decide the matter regardless of what the possible political implications may be.

Of course, many such motions to suppress are filed by defense attorneys even though they know they have virtually no chance of success. Their professional responsibility and reputation simply require them to be diligent in the defense of their clients. But sometimes the law governing a situation can go either way, and frequently the situation can be complicated by disputed issues of fact. Once again, in these cases judges must remember the burden of proof gives assistance in these issues. (For more on the "burden of proof" issue, see the inset "Should We Add Another Form of Verdict?" on page 31.) So judges must listen

SHOULD WE ADD ANOTHER FORM OF VERDICT?

To accent the importance of the fact that defendants themselves are not required to prove anything at trial, i.e., that the burden of proof is on the prosecutors, I believe that we would be well served to copy the forms of verdicts used today in Great Britain. In addition to the verdicts of "guilty" or "not guilty" that can be entered by a judge or a jury, Great Britain's judicial system also has a verdict that concludes that the charge is "not proved." Many defendants have been found "*probably* to have done the criminal deed," but that is not enough to convict a defendant under criminal justice systems in either Great Britain or the United States. The finder of fact must be convinced by the evidence *beyond a doubt based upon reason* before a guilty verdict can be returned. The additional form of verdict already used in Great Britain would reinforce that protection to ensure the jury is utilizing the proper burden of proof.

to and consider all of the evidence before making a ruling. Therefore, on those infrequent occasions in which the law enforcement officer might appear to be mistaken, wrong, or even not telling the truth, it is the absolute responsibility of the judicial officers to rule based upon the evidence, regardless of where the political chips may fall. This comes with the job. It is critically important that the integrity of the judicial system be upheld, and that the judicial officers honestly "call 'em as they see 'em."

Find a Little Humor When Possible

Although Criminal Court assignments obviously deal with serious matters, sometimes humorous things come up. It is okay to recognize and enjoy the humor, as long as it is not overdone and does not interfere with the important business at hand. For example, I often express wonder at a defense attorney's request to continue or postpone a trial so that she can prepare a motion to dismiss the case for the lack of a speedy trial.

As another example of humor, I present you with the following comments from a defendant in an actual criminal proceeding:

The Court: I have a letter in the file purportedly signed by you stating why you missed your court date. Is this your letter, and is this your signature?

Defendant: Yes, Your Honor.

The Court: The letter says you missed your last court date because your aunt was in the hospital dying of prostate cancer.

Defendant: That's right, Judge, and she's still in there, too.

The Court: Sir, your aunt does not have a prostate.

Defendant: Wow! I'll bet she'll be glad to hear that!

Every judge has stories about certain defendants who have done things that are actually unintentionally quite funny. For example, once as a prosecutor I was confronted with a bank robber who had used a written note saying he had a gun and demanding cash from the teller. But he happened to have used his own bank deposit slip as his stationery, and that slip had his name and address printed on the other side. In that case, the FBI agents actually got to his house before he did and arrested him as soon as he arrived home with the stolen money.

There was another time in which a judge was arraigning a criminal defendant by explaining the charges against him, advising him of his rights, and taking his plea of either guilty or not guilty. But when the judge asked the defendant if he wanted a good attorney, the defendant honestly responded, "Actually, your Honor, what I really need is a good witness."

Admittedly, these types of excuses make the judges chuckle. And that is okay. Given the heavy type of work felony judges do, a few laughs are truly necessary and healthy.

Believe in the Power of Your Words

I have frequently tried to talk to defendants in criminal cases, tell them what a waste of time it is for them to be in jail, and encourage them to get into constructive programs or to get their education. Another strong recommendation I give is for them to stay away from people who use drugs, because if they hang around people who use them, the odds are overwhelming that these defendants will return to using them again as well. Some attorneys and judges believe talking with defendants is a naïve approach. And it is true that my own estimate is that probably 50 percent of the defendants are not really listening to me even while I am talking to them. About 30 percent will probably have forgotten all about my advice by the time they leave the courthouse. But of the remaining 20 percent, maybe half will actually take the thoughts to heart and change their attitudes. If that is actually true, those few minutes of talk constitute time well spent. So I continue this practice at every "teachable moment" chance I get, and I recommend the same approach to you.

In that regard, I remember an occasion in which a middle-aged female defendant had already been convicted of negligent homicide. She was testifying in my court about her ability to make restitution to the estate of the deceased over a period of time. At the end of her testimony, I remember being impressed with her candor and remorse. Therefore I mentioned to her that, by the very nature of the offense of which she had been convicted, I knew it had been an accident, and I said that I was sorry that this had happened to her. Several months later I received a note from the woman, which read as follows: "Thank you for your kindness and understanding. Your words to me when I was on the witness stand meant a great deal to me. This has been a very difficult fourteen months, trying to deal with this accident." The woman had done something wrong that resulted in the death of another person and in the terrible grief of the family that was left behind. But we should remember that these matters can also be tragedies for some of the defendants as well, and some occasional expressions of honest sympathy can be helpful and appropriate.

Do Not Showcase Your Toughness

Unfortunately, for some judges criminal sentencing can be an exercise in showing off their "toughness." For example, there was once a federal court judge in Los Angeles who was known as "Maximum Mathis," because he almost always gave criminal defendants the maximum sentence. In fact, a story is attributed to him that one day he sentenced a relatively aged man to the maximum thirty years in prison for a particular offense. The man responded, "Your Honor, I am now 64 years old. There is no way that I can serve such a long sentence." Judge Mathis was heard to reply, "Well, just do the best you can."

Obviously, sometimes a maximum sentence is appropriate. But the sentence should be imposed on merit—or demerit, if you prefer. Judges should not use the occasion to show off their machismo, or even their insecurities.

To emphasize a similar point further: when I was a federal prosecutor I was leaving the courthouse for lunch one day when a judge who was widely known for his harsh sentences was standing next to me. While we were waiting for a traffic light to change, I greeted him and asked him how his day was going. He surprised me by saying, "Well, Jim, Mondays are always hard for me because I have to sentence people, and it hurts." I responded to him by saying: "Well, Your Honor, I believe it is supposed to hurt, and when it stops hurting you should be in a different job." He looked at me in surprise, but I stand by that comment. Without a doubt it is sometimes appropriate to remove some offenders from society for a long time, but it should hurt to do so. If judges do not feel any pain in doing so, my view is that they should be on a different calendar.

Look Beyond the Obvious

Many of the decisions that judges in Criminal Courts are called upon to make can actually be deceptively difficult, and even counterintuitive. For example, disagreements can arise between criminal defendants and their attorneys. These can be a result of ethical dilemmas, such as the desire of the defendant to call witnesses to the stand who the attorney is convinced will present perjured testimony. Or they can be the result of tactical decisions, such as whether or not to plead guilty to one or more of the lesser offenses. (A guilty plea might be suggested so that the jury will not hear some of the facts of the case that might prejudice them against the defendant on the more severe charges.) The defense attorney has the ethical duty not to violate the professional code of ethics, so she must call the shots in the ethically challenging situations. But it is the defendant's case and the defendant's life, so the defendant should have the ultimate decision-making power on the tactical decisions—unless they involve ethical violations. Active disagreements can occur, and on some occasions they have actually given rise to the defendant's simply hitting the defense attorney in open court in an attempt to show the court that the defendant and attorney have "irreconcilable differences." With that finding, the defendant would be allowed to be appointed a new attorney.

The natural response to this situation would ostensibly be for the judge to agree and to appoint new counsel. But it is the judge's duty to look beyond the apparent and consider the entire picture. If she were to appoint a new attorney in such a situation, it would quickly become "open season" on appointed defense attorneys. Literally every time a defendant wanted a different attorney, all that person would have to do would be to assault the present one. As a result, judges have uniformly held that assaults are not sufficient to cause the appointment of new counsel. Effective judges always try to look beyond the obvious to the eventual result and impact of their decisions.

Be Vigilant Concerning Warrants

As previously touched upon, judges in Criminal calendars must also be very careful about their involvement in arrest warrants and search warrants. In reviewing requests for warrants, judges must make it a strict policy not to base their decisions upon any oral discussions with the police officers. Only the sworn information that is "within the four corners of the declaration" can be considered when deciding upon the issue of probable cause, both for the reviewing judicial magistrate and for the reviewing trial and appellate court judges. For purposes of the warrant, if it is not written in the declaration the information does not exist.

But there is nothing wrong with the magistrate's asking the peace officers questions or asking them to add to their declarations if they have the answers. There is also nothing wrong with a peace officer's taking a declaration back and adding to it when he discovers additional information. No one gains by playing games; if there is not probable cause for the warrant to be issued, it should not be issued. But if the information is there, judges should not play "hide the ball" by refusing the warrant and making the officers guess as to what is lacking.

As an example, I presided over a situation in which a peace officer requested a warrant to put a tracking device upon the automobile of a criminal suspect. The police ostensibly had probable cause to do this, but the declaration said that the suspect had already been arrested. So as far as the declaration was concerned, the subject of the warrant was still in custody. Had I signed the warrant, it probably would have been reversed, because it would not have been appropriate—on those facts—to have put the device on the subject's car while in custody. The device would then have been tracking other people who might have been driving the car even though there was no probable cause stated against them. When I expressed my concerns, the officer said that the subject had actually posted bail and was back out on the streets. With that, I allowed the officer to augment the declaration with those additional facts. And after the officer initialed the changes, I signed the warrant.

Before I leave the subject of warrants, I will also pass along a recommendation that an experienced judge made to me long ago. He instructed that a judge should always have the peace officer number the pages of the declaration seeking the warrant, and then the judge should put her initials upon each page that she reviews. Following this procedure will enable anyone working on the case in the future to know exactly what was and was not presented to and considered by the magistrate. This protocol works to everyone's advantage. Consider a situation in which a judge's decision is reversed on appeal. I know I would much prefer to be reversed on appeal for what I actually did than for what someone thinks I might have done. My initials on each page would confirm that I thoroughly did my job when the declaration was handed to me. Initialing each page also helps the court to avoid confusion and keeps to a minimum the subsequent temptations for someone to add to or subtract from what was presented to the judge on the date that the warrant was signed. These small matters can get critically important at times. It is not unheard of for judges to get publicly castigated for something that simply looked like it happened but actually did not. In this matter, like in many others, a little care in your procedures will protect you from an unjust and sometimes cruel fate, and it will allow the right decisions to be made.

Consider the Right Issues When Deciding upon Bail

This chapter's introduction briefly introduced issues involving bail. The Felony calendar judge deals with this matter quite often. Every judge lives in fear of releasing a defendant on bail and then having that defendant harm someone before trial. Of course, that problem could be negated by *never* setting a low bail. Yet not only would that be a violation of the Eighth Amendment guarantee against excessive bail, but it would also be an abrogation of the judge's responsibility. And, of course, it would further seriously overcrowd our nation's jails.

Judges are called upon every day to make decisions on bail, sometimes in the presence of a cry from the prosecutors, law enforcement officials, and even the general public that the person must be punished *now* for the alleged violations. But judges must be prepared to stand up and do what is right under our laws, regardless of the public sentiment. That means that judges should consider only the two factors discussed earlier: Will the defendants show up for all court appearances, and will the defendants be a threat to society if they are released from custody pending that trial? It is fundamental to our System of Justice that a defendant not be punished before she is convicted of an offense.

Provide Civilian Clothing for In-Custody Defendants in Trial

In most jurisdictions it is considered unduly prejudicial for in-custody defendants to be seen by the jury in jail attire during their trial. So consider gathering some acceptable trousers, shirts, blouses, skirts, and jackets at the courthouse for those defendants to wear. Obviously, they must be continuously searched and monitored for contraband of all sorts. But on many occasions this will save you lots of time that will otherwise be spent waiting for the arrival of proper clothing.

Consider Counseling for Jurors

Increasingly it is becoming apparent that really horrendous cases can adversely affect the psychological well being of jurors. So consider setting up a counseling program funded by the court for jurors *after the case is completely over.* In my view, we owe this to them.

Felony assignments are probably the most glorified that judges have, because the cases are generally what the media covers and what the movies depict. In many ways they deserve the attention, because this is where the heavy-duty, serious cases are tried. But as you will see, Felony Court is not particularly where the most important criminal judging takes place. When it comes down to it, what difference does it make in the long run if a burglar gets three, five, or seven years in prison? The judging that affects more people's lives is done in the Misdemeanor Courts, and that is where we will now turn our attention.

MISDEMEANOR COURTS

Misdemeanors are crimes punishable by up to a year in a local jail. One of the failings of many judicial systems is that most of the public and most of the judges look at Misdemeanor Courts as a training ground in preparation for the "important" work of judging in criminal matters—which, as stated above, is understood to be the Felony calendars. In my view, that is simply misguided. Although most of the Misdemeanor Court cases are not played up as much in the newspapers or in the eyes of the public, this is an arena in which the judicious use of ten days, or even a couple of weekends, in jail can often change the direction of people's lives permanently, and for the better.

The Basics of Misdemeanor Calendars

The original concept of a misdemeanor was that it was closer to "bad behavior" than serious criminal conduct, or as Judge David Rothman of the Los Angeles

Superior Court puts it, "People's (mis)demeanor mostly does not arise after reflective thought." The following are common examples of misdemeanors: petty theft offenses; assaults or batteries without weapons that do not result in serious injuries; relatively serious traffic offenses, such as driving under the influence of alcohol or other drugs, or "hit and run" automobile collisions in which no one is injured; prostitution; vandalism, or other property damage below a certain monetary value; and being drunk or disorderly in public.

In some ways offenses of this kind are less serious and should be treated accordingly. But they can also become a lifestyle that can be a substantial drain on society, the defendants themselves, and their families. Moreover, these offenses can be a symptom of more serious problems, such as mental disorders, and can become a stepping stone for young people and also those with increasingly serious alcohol and other drug usage problems toward more serious criminal conduct. As a result, judges in the Misdemeanor Courts have an enormous opportunity to address these problem areas and turn this pattern of conduct around. In short, proactive judges can play a major part in changing people's lives for the better, and in that way they can contribute enormously to our society.

Advice for the Misdemeanor Court Judge

Depending upon how they see their role, judges on Misdemeanor calendars have their own set of challenges. I will share with you some of my thoughts about what I have found to work in these areas. I hope that you will also see that in the Misdemeanor Court judge's adopted role as parent, counselor, psychiatrist, mentor, and jail warden, she can receive the gratification of changing people and lives for the better, and eventually receiving the heartfelt and often even tearful thanks of the defendants themselves and their families. I will also explain why I do not accept the argument that there are too many cases in Misdemeanor Courts for judges to attempt to rehabilitate those who are convicted.

Aim for Sentences That Do More Than Punish

Misdemeanor judges are in a unique position to encourage convicted defendants to straighten out their lives. Let me explain by providing an in-depth look at one type of misdemeanor crime. Prostitution is a big-scale occupation for numbers of people. Prostitutes often have their own pimps, their own culture, their own rules, and their own lifestyles. In fact, large prostitution rings can get so sophisticated that the ladies (and increasingly the men) are actually scheduled to move around from one city to another in order to keep the police from getting to know them.

Unfortunately in today's world jail can be a normal part of a prostitute's life, and it has reached the point that jail often has virtually no deterrent effect. In fact, when I go by the lockup in the courthouse at which I work, it will almost always sound as if the prostitutes inside are having a party. Laughing and merriment are commonplace, and I find this frustrating. What is the use of these jail sentences if they actually enjoy themselves? So I began a program that involves sentencing prostitutes to jail, but staying a large part of those sentences by putting them on probation so that they can job hunt and ultimately obtain honest employment. Why? Because as explained to me by one of our public defenders, the biggest antidote to prostitution is full-time employment.

Under this program, when the prostitute is granted probation she is also issued the requirement that she come back to my courtroom every Friday. At this time, she must bring with her a list of fifteen companies to which she has provided her resume and with whom she has interviewed in seeking full-time employment. All the details need to be there, such as the names of the people who interviewed her and those individuals' phone numbers. That means the defendant must obtain three interviews per working day, and she is told that either my bailiff or I will call the prospective employers in order to check up on the situation. Moreover, the woman is required to continue this program until she actually has *started* a job—not just found a job, but actually started it. Then, after she has begun working, I continue to order her to report back to me once per month for three months, so that she can show me her pay stubs. After this three-month period I feel that I have done as much as I can do, and I permanently stay the remainder of the jail sentence.

The results of this program have been encouraging. About 80 percent of the women have complied with the terms of probation and have found a job. Then I ask these success stories, in the hearing of the other women who have not yet found employment, how their lives have been changed. Uniformly, the women who were prostitutes but are now legally employed say they really had not wanted to be involved in prostitution and are happier and much more proud of their lives now.

I use this example to illustrate the power the misdemeanor court judge has to redirect people's lives. Several other examples of similar programs are discussed under Specialty Courts later in the chapter. At this point though, it is important that I confirm that I am not disregarding the importance of prison sentences for some crimes and their offenders.

Do Not Make False Threats

Most of the defendants in a judge's Misdemeanor Court do not generally believe the judge when she tells them what they will be required to do. They do not think that she will hold them to it. Why? Because they have not been held accountable for their actions for large parts of their lives due to many threats of punishment that were no more than threats.

Do not contribute to this problem! Be thoughtful and careful about what you order sentenced defendants to do, but then follow through on your orders. The word will get out one way or the other. Make sure that the word on you as a judge is that you are caring but stern, and that people under your jurisdiction who fail to perform end up back in jail right away (usually for a short time). If this is not your modus operandi and your reputation, you will probably not be successful as a judge on these calendars.

Be Conservative Concerning Demands for Court Appearances

It is critically important to realize that in many of our courts the system can actually work against itself. What we are striving for in the criminal justice system is to reduce criminal conduct instead of simply punishing it. As discussed, most of the time our best hope of that is for people to obtain and hold onto full-time employment. Tracking such employment involves "report backs" to the courtroom. But if we require defendants to come back to court too often, that can have a harmful effect upon their ability to keep their jobs.

Because of such possible complications, programs geared toward revising the lifestyles of sentenced defendants should be as "user-friendly" as they can be, as long as they still get the job done effectively. So the number and length of court appearances must be judiciously ordered. For example, understanding judges will ask the defendants what day of the week would be best for them to return to court, and whether 8:30 in the morning or 1:30 in the afternoon would be more convenient. When defendants are required to miss several hours of work to come to court, judges should try diligently to be sure that those defendants' cases are addressed at least by the end of the morning so that the defendants will not be required to miss work that afternoon as well.

The same is true if defendants are required to miss work because of time in jail. That does not mean that jail sentences should not be ordered. (See the inset "Questions of Prison vs. Rehabilitation" on page 40 for more on this issue.) It simply means that judges must constantly be aware of the impact their sentences will have, both positive and negative, and that they should consider all options, such as work-release programs in which defendants stay in jail at night and on weekends but are released to perform their jobs during the day.

Avoid Using the Volume of Cases As an Excuse

Some judges do not see the establishment and enforcement of accountability and rehabilitation programs as the proper role of a judge. "I did not go to law school and become a judge in order to become a social worker," is a comment heard from some of them. But an increasing number of judges are recognizing this actually to be one of their major functions. The other comment often heard from judges is, "Yes, that would be a good idea, but we have so much volume in our caseload that we don't have time." In my view, that type of thinking is a trap.

Judges simply must not use the excuse of volume to keep from fully representing their constituency—namely the people of the jurisdictions that they work

---

QUESTIONS OF PRISON VS. REHABILITATION

As all experienced judges know, different crimes and criminal defendants call for different responses from the criminal justice system. Just because there is more of a discussion in these pages about rehabilitative and community programs than simply sending an offender to prison for long periods of time does not mean that prison is never the answer. But in this regard, you should keep two things in mind. The first is that once you decide upon prison there is not much else to talk about. The second is that 95 percent of those who are sent to prison will get out at some point, and then what will they be like?

---

for. The job of a judge is both to do justice and to use the powers that come with the position to reduce not only crime but also all of the costs and misery that accompanies it.

The same excuse of volume is often inappropriately used to justify the pushing of defendants through the system without those individuals' knowing what their rights and options are. This results in treating defendants as statistics instead of human beings. Good and effective judges fully resist such temptations. At arraignments, such judges tell defendants that if there is any question in their minds about whether they are acting in their own best legal interest in entering a plea of guilty, they should enter a plea of not guilty, reflect further, and get additional legal advice. If the defendants continue to feel as though they are not acting in their own best interest, they are counseled—by good and effective judges—that they should plead not guilty and go to trial instead of entering a guilty plea.

Foster Hope and Encouragement

One final issue I would like you to consider under this section on misdemeanors is one not often thought about or discussed. Some defendants can be so completely overwhelmed by the system that they begin to lose hope. This, of course, almost always leads to despair, which in turn leads to the downward spiral of additional crime, drug abuse, and further sanctions. For example, if someone who is out of work and trying to find a job and support a family is facing fines of $2,900, the situation often looks pretty hopeless. This is an opportunity for judges to shape their decisions to the particular situation at hand.

Experienced judges will try to blend individual responsibility with what I call a "sophisticated understanding," so that they do not simply compound the problems. A reasonable program of monthly payments helps, as do programs of "community service" with charitable organizations, or even picking up trash in local parks or on the freeways in lieu of paying a fine. In addition, judges should not underrate just listening to these people, and even giving them some honest encouragement. Most defendants are accustomed to getting "spanked" by sanctimonious people in black robes. But when those authority figures actually give them a little appropriate praise and encouragement, it often can be of genuine and even lasting assistance to them.

Our Misdemeanor Courts are where the "rubber meets the road" in our society's attempts to turn people away from socially unacceptable conduct. Judges on Misdemeanor calendars are in a singular position to put a large number of people back on the right track. Drill sergeants in the military will tell you that they can make upright men and women out of most of their recruits by providing them with discipline, motivation, and a "cause." I believe, to an appreciable degree, judges can do the same through our court system, with the "cause" being the futures of the defendants and even our society.

SPECIALTY COURTS

As mentioned earlier, there are a number of Specialty Courts that have been developed on Misdemeanor calendars. The following ones are discussed in this chapter: Traffic Court; Domestic and Elder Abuse Court; Alcohol-Related Offenses Court; Drug Court; and Co-Occurring Disorders/Homeless Outreach/Community Court. The sentences for the defendants can and often do include time in jail, except for traffic infractions, but the programs normally are used only for defendants who are out of custody.

Traffic Court Calendars

Most judges do not like to sit on Traffic calendars, mostly because such calendars are seen as repetitive, non-challenging, and even boring. As a result, traffic assignments are usually given to the most junior judges and to other judicial officers such as commissioners, referees, and what we call *judge pro tems*—attorneys who volunteer to do judicial assignments without compensation. In many ways, it is really unfortunate that more experienced judges do not value the potential of this area of service because this is one of the calendars that allows for close contact with large numbers of our constituents. In fact, in California a full 64 percent of all court filings are for Traffic Court cases. The majority of the people involved will never again be in touch either with the judicial system or with any other system of government. Therefore, the judges of Traffic Courts have a chance to touch these people's lives in helpful and meaningful ways and leave them with a positive perception of not only the judicial system but also the government in general.

The cases that are adjudicated in Traffic Courts consist of violations by drivers of bicycles and various motor vehicles, including boats. These involve, depending upon the circumstances, moving violations such as speeding, turn violations, failures to stop for traffic signals, and other violations of traffic regulations. They can also include issues involving weight, cargo, and equipment restrictions for trucks. Violations by pedestrians, such as jaywalking and crossing the street against red lights, are also brought into Traffic Courts. Some of these matters sound boring and even esoteric, but if you think about it, they all can have a direct effect upon everyone's safety on our streets and highways. So each case is important in itself. But as the demand for judicial resources continues to expand, more jurisdictions do not authorize jury trials for these infractions and have even taken citations for parking violations out of the court systems completely, handling them administratively.

Naturally, most people will not agree with the judge if they lose their traffic trial. But as in any other case, if they come away with the feeling that the judge listened, considered their side of the case, and fairly explained the reason for the rulings, they will more easily accept the result. The real anger mostly comes from situations in which defendants feel they did not get a fair hearing. Accordingly, if the courts are going to assign inexperienced judicial officers to the Traffic (or any other) calendar, they have an obligation to educate and otherwise train the judicial officers extremely well before they are allowed to put on a robe.

Unfortunately, I have heard of instances in which the judicial officer presiding in traffic trials was unaware that the burden of proof in traffic cases is the criminal standard of "guilt beyond a reasonable doubt." That lack of knowledge is inexcusable and can cause a great deal of harm to and bad feelings about our judicial institutions. Now let me share with you some of my personal advice on serving Traffic Court calendars.

Be Thorough and Attentive

When I preside in traffic trials, I try to be somewhat easygoing but firm. I first try to make sure I pronounce the names of both the defendants and the police officers correctly, and I ask them to assist me if I do not. Then I ask the officers a compound question eliciting testimony that they were employed with a police department, on duty, in uniform, and in a marked vehicle of some kind on the day in question. Thereafter, I ask if their attention was directed to a vehicle driven by the defendant on that particular day and, if so, what time of day it was. Following that, I ask for a narrative as to where the officers were and what they saw.

At that point I listen, try to understand what happened, and continue to ask clarifying questions as they arise until I do. After the officers have testified about how they saw the infraction committed, I ask if they pulled over the driver and if they recognize the defendant present in court as the driver. Did the officers explain the reason for the stop, and thereafter did the defendant make any form of statement after being so advised?

After I question the police officers, the defendant or defendant's attorney is allowed to ask questions in cross-examination. Frequently the defendants try at that point to present their side of the case. I remind them that they will have an opportunity to testify if they so choose, but now is the time just to ask the police officers any relevant questions they may have.

Once the officers' testimony before the court has been completed, I thank the officers and ask them to step down from the stand. Then I advise the defendants that they have the opportunity to testify if they so choose—it is not at all required, but the option is certainly available to them if they wish. Most of the time, unless they simply came to court hoping that the officers would not appear and the case would therefore be dismissed, defendants will want to give their side of the case to the court.

When I sit on Traffic Court cases, my approach is to see if I can find at least one problem or inconsistency in the story presented by the defendant. For example, if a defendant says he parked his truck illegally on the freeway because he had engine trouble, I ask him why he did not bring that up with the citing officer. Or if a defendant had had her car on "cruise control" at or slightly above the speed limit, why did she not say so to the officer at the time? Or if a defendant says he was not going the speed that the officer said he was going, I say, "Okay, but how fast *were* you going?" If he says something that is more than slightly above the speed limit, the case is over, because most of the time the actual speed over the speed limit is not a necessary finding. Being detail-oriented and honing your listening skills are important endeavors when fulfilling a Traffic Court calendar.

Yet sometimes, at the end of the trial, I am not sure if the driver truly committed an offense. In my traffic trials, I have had defendants tell me that they were not even driving the same car that the officer put down on the citation. I have also heard defendants claim someone else was using their identification. And, of course, there is always the judgment call about whether the signal was red or green or yellow. So what is a judge to do? Well, that is where the burden of proof enters the fray.

If after all of the evidence there remains a doubt that is based upon reason, the judge must—under our country's laws—enter a finding of not guilty. End of discussion. Yes, applying this concept means that sometimes people who are flat out lying will be acquitted. But it also means that a few people who actually did not commit offenses will not be unjustly convicted, and that is undoubtedly a good thing. Under those circumstances, for the benefit of both the police officers and the defendants (and also sometimes just to make myself feel better), I tell the defendants that I believe, based upon the evidence, that they actually went through the traffic light when it was red, or that they were in fact going above the speed limit. But I do have a doubt based upon reason, and I am required to follow the law as well, I tell them, so I am going to enter a finding of not guilty. That is the answer, and I think most of the police officers understand that concept and explanation as well.

Hold Drivers Accountable When Excuses Are Flimsy

People frequently "lie through their teeth" in traffic trials. Unfortunately, our traffic system has linked a conviction so heavily with increases in insurance premiums or even insurance cancellations, as well as with possible suspensions of licenses from the state's department of motor vehicles, that some people will say almost anything to avoid a guilty verdict. In other words, large numbers of people fully compromise their integrity to get out of a citation. The trick is, as with any other type of trial, to determine which person is and which person is not telling the truth. If I am sure that I have found defendants who are not telling the truth, I will frequently *increase* their traffic fines. These are probably the ones who will continue their unsafe conduct if they feel they can get away with it, so we need the higher fine for increased deterrence.

Of course, sometimes people simply see things from their own unique perspective, and when the law is explained to them, they understand and accept the judgment. A common example is, "Maybe I was speeding, but I was just going with the flow of traffic." The response to that is that if they happen to be cruising on the highway with ten racecar drivers going 95 miles per hour, that is not a defense. Each individual driver is required to follow the law regardless of what other drivers do. How about when people claim that their vision of a traffic light was obscured by the big truck right in front of them? Should they not be found guilty of going through a red light? Or what if, according to the defendant, the speedometer did not work in the borrowed car she was driving, so she claims it is not really her fault? There is even the celebrity-involving excuse: "I was distracted because I thought I saw Marilyn Monroe standing on the side of the road." The answer to all of these scenarios is that all drivers are responsible—and must be held to be responsible—for the operation of their vehicles, regardless of anything else. Obviously it is also not a valid defense if a driver says her car has no brakes. I tell such people to be sure the car they are driving is safe and legal under all circumstances before going on the road.

Acknowledge That Police Officers Can Be Wrong Too

We have covered inconsistencies and flimsy excuses on the part of defendants, so I feel we must now discuss when drivers are not necessarily at fault. There *is* such a thing as a "bad ticket." Sometimes the officers simply did not accurately see the defendant's driving, and at other times police officers may not be as accurate in their testimony as they should be. So it is best to apply the same scrutiny to the testimony of the officers as that applied to the defendants and/or other witnesses.

Police officers do not like to lose traffic cases either, but if they see that a few times their citations have been excused with a warning, they will begin to give warnings—instead of tickets—for appropriate types of cases in the future. One time I heard a police officer testify that the procedure adopted in his office was that if there was an automobile collision and someone insisted upon having a police report, the officer was *required* to issue a citation to somebody. That case resulted in my finding the defendant not guilty, because I believed that an automatic procedure of this kind was inappropriate and even harmful. Was I exceeding my judicial authority? Maybe some reasonable people could argue so, but I believe that judicial officers are required to use common sense and that the appearance of justice in traffic cases, like in everything else, is critically important.

Remember That Traffic Court Means More Than Revenue

It is important to mention that most counties and states are continually grasping for funding, so they factor revenue from traffic fines and fees in advance into their annual budgets. As a result, traffic cases are seen as providing a needed source of revenue to the various governmental agencies. If a trial judge believes a particular fine is appropriate under the law and the facts, then that fine should be imposed. But judges must resist being used as revenue-producing agencies. It is our assignment to do justice, not to raise money.

In addition, we should remember that many defendants in Traffic Court come from the lower economic levels of our society. So a fine of $100 can be quite a bit more significant to them than it is to many other people. Furthermore, often the purpose of a citation is to get the defendants to fix a particular problem: get the car registered; put license plates on both the front and rear of the car; replace the worn-out tires; fix the broken tail light. Personally, I think these "fix-it tickets" should not be seen as a source of revenue for the government; they should be used as a means to keep us all safer on the highways. So once the required repairs have been made, the cases should be dismissed with only a small administration fee assessed.

Practice Discretion, Clarity, and Flexibility

There are a few things Traffic Court judges must allow themselves. One of these is "not guilty" verdicts—otherwise known as acquittals—when justly called for. In addition, a good and effective judge uses discretion and sometimes enters a finding of "not guilty with a warning." Or maybe she allows a defendant to attend traffic school when not otherwise strictly eligible.

Moreover, an effective judge *explains* why she feels an "acquittal with a warning" is the appropriate conclusion—when such an outcome is decided—for two primary reasons. First, the defendant, as well as others who may be listening inside the courtroom, should know why this particular case gave rise to an exception. Second, the police officers should be able to understand why the defendant was given this warning so they can utilize that discretion in future cases out in the field.

Along the way, judges should also remember that most of the people they are dealing with are normal citizens who happened to have made traffic mistakes. So there are often some seemingly small things the judges can do to help these people, or at least not to beat them up too badly, when a defendant has, for example, failed to come back to court to pay a fine. In most of those circumstances, a judge could issue an arrest warrant for the person. But in appropriate cases, instead of requiring the defendant actually to appear in court, the judge can simply set forth the amount of the fine that is unpaid as "forfeitable bail." Or she could add a civil administrative assessment for the failure to appear and put a "hold" on that person's driver's license until it has been paid. This will still require the defendants to pay their appropriate fines, but once that occurs, the matter will be ended and the defendants will not be held in jail. The result will be less clogging up of the system and also the reduced sapping of precious time and energy by judges and their staffs.

Flexibility is demanded of judges as well, and judges should give themselves the room to be flexible. They must be aware that they will be called upon, even in traffic matters, to adjust various advances in technology to the real world. One of those areas is the increasing presence of video cameras to monitor red-light violations at intersections and other cameras to issue citations for speeding. These circumstances present judges with yet another balancing of "security" versus "freedom from undue government intrusions into our lives." Yes, automatic cameras can certainly be an effective tool for traffic law enforcement, but they can also allow another encroachment of the notorious "Big Brother." So once again, judges are on the front lines of society's conflicts and are called upon to strike a proper balance.

Offer Relatable, Practical Safety Reminders

In the process of finding people guilty of traffic offenses, I frequently tell them that we all need reminders to drive more safely. For example, I sometimes ask the defendants to try to keep their eyes open the next time they sneeze. They will quickly learn that the body will not allow this to be done. I then tell them to remember that if they are driving at 80 miles per hour, they will probably be driving blind for about a full second. My calculations tell me that means they will have traveled more than 115 feet with their eyes closed, which in my view is an unacceptably high risk of danger.

I often also pass along a comment that I heard a long time ago. I was complaining to a friend about what some inconsiderate driver did to me while we were on the road. My friend responded by asking me a question: "Jim, what would you have done under those circumstances if you actually *knew* that this person was under the influence of drugs?" I responded that I would get out of his way and let him go, being thankful that he did not crash into me. My friend agreed, and then said that whenever he finds an aggressive, incompetent driver on the road, instead of getting mad and trying to keep that driver from cutting him off or the like, he simply pretends that the other driver is on drugs and acts accordingly. Since that time, I have adopted the same approach on numbers of occasions, and I recommend it to those who are in my court. Unfortunately these days, many of these bad drivers might actually be on drugs, so you might not really be pretending.

Finally, I tell the defendants that it is not the purpose of the traffic patrol officers unnecessarily to take our time and money, or to increase our insurance rates. In fact, we could probably take the rest of the morning to have these officers testify about what they have seen in cleaning up after our mistakes out on the highway. They are the ones who hear the screams and see the blood on the streets, and they have to tell family members that their loved ones have been seriously injured or have even been killed. So all the police are trying to do is to have us drive more safely. I believe that is true, and I hope that most of the defendants in my courtroom believe it as well.

In summary, judges can both "do justice" in traffic cases and make the system work by listening to each case, applying the law, and explaining the reasons for their rulings. Importantly, in doing this they can also promote safer driving on our streets and highways by enforcing the "rules of the road." To repeat, traffic cases involve some of the most important matters in our court systems. Yes, it can be tedious to hear them on a regular basis. But Traffic calendars provide judges with a significant opportunity to blend the firm but not severe enforcement of our laws with education about safety on our streets and highways. Not to mention that they are good sources of occasional humor; see the inset "A Little Traffic Court Humor" on page 48.

Domestic Violence and Elder Abuse Court Calendars

In many jurisdictions, specific calendars have been created fairly recently to address domestic violence offenses and elder abuse. Problems involving violence directed toward spouses, domestic partners, children, the elderly, and even non-family members have been around for centuries, but these calendars are making positive headway regarding breaking—or at least reducing—these terrible cycles. This attention is critically necessary because today about one in twenty adults in California is a victim of neglect or abuse (physical, psychological, or financial), and most other states have similar statistics. Furthermore, two-thirds of the abuses are committed against family members. And since Americans are living longer and having fewer children, it is estimated that by the year 2050, seniors will outnumber children and youth.

Numbers of individual judges have also taken notice of these problems more recently and are helping to combat them. In this regard, consider the following comment Judge Julie Conger of the Oakland Superior Court made to me:

A LITTLE TRAFFIC COURT HUMOR

A defendant who was given a citation for driving on the wrong side of the street at night without any headlights appeared in court. His explanation was that he had forgotten to turn on his lights. When asked why he was on the wrong side of the street, he said, "Well, I couldn't tell because it was dark!"

In another case, a man heard on the radio that there was a wrong-way driver on a particular freeway. Knowing that his elderly father was driving somewhere in that area, the man called his father on his cell phone to warn him to look out for a car going the wrong way. "What do you mean one car, there are hundreds!" yelled his father.

These anecdotes emphasize the lighter side of serving on a Traffic Court calendar. As the old saying goes, sometimes truth is stranger than fiction!

When I first became a judge, I wish I had striven to be more visionary, more proactive and more perceptive of how my position affects the community in which I reside. . . . It was through . . . community meetings that I became growingly aware of the problem of Elder Abuse and the obstacles seniors encounter in access to the courts. This has led to the development of our Elder Access program, which encompasses outreach to seniors throughout the country and the innovative Elder Protection Court. I mention this to illustrate how responsiveness to community needs can assist judges in leaving the "ivory tower" that is so often the hallmark of the judiciary.

Quite a few jurisdictions now require that law enforcement officers be educated to detect the indications of domestic violence and abuse of the elderly. These officers are also trained immediately to arrest the alleged perpetrators. Then temporary restraining orders are often issued against the perpetrators to prohibit them from any contact with their victims until a hearing can be held within a few days. The hearing would determine the appropriate course to follow thereafter.

In most jurisdictions, if serious injuries or abuse are involved, the cases are handled in general Felony calendars, and often the perpetrators who are convicted are incarcerated for lengthy periods of time. This type of perpetrator would also be permanently restrained from having any contact with the victims whatsoever, unless or until a judge modifies the restraining order. But most of the cases are less serious and result in the perpetrator's, after spending a short time in jail, being ordered to perform some physical labor, such as picking up trash on the freeways, and then enrolling in and successfully completing a batterer's treatment program. There are a variety of programs out there, but one example is a behavior rehabilitation program that lasts for fifty-two weeks. If alcohol or other drugs were involved, the program would also be likely to include additional drug education and counseling components. But most of the programs are primarily anger management classes that educate participants about peaceful dispute resolution techniques.

It is clear that Domestic Violence and Elder Abuse calendars—like the Misdemeanor calendar discussed previously—give judges the opportunity to devise and/or promote rehabilitative programs. That means the judges and their staffs do a lot more work, but the work is rewarding. The programs and the judges who preside over them have significant power to change the anti-social conduct that gives rise to domestic violence and elder abuse. As a result, everybody wins.

A necessary perspective required of the professionals involved in this area of law is that they understand that, for the most part, they are not dealing with hardened criminals. Instead, they are dealing with people who have been exposed to a history of abuse. Frequently the perpetrators were raised in families in which (most often) their mothers were repeatedly beaten or otherwise abused by their fathers—although sometimes the husband was the victim of violence. The fact that the perpetrators witnessed domestic abuse is not at all an excuse for their violent behaviors; they must still be held strictly accountable for their conduct. But there are ways to encourage convicted defendants to change. One way to help them change is to assert that they can be truly important people in their families' histories, because they can be the ones who break that cycle of abuse. The following sections will offer a little more advice if you would like to serve on a Domestic Violence or Elder Abuse calendar.

Speak Effectively to the Perpetrators About Anger

I believe it is important to talk with many of the defendants I come into contact with in this type of Specialty Court, and when I do, I discuss anger with them. For example, I ask them if they think that I, myself, ever get angry. What about my clerk or bailiff, or the nice person who is the court interpreter on the case? Of course, the answer (eventually) is yes. Everyone gets angry; that is normal. But it is a question of what one does with the anger that separates an adult from a child, or a mature person from one who is immature.

I suggest that when individuals get angry, they should back off or immediately take some time out. At that point, people should turn to an activity that will calm them down. My own therapy throughout my life has been to shoot baskets. When the anger has passed, it is time to talk like a reasonable adult about the problems or frustrations. Regarding spousal beatings, I always try to get the perpetrators to agree that just as it is always wrong for an adult to hit a child, it is also always wrong for a man to hit a woman. Likewise, of course, it is wrong for a woman to hit a man.

Hold Perpetrators Accountable for Program Performance

Most of the courts that have behavior modification programs also have report-back calendars that are assigned to individual judges. The defendants return to court at designated intervals to present progress reports concerning their participation in batterers' and other programs. Usually "report cards" filled out by program staff members grade the subjects with a score—for example, from one to five. A "five" signifies an active, responsible, and helpful participant, while a "one" identifies an irresponsible, unhelpful participant with attendance problems. As you can guess, a "three" represents satisfactory participation. Frequently, those with very low scores are terminated from the programs.

I have a special policy with the court staff regarding returning defendants—also called "report-backs"—who have been terminated from the programs and sent back to court. I have those defendants called at the beginning of the calendar, and I tell them that they are considered to be in violation of their probation due to their failures. If they want a hearing, they are entitled to it, usually within one week. But if they decide to admit the violation, they can have a choice. If they simply do not want to take the program seriously, I understand; they can serve the next ninety or so days in jail, and I will not make them complete the program. Of course, the restraining order will also remain in effect. On the other hand, if they do want to take the program seriously, I will put them in jail for the next five to ten days, depending upon the circumstances, and then allow them to re-enroll in and successfully complete the program.

Once again, in my view it is virtually always essential that the defendants *feel* that they have a choice, which enables them to "buy into" the program. But, of course, I try to weight the scales rather heavily in one direction so that they make the choice to get themselves the tools they need to grapple with future anger management situations. Which do they prefer—a month in jail or re-enrollment in the program? Most of them apologize for their past behavior, choose to serve the short time in jail, and go back into the program. Then I usually take them into custody right away, in front of the other defendants.

What is the result of this scenario? The subjects themselves see that they will be held accountable for their lack of results, but also that they have another meaningful chance to move forward. The counselors and staff members of the treatment programs come out ahead because it becomes evident that their assessments carry weight with the judges, and thus their clients will treat them with more respect. Lastly, the other forty or so defendants in the courtroom will clearly understand that they had better continue to take the program seriously or they will soon be required to make a similar decision. In other words, once again, everyone wins!

I also try to help people understand that programs for domestic and elder abusers should not be seen as punishments. Instead, these programs provide opportunities to learn from the experiences of others. And as time goes along, others will learn from the participants' experiences as well. In other words, all of us can help each other.

Regarding those who report back with reviews that are just satisfactory, I tell them that I can ensure only that they be present at the programs. I cannot effectively make them learn. But since they are going to be there anyway, would it not be more productive of their time to give a bit more of themselves and learn from the experiences of others? And would it not be constructive to pass along their experiences to others as well? In my view, if this discussion works with even 10 percent of my "clients," it is worth all of the effort.

Use Discretion Regarding Restraining Orders

It is true that Domestic Violence and Elder Abuse calendars present situations in which judges can intercede in the lives of individuals and break a cycle of violence and other anti-social behavior. But these calendars also furnish the opportunity for the courts *inappropriately* to meddle in other people's lives. So how do we decide which situation is which? Well, that is why judges are paid all the "big money"—they have to use their discretion.

Since many courts now have procedures for restraining orders to be issued, some people try to take advantage of them for their own selfish purposes. Often, people involved in child custody disputes on the Domestic Violence calendar will bring exaggerated or even false charges against the other party. What do we do about that? Often one side will agree voluntarily to a restraining order, as long as the court will issue a similar order against the other side. That can be an easy way out for the judge, but is that the appropriate way for the courts to go? The answer to these questions is, "It depends."

Judges must do their best, within reasonable time constraints and given incomplete information, to do what is right in each case. In practice, that often means to err on the side of caution and issue temporary orders that may later be determined not to have been completely necessary. The worst thing would be for someone to be harmed when a judge reasonably could have prevented it—and believe me, all judges feel those pressures and concerns.

Sometimes, though, with a little thought and analysis, a judge can determine that a restraining order is simply not the appropriate response. For example, I once had a petitioner who requested a temporary restraining order against her ex-father-in-law. The problem was that the ex-parent-in-law, referred to as the *respondent,* was telling the petitioner's sisters that he thought the petitioner's new husband was dangerous and that the wife should immediately leave him. The petitioner wanted the court to restrain the respondent from saying those things. Surprisingly enough, the petitioner had even found an attorney to represent her in this request. My official response was that her sisters are adults, and they can choose to listen or not listen to the respondent as they wished. I further reminded her that a restraining order is meant to protect people from *imminent physical harm*, not to keep people from talking about each other. Then, having dismissed the petitioner, I unofficially looked at the respondent and strongly suggested that, in the future, he mind his own business.

On other occasions, judges are presented with what I call the "jilted lover" situation. In these cases, one of the former partners simply does not seem to be able to let the relationship go, and so continues to call the former lover with apologies or hopes of reconciliation. In some of these situations, restraining orders are appropriately issued and kept in place, particularly if there is any threatened violence. But at other times, I have found it beneficial to tell the offending party that I have the power to hurt her by issuing a restraining order against her. So if she promises me that she will completely let this go without any further contact at all, I will not issue the order. *If* I believe her, then I ask the two parties to face each other. If the alleged perpetrator wants to apologize, I let her voice her apology, and then I ask the other party if he has heard the apology. Next, I ask each party in turn to say goodbye to the other, which they do, and then I tell them both that their relationship is over. Finally, I tell the perpetrator to stay in my courtroom for the next fifteen minutes while the other party leaves the courthouse. Hopefully the whole thing is now completed. I know this can be risky, and if anything untoward happens later, I could publicly be blamed. But I have done this about fifteen or twenty times, and to my knowledge none of the cases has ever come back.

I often get frustrated when I hear yet another account about violence that is perpetrated upon a weak and vulnerable spouse, domestic partner, other family member, or elderly person. And I am consumed by the thought, "Why doesn't somebody do something?" Well, in this and other similar areas, judges can do wonders when it comes to protecting the vulnerable and even reshaping failing relationships. Helping in this manner is a wonderful and gratifying feeling that I hope some day you too will experience.

Alcohol-Related Offense Court Calendars

Decades ago, many courts around the nation created a separate Specialty Court for alcohol-related offenses. This occurred in large part as a result of the frustration of judges and other people in handling numbers of senseless alcohol-related vehicular manslaughter cases. In fact, motor vehicle accidents are the leading cause of death among young people aged sixteen to twenty, and one-third of the fatalities involves alcohol. So a number of people in the judicial system believed that just maybe they could put together a program that would head off the number of such tragedies in the future. The other impetus for the formation of this type of court and its associated alcohol-recovery programs was the sheer numbers of offenses in our society due to alcohol use and abuse. Judge Peggy Hora of the Hayward, California, Superior Court put this into perspective when she made the following comment to me:

> Given that 90 percent of the criminal cases and at least 70 percent of child abuse and neglect cases are fueled by alcohol and other drugs, it is imperative that judges understand alcoholism and other addictions. . . . I would urge all new judges to educate themselves on these issues because supervising cases where people actually get better is so much more satisfying than recycling the same people through the system.

Most of the alcohol-related offense cases center around the driving of a motor vehicle while under the influence of alcohol, and the related offenses of driving with a suspended license, no license, no insurance, etc., because frequently these alcohol-addicted people are irresponsible. Unfortunately, for years many of these calendars have been seen as big moneymakers for the local governments, since they have mostly resulted in cases in which large fines are imposed instead of incarceration. The other problem has been that alcoholism is an equal-opportunity disease—it strikes at all levels of society. Accordingly, right or wrong, sometimes judges feel as if they are sentencing their next-door neighbor and are less inclined to issue tough sentences. In fact, many judges in the past have been quite lenient with these offenses.

Alcohol-related traffic cases are still seen as large sources of revenue, but now many states also require that first-time offenders of "driving under the influence" (DUI) or "driving while intoxicated" (DWI) enroll in and successfully complete a three-month program on alcohol awareness. Those defendants with higher levels of alcohol in their bodies must often complete programs lasting twelve to eighteen months. Many of these longer programs require counseling, total abstinence from alcohol, and attendance at meetings of groups like Alcoholics Anonymous, which has successfully mainstreamed the concept of "12-Step Programs."

As of the end of 2005, there were more than 200 programs of this kind around the country, and most of them have been successful. For example, one study in 2005 revealed the average re-arrest rate, after two years, for traditionally-sentenced DUI offenders was about 25 percent. But for those who completed DUI programs, the re-arrest rate was only about 15 percent. A similar study showed that a DUI program in Kootenai County, Idaho, reduced the recidivism (or re-arrest) rate from 25 percent to 4 percent. One graduate put it best when he said, "If my sentence had been thirty days in jail [rather than] DUI court, I would have been drinking on my thirty-first day."[3]

Many courts also often require all convicted defendants to attend a two-hour Mothers Against Drunk Drivers' Victims Panel. Such a panel presents, in a nonaccusatory fashion, the stories of victims of drunk driving. I have monitored these sessions on two occasions, and I got tears in my eyes both times. This and other experiences I have had in the area of Alcohol-Related Offense Courts have allowed me to develop helpful pointers for judges working in these courts.

Consider Furthering the Existing Programs for Problem Drinkers

The courts in Orange County, California, took the approach to DUI calendars a large step farther in 1984, when we established a screening process for "first-time offenders." I put that label in quotation marks because everyone who is knowledgeable in this area understands that most of these defendants have driven in an intoxicated condition at least 100 times before they have ever been arrested. So there literally is almost no such thing as a first-time offender.

In any case, we put the defendants through a screening process in order to determine whether they were alcoholics or not.[4] In this process, we relied upon professionals to conduct the screening process, which was based upon three different factors. The first factor was the blood alcohol level reported by the arresting police agency. The second factor was the Mortimer-Filkins Test, which is also called the Court Procedures for Identifying Problem Drinkers. This is a self-administered questionnaire, consisting of fifty-seven items, originally compiled for the National Highway Traffic Safety Administration. On a side note, we developed Spanish versions of the test and gave assistance to those who could not read at all. The third factor was a personal interview that orally asked the defendants seventeen questions and included a subset of questions known as the "CAGE" test. The name comes from key letters in four of those questions: (1) Do you feel you should Cut down on your drinking?; (2) Do you feel Annoyed when someone criticizes your drinking?; (3) Do you feel Guilty about your drinking?; and (4) Do you Ever take a drink to cure a hangover?

But identifying the problem drinkers is useless unless the courts have a place to send them for help. So, with the substantial assistance of our local county healthcare agency, we developed an eight-month program of counseling, group meetings, sessions of Alcoholics Anonymous, and total abstinence from the ingestion of alcohol. Along those lines, I told those I sent to the program that if they even ate rum cake and I found out about it, I would put them in jail. And as some people found out, this was not an idle threat. The counseling sessions included discussion groups led by recovering alcoholics who were attuned to the excuses for non-performance and the whining about how "you just don't understand," as well as honest education about healthcare issues brought about by the overuse of alcohol.

Once convicted and sentenced for their alcohol-related offenses, the defendants had to enroll in our program and then return to court thirty days later with proof of that enrollment. Then on my report-back calendar I tried to take the ones who had not successfully completed their enrollment first. I would tell them they were considered to be in violation of their probation, and, if they wished, they could have a hearing in a week. Or, if they admitted their violation, I would give them a choice. I would either put them in jail for ninety days, suspend their driver's license for six months, and terminate probation so they "would not have to be bothered" about the program, or if they so chose I would put them back on the program after they served three to ten days in jail. (Sound familiar? This is the same protocol as with domestic and elder abuse cases.) Again the theory is for the defendants at least to feel that they have a choice. Most of them chose to go back on the program, which was, of course, the intended result.

At the report-back sessions, most of the defendants on our program looked quite a bit better after just that first thirty-day period. In fact, I remember one particular young man who had looked quite slovenly when he first pleaded guilty and was sentenced to our program. When he returned thirty days later, he was much better groomed and was actually wearing a short-sleeved dress shirt and a tie. I also noticed that the large tattoo he had on his arm was different, and I asked him about it. He responded that the old tattoo had been of a marijuana leaf. He did not have the money to have it removed, so he had it changed into the form of a peacock. To this day, I am really proud of the change.

Our program was modeled after the "Lucky Deuce" program, which was established by Dr. Mark F. Joseff of the American Public Health Foundation. We also adopted Dr. Joseff's credo that we were attempting to "replace a drinking driver with a sober one." And we were successful! Our statistics showed that nine months after graduation from the program, 65 percent of these problem drinkers had been able to stay off alcohol completely. And besides, as Dr. Joseff said, we were also probably successful in "spoiling the drinking" of the remaining 35 percent, so there was greater hope for those people as well.

Based upon our success rates, we soon increased the scope of our program to include any misdemeanor offenses committed by a defendant who was found to be under the influence of alcohol. Those results were gratifying as well, because not only did defendants convicted of thefts, spousal abuse, and other assaults respond well to the program, but we also found that people charged with things like the failure to pay child support began to make their payments like clockwork once they got off the alcohol.

Even though the programs cost about $1,000 over the course of the eight months, virtually all of the people actually had more money when they were on the program than they did before, because they were not spending it on alcohol and the lifestyle that frequently accompanies it. Just think of it this way: if people are supporting their alcoholism at a bar, which is frequently the case, imagine how much money that is costing them per drink and per night. That money is saved, and it stays in their pockets. So the occasional arguments by the defendants that these programs are unaffordable almost never turn out to be true.

If as a judge you involve yourself in approaches like these, I am sure your experience will be the same as mine. Over the course of time, I have received a stack of letters from family members of the defendants offering positive feedback such as, "I was going to divorce my husband because I couldn't trust him. He would get drunk and beat up our children. But now that he is on your program, you have given me back my husband, and the children their father. Thank you!" We do not need to receive too many of these letters to know that we are on the right track.[5]

Throughout the entire process we understand that people must be given a fair opportunity to do what they have been ordered to do. Nevertheless, if a court grants multiple extensions to accomplish those requirements, that really leads people to conclude that the court is not serious about what it is requiring. In short, that results in the court's becoming an "enabler." Judges therefore must realize that giving offenders multiple extensions to do what they are required to do in rehabilitation programs and other venues without first remanding them to jail really means only that the judges lack the strength or resolve to remand dilatory defendants into custody.

Use Positive Language

In discussing programs like those offered to convicted offenders of alcohol-related offenses, it is important to recognize the profound power of psychology found in what judges do and say. Accordingly, try to phrase things in the positive and have the defendants focus upon the positive as well.

For example, instead of emphasizing that a client will go to jail if she does not take the program seriously and obey the orders given to her (even though she will, in fact, go to jail), focus on how she probably will be able to live a more normal life again, keep her job and family, and have a lot more money in her pocket if and when she completes the program successfully. This is a variation of the truism that when you lead people by the hand they will probably follow you, but if you push them, they will most likely resist.

Take Advantage of Available Technology and Science

The worlds of technology and science have developed a number of useful tools that are allowing better monitoring of convicted defendants' actions. One of these is a monitoring bracelet that is a non-removable and water-resistant device. It is strapped upon a defendant's ankle for weeks at a time and allows a monitor remotely to determine if the defendant has consumed any alcoholic beverages at all.[6] These bracelets can be enormously helpful for those who have trouble with our orders for abstinence.

The medical community is also making strides. Many counseling sessions now include the newly discovered medical information that alcohol actually shrinks a person's brain by drying it out, thus eroding memory and organizational abilities. But the brain in many ways actually can regenerate itself and regain some of these functions when people again follow a path of sobriety.[7] Revealing scientific *proof* of the harmful effects of alcohol to the defendants can be a truly effective measure.

Finally, medical research is continuing to explore the area of "addiction medicine" and develop new drugs like Naltrexone and Topamax. These new medications hold the promise of reducing an addict's cravings. So the future will hold even more ways for the judicial system to promote rehabilitation for heavy drinkers. For additional information on science and alcoholism, see the inset "Defining Alcoholism as a Disease" on page 58.

When I was first appointed as a trial court judge in 1983, I quickly realized that alcohol-related offenses were the largest problem area we faced at the misdemeanor level, and that we really were not doing nearly enough to address them. So I helped to establish a Specialty Court to break the cycle of harms caused by people's addiction to this prevalent drug. And by employing the techniques outlined above, I am proud to say that we were quite successful. In all honesty, I believe that this is the most important contribution I have made in my professional life, and I recommend that you involve yourself in this type of program development as well.

Drug Court Calendars

Basically, Drug Courts have adapted the concepts that were discussed above in the Alcohol-Related Offense Court calendars to offenders who use other mind-altering and sometimes addictive substances such as heroin, cocaine, and methamphetamines. Whereas previously these defendants were most often simply sent to jail, now substantial efforts are being made to address the underlying problems so that they will have a meaningful chance of breaking the cycle of their addictions and criminal behavior. These programs have been so successful that they have spread all around the country, to the degree that today it is virtually indisputable to say that drug courts have been a positive revolution in the country's criminal justice system.

The first Drug Court began in Miami in 1989. It was so successful that Congress passed Title V of the Violent Crime Control and Law Enforcement Act of 1994, which authorized the United States Attorney General to grant federal funds to the states in order to set up similar programs. With this funding, these rehabilitative programs are now in full swing all around the country.

Of course, Drug Court programs vary from court to court and state to state, and the types of defendants considered eligible for them can vary as well. For example, some states use "diversion programs" for their Drug Courts, and some do not. In those states that use them, the defendants are sent to programs that are meant to address their specific problem areas, and then if they successfully complete the programs and do not violate any additional laws, their charges are subsequently dismissed. Other states do similar things, but they require the

DEFINING ALCOHOLISM AS A DISEASE

Make no mistake about it: Alcoholism is a disease. The condition was aptly described by Betty Ford when she explained, "In our society, we get to know one another over drinks, we associate feasts and celebrations with liquor. We think we have to drink, that it's a social necessity. It's romantic as long as you can handle it—for years I could and did—but it's misery when you become addicted."[1] Although alcoholics can never *recover* from the disease, for they are always *recovering,* they can fully recover from the *symptoms* of the disease of alcoholism if they stop drinking. But that is not always easy.

Most medical doctors who have studied alcoholism not only agree it is a disease, but they also agree that it can be genetic. This means that children of alcoholic parents are at a much greater risk of having this disease than other people whose family bloodlines do not have the same genetic makeup. In addition, some ethnic groups are particularly sensitive to alcohol. For example, many Native Americans have been found to lack a particular gene that allows their bodies to process and absorb alcohol without problems.

Those who are still not convinced that alcoholism is a disease should consider that alcoholism is almost completely medically diagnosable. This is done by measuring the amount of a chemical called dihydroisoquinolone (DHIQ), which is found in the fluids surrounding a person's brain. Unfortunately, this is only detectable by autopsy, so that tends to reduce the number of volunteers for the procedure!

Suffering from alcoholism is not a crime, which is to say that it is not a criminal offense to have a disease. But if someone drives a motor vehicle while displaying the symptoms of alcoholism, that *is* a crime. Why? Because now that individual, by her actions, is putting the safety of other people at risk.

Fortunately, in addition to many people at all levels of our society, the courts are beginning to understand that alcoholism is a disease, and also realizing that it is not a laughing matter. The movie *Arthur* starring Dudley Moore, which was about an eccentric alcoholic, was considered quite funny when it was released back in 1981. But I do not believe that this movie would be at all successful now, because most people today do not consider alcoholism to be funny.

defendants to plead guilty to the charges and then enroll in and successfully complete a particular program. Once the program is completed and no further law violations occur, the defendants are allowed to withdraw their guilty pleas and the charges are then similarly dismissed. This latter type of program is more popular with prosecutors because they get their convictions, and if there is a problem in the future the prosecutors are not required to locate the witnesses and resurrect the cases. But defendants and their attorneys are less enthusiastic about these programs because if the defendants have problems in the future they potentially can and sometimes do receive a maximum sentence.

Most Drug Courts began by allowing eligibility only to drug users who were charged with drug possession or use but who had not been involved either in the sales of drugs or any crimes of violence. The resistance by prosecutors and the police agencies was simply too high politically to allow any of the other defendants to be included. The basic reason for the resistance was that the programs appeared to them to be the "liberal coddling of criminals." But these eligibility requirements have been softened in many places, so more of the drug-addicted defendants who are causing harm to other people—even violent harm—are now becoming eligible for participation. In a lot of ways this makes sense. Drug Courts require a large number of resources, so it seems logical to use them to address the cases of those defendants who are burglarizing our houses and cars, as well as assaulting and otherwise causing harm to other people in addition to themselves.

As we have seen in similar program situations earlier in this chapter, Drug Courts are a therapeutic "carrot and stick" approach to dealing with addiction. The programs require accountability, responsibility, and an enormous amount of effort from everybody concerned. The counseling phases of the programs mostly focus upon healthcare issues, job skills, the importance of being a reliable employee, and the critical choices concerning whom the defendants decide to choose as friends. They also address the downward spiral of reality that all of the addicted people have experienced: At first the drugs became their friend, but then after a short time their best friend, and soon after that their only friend. As a result, the programs take a holistic approach to rebuilding addicted people's lives. That means reunions with spouses, children, and other family members, as well as payment of child support, and generally more responsible living are all addressed.

Virtually every Drug Court program emphasizes promptness in its response to the problems. As soon as defendants are determined to be eligible and agree to enter the program, they are taken to a counselor, drug tested, provided with a list of the requirements, and given a short period of time to enroll and return to court. The rigorous requirements of these programs almost always include orders to violate no laws and also include the following: not using or possessing any non-prescription mind-altering drugs or related paraphernalia, making timely appearances for all court and counseling dates, not making any threats toward any other participants or staff, reporting regularly to probation officers, having regular drug testing, attending educational and counseling sessions and dressing appropriately for them, not associating with people who are still in the drug-using community, writing essays to organize their thoughts, and making frequent report-back appearances in court.

If things begin to go well, the participants are congratulated by the judge, staff, and their fellow Drug Court peers. They can also be rewarded with incentives such as movie passes, a later curfew, less frequent court appearances, and progressing to the next phase of the program. If participants do not do well, at first the length of the program is increased. With no improvement, they will soon be forced to serve time back in jail.

At first it is not conducive for the participants in Drug Court programs to go back to school or to hold full-time jobs because the programs and report backs

---

JUDGES COMMENT ON THE POWER OF DRUG COURT PROGRAMS

If you have never attended a Drug Court graduation ceremony, you should. Tears flow, and hearty applause and embraces abound. Frequently the graduates hug their arresting officers and thank them for the arrest that brought them into the program. Testimonials from the graduates and their families are often truly inspiring and heartwarming; positive comments from the presiding judges are legion.

I have never heard a judicial comment about a Drug Court approach that was not laudatory. Below you will find several judges' comments. Some are practical, and others are emotional.

Other than raising my own children, the Drug Court is the most satisfying thing I have ever done.

I have handled a criminal calendar almost all 16 years of my time on the bench, and have sent, as you surely know, thousands of people to jail and prison, if not tens of thousands. I have also had a very satisfying career as a parent, with seven children (and I am proud to say, they have been highly successful).

I tell you that only because for me to compare working in the Drug Court with raising my children is high praise from me, and I am not one to praise highly. We have graduated almost 2,000 people from the Drug Court over the last 10 years, and to see them later in a store or at a park,

take so much time. But as the participants progress in their courses, school and employment are increasingly emphasized. Most of the time the programs take between twelve and eighteen months.[8] Then the participant "graduates." For judges' thoughts and feelings about the gratifying feedback from such program participants, see the inset "Judges Comment on the Power of Drug Court Programs" below.

We are beginning to see some substantial progress in reducing the recidivism rates, crime rates, and prison population of drug users. This began in 1994, when the U.S. Department of Justice reported that where 67.5 percent of drug-related offenders were re-arrested within the first three years of their offense, nearly 80 percent of the Drug Court graduates have been drug-free with no new drug arrests during that same period of time.[9]

Furthermore, according to the 2006 Orange County Collaborative Annual Report, the Administrative Office of the Courts in California has determined that

---

doing well, grateful still to be clean and sober, happy, employed, and productive is most gratifying. Some have obviously returned to drug use, but hundreds have not, and I see them periodically in various places around the community. Compared with seeing them come back for yet another trip to prison under the traditional system, the Drug Court is very rewarding.

—*Glade F. Roper, Judge of the Superior Court, Porterville, California*

If I have someone clean and sober for a year, that is $23,000 saved in keeping him or her in prison, plus at least $20,000 to $30,000 saved in property crime, multiplied by 1,000 people per year in our Drug Court. You do the math.

—*Jack Lehman, Senior Judge of the District Court, Las Vegas, Nevada*

[In a typical judicial setting,] the natural response is a jail sentence. [But in drug court,] you have to become more interactive, more involved with defendants and their families. I saw people change, and I can honestly say it changed me.[1]

—*Marcelita V. Haynes, Judge of the Superior Court, Los Angeles, California*

When a mom comes in and says thank you for saving my child's life, it just hits you in the heart. We can't save them all, but the ones we do, it sure makes the job worthwhile.[2]

—*Dorothy B. Reyes, Judge of the Superior Court, Los Angeles, California*

every dollar invested in Drug Courts in Orange County, California, has resulted in a cost savings of $7.30 for law enforcement agencies. That translates to a cost savings of about $12,822 per participant. Moreover, from 2000 through 2006, Drug Courts also saved about 129,680 jail bed days and 65,250 prison bed days for a total savings of approximately $16,321,000. And 89 children who had been removed from their homes by the county were reunited with their newly clean and sober parents—who had completed drug programs—an average of 183 days earlier than those whose parents were non-participants. Finally, 102 drug-free babies were born to mothers who were participants in the program and were drug-free themselves.

Below I provide some suggestions for sitting on Drug Court calendars. They involve several key issues. These include staying true to the law and knowing what works in the fight against mind-altering, sometimes addictive and dangerous drugs.

Recognize the Power of Drug Courts to Tear Down Stereotypes

In addition to all the benefits already discussed, Drug Courts have resulted in an additional significant benefit that is a part of the "revolution" that was addressed above. Instead of seeing most drug-addicted people as statistics, "hypes," "junkies," or "dirt-bags," more judges, probation officers, and police officers are now actually seeing drug users as human beings with many of the same needs, desires, and failings that all of the rest of us have. That does not at all mean that these defendants are not held accountable for their conduct, but it does mean that they are seen as real people with real problems that can be addressed and often overcome. Just like alcohol addiction, addiction to these other mind-altering and sometimes addicting drugs is a disease.

Fortunately scientists and other healthcare researchers are beginning to make the discovery that addiction is most often not the result of a flawed character but instead mostly the result of altered brain function. And these increased understandings about addictions are beginning to yield numbers of medical treatments that work. One cause for optimism is a drug called Naltrexone, which seems to be able to reverse the pleasurable effects of narcotics like heroin and at least slow down the pleasurable response to drinking alcohol.[10] Hopefully, approaches like Drug Courts will increasingly be able to succeed in reducing the harms of the presence of these drugs in our communities until modern science can make additional strides.

Unfortunately, though, we still have much progress to make. Society in general and most courts in particular still are not making distinctions among drug *use,* drug *misuse,* drug *abuse,* and drug *addiction.* Usually when a defendant is found to be using drugs the court response is uniform: to address the situation as one calling for drug treatment. This is often simply not the case, but if the defendant must choose between drug treatment and a criminal conviction, the

An Opinion on Drug Control in Our Country

My personal libertarian belief is represented by the following words I saw one day on a t-shirt: "Other People Are Not Your Property." The government should not have any more right to control what adults put into their bodies than it should have to control what adults put into their minds. Instead, the government should focus upon a person's *conduct* that could cause harm to other people. Another way of putting this is that it makes as much sense to me to put the gifted actor Robert Downey, Jr., in jail for his cocaine problem—and he certainly seems to have one—as it would have to put Betty Ford in jail for her addiction to alcohol. Fundamentally, it is a medical issue! And besides, most of the *problem* users will find their way into court due to their conduct anyway.

Additionally, just because our culture chooses to make these sometimes dangerous and addicting drugs illegal does not at all mean that the drugs are unavailable. As a point of fact, people can get all the drugs they want in prison. The drugs cost more, but they are fully available. For example, a few years ago Charles Manson was moved from Corcoran State Prison to a different facility because he was found to be selling drugs from his prison cell. And he was in solitary confinement! So if we cannot keep these drugs out of prison, how can we expect to keep drugs off the streets of all of our towns and cities?

The basic truth is that there is no such thing as a free society that is also a drug-free society. This fact was made brutally clear with the fall of the former Soviet Union, since the first people to take advantage of a less-authoritarian society were the big-time drug dealers (who since that time have been thriving). The same is true in our country, where marijuana is probably our nation's biggest cash crop today.[1] As soon as we face these realities—and as soon as we focus on the fact that the "tougher" we get on drugs, the "softer" we get on the prosecution of all other crimes because we have only so many resources to devote to law enforcement—the sooner we will change away from this failed system of drug prohibition.

In this regard, maybe we should follow the advice of George Shultz, the former United States Secretary of Labor, who said, "We need at least to consider and examine forms of controlled legalization of drugs."[2] Or that of Gary Johnson, who said, "Take it from a businessman: The War on Drugs is just money down the drain."[3]

choice is almost always for the former. See the inset "An Opinion on Drug Control in Our Country" on the previous page for a related discussion.

Observe the Law or Resign

Drug issues are definitely complex. Even if judges do not agree with some of the laws that come before them, by their oath of office they must either enforce those laws or resign their position. Let us consider an example. In California it is still a violation of law to possess a hypodermic needle and syringe without a prescription, even though the absence of clean needles—that is, the sharing of dirty needles—is directly responsible for the fact that large numbers of people unnecessarily contract the AIDS virus, hepatitis, and other blood-borne diseases. Yes, as a judge, I enforce all of these laws, but I am not required to do so quietly.[11] For example, I often speak to civic, service, religious, and political groups about the fact that needle exchange programs, in which dirty needles are exchanged for clean ones—no money changes hands and no questions are asked—do not increase or decrease drug usage; they are neutral. But they do decrease the incidence of AIDS by about 50 percent! Yet until the laws are changed, I will continue to enforce them.

Know What Works

Our elected officials, courts, and average citizens nationwide are beginning to understand that there are basically four things that work with regard to the nagging and complicated problems that arise from the presence of mind-altering drugs in our communities. The four pillars of productivity are listed below.

- Education: Virtually every social problem adversely affecting our society can be mitigated by strong programs that provide full and honest education, and this is certainly true with regard to drug abuse as well. A major example is the progress we have made in reducing the use of tobacco because of honest education about its effects. These programs can and should be implemented through the parents, the schools, and the public media.

- Prevention and Treatment: Programs of preventive maintenance and repair are effective for our automobiles, our airplanes, and our own bodies. They work in the area of drug abuse as well.

- Positive Incentives: These involve setting up a system that encourages people to do what is socially acceptable, instead of providing such strong financial incentives to sell drugs and otherwise violate the law. For example, in my opinion, a number of drug problems that we are facing today can be reduced by treating marijuana like alcohol. That would get rid of the criminal element in these transactions along with all of the violence, corruption, and enticement to children that accompanies it. It would also bring in large tax revenues, which should be used expressly for drug treatment and honest drug education.

- Individual Responsibility: Hold people strictly accountable for their *actions,* but not for what they put into their bodies.

Judges who serve on Drug Courts are positively affecting our entire nation. Several studies released by the Physician Leadership on National Drug Policy (which is a bi-partisan group of doctors and public health leaders that includes former members of the Bill Clinton, George H. W. Bush, and Ronald Reagan administrations) document that placing drug users into rehabilitation programs significantly reduces drug use and re-arrest rates. Since programs like these cost only about $3,000 per year per person—as opposed to about $25,000 per year to keep one person in prison—this group calculated that Drug Courts will help to save tens of millions of taxpayer dollars per year, reduce the prison population by about 250,000 within five years, and reduce crime.[12] The programs promoted by Drug Courts truly do work.

Plus, if you serve on a Drug Court, you will be gratified by the positive results you see and the appreciation of others for those results. Take, for instance, the words of a nine-year-old boy thanking the Drug Court team by saying, "Now I don't have to sleep in the car anymore or worry if my mom will come home at night or be in jail." You will feel fulfilled when holding a newborn drug-free baby that would not, but for your drug team's efforts, be so lucky. And by the way, the taxpayers around the country will be grateful as well.

Co-Occurring Disorders, Homeless Outreach, and Community Court Calendars

Co-Occurring Disorders, Homeless Outreach, and Community Courts are fairly recent additions to some of our trial courts around the country, and they generally operate on the same basic principles as Drug Courts. In a genuine sense, they offer therapeutic, life-changing alternatives to incarceration and the revolving door of re-arrest. The Co-Occurring Disorders Court (CODC) teams administer the sentences of people with mental illnesses who have been convicted of mostly felony drug offenses and who have previously failed in drug rehabilitation programs. The Homeless Outreach Courts serve people who are homeless and charged with non-violent, victimless misdemeanors and infractions—with an eye toward helping them to become self-sufficient once again. And the Community Courts, in addition to addressing cases involving drugs, prostitution, trespassing, jaywalking, and vandalism, also frequently address so-called "quality of life" cases, such as playing music too loudly, drinking or urinating in public, illegal camping, and being in a public park after hours. Actually, almost all of these courts employ "quality of life" sentences that try to instruct, coerce, or otherwise help the defendants/clients to improve their conditions in life and those of the people around them.[13]

Based upon a 2005 survey of national representative samples, the U.S. Department of Justice estimated that 56 percent of the nation's 747,000 jail inmates and 45 percent of its federal prisoners reported treatment for or symptoms of major depression, mania, or psychotic disorders such as hallucinations or delusions. Disturbingly, fewer than one-third have gotten any beneficial treatment at all behind bars.[14] In addition, about 30 percent of the inmates in jails and prisons have been diagnosed as being *chronically and persistently mentally ill*— usually schizophrenic, bipolar, or suffering from major depressive disorders— and about 72 percent of these people have a co-occurring disorder of alcohol or drug abuse. These are the defendants who typically have been shuffled through the criminal courts, jails, and prisons without much hope of any positive change.

Actually, most of these jails and prisons have mental health facilities, but virtually all of them are critically overcrowded. For example, the mental health unit at the jail in Broward County, Florida, has 375 beds, but only the most critical get a spot. The other 600 who are on a regular program of psychotropic medications are housed with the general population. Suicide attempts are common, as are numbers of inmates talking to people who are not there. As Ana Mourer, the Supervisor of Psychiatric Nurses, said, "A lot of these inmates shouldn't be here. They're charged with misdemeanors. They just have nowhere else to go." Tim Ludwig, the jail's Mental Health Coordinator, put the case more starkly: "This is how we cared for the mentally ill in the 1700s."[15]

But now there is hope, because in a small but growing number of courts there are Co-Occurring Disorders Court calendars. And there is increasing proof that the above-described humanly and financially expensive and discouraging cycle of failure and lost opportunities can be broken. Participation in the programs is voluntary, which means that the defendants can choose to have their offenses addressed in the traditional fashion if they prefer. But once enrolled, the participants are required to comply with all court orders for treatment, take prescribed medications, and attend court progress review hearings. The goal of CODC programs all around the country is to reduce the recidivism of the mentally ill drug offenders by engaging them in comprehensive treatment plans and intensive supervision by the court and probation department. The specific goals are individualized based upon the participants' observed abilities.

Some jurisdictions are getting pretty advanced in their approaches to these problems. For example, in Pennsylvania every jail and prison inmate has a psychological profile developed. The state has set up medical diagnoses and treatments for all of their mentally ill prisoners, as well as community correction centers to help get them back out to and functioning in the real world.[16] Not only is this the practical and humane thing to do, but the RAND Corporation has determined that it is also the economic thing to do. For example, the first year of outreach and wrap-around services for an individual with a mental illness costs about $16,000 to $17,000, as opposed to $25,000 to $30,000 to lock that person up. As California State Senator Darrell Steinberg said after looking at the study, "People are looking for answers. There is no single answer, but treating people with mental-health and substance-abuse issues is the biggest missing part of corrections reform."[17]

The Co-Occurring Disorders Court program in Orange County, California, lasts a minimum of eighteen months and often is quite a bit longer, depending upon the level at which the given participant is able to function. Generally, the screening phase of the program lasts about sixty days. It consists of a client interview and a thorough review by the probation officer and mental healthcare coordinator of the client's medical information and treatment history. Only then is a program suitability determined. Once participants are admitted into a program, they are immediately assigned to a counselor and a psychiatrist who monitor each individual's progress throughout the program. Individual life plans are prepared for each participant that are consistent with the participant's treatment plan developed by the contracted treatment provider. It is mandatory that the participants comply with the taking of all prescribed medication. All participants receive regular and random drug and alcohol testing as well. The program staff meet weekly to discuss each participant and make recommendations to the judge based upon the observed performance. These observed performances also determine the frequency of court appearance dates.

The comprehensive individual treatment plans often include employment assessment and training, job placement, safe and secure housing, and the obtaining of Social Security Insurance if appropriate. They also involve the addressing of medical and dental needs, general individual counseling, medication compliance, consistent attendance at self-help meetings and counseling sessions, the accomplishment of a G.E.D. (high school graduation equivalency degree), the handling of outstanding legal obligations, the obtaining of a driver's license, and developing a plan for the individual's productive usage of time. But any participant who commits a new offense that constitutes a threat to public safety is immediately terminated from the program.

To graduate from the CODC program, the participants must be drug- and alcohol-free for a minimum of nine months, have had no program violations for a minimum of six months, have continued attendance at self-help meetings, be compliant with all of the conditions of probation, have completed their treatment programs as directed, have achieved their Individual Life Plan goals, and have developed appropriate aftercare plans for the future. Successful completion of the program results in the dismissal of the original charges that were brought against them.

The programs, procedures, and goals of the Homeless Outreach Courts and the Community Courts are similar to those of the Co-Occurring Disorders

Courts. Sadly, about a third of the participants in these programs are veterans of our armed forces.

Although it is a hard fact to swallow, the largest mental institutions throughout our country are most often the local county jails. This is frequently due to the fact that these emotionally fragile people enter the criminal justice system because they self-medicate the symptoms of their diseases with illicit drugs, or they fail to come to court after being cited for various offenses, and they end up in jail after an arrest warrant for them has been issued. But once the issues of these mentally ill and homeless people start to be addressed, those individuals usually have a better appearance rate at court than the defendants at the traditional courts. Orange County, California, has found their re-arrest rate to be only about 7 percent. The reason for the more faithful attendance and success seems to be that the mentally ill and homeless are so grateful for the help and encouragement the teams provide them. As Judge Wendy Lindley stated, "They come to us homeless and helpless and graduate at the highest level their individual treatment plan dictates. We have activities for them to learn to interact with others. I remember scanning the softball field and feeling tremendous satisfaction to witness three schizophrenic clients actually enjoying themselves."

The Homeless Outreach and Community Courts provide special court sessions that are often convened in local homeless shelters or other locations readily accessible to the homeless and to people who are at the lower end of the economic scale. The programs attempt, among other things, to resolve all infractions, misdemeanors, and arrest warrants that are outstanding against the participants. But the offenses must be non-violent and victimless misdemeanors or infractions. The courts also address probation violations for the failure to pay fines in other cases as well. Court teams frequently consist of partnerships among the courts, local shelters, community service agencies, district or city attorneys, and public defenders.

The thrust of these programs is to try to meet the problems of homelessness and lower-end living with practical solutions. This results mostly in court orders to participate in agency programs and also in self-help activities and community service at agencies that serve the homeless, instead of the more traditional court sanctions of fines and time in jail. If homeless people are accepted into the outreach programs, most of the courts will resolve all of the outstanding charges against them by sentencing them to various activities in the shelter programs. Examples of these activities are building life-skills, self-help meetings such as Alcoholics Anonymous or Narcotics Anonymous, job training, literacy classes, searching for employment, counseling, and volunteer work. Then when participants have completed their sentences, the pending case records are cleared and the individuals have a fresh start. In addition, the graduates are free from the sometimes oppressive fines that have built up over the years for numbers of these offenses, and that helps to give them some hope. As Judge Jerome Nadler of the Santa Clara, California, Outreach Court put it, "All of a sudden, they've dug themselves such a deep hole that they don't see a way out and so they sort of give up. Being able to clear those is a godsend to them."[18]

The sanctions that are employed for participants on the programs can be anything from writing an essay to performing community service work, or, if necessary, spending time in jail. But since jail time can disrupt medication schedules, the courts try to use jail only for overnights when it comes to those who are on medications. Otherwise, if longer periods of incarceration are deemed necessary, the court staff try to provide as much information and notice to the jails as possible.

Now you have a good idea about what CODC, Homeless Outreach, and Community Court calendars demand from the judges, and what the court teams do in general. The work is intense but rewarding. Here are a few of my personal suggestions if you decide to pursue this type of judging or if you are currently involved in it.

Always Be Prudent in Selecting Sentences

In the various Specialty Courts, the threat of short periods of incarceration is used in order to give people the extra fortitude to improve their position in life. But, like in all calendars, it must be a *meaningful* threat! We are in the "incentives business," and we can never be seen as making false threats. In other words, the defendants (or our "clients") must believe that they have a choice, and that they are choosing to accept responsibility for their actions and to be involved in the program.

It is critical to understand in this process that once judges have sentenced the defendants, they have played almost all of their cards. Judges cannot later increase any part of the sentence unless a defendant later violates a part of the probationary sentence. Therefore, we judges must do it right the first time in sentencing, because once the sentence is ordered, there is no second chance. In general, Criminal Court sentencing can be very complicated and will be discussed at length beginning on page 70.

Join Forces with County Healthcare Workers

When I became a judge I confess I had a built-in bias against county healthcare organizations. For some reason, I felt the staff would be uncaring, uneducated, and lazy. To my surprise, I found that the contrary was true: Most of the agencies employed people who were well-equipped and dedicated to help alcohol- and other drug-addicted people, the homeless, and the mentally ill. In fact, I found out that they too were frustrated with our system because they felt that, in this area, most judges were uncaring, uneducated, and lazy. And strangely enough, I discovered that they were more correct in their assessments than I was in mine.

I say all of this to encourage you to seek out and work with the county healthcare workers in your community. I anticipate that you will be pleasantly surprised—and so will they. And the more we work together, the more we can accomplish.

Do Not Ignore the Receptivity of Those in Need

Another thing that surprised me about working on the Homeless Outreach, CODC, and Community Court calendars was how receptive these defendants were to what we were trying to do for them—after an initial phase of lack of trust. When it comes down to it, most of the defendants realize that they need some help, and when they grow to understand that it is coming their way if they do their part, they can be amazingly successful—and grateful!

So do not believe the stereotypes. People *can* change. Appreciable and beneficial change can be realized on these calendars if you, as the judge, simply adopt the "old one-two" of individual responsibility on the one hand, combined with caring and respect on the other.

In general, the goal of the specialty courts discussed in this section is to take people who are terribly challenged by cycles of addiction, violence, self-destructive behavior, and/or mental illness and assist them with rehabilitative programs. Those programs eventually bring them toward or to self-sufficiency and generally increase their station in life. Typically, the time spent by the participants in the programs far exceeds the time that they would have had to spend in jail or performing other community service work. But once they have completed their programs, all of the participants have something positive and tangible to show for their efforts. It takes time for people who have experienced failure and deprivation to overcome their fears and face their lives and their future. But the results have been positive, and the work deeply gratifying.

THE ART OF SENTENCING IN A CRIMINAL CASE

In those cases in which a defendant either pleads or is found guilty, the judge becomes the voice of society. I myself have sent substantial numbers of convicted defendants to jail and prison, and I must say that sometimes I have felt quite good about the decision. In many ways, individual responsibility has become a rare commodity in our society, but on numbers of occasions judges are in a position to uphold and enforce it, and to punish the wrongdoer. Of course, in their sentencing judges want to do the right thing. But it can be hard. As Judge Frank J. Johnson of the Los Angeles Superior Court has said, "It's easy when somebody comes in with a rap sheet that's a yard long. That's easy. And it's fairly easy when it's a relatively minor crime with no record. It's the ones in the middle that make everyone sweat a little bit."[19] In addition, contrary to the perceptions of many people, criminal sentencing can be a complex and technical matter. In fact, sentencing gives rise to more successful appeals in many jurisdictions than anything else in the criminal justice field, with the exception of instructing the jury on the law at the end of a trial.

Judges must be familiar with all the nuances of sentencing and the law in order not to have their sentences successfully appealed. For example, there can be a major difference between a jail sentence being "consecutive to" as opposed to "concurrent with" any other sentence a defendant may be serving. If it is consecutive, the sentence will be served after whatever other sentence the defendant may be serving is finished. If it is concurrent, it may be served at the same time as any other sentence already imposed. If the judge does not actually state at the time of sentencing that the sentence is to be consecutive, the laws of most jurisdictions require that the sentence be concurrent. And this is one of the more straightforward of the issues! You can imagine how complicated sentencing and subsequent appeals can get with laws dealing with the use of prior convictions, enhancements, mandatory minimum sentences, and more.

In addition, in criminal sentencing the judges are directly affecting the lives of not only the defendants themselves, but also frequently their families, their employers, the victims of the offenses, and society in general. Sentencing in criminal courts is so complicated that I have dedicated a whole section to it below, where I discuss some key issues that should be considered when deciding upon appropriate criminal sentences.[20]

The Uniqueness of Each Case

Obviously, each criminal case is different because each defendant has a unique story, background, and criminal history or lack thereof. So every time judges sentence a defendant, in my opinion they should consider at least the following six issues.

The Range of Possible Sentences According to the Law

Like it or not, judges must follow the law, which is to say that they must stay within the boundaries of sentences that the law prescribes for the crime. Sometimes that means judges must give sentences that are more severe or more lenient than they otherwise would give. But that is one of the challenges of the job. So when deciding upon sentences, judges must ask themselves the following questions: what range of sentences is permitted or required by the law, and are there any mandatory provisions or enhancements?

The Extent of Violence or Threat of Violence

If a person who committed a crime used, showed, or even possessed a weapon—a gun, knife, or any other form of device that can be classified as a weapon—that should be seen as a significant factor in aggravation. The sentence should take this into account.

The Likelihood of Deterrence

Judges must also ask themselves whether or not this sentence is likely to deter similar offenses in the future, both for this individual defendant and for other people in general. The basis for deterrence is the old saying, "People respect wisdom but they obey pain."

There are a few more questions that fall within this issue. Was this criminal act pre-meditated or carried out on the spur of the moment? If it was pre-meditated, then deterrence will be more likely. But if it was done on the spur of the moment, deterrence will be much less of a factor. In addition, judges should ask if there was an influence of third persons upon the defendant that contributed to the offense—such as a girlfriend, boyfriend, or a criminal street gang? If so, is that influence likely to re-occur in the future? For more on the subject of factors involved in sentencing, see the inset "Should Some Defendants Get Celebrity Treatment?" at right.

But contrary to some people's thoughts, there are several ways of deterring people from Criminal Courts in addition to incarceration sentences. Sometimes simply being charged and convicted, along with the accompanying notoriety and social ridicule, is sufficient. Sometimes the payment of a substantial fine and restitution provides enough incentive for the offender and others in the offender's position to be deterred. Sometimes losing one's hob is an enormous deterrence. And actually some judges have forced offenders to wear signs in public places saying things like, "I stole from a local store," or showing a picture of a pig with the language, "This is not a police officer" on it. There is even a judge in Florida who ordered three men who had been convicted in a prostitution sting to wear a chicken suit and carry a sign that read, "There is no chicken ranch in Painesville." I cannot say I agree with these sentences of humiliation, but they seem to be effective. And although they may be "unusual," many people do not think they are "cruel."[21]

The Impact of the Offense upon the Victims

After the accused has been convicted, the crime victims should be contacted by the authorities, made aware well in advance of the sentencing date, and given the opportunity to make an appearance in court. Then they should usually be allowed to make statements to the sentencing judge—in open court, in the presence of the defendant and all counsel—about the negative impact the offense has had upon them. Ultimately, the sentence should, to some reasonable degree, be influenced by the impact described.

The Defendant's Record and Life Connections

Is this the first time the defendant has been in trouble, or the seventh? How long ago was the last criminal violation, and for how long was the defendant out of custody and off parole or probation before having committed this offense? These

SHOULD SOME DEFENDANTS GET CELEBRITY TREATMENT WHEN BEING SENTENCED?

Should a sentence in a criminal case be affected because the defendant happens to be a celebrity? In my view, the answer is yes—to the degree that it will affect the issue of deterrence, and also to the degree that it will affect the population's view of and support for our judicial system. But that is all.

Unfortunately, there is a widespread view in society that people are held accountable for their actions unless those people are celebrities or otherwise wealthy. Actually, that view goes back at least as far as Ancient Greece, when Plutarch observed, "Laws are like spiders' webs; they hold the weak and delicate who are caught in their meshes, but are torn to pieces by the rich and powerful."[1]

So if a judge determines that sentencing a celebrity to a short time in jail for a particular offense would have more of a beneficial effect upon deterrence for the rest of us, then that possibility should be considered. Otherwise, people should not be punished by their celebrity status or receive a benefit from it either. Instead, to the degree that it is humanly possible, everyone should be treated equally in a court of law, and judges should try to follow the challenge from poet Robert G. Ingersoll, who said, "Justice should remove the bandage from her eyes long enough to distinguish between the vicious and the unfortunate."[2]

Let us consider a particular example with regard to deterrence. My father once had a case in his court involving a medical doctor from Beverly Hills who had pleaded guilty to evasion of his income taxes. After reading the probation officer's pre-sentencing report and listening to the arguments and statements of the appropriate participants, my father sentenced the doctor to something like thirty days in jail, and then gave him a delay of the sentence so that he could re-arrange his schedule. About six months after imposing the sentence, my father received a letter from the case agent for the Internal Revenue Service. In effect, it read, "Dear Judge Gray, since you sentenced that doctor to jail, I thought you would be interested to know that we have received a large number of amended tax returns from Beverly Hills doctors." This is a situation in which efforts to deter additional crime worked. Sentencing this doctor to years and years in prison would probably have been counterproductive. But for non-violent offenses where recidivism is probably not going to occur, short periods of time in jail are often sufficient for the word to get out that these matters are to be taken seriously, and that people who commit these offenses will be held accountable for their actions.

questions consider the fact that the defendant's past cannot be ignored as the judge decides upon a sentence.

Nor can the defendant's personal life be ignored. For example, what impact will the proposed sentence have upon the defendant's family? Will the defendant lose his job as a result of the sentence? If so, is that avoidable or not, or should it be?

The Chance of Rehabilitation

What is the likelihood that this defendant will repeat this or any other violation of the law? Was the defendant under the influence of alcohol or other drugs at the time of the offense, and how seriously is the defendant addressing this problem? The defendant's level of *honest* remorse for the violation should also have an impact upon the sentence. That level will give the judge an idea of how likely rehabilitation actually is, so that the sentence can be adjusted accordingly.

Restitution to the Victims, Balanced with Justice for the Defendant

A further complication at sentencing is requiring the defendants to make restitution to their victims. In this matter, the actual ability of defendants to pay is not a relevant factor in deciding the appropriate amount of restitution. Instead, the only determination judges are required to make at this point is the amount of damage that has been directly and reasonably caused to the victim by the defendant's conduct. Of course, we do not have debtors' prisons in this country, so the defendants' ability to pay does become relevant once they begin to make the actual payments.

Experienced judges try to take matters of criminal sentencing out of the sphere of politics and stay focused on proper restitution for the victims, while being fair to the defendant at the same time. But it is not always easy for this to be done, especially if there is a lot of media and emotional pressure on the judge to give a particular sentence. For example, Orange County had a highly publicized case in which one group of high school boys was driving by another group of boys from a different high school in a parking lot on a weekend night. Generally all of the boys were yelling obscenities and showing off their machismo. At one point, one of the young men lost his head and hurled a paint roller from where he was standing toward those in the car. In what could only be called a freak occurrence, the roller hit one of the boys in the car in the side of the head, entered his skull, and eventually killed him. So the young man who threw the paint roller was charged with murder, and he was convicted. The case involved great political emotion. Now what does the judge do in sentencing?

On the one hand, we had a true tragedy that left a young man dead, and his parents, friends, and political representatives calling for a life sentence for the offender. On the other hand, we had a young man with no prior criminal record to speak of who had certainly intended to throw the paint roller, and did so with a "man-endangering" frame of mind, but ended up killing the boy only because of a freak occurrence. Put yourself in the judicial robe. What would you do? The fact that most state judges are elected can work against a defendant convicted of a criminal offense. Some judges, if up for reelection or a promotion to the court of appeals, might sway toward the side of what is politically advantageous. Would that have affected you as a judge?

The situation called for just about everything: punishment, accountability, deterrence, understanding, and reason. The judge—a senior and experienced judge—looked at the case outside of politics. At the sentencing hearing, he allowed all parties to have their say, certainly including the parents of the deceased. Then he stated the obvious: This was a tragedy from everyone's point of view, but nothing could be done at that time to bring back the deceased young man. That said, our senior judge sentenced the defendant to several years in prison—not as much as the prosecution and the victim's parents had been requesting, and not the probationary sentence that would have occurred had the paint roller not killed or even injured the other boy. The sentence showed that the judge recognized two important things: that this conduct did not arise after reflective thought, and that it would have served no useful purpose to waste a second life as a result of this tragedy.

As suggested above, the problem of politics' potentially influencing the actions of judges can be compounded in the state systems where judges must run for reelection, because this can deeply work to the disadvantage of criminal defendants. I believe all judges try to live up to the words of Robert A. Baines of the Santa Clara Superior Court in California: "My job is pretty clear. None of us should be judges if we can't bear the heat when it comes to making unpopular decisions."[22] But do we always?

Sometimes judges simply cannot help but wonder whether a correct but unpopular decision in a visible case will cost them their upcoming reelection or will torpedo their pending promotional appointment to the court of appeal. One of my finest colleagues, Judge Nancy Wieben Stock, was assigned to try the O. J. Simpson child custody case when she was in Juvenile Court, and it happened to be during a time when she was being strongly considered for an appointment to the court of appeal. As is customary in juvenile proceedings, the courtroom in the case before her was closed to the public in order to protect the privacy of the children. But according to what several knowledgeable sources told me firsthand, the decision Judge Wieben Stock made to allow the children to remain in the custody of their father—whom many consider to have murdered their mother and their mother's friend, despite a not guilty verdict in court—was the correct one *under the evidence* produced in the trial. Nevertheless, when that decision became public, there was such outrage that her appointment to the court of appeals never was realized.

If Judge Wieben Stock had known that her decision would have taken away the possibility of her appointment, would that have made any difference in her decision? Certainly not—not this judge. But these are the practicalities of life for a judge, and sometimes some judges, being only human, can succumb to or at least be influenced by the pressure.

The Weight of Intention and Fate

The example of the case involving a boy who threw a paint roller at another boy in a car brings up an additional issue, which is that of intention. Some people put themselves into a position to cause severe harm to others, but for reasons of fate do not actually do so. These people are frequently not punished as severely as their actions might warrant. Conversely, others who do the same things but have fate, in all of its fickleness, intercede to cause a tragedy are frequently punished quite severely.

In the prior example, had fate not interceded with the paint roller, the young defendant would probably have received a misdemeanor conviction, a scolding, and some community service work picking up trash on the freeway. Similarly, many people who drive a motor vehicle under the influence of alcohol or other drugs put themselves in a position to cause substantial harm to others. For some, due to one lucky reason or another, nothing happens when they drive through an intersection against a red light other than that they get arrested, prosecuted, convicted, and sentenced to pay a fine. They also have their license restricted for a while and attend a program. Others who did the exact same thing but found that fate intervened and resulted in the killing of an innocent person in the intersection will most often be sent to prison for a substantial period of time.

Now judges simply cannot and should not close their eyes to the consequences of criminal behavior. But judges should also understand that much of what happens is simply the "luck of the draw." That means that the more sophisticated judges will impose more severe sentences upon the defendants whose identical actions fortunately caused no harm, and they will impose somewhat less severe sentences upon those whose same actions through quirks of fate caused some real harm. This brings up the issue of minimum sentences, which is explored in the inset "Should Legislatures Set Minimum Sentences?" on the following page.

So, when it comes down to it, how do judges decide what sentence to give to a criminal defendant? Basically most judges will tell you that they have a standard sentence for particular offenses, and then they either move up or down from that sentence depending upon various factors in aggravation or mitigation. One of the most important factors is almost always based upon the amount of actual harm done to the victims or to society itself, and whether there was a betrayal of any position of trust. Other factors are the presence or absence of the defendant's record of prior convictions, on the one hand, or good works on the

SHOULD LEGISLATURES SET MINIMUM SENTENCES?

For many years, people at large, and certainly the politicians who represented them, argued that many judges were so weak in their sentences that the legislatures were "forced" to pass statutes with mandatory minimum sentences for various offenses. Naturally, judges have always resisted the imposition of minimum sentences, because they are seen as severe encroachments upon judicial discretion. Judges argue that without judicial discretion we might as well use computers instead of judges for the determination of sentences. I personally believe it is simply not possible for anyone in the legislature, or anywhere else, to decide upon a reasonable and just punishment in advance without knowing who the perpetrators are, their backgrounds and records, the circumstances of the offenses, and the effects the offenses have had upon the specific individuals involved, as well as upon society in general.

So to this day the debate about mandatory minimum sentences continues to go back and forth. But one suggested compromise in this debate that makes sense to me would be to have a "panel" of three judges who would decide upon the sentences for all of the criminal cases handled by those three judges. Having this consortium of judges would tend to provide more middle-of-the-road consistency in sentencing without taking away important judicial discretion in sentencing.

other, and the presence or absence of remorse, mostly as shown by the defendant's conduct instead of words.

Many judges also consider whether the defendant testified untruthfully during the trial. If a defendant took the stand and lied, then she is not seen as being particularly remorseful. Note that defendants are not actually punished for testifying untruthfully, but they appear not to have learned from their mistakes and therefore do not get much favorable consideration. Finally, of course, issues of punishment, deterrence, and possibilities for either rehabilitation or recidivism have an important effect upon the sentence that is ultimately imposed.

CONCLUSION

This chapter has highlighted many things for you to consider regarding the criminal court system and the role of judges within it. It is one of the most vibrant areas of the law and certainly will remain so in the future. For example, as modern neuroscience is more able to "map" the brain and modify it, how will the courts grapple with those changes? If a defendant committed an offense but subsequently his brain makeup has been changed, should he still be punished for his previous behavior? Or how will the legal system deal with testimony itself if modern technology develops a way to "plant" memories in a person's brain? These fascinating issues and more will be thrust upon judges on Criminal calendars. We should not shy away from such challenges; we should embrace them.

But I hope that you now have a more in-depth understanding of Felony, Misdemeanor, and Specialty Court calendars. And I also hope you have gained a large number of pointers that, if personalized and practiced, will make you a more insightful Criminal Court judge who will deal ably with the upcoming challenges of the future. Many of these skills and suggestions will be further discussed in Part II of this book as we go more deeply into issues about how you can be the most effective judge you can be. But for now, we still have a number of court calendars to review. The next court calendar to consider is the Civil Court system, which is addressed in Chapter 3.

Chapter 3

The Civil Court System

*"Through the centuries, men of law have been persistently
concerned with the resolution of disputes . . . in ways that enable
society to achieve its goals with a minimum of force and
maximum of reason."*[1]

—ARCHIBALD COX

Civil disputes usually involve quite different types of calendars than criminal cases do. The former are lawsuits brought by individuals or groups of people—such as corporations or other businesses, governmental agencies, or any type of public or private organizations—against other entities or parties, and money damages are usually the main issue. These cases are resolved on what is referred to as a "preponderance of the evidence" standard, which is basically a "more likely than not" burden of proof. A few issues, such as exemplary or punitive damages, are also resolved on a "clear and convincing" standard, as opposed to the more strict "beyond a reasonable doubt" standard used in criminal cases. Although the types of cases in a Civil Court calendar are almost limitless, they are usually based upon either a breach of contract or a tort.

If you think about it, many of the things we do in life are based upon voluntary contracts, such as the buying and selling of goods, services, and labor. When people fail to perform their obligations under their contracts, and others are damaged or harmed as a result, a lawsuit may ensue. The law of torts deals with either negligent or intentional acts by one entity that wrongly inflict damage upon another. Damages can be sustained to one's person; reputation; mental state; or real, personal, or intellectual property.

Unlike criminal prosecutions, civil cases do not result in incarceration or the imposition of fines; instead, they mostly involve judgments concerning the payment of money to injured or wronged parties. But civil cases can also result in enforceable judicial orders requiring a party either to do or not to do an almost limitless number of acts. For example, a party might be ordered to return property, sign documents, keep within specified noise levels, or refrain from competing in a certain manner—just to name a few possibilities. It all depends upon the nature of the case. In addition, people naturally see things differently, depending upon what side of the case they are on. Aesop's *Fables* expressed this concept well with the following quote: "The injuries we do and those we suffer are seldom weighted in the same scales."[2] In course, we judges are always placed between the people of these different viewpoints, so get used to it!

Ideally, civil cases would be handled in the courts local to where the injury is alleged to have occurred. The federal civil system was originally designed only for more sophisticated civil matters that involve interstate transactions or particularly federal matters like patent or copyright infringements. But federal courts also have jurisdiction to try cases among entities that have their residences in dif-

WHERE DO THE CASES COME FROM?

Imagine you are a judge in a large jurisdiction that has many cases to assign. How can this be done? In small jurisdictions the cases are usually assigned directly to each judge on a rotating basis. But in large jurisdictions that is almost unworkable. So large jurisdictions usually adopt one of two approaches.

Some courts use what is called a *master calendar system,* in which all cases are administered by one central court. Under this system, each case is referred to a Specialty Court for one or more facets of the procedure, such as pre-trial motions and settlement discussions, and eventually for trial. When a trial judge under the master calendar system finishes one trial, the judge is sent another one from the master calendar. The other system is called the *direct calendar system.* Under this system, a judge is assigned to a case for all purposes as soon as it is filed.

When our courts in Orange County, California, switched to a direct calendaring system, we went from a substantial backlog in getting our cases to trial to a situation in which we were basically ready for trial whenever the litigants were ready to go forward. And the same results have mostly been achieved throughout our entire state because all counties now use the direct calendar system. For example, in 2005–2006, 68 percent of Civil Unlimited Court cases were disposed of within twelve months, 85 percent within eighteen months, and 91 percent within twenty-four months. I think you will agree that those are good numbers.

ferent states. The purpose of this is to reduce the likelihood that a local state judge will succumb to the temptation of ruling for the "hometown" litigant because the judge has to run for office in that local community.

For decades the jurisdictional threshold for cases brought to federal court was $10,000. Cases below that amount would be litigated in state courts. More recently that amount has been raised to $75,000. But the newer threshold amount still screens out only a small number of cases, so the federal system has evolved into trying many matters that were once solely within the province of the state courts.

In moderately- to small-sized civil jurisdictions, each judge hears every type of civil case. But in the larger jurisdictions the calendars are mostly broken down into subdivisions, usually determined by the amount of money that is at issue. Keep in mind that the more money that is involved, the more protections the parties will have in being represented by an attorney, having a jury, and being

---

In my view, there is a good reason for these positive results. Let us say the defendant's attorney in a civil case has a special tactic he wants to use during trial. If that tactic is unsuccessful early in the process but the same judge is staying with the case throughout its entire life—that is, if the direct calendar system is being used—that attorney and his client are less likely to repeat that tactic. Quite differently, if it is going to be a new judge at the next stage of trial—through the master calendar system—that same tactic can be recycled. The practical reality is that the direct calendaring system with one judge assigned for all purposes tends to keep the cases moving forward.

Also, if the trial judge is the one who hears the argument and rules upon it, the odds are strong that this ruling will not subsequently be changed as the case progresses. That means that the litigants could quickly get a flavor about the way the case will likely be resolved, and they will adjust accordingly. Furthermore, there is much less of an incentive for counsel to act like "jerks" during discovery if they know that they will have to stay with the same judge for trial.

Finally, trial judges who do not work hard to settle their cases under the direct calendar system know they will have to keep them for trial. And, although there is no formal requirement to reduce one's caseload, in many jurisdictions statistics setting forth the number of cases in one's inventory are released to all of the civil judges. The statistics also make note of the age of those cases. So there is a natural incentive for the judges to try to look better to their peers. As all sophisticated people understand, incentives matter. It should not be a secret that this eternal rule holds true with regard to judges and their diligence as well.

afforded access to evidence before trial. Of course, these protections also increase the time and expense that will be involved. In most jurisdictions, regardless of the specific terminology used, these civil calendars are broken down into General Unlimited, Limited, Complex, and Small Claims. For more information on how a given jurisdiction distributes cases, see the inset "Where Do the Cases Come From?" on pages 80 and 81.

GENERAL UNLIMITED CIVIL COURTS

Depending upon the jurisdiction, General Unlimited Civil calendars address any civil case in which the alleged money damages exceed a minimum value. This is usually between $15,000 and $50,000. In addition, these calendars will also handle cases in which one or more of the parties are hoping for some type of court order for which money is deemed insufficient, such as a restraining order to prohibit some type of conduct, the specific performance of a contract, or a mandamus action that would require a party to do something such as to remove a fence or deliver a deed to some real property. Now we will address some of the specific judicial responsibilities of this type of calendar.

The Basics of General Unlimited Court Calendars

General Unlimited Civil Court cases generally run the gamut of all kinds of torts and breaches of contract. I use the term "the gamut" because these cases can involve factual patterns that are limited only by humankind's creativity, emotion, negligence, carelessness, and stupidity. As a result, judges are called upon to decide things as diverse as disputes between parents about the final resting place for a son killed in battle, whether or not a particular Environmental Impact Report is sufficient to support the building of a particular project, what work stoppages are authorized under the law, whether the wording on a ballot election statement is within the law, the rights to publicity of dead celebrities, whether pesticides applied to a river under a program to eliminate non-native trout are "pollutants" under the law, whether pets have rights when it is decided which "owner" they should be returned to, or even whether the CIA should be ordered to report upon the number of alternative fuel vehicles their personnel have been operating. And, putting it mildly, sometimes the decisions we are forced to make are distasteful to us and a majority of people around us. This issue is well addressed by Justice Anthony Kennedy, who said, "The hard fact is that sometimes we must make decisions we don't like. We make them because they are right. Right in the sense that the law and the Constitution as we see them compel the result."[3]

General Unlimited Civil judges are also occasionally called upon to decide difficult ethical problems, such as whether research may be conducted in third-world countries on drugs that will primarily be used by people in wealthy countries. Another example would be the question of who should be able to get scarce antiviral drugs or vaccines when a flu epidemic hits. There are even cases concerning whether the public or private sector should be allowed to pay living donors for organs that will increase the number of life-saving transplants. In other words, judges in civil calendars are frequently called upon to make difficult decisions that can have a large effect upon the safety of or potential harm to people and property.

In addition, these judges are called upon to protect minority rights as provided by the U.S. Constitution. The circumstances of some of these cases can be quite political, emotional, and controversial. In that regard, I believe it is a judge's duty to follow the lead of Justice Robert Jackson who—even in the year 1943, while a world war was raging—held that no one in our country could, under our Constitution, be *forced* to salute our flag or even to recite the Pledge of Allegiance. Justice Jackson said:

> The very purpose of our Bill of Rights was to withdraw certain subjects from the vicissitudes of political controversy, to place them beyond the reach of majorities and officials, and to establish them as legal principles to be applied by the courts. One's right to life, liberty and property, to free speech, a free press, freedom of worship and assembly, and other fundamental rights may not be submitted to vote; they depend on the outcome of no elections.[4]

The less difficult cases for judges to try are those that are submitted for resolution to a jury. Of course, judges must always be attentive to objections regarding the offering of evidence, provide the correct legal instructions to the jury, and be cognizant of all of the issues. But otherwise the judge can mostly sit back and simply let the trial take its course. It is a lot more work for judges when all parties waive (or give up) their rights to a jury, because then they are called upon to decide the case and give the reasons for their decisions. In such cases, regardless of the situation, judges *must* issue a judgment. That can be difficult. Even after judges decide who the prevailing party should be, they still must decide upon the exact amount of the judgment if the plaintiff prevails or the appropriate actions to be ordered. These tasks can be quite complicated, and the judge's explanations must be thoughtful and clear. For more on difficult situations in which Civil Court judges can find themselves, see the inset "A Dilemma to Think About" on the following page.

Advice for the General Unlimited Civil Court Judge

Obviously, this type of judicial calendar covers a myriad of subjects and responsibilities. Below you will find several pointers for the General Unlimited Civil Court judge, addressing just some of the challenges that come up in this particular field.

A Dilemma to Think About

Many years ago in a civil case that was tried before me without a jury, it increasingly became apparent that there was an affirmative defense that was at least viable for the defendant. When I could stand it no longer, I asked the defendant's counsel if he was pursuing this defense. When he naturally said he was, I told him that it had not been raised in his Answer to the Complaint and asked him if he was moving to amend his Answer. Of course, the counsel's answer was yes.

Then I asked plaintiff's counsel if he objected to the motion, and, if so, could he show "surprise or prejudice." The plaintiff's counsel did object, but he did not convince me that either surprise or prejudice was present, so I granted the defendant's oral motion. Subsequently, the case was decided by that affirmative defense, and judgment was entered for the defendant.

A week or two later I received a letter from the plaintiff's counsel that was completely respectful but complained that I, as the trial judge, had found this affirmative defense, talked defense counsel into moving to amend, and then decided the case for the defense because of it. I wrote back to counsel, thanked him for his letter, and cited this as a dilemma. What is a trial judge in a non-jury trial supposed to do in a situation like this one? On the one hand, we have an adversarial system in which the actions of the attorneys ideally are supposed to cancel each other out. In that way the "truth" can prevail. On the other hand, life is not perfect, and it is a judge's responsibility to do justice. That means that a party should not be penalized because his attorneys are less schooled or insightful than those of the other party. As I sit here writing these words, I have still not satisfactorily resolved that dilemma in my own mind. Instead, I am simply passing it along to you for your consideration.

Accept the Fact That There Will Be Unresolved Problems with Witness Credibility

The reality is that some cases, including civil cases, are hard to decide based upon the credibility—or lack of credibility—of some of the witnesses. One time I had a case involving a former partnership that was formed to purchase and move several small buildings to another location and then sell them. None of the partners had any background in these types of activities, and so the endeavor eventually failed. As a result, the "investing partner" brought suit against the others to get back some of his money. Unfortunately, the only things that were put down in writing about the responsibilities of the partners were several comments on a paper napkin at a coffee shop about how the "profits" were to be distributed. Naturally, the oral testimony of the various partners and witnesses was inconsistent.

Another case of this kind involved two former business partners who were dissolving their partnership. I concluded that both of them would testify to *anything* if they simply thought it would "move their chess pieces forward even a little bit." As a result, none of the oral testimony was reliable.

So what does a judge do in these situations? In my cases, I set forth my conclusions as best I could on the record, stated what I did and did not believe from the testimony, and drew the best inferences I could based on the limited amount of believable evidence submitted. Finally, taking into account the appropriate burden of proof, I issued a judgment and moved on to the next case. Judges cannot allow themselves to labor too long and emotionally over the questionable testimony of witnesses. Just listen, reflect, and then do the best you can.

On some occasions you will have cases in which a defendant is incarcerated for an offense that gave rise to the civil case. Examples would be a collision in which the defendant was driving under the influence of alcohol, or a defendant having assaulted the plaintiff in some way. Usually those cases will result in a default judgment's being issued against the defendant. But what happens if the defendant writes you a letter and wants to defend the case but is virtually prohibited because he is in custody? My view is that he is in an unfair situation, and that the judge on the case should use best efforts to find the defendant an attorney who will take the case pro bono. Yes, you are right, it probably will not affect the ultimate result. But without this assistance the "appearance of justice" would be lacking. And that is what we judges should try to uphold.

Anticipate Some Frivolous Lawsuits

Civil Court judges do see some truly righteous tort cases. For example, having seen numbers of medical malpractice suits, I myself have gone to great lengths not to be administered general anesthetic in medical procedures unless it is absolutely necessary! I refer to the time I heard of the testimony of a plaintiff in a medical malpractice case who was complaining that several times during the operation she heard her doctor say a disturbing four-letter word, which was, "Oops!" Although medical doctors try to follow their oath to "first do no harm," sometimes mistakes happen, just like with everybody else. But we must acknowledge that there are quite a few exaggerated or even baseless malpractice cases as well.

Unfortunately, some folks in our society feel that other people should be guarantors that nothing will ever go wrong. And if something does goes wrong, such folks believe that they, as "victims," should be paid for all damages, real or imagined. But that is simply not the way that life, or our civil justice system, works. (And it does work! For more comments on this issue, see the inset "By and Large, the Civil Justice System Is Working" on pages 86 and 87.) Additionally, some situations can involve plaintiffs who are simply frauds. For example, there is the story about a plaintiff's being asked on the witness stand how high he now can raise his arm. He is able, with visible pain, to raise it only to shoul-

By and Large, the Civil Justice System Is Working

Many people, including numerous politicians, routinely demonize our trial system for civil cases—that is, until they need a lawyer. Many noisy activists cry out for reform, until they are in an automobile collision. Many large institutions complain about the high number of lawsuits they must endure, but they bring numerous lawsuits to court themselves. Yes, there are certainly problems with our civil justice system. But in my view there are basically only two ways to oversee and maximize safety in the marketplace, workplace, and society in general. One would be to increase even further the bureaucratic regulations at all levels of government—and no one I know wants to do that except the regulators. The other is to employ our civil justice system, with all of its perceived imperfections.

For all their complaining, most people also inherently seem to understand that our civil justice system is better than any other alternative. I clearly remember a fundraising dinner at which I sat next to a woman who learned that I was a judge. During the entire dinner she harangued me with stories about how the "shyster lawyers" and the civil justice system were responsible for large numbers of the problems in our world. Finally at about the time of dessert I tried to change the subject. In desperation, I asked her if she had any children. "Oh yes," she gushed, "and my oldest son is in law school!"

Life unavoidably entails risks, particularly in a free society, and the more we allow the regulation of risk, curtailing of rewards, and increased government bureaucracy to dominate our lives, the more we will strangle creative risk-taking and innovations and make our lives more bland. So with an understanding that there is a difference between taking risks on the one hand and gambling on the other, we must continually strive for the enforcement of our laws to strike a reasonable balance between risks and safety. I believe that our civil system best and most efficiently strikes the proper balance.

That being said, it is true that sometimes the civil justice system pushes seemingly silly results. For example, there are the spectacularly unhelpful "warning labels" on some cans of soda that read, "Open. Drink." Or how about the labels on the bottles of over-the-counter medications that state, "If

der level. Then on cross-examination the plaintiff is asked how high he could raise it before the collision, and he raises his arm well over his head.

I myself have been involved in a case in which a plaintiff who was complaining about serious back injuries had actually been videotaped about a week before when he was carrying a garage door on his back while assisting his brother-in-you are allergic to this medication, don't use it." Then there are the signs inside a movie theater that advise, "In case of emergency, please go to the nearest exit." I once even saw printed, "The FDA is issuing a warning not to eat things you find on the sidewalk." In large part we in the legal profession are responsible for these transparently exaggerated warnings. But they are fundamentally due to lawsuits that found the manufacturers of products liable for injuries that resulted from a lack of labels' warning customers of various risks inherent in the use of the products. Similar lawsuits have had the result of medical doctors' ordering numbers of tests not so much to diagnose illnesses but instead to protect themselves from malpractice suits brought by their patients if anything goes wrong. But overall the marketplace, as overseen by our judicial system of enforced responsibility, seems to me to be working quite well.

Yes, some people argue that there have been "outrageous verdicts" by which plaintiffs were awarded "unbelievable" amounts of money. But we seldom hear about the substantial majority of verdicts when plaintiffs are successful that order defendants to pay amounts that are *not* unusually high. And do not forget, all of these verdicts were rendered by neutral people on juries who had no vested interest in the outcome of the case except to do what they felt was right under the facts and the law. In addition, those juries *actually heard the evidence* in the case and were instructed in the law before rendering their verdicts. For example, although I did not actually hear the evidence in the "McDonald's coffee case," in which a woman was scalded by a cup of coffee she placed between her legs while driving a car, I do understand that the evidence also included the fact that similar incidents had resulted in severe injuries on numbers of prior occasions, without the company's taking any corrective action. In addition, a sizeable percentage of that verdict was reduced as a direct result of the plaintiff's own negligence. Many of the "extreme verdicts" are subjected to the additional protections of the judicial system and are often substantially reduced before they ever are entered as final judgments. So when the issue comes up I often tell my jurors that we should leave other cases to their juries and judges and should instead devote our full attention to doing the right thing in our particular case, whatever that right thing might be.

law in the door's installation. The defense's counsel wanted to keep the tape a secret until trial, but I persuaded him to disclose it. When confronted by the tape, the plaintiff dismissed the case.

I have also worked on other cases in which the defendants told me that they believed that automobile collisions or "slip and fall" incidents had simply been staged. If I am confronted with one of those types of cases, I look the plaintiff's counsel in the eye and say that if he ever has reason to believe he is representing a fraudulent plaintiff, he is ethically bound to dismiss the case immediately. I also look at the defense counsel and say that if she truly believes the plaintiff's case is a sham, she will be performing a public service by not offering one penny for settlement and taking the case to trial. Frivolous cases are actually more rare than most people think, but they do happen.

Under our laws, judges are frequently prevented from being able to do much about frivolous lawsuits until such cases have been decided at the close of trial. But they almost always have some ability to affect the outcome at least to some degree. For example, in most jurisdictions there are statutes that give judges the discretion to award some or all of the fees and costs incurred by a party as a result of actions by an opposing party that clearly and transparently have no merit. In circumstances in which it appears that this might be one of those cases, I recommend the judge put both sides on notice—on the record—that the reimbursement of such fees and costs is being contemplated.

Anticipate the Possibility of Problems in Default Judgment Cases

Default judgment cases arise when defendants have been properly served with civil complaints and then have failed to respond within a specified period of time. The first thing to establish, of course, is that the defendant *was* properly served and that the complaint furnished adequate notice of the relief being requested. I also recommend to all plaintiffs that even though they have taken a default, they should send a copy of the notice for a "default prove-up hearing" to all of the possible addresses they have for all defendants. This actually works in favor of all parties, because if it is shown later that a defendant did not get actual notice of the lawsuit, most of the time the default is set aside and lots of time and effort are wasted. But if it is shown that defendants actually received the notice of one of these hearings and still do not appear, it may be that defendants were simply ignoring the case. In those situations, the default will probably not be set aside.

But at the default prove-up hearings, plaintiffs still must prove their cases. The hearings are still trials, and, to the surprise of many plaintiffs' counsel, the burden of proof and rules of evidence still apply. So plaintiffs must present testimony, writings, or other evidence that satisfy each of the elements of their causes of action, including actual causation and damages. In that regard, there was one occasion in which, even after I granted the plaintiff a continuance to produce additional evidence, I actually ordered a judgment for the defendant in the defaulted case based upon the plaintiff's failure of proof.

Keep "Special Notes"

Whether you use a computer to take notes or you still use a pad of paper, reserve a place for "special notes" to be taken that set forth some insightful pieces of evidence—the pieces that can help you decide the case. For example, in a case alleging that an employee had stolen his employer's testing equipment, the defense was that he simply had taken the equipment home so that he could conduct company experiments on the weekends. But the fact that he had also taken a *telephone* from his employer found its way onto my separate pad of notes, which I cited as important evidence in showing the defendant's state of mind.

So why not avoid the trouble of relying upon yourself to highlight special points on your main note pads only then to have to review and find them when ultimately gathering your thoughts? It is helpful to have them all in one place and easily accessible on a separate pad.

Give Tentative Judgments

In cases tried to a judge without a jury, counsel appreciate hearing where the Court tentatively stands at the close of the evidence but before their closing arguments. That includes all material matters in dispute, including a review of controlling case law, possible failures of proof by the various parties, credibility of witnesses, amount and specific computations or even just estimates of damages, where appropriate, and more. The tentative judgment should also set forth areas in which the Court may still not be sure about a decision or is hesitant to reveal its tentative thoughts until the arguments of counsel have been received. This approach has two benefits: It gives counsel for the potentially losing side a "fighting chance" to change the Court's mind before the judgment is entered, and it provides an opportunity for judges to test their tentative conclusions "by fire" before the final decisions are entered.

If and when you give your tentative statements, try to be as precise as you can be. First of all, counsel will rightfully take your tentative comments seriously, and they deserve clear statements from the judge. Secondly, this can be a main record of your thoughts and rationale if the case is appealed, so it will be helpful for the appellate court to have an unambiguous statement as well. As an example, on one of my cases an attorney argued on appeal that the testimony of its main witness was inconsistent with the judgment I had entered. But when the appellate court cited the statement in my tentative opinion (which I later expressly adopted as my final thoughts) that I had found that witness to have been "sneaky, shady, slick, and suspicious," the appellate court had little difficulty finding that I had discounted that witness' testimony and upheld the verdict. I do not make derogatory comments like those very often, but in that case they were appropriate. In any case, the fact that I had provided clear, observant notes in my tentative judgment ended up helping the parties and making a fuller, more lucid record.

Be Prepared Concerning Your Statements of Decision

Many jurisdictions require that a court provide a written Statement of Decision in a non-jury civil trial if it is requested by counsel in a timely fashion. In those situations, I suggest that you request a stipulation from *all* counsel on the record that the tentative decision that you are about to give, as discussed previously and as subsequently amplified by your final comments *and* answers to any clarifying questions of counsel, will constitute your Statement of Decision. Then, if a party wishes to have the statement reduced to writing and signed by the Court, that party may order the transcript of the statements from the court reporter and then submit it to the Court for signature. Most likely, if the stipulation is requested *before* the tentative statement is given, all parties will accept this procedure. But if you wait until you have already shared your tentative thoughts with them, you can be sure that the side that has not prevailed will decline your invitation for such a stipulation.

The process of combining the tentative decision with the Statement of Decision has three benefits. First, it gives counsel a chance "while the iron is hot" to ask clarifying questions to the Court. Second, it saves the trial court judge a large amount of time in trying to resurrect his thoughts and rationale at a later date and then laboriously reduce them to writing. Finally, it reduces the practice of the trial judge's simply ordering counsel for the prevailing party to prepare the Court's Statement, which the judge later signs. Most of the time when this happens the prevailing party largely exaggerates the judge's findings in its favor, and often the judge can be too hurried or inattentive to make the appropriate changes. So in my view this process proves to be much more straightforward, accurate, and helpful to everyone.

Understand That a Signed Verdict or Final Order Belongs to You

Once a final order or final judgment has been issued, that order or judgment and everything that led up to it will be attributed to you as the trial judge. That means that the facts of the case should be documented, the proper jury instructions given, the proper verdict forms used, and the appropriate law employed. And this is true no matter how the trial went, how weak or impossible the trial counsel or witnesses were, how sick you were with the flu, or what time pressures you faced.

So stand advised, and perform all of your responsibilities as correctly as you can under all circumstances because everything else will be irrelevant and forgotten. The ultimate outcome, except for an actual jury verdict, will belong to the judge. And that judge will be held publicly accountable for it.

Refer Perjury Cases to the Proper Authorities

Nothing undercuts our system of justice more than the feeling some people have that they can knowingly give false testimony under penalty of perjury and not be held accountable for it. If you face a clear case of perjury, refer the matter—with a letter of explanation and a transcript, if possible—to the local prosecutor's office for possible prosecution. Unfortunately, prosecutions for perjury are rare in today's world. But in my view, being in the presence of perjury without doing anything about it is tantamount to condoning it.

Be Courageous and Speak Your Mind, When It Is Appropriate

It is generally considered an ethical violation for a trial judge to comment in front of the jury about its verdict. There are obvious reasons for this: The comments could undermine the jurors' confidence in their verdict or the system of justice in general and also could affect the jurors' decision in future cases. But sometimes there are exceptions to this rule. Allow me to provide an example.

A fairly long time ago I had a medical malpractice jury trial in which I felt that the young male plaintiff, and especially his mother, had wrongly blamed the medical doctor for fouling up the plaintiff's medical condition and even his life. So when the jury brought back a unanimous defense verdict, I told the plaintiff and his mother in open court that, based on all of the evidence, I agreed with the jury. Moreover, as a fellow human being I strongly recommended that the plaintiff should take much more responsibility for his own life and his future, and that he should stop blaming other people for his problems.

After we adjourned, several jurors volunteered to me that they had agreed so strongly with what I had said that they had even debated attaching an addendum to their verdict putting forth similar comments. As a sequel, more than five years later I ran into the defendant doctor at a social function. He sought me out, reminded me of what I had done, and thanked me for doing so. He told me that he had been professionally and personally mortified about having been sued in the case, but that my comments from the bench at the very end of the trial had gone a long way to soothe his damaged psyche. And he actually told me this with tears in his eyes.

The bottom line is that judges still have a position of prominence and authority in our society, and what they say and do can carry sometimes unimaginable weight with others—for good or for harm. That means that after the facts and the law have been fully considered, judges should, on appropriate occasions, look some people in the courtroom squarely in the eye and remind them that, as adults, they are responsible for themselves and their actions, and that they should pay their own way and stop making excuses. On some rare occasions judges should even recommend that the party get over whatever the problem is and get on with their lives. Of course, judges should always be guided by ethical rules and regulations, and mostly those rules tell them not to comment to the jury about their verdict. But if we believe that all procedural rules must be blindly followed at all times, we might as well put a judicial robe on a computer.

Support the Adoption of the Federal Approach

Today's discovery rules in most state jurisdictions often unnecessarily drive up the cost of litigation. Alternatively, Federal Rule of Civil Procedure 26 basically requires all parties—with only limited exceptions—to serve upon each other all relevant documents and a list of their witnesses with their addresses, as well as a summary of their testimony, that they will present in their case-in-chief. And all of this must be done automatically within forty days after the filing of the defendants' Answers to the Complaints. Rule 26 also requires each party automatically to produce all accessible data by computer, where available, and to describe the path by which it can be accessed. Parties that withhold any of this information do so at their peril.

The federal rule described above has had a substantial effect upon the reduction of litigation expenses and bickering about discovery in federal courts. Since the thrust of the discovery rules in most state jurisdictions is to allow full discovery of this information anyway, the states could materially reduce the expense, delay, and bickering of *their* civil cases by adopting this federal rule as well.

Try to Avoid Judicial Site Visits for Juries

On eight to ten occasions in my years as a judge, I have personally visited the site of the dispute at issue. One site was an office building, where I went to see whether the marble walls in the entryway appeared from all angles to be well polished. The rest were apartment complexes, and I was observing the state of disrepair. I did not take my court reporter and did not take testimony, but I found the visits to be helpful either to settle or to adjudicate disputes. So I recommend site visits to *judges*. But it has almost never seemed worth the effort to take a jury for a site visit.

A jury site visit can be a major production, and I recommend it be avoided if possible. There can be lots of confusion and things can go irreparably wrong if you have twelve to fourteen jurors, along with counsel, parties, and staff "on the loose," seeing and hearing different things and from a different perspective outside the courthouse.

Utilize a Modified English Plan for Awarding Attorney's Fees to the Prevailing Party

In most jurisdictions in our country, attorney's fees are awarded only in cases in which there is a written contract among the parties that provides for them to the prevailing party, and also in those relatively few circumstances in which they are awarded to the prevailing party by statute. As a result, the prevailing parties in a majority of our cases are still not reimbursed for their reasonable attorney's fees. In the "English Plan," the prevailing parties are always awarded all of their reasonable attorney's fees. Of course, that can have a substantial chilling effect upon bringing even a meritorious case against a party that has lots of resources.

Here is my suggestion: Employ a "Modified English Plan," in which the trial judge has the *discretion* to award reasonable attorney's fees to the prevailing party in every given case. That way the courts could award attorney's fees for cases that should not reasonably have been filed or that should have been abandoned as soon as the facts had been disclosed. But it still would not be potentially ruinous for parties to pursue the righteous prosecution or defense of appropriate cases. I call it a "Modified English Plan" because it is a spin-off of a procedure followed by the British court systems. While this is part of my larger vision for the future of our justice system, I mention it here for your consideration.

Aim to Create and Adopt a Reasonable Alternative System for Standard Automobile Collision Cases

One of the areas covered by General Unlimited Civil Court is standard automobile collision cases. Generally no one is winning under our present trial system for these cases—except the attorneys. So we should all put our heads together and come up with a better system. One alternative would be to keep our present system for cases in which there are severe injuries or damages, or for those that involve egregious conduct like drunk driving or reckless driving. But for the standard cases up to a maximum recovery of $50,000, we could implement a system of no-fault insurance in which drivers would, with a provision for judicial review, look only to their own insurance companies to compensate them for their own property damage and personal injuries according to a set plan. Even though some of the recoveries might be lower than they otherwise might be, at least the monies would be paid fairly promptly throughout and at the end of the recovery period. *And* the party also would not be forced to pay around one-third to two-fifths of that recovery to an attorney.

Under today's system, injured drivers have many reasons to delay their medical recovery, because getting better would probably reduce their compensation at trial. No-fault insurance would appreciably reduce this problem. Moreover, in many ways it is hard to justify the use of a courtroom and staff, and require numbers of jurors to take about three to four days out of their personal or professional lives, to sit and listen to another "fender bender" that could not be settled because the plaintiff was demanding $5,000 and the defense was only willing to offer $4,250. In my view, that is simply not a proper use of our scarce judicial resources.

On that subject, I will never forget one morning when I was driving to the judges' parking area at my courthouse and I saw a fairly young man with a neck brace walking on crutches toward the main entrance of the building. It seemed obvious from the expression on his face that he was in substantial pain. However, when I left the courthouse at noon for a lunch meeting, I happened to see the same fellow with his neck brace off and his crutches tucked under his arm as he briskly walked away. It is very likely he had received his settlement agreement, so the game was over.

Of course, I know that nothing involving human beings will do away with gamesmanship or even fraud, but in my view each state would be well advised to investigate, create, and adopt its own system of no-fault insurance. What most states are now doing in this area is largely not working. Under this new system, if a driver chose not to have insurance, that driver would not be covered. This result not only would promote individual responsibility, but it would also enormously reduce everyone else's insurance rates—not only for present uninsured motorists' coverage, but also for the material reduction of litigation expenses. In short, based upon my many years of sitting on the bench, I believe this new system would be worth exploring.

Another alternative would be for the insureds and insurance companies to agree in advance, along with the participating plaintiffs' attorneys, to utilize a system of binding arbitration for cases that had a potential value below a specified amount, such as $50,000. This would be accompanied by an agreement for the plaintiff's attorneys to cap their contingency fee at 25 percent. There would also be a penalty for plaintiffs who went to trial if it was later shown that the value of their case was reasonably less than the minimum specified amount. Both of these alternative systems would probably be much more effective, as long as laws were in place for bad faith insurance actions against unreasonable insurance companies.

Be Aware of the Laws of Economics in Your Rulings

As Justice Antonin Scalia once said, "A law can be both economic folly and constitutional."[5] That means that judges must not substitute their own economic wisdom for the implementation of the current law that applies to their cases. But fundamentally judges should also be aware that it is the intent of most statutes to place liability upon the parties who are in the best position to prevent the subject loss or damages.

For example, the Uniform Commercial Code requires bank customers to notify their banks of all questionable transactions on their accounts within thirty days of the receipt of their bank statements. This makes economic sense. Why? Because the customers are in a far better position to detect a forged check, unauthorized withdrawal, or other suspicious activity than the bank is. And, when it comes down to it, most people do not want their banks to become familiar enough with their financial transactions to be *able* to detect that abnormal activity. So judges should at least be aware of the force of economic rationale when interpreting the law that covers their factual patterns. They also should be able to explain the impact of that rationale to the litigants.

Embrace the Challenges of New Technology

To state the obvious, we will continue to see enormous changes in technology. For example, it probably will not be long until science is able to map the human brain and its response to pain. The impact of this new technology on our personal injury and workers' compensation cases could be revolutionary! We judges should not be intimidated by these changes, but instead we should embrace them.

Concerning even the current strides in technology, do not try to tackle these advances by yourself. First, remember to use the attorneys to convince you of the reliability of new technology. And second, tap the knowledge of your fellow judges and use the seminars in technology that are available. Remember at all times, you are not alone in these situations. You have resources.

Well, now you have some advice regarding the General Unlimited Civil Court calendar. Of course, it applies to other civil cases as well. Judges who serve the civil courts are in a position to—and must remember to—speak out for our system of justice. Dr. Martin Luther King, Jr., once said, "Morality cannot be legislated, but behavior can be regulated. Judicial decrees may not change the heart, but they can restrain the heartless."[6] It is probably true that only time and social mores can change people's hearts, but our system of justice can and does have an effect upon people's conduct. See the inset "The Laws Do Affect Public Conduct" below on the judicial system and public conduct for more on this issue.

THE LAWS DO AFFECT PUBLIC CONDUCT

Quite a few years ago a new ordinance was passed in New York City requiring people to pick up after their dogs. For the weeks prior to the effective date of the new ordinance, people were mocking the law and saying that there was no way an elderly aristocratic gentleman would follow after his dog with a "pooper scooper." But once the effective date arrived, the program worked right from the start, and the amount of dog waste was reduced immediately and permanently. This is one example of how laws can and do affect conduct. Most people consider themselves to be law-abiding, and when the laws are seen as being at least somewhat reasonable and fairly enforced, most people—including even the hard-hearted—will change their conduct in order to comply with those laws. That is what Dr. Martin Luther King, Jr., suggested in the quotation above.

That is where a judge comes in. Not only should judges act tirelessly to adjudicate our laws fairly, but they should also be *seen* as attempting to do so. In addition, they should devote a fair amount of their efforts, as a natural part of their job, to promoting that feeling and understanding as widely as possible throughout our society. And lastly, judges should be eminently proud of our system in doing so, and of the beneficial effect they can have upon it!

LIMITED CIVIL COURTS

Most of the procedures described for General Unlimited Courts are also applicable to Limited Civil Courts. And the same is true for the recommendations to address and improve them. The only major difference between the calendars is the amount of money at stake. By definition, there is less money at issue in Limited Jurisdiction Court cases than in General Unlimited Court cases. Once again, the amount varies by each jurisdiction, but Limited Civil Court cases usually involve an amount less than $15,000 to $50,000.

The Basics of Limited Court Calendars

Because there is less money involved in this type of calendar, the cases handled are designed to be more streamlined and less expensive to the litigants. To varying degrees, less discovery is allowed, unless the trial court modifies the rules for that particular case. The time period is also shorter between the filing of the Complaint and the beginning of the trial. Fewer types of challenges to the pleadings are allowed, and there is often a procedure for expert witnesses to testify by written declaration instead of having to come into court. Otherwise, the proceedings are similar to those of General Civil Courts.

So just like a judge in other cases, the Limited Civil Court judge should be the force that reasonably keeps things moving forward. That means that even though taking an additional witness deposition before trial may be somewhat helpful for the attorneys' preparation, if the case does not justify the expense, the Court should discourage it or sometimes not even allow it. And at all times for these smaller cases the judges should emphasize settlement, so that the parties can "stop the bleeding" as soon as possible.

Within reason, the same rules of evidence also apply for Small Limited Civil Court cases as with larger Unlimited ones, and also for parties who represent themselves and for those who have competent counsel. All are entitled to patience, judicial competence, caring, explanations, and respect. And in my view judges can get at least as much gratification working on smaller cases as they can from the larger and "more important" ones.

Advice for the Limited Civil Court Judge

Here are some helpful hints for those considering or currently fulfilling the role of judge in the Limited Civil Courts. Because this type of service is so similar to that performed in General Unlimited Court calendars, please also see the advice provided under the previous section, beginning on page 82.

Work Toward Settlements Whenever Possible

Chapter 7 is entirely dedicated to settlements, negotiations, and dispute resolution. But it is worth studying how a Civil Court judge—here, a Limited Civil

Court judge—can actually resolve a case through settlement before it eats up a large amount of money and time in the court system.

One approach that has been consistently successful is useful for Law and Motion hearings with yet another motion to compel discovery. Look at the underlying Complaint and see how much money is at issue. Then call that case first on the calendar, hold up the increasingly thickening file, and ask counsel to go out into the hallway and settle this small case. It has been gratifying to see how this works; often within fifteen minutes counsel come back into court and express thanks for the guidance in settling their case.

Try to Put the Train Back on the Track in Unlawful Detainer Cases

Unlawful Detainer cases present a particular area in which judges may be unusually helpful to all of the litigants. These are landlord/tenant disputes that frequently involve defendants/tenants who are unsophisticated and not represented by an attorney.

Consider that a couple is being sued by their landlord for delinquent payments of rent. In such a case, the first thing I do is to ask the tenants—before the trial has started—what result they are actually hoping for. If at this point the tenants *do not want* to stay in the property, I try to get both sides to agree upon a lockout date at some time in the future, so that the tenants can transition their lives with as little disruption as possible. However, they will have to pay the landlord in advance for that period of time until they vacate the property, and they will be agreeing to a judgment of eviction as well as some specified damages to be entered against them.

If the tenants *want* to stay in the property, I ask the landlord if there is still money owed in the matter. If so, I tell the tenants that I could never convince the landlord to allow them to stay in the unit unless they not only make concrete arrangements to pay the past-due rent, but that they also convince the landlord that he will not have trouble receiving all payments of rent on time in the months to come. If the tenants can put together a payment plan that seems reasonable to me, then I suggest that the landlord accept it. But that agreement is also directly conditional upon not only a material and immediate payment's being received by cashier's check, but also an additional provision. That provision calls for a judgment to be entered in favor of the landlord for immediate restitution of the premises to the landlord and a judgment for the balance of payment if the tenants do not continue to perform in a timely fashion for a specified number of months. During this discussion, I remind the tenants that the landlord is not a philanthropic organization, and in most circumstances landlords are legally entitled to their rent without having to go to court.

In cases that argue that the premises are not habitable, I first ask the tenants if they still desire to stay in their unit. If so, I ask both if they will agree to pay some negotiated reduced rent to the landlord for the past and future months until all repairs are completed, and if they will make the premises available to the landlord for those repairs. Then I ask the landlords if something like this would be agreeable to them as well. If it is, we set a time schedule for all repairs to be made. After the repairs are made, full rent will be payable from that point on. As an aside, sometimes in these cases judges literally hear tenants ask the court, "Please do not evict me from this house because it is uninhabitable." It is internally inconsistent, but this is simply one of the ironies of life that judges sometimes see in our profession.

In my view, if all parties are able to agree to settlements of these kinds, everyone will come out ahead. The tenants will benefit because we are delaying or even avoiding the potential disruption of their homelife. Considering that many tenants frequently have small children, this is important. To be forced to move immediately, or at all, almost always presents the tenants with some serious financial, emotional, and logistical problems. But, of course, if the tenants fail to keep up their part of the agreement, they will know that they really have only themselves to blame. The landlords will also come out ahead because they will be assured of receiving either their rent in a scheduled fashion or a judgment that includes the remaining damages and an eviction. Moreover, the landlords probably will be receiving at least some money from the tenant that they never would have received without this agreement.

I have been successful in settling about 75 percent of all of these Unlawful Detainer cases that have been assigned to me without a trial, and I have felt pretty good about doing it. So I recommend these procedures to you. Of course, you can adjust this type of settlement approach to cases other than Unlawful Detainers as well.

If you are the kind of person who likes to work with "regular folk" and feels good about helping to resolve their daily problems in your community, Limited Civil is the calendar for you. Although some of the cases can be quite complicated, most of them usually involve "nuts and bolts" issues of everyday life. Also, they can move along quite quickly.

COMPLEX CIVIL COURTS

A Complex Civil Court calendar is almost the opposite of a Limited Civil Court calendar. Complex Civil Court calendars handle cases in which there are usually large numbers of parties, large numbers of documents and witnesses, lots of discovery problems, much Law and Motion activity, many settlement conferences, and/or lengthy trial estimates. Therefore, these cases require the utilization of extra judicial time and resources for monitoring and for trial in an effort to avoid placing unnecessary burdens on the court or on the litigants, to expedite the cases as much as possible, to promote effective decision-making, and to keep costs as reasonable as possible.

The Basics of Complex Civil Court Calendars

Usually, Complex Civil Court cases are exempted from the typical time standards governing General Unlimited calendar cases, such as the time by which a complaint must be served, an Answer or other responsive pleading filed, and discovery provided. On this calendar, innovation designed to resolve the cases more efficiently and monitor them more economically is the name of the game. In fact, Complex Civil courtrooms are increasingly being equipped with the ability to increase the accessibility of the courts with things like telephone conference calling, and to accommodate the electronic presentation of evidence at the trials. More and more of these courtrooms are hard-wired at trial to connect laptop computers, elmos, and monitors to all of the participants. That includes the parties, counsel, witnesses, jury, and the judges.

Typical examples of matters handled in Complex Civil Courts are class action cases, environmental impact cases, and construction defect cases. As suggested previously, these cases are not necessarily more complicated or confusing than those assigned to Unlimited Civil Court jurisdictions, nor do they necessarily involve more money. But they usually have more parties, take longer to try, or require much more effort to oversee.

Finally, multiple settlement conferences are the norm in Complex Civil Court cases. Surprisingly, most of the complex litigation cases usually settle before trial. Part of the reason for that is that it is expensive and unusually cumbersome to try the cases, and the risks for all parties in leaving their fate to a judge or jury are often unacceptably high. Another reason is that the attorneys on these cases are usually more experienced and are thus more able and willing to put clients into a posture of settlement. As a result, the largest of the judge's problems involved in these calendars are most often administrative—keeping all parties straight and not forgotten or excluded, being flexible in responding to emerging litigation problems, arranging complicated settlement conferences, and moving the cases along toward trial.

From the judges' standpoint, being on a Complex calendar is like a cross between trial work, appellate work, and executive assistant work. Judges have much more time to read cases in preparation for a large volume of Law and Motion issues, and they are involved in a great deal of planning for discovery in the cases. But frequently the issues are interesting, and, as mentioned above, the competency level of most of the attorneys is usually quite high.

Advice for the Complex Civil Court Judge

Obviously, most of the advice about things that work in other Civil calendars will equally work in Complex Civil calendars. But the things that are considered by attorneys that judges can do to be most helpful in Complex Civil cases are to provide comprehensive written orders, to be familiar with the record on Law and Motion matters, to supervise discovery in order to reduce the overall costs of the cases, and to be flexible, creative, and available in addressing litigation problems as they arise.[7]

It can be quite satisfying to work on Complex Civil Court cases. These judges have the opportunity to appreciate all the nuances of dispute resolution and skilled techniques that the cases inevitably present. And usually the quality of the attorneys is well above average. There are challenges presented as well, of course, and judges who do not have good organizational skills or who cannot usually see the "forest for the trees" should probably seek a different assignment. But otherwise this can be considered a great place to do business.

SMALL CLAIMS COURTS

I believe that with the exception of the Juvenile Court calendars (see Chapter 4), Small Claims calendars and Traffic Court calendars (the latter of which is discussed in Chapter 2) are the most important calendars in the judicial system. That is so because Small Claims and Traffic Court calendars allow for a great deal of contact with people in all walks of life. Forevermore, when those people think of "The Government," rightly or wrongly they will often think of the judge in their Small Claims or Traffic Court trial. And most of the matters that will come before you are legitimate business disputes or the result of honest misunderstandings among good people. Thus, Small Claims judges are in a position to encourage many Americans in all walks of life to honor and respect our System of Justice. Or, as Chief Justice Earl Warren was quoted as saying, "You sit up there, and you see the whole gamut of human nature. Even if the case being argued involves only a little fellow and $50, it involves justice. That's what is important."[8]

The Basics of Small Claims Calendars

Small Claims Court is designed to be a "Town Hall" system of justice, but the issues are still decided according to the law. In most jurisdictions Small Claims Court cases are the only civil cases for which a jury is unavailable. In addition, there is no discovery, and no pleadings except for a short complaint from the plaintiff (and occasionally one from the defendant/cross-complainant) requesting money damages. Moreover, no attorneys are allowed to represent any of the parties or even stand up in court with them. This also means that non-attorney employees may appear in court for a corporation.

But some judgments can be conditioned upon some equitable relief, such as a return of the subject property before the payments are refunded. In addition, since these are rather summary proceedings in which the rules of evidence barely apply, they have no collateral estoppel effect (except among the same parties regarding the identical claim). Therefore, if a party loses a case in Small Claims Court, it may re-litigate the same issue in a later case with different parties.

In Small Claims Court, a party may bring a written statement or other document from another person, or may even testify about what another person would say if he were present in court. As a result, the jurisdictional limit is kept small, usually between $2,500 and $7,500, and for multiple filers like finance companies and jewelry dealers, it is usually lower than that. Most of the time, if the plaintiffs are unsuccessful, the Small Claims matter is over. But an unsuccessful defendant may file an appeal, which results in an automatic new trial before a different judge.

Judges in a Small Claims Court can sometimes fill the roles of teacher, therapist, police officer, social worker, and parent, in addition to their formal role as arbiter. In some jurisdictions the judges are even permitted to be investigators and to gather evidence on their own. That means that a judge on a case might take a recess and, for example, place a telephone call to the mechanic who worked to repair the plaintiff's car after the defendant had allegedly damaged it. Or maybe the judge will decide to call and get additional information from the photographer who touched up the allegedly defective wedding photos taken by the defendant. Or the judge might, as I have done on numbers of occasions, go through the telephone book, locate his own experts, and obtain their cooperation as a public service. Then the judge might, for example, have the plaintiff take his automobile to a paint shop that is not at all involved with the case and obtain an explanation for why the paint job has to be redone or not. Afterward, the "expert witness" can telephone back to the judge and give an oral report as to his opinions on the matter at issue. The possibilities are endless.

Advice for the Small Claims Judge

Small Claims Court judges see a wide variety of issues and people. In that regard, judges must serve as arbitrators between neighbors, family, friends, and business contacts, as well as often be peacemakers between the public and the county, town, or state. In the following paragraphs, I provide a sketch of what it is like to be a Small Claims judge by relating the scenarios of a few of the cases I have worked on over the years. Hopefully you will find some of my approaches to be helpful.

Be Prepared to Deal with Emotional Battles

All Small Claims judges have stories about their cases. Some of them can be wonderful, some of them can be funny, and some of them can be quite sad. The ones that deal with disputes among people who could so easily be close and friendly are particularly frustrating.

For example, one time I had a case between an elderly widow who lived uphill from another elderly widow, and they did not get along at all. Here was an opportunity for two women who shared a similar lifestyle to become friends and confidants, in addition to friendly neighbors, but they took the opposite route. It happened that the uphill widow got upset that the downhill widow's juniper trees were blocking her view and thus were in violation of the homeowners' association's Covenants, Conditions, and Restrictions (CC&Rs). So after the bickering with her neighbor about the situation brought no results, the uphill widow hired a laborer to top the trees. In response, the downhill widow hired her own laborer to wire the now dead branches back onto the juniper trees, thus again blocking the view but now with brown branches instead of green ones. Thereafter, the downhill widow sought damages in Small Claims Court for her ruined trees.

What would you do? My response was to encourage them to get along together better because, one way or the other, they were going to be neighbors. I also said that I sympathized with the uphill neighbor's problem, but I told her that if they could not work the problem out with her neighbor like two adults, the proper course of action would have been to call the homeowners' association and secure its assistance in the matter. Taking matters into their own hands was the wrong thing to do—for both of them. As a result, I ordered a judgment for the plaintiff—the downhill widow—for the cost of new juniper trees and recommended that she not allow them to grow above the height approved by the CC&Rs.

On another occasion I had a sister suing her brother for the repayment of a loan. The brother responded that he had already repaid the loan to her. When I asked if there had been anyone else present when the loan was repaid, he said their mother had been there. In my wisdom, I continued the case for a week and told them to ask their mother either to resolve it or to come back to court, feeling that once the mother got involved I would probably never see them again. Surprisingly, the next week they were back in court, with their mother in tow. When I asked the mother whether she had ever seen her son repay the loan to her daughter, she responded that this had never happened in her presence. The brother/son exploded, shouting out to his mother, "You're a liar!" What a sorry situation. I had done what I could. Judgment for plaintiff.

Another case I heard two days before Christmas had a plaintiff suing her long-time but newly former friend for the charges on her cellular phone bill in the amount of $491 that were incurred while the defendant had possession of the telephone. As they continued to talk, I discovered that the defendant had been such a good friend that the plaintiff's family had virtually treated her as a daughter for years. So after listening to all of them present their case, I told them that the money in this matter was unimportant. What I wanted to talk about was important things, like family and friends. Here they had something truly beautiful and special, and if they let it get away, they would always regret it. So I asked the plaintiff's mother if she still had an affection for the defendant, and if she did to give the defendant a hug, please. She did, and she did. Soon there were hugs and tears all around. They all agreed to work out the problem of the payment of the bill, dismissed the case, and walked out of my courtroom arm in arm, thanking me and wishing me a Merry Christmas.

Obviously, the details and outcomes of these stories are very different. But they have one thing in common: high emotions between people who really should not be fighting. The Small Claims judge must try to trudge through these heated and sad circumstances, always with an eye on how to make peace between neighbors, friends, and family.

When Appropriate, Reinforce the Power of Justice for the Individual

In many cases, Small Claims Court presents the judge with an extraordinary opportunity to see that justice is provided for "the little guy," or the individual who is being taken advantage of by a system. For example, in one case I found that our county had impounded the plaintiff's $500 tax rebate check for an unreasonably long period of time before returning it shortly after the plaintiff had filed his complaint. Even the plaintiff agreed that the basis for the original impounding of the check was understandable and reasonable, but quickly the plaintiff had presented persuasive evidence to the county that it had been unfounded. Under the circumstances, in an effort to compensate the plaintiff for his months of frustration and to encourage the county agency to be more diligent in the future with other people's money, I ordered a judgment for the plaintiff for $100. I recommended he use it to take himself and his wife out to dinner, courtesy of the county.

In another case, a defendant who sold pet birds from his house as a "hobby" was sued by a county agency because he had engaged in this activity without a license for the past two years. I asked him if he was selling to any commercial pet shops at all, and he said that such sales comprised about 10 percent of his transactions. That being the case, I concluded that he was conducting a commercial business for which he needed a business license. But then he said that the county had actually prohibited him from selling any birds out of the county for the entire year because of the presence of a particular type of bird flu. Accordingly, I told the county that since it had kept the defendant from doing any business for a year, it did not seem reasonable to charge him for a business license during that year. As a result, I ordered the defendant to pay the county the money for a business license for the current year only, not for the one in which he had not been able to do business. To be honest, I am not sure whether this exception was within appropriate business license regulations, but I believed it to be fair and just under the law, and that is what I did.

Accept That You Might Never Be Sure About What Is True

Years ago I had a woman in a Small Claims case who had been involved as a defendant in a rear-end collision case on the freeway. Minor damage was done to the plaintiff's car. But the defendant's testimony was that after all cars had stopped, the plaintiff actually backed up, hit her, and then took an off-ramp that had been behind her. The defendant also stated that her husband had previously recommended to her that if she was ever in a collision she should make a note of the license plates of nearby cars so that she could later call them as witnesses if necessary. Well, in this case she had followed that advice, and she gave me the license number of the car that had been next to her.

I had my bailiff run the plate, and then I called the witness. I explained who I was and what had happened, and I then asked the person if she had seen and remembered a minor collision on the freeway on the day in question. The woman responded that the collision had happened just as the defendant had described it. As a result, I entered a judgment for the defendant. However, I must confess that to this day I do not know if I was deceived by the defendant. It would not have been hard for her to give me the license plate number of a friend of hers who then passed along the story. I will never know. But at the time I believed the defendant's testimony, and I felt that she had presented evidence that kept the plaintiff from meeting her burden of proof. Yes, upon reflection, I still believe today that I did the right thing.

There is an extra piece of advice linked with the story above. For summary proceedings involving limited amounts of money, hearings and procedures like the one I described are fine and appropriate. But for situations in which there is more at stake, it is good to have the protections of the evidence code and actual cross-examination of witnesses in court for the reliability of the witnesses' testimony to be established.

Keep Things Moving

You do have to move the cases along. After all, you do not want the parties to think and act like they can take the entire morning, because they will if you let them. One way is to have them remain standing instead of seated. Another way is to be sure to make the courtroom objectives and boundaries clear by telling them you are there to resolve a dispute and not to hear their life stories.

Similarly, do not allow the parties to talk to each other. That situation can quickly deteriorate. Instead, have them talk only to you. If you feel it is necessary, you can pass along one party's questions to the other.

Finally, let each party have his say uninterrupted for two to three minutes. All sides should feel that they have been justly heard. The plaintiff's side presents first, and then the defendant's. And *never* allow one side to interrupt the other, on penalty of being banished from your courtroom.

Promote Settlements

I have found that one of the best questions to ask during a case that involves a business situation is whether the parties would be able to resolve their dispute by doing business together in the future. For example, while discussing a case involving alleged damage to a good client's car at a car wash, I asked the parties if they would be willing to resolve the matter through a "services" agreement. The defendant could provide the plaintiff with a certain number of coupons for his "deluxe treatment" car wash. Actually, the number of treatments I suggested was for an amount that was greater than the requested compensation, so that the plaintiff would actually stand to benefit. But the defendant would also benefit because he could resolve the matter with services instead of cash, and he would probably also be able to keep a good customer. Employing an approach like this can actually satisfy all of the parties, and that is what happened in this case.

So the first thing to do is to state that the Complaint says that the plaintiff is asking for $625. Then ask the defendants if they agree that they owe *any* amount of money at all to the plaintiff. This is not the time for defendants to *defend* their cases. Instead it is a chance for them to identify the issues of the case. Sometimes the defendants agree that paying a reduced amount of money or offering compensation in services would be reasonable, and the plaintiffs then agree that the latter monetary amount or services are really all that is owing. So at that point the case is over and both parties are happy. For much more on settlement and other related issues, see Chapter 7.

If You at All Can, Rule from the Bench

The judicial advice I received as soon as I started presiding over Small Claims Court calendars was to take everything under submission and notify parties of the result by mail. The rationale for this advice was that once the matter was over, there was a substantial possibility that the losing party would start yelling at the winner in the hallway or even resort to violence. Only rarely have I felt that this would occur, but in those situations, I listened to the advice given to me and simply told the parties that I would submit my decision to them in the mail. But in all other circumstances I believe it is helpful and appropriate for the losing parties to hear directly from the judge about the reasons why they have not been successful based upon the facts and the law. They will be much more likely to accept the decision and learn from the experience after the judge's in-person explanation.

For example, I believe that I, as a judge, should tell a carpet layer that he is the professional. As such, he is in a much better position than his customer to know when there will be problems with the job and to give an estimate based upon those possibilities. This information will help to guide the carpet layer in his future business relationships and avoid future misunderstandings and litigation. The carpet layer is likely to benefit from hearing such an opinion from a judge, considering that judges are still respected as authority figures. However, once I have ordered the judgment to be entered and explained my reasons for it, I do not allow any further argument, and I do not accept anything more from the parties other than clarifying questions, which I am happy to answer. It is time to move on to the next case.

Send Letters of Appreciation to Citizens
Who Served as Court Experts

One time I took a picture of the damage to the front end of a big rig truck to one of my own selected "experts," and I asked him if he believed that the damage shown in the picture could have caused problems to the truck's transmission. My eventual judgment in the case was based upon the expert's opinion that it could not. Thereafter, I sent a letter to my expert, thanking him for his time and his community service.

In my view, a material part of a judge's job is community relations and education. As such, letters of appreciation are also a part of our job. So I encourage you to follow a protocol that makes citizens feel that their time and skills are valuable to and respected by the judicial system.

Small Claims Court cases can be interesting and fun. But they are best adjudicated by a "people person" who can let everyone have his say and who can also move the cases along. If you sit on this assignment you will be surprised at the variation of issues that are presented to you. In addition, you will be gratified by being able to help many good people resolve their disputes and move on to other, more pleasant matters.

CONCLUSION

No matter what the situation is, judges should never feel that they are simply reduced to being onlookers. Mostly we should be quiet, but we should nevertheless see ourselves as active participants in every court case. And at all times, whether sitting on a General Unlimited, Limited, Complex, or Small Claims calendar, we must remember that we speak for our government and for our society in general. We also speak for "Justice Under the Law." So we should marshal our experience, wisdom, and resources to render the best justice we can. We should also clearly communicate the appearance of justice by being attentive and patient. It is important to explain the reasons for our decisions fully and then to move on to the next case.

Chapter 4

"Relationship" Calendars

"Fundamentally the decisions that you're making as a judge are decisions that you would be making as a parent in your own family. They call upon your values and your parenting skills."[1]

—Brian J. Lamb, Judge of the Superior Court,
Independence, California

In my view, the majority of the most important judging occurs in calendars for Juvenile, Family Law, and Probate Court cases in the state court systems. (My opinion, especially regarding Juvenile and Family Law Courts, is further explained in the inset "The Significant Work of Juvenile and Family Courts"on page 109.) Although these calendars are truly separate and calendars in their own right, I have placed them together in this chapter because all deal with intensely personal family matters involving people who are under stress, often sorry about their past, and worried about their future. And although in California Family and Juvenile Courts cases represent only about 7 percent of all court filings, they account for almost a third of the trial court's judicial workload.

Many times per day, judges assigned to these calendars address critically important issues, including the well being, liberty, placement, and future of children and of the aged. Of course, many of the issues, approaches, and pieces of advice in the following discussions apply to all calendars covered within this chapter and are therefore somewhat interchangeable. But with that understanding, it is now time to explore some of the most difficult, emotional, and critically important calendars upon which judges can serve.

JUVENILE COURT

No legal training prepares judges—or attorneys either, for that matter—for decisions they must make on Juvenile Court calendars, or what they must learn to intuit. But the judges are faced with some of the most important decisions that society is forced to make. How can judges possibly have answers to questions like where a toddler should attend nursery school, or in which religion the children should be raised? How can judges really know what the self-employed spouse's true income is, or when permanent spousal support should end?

Similarly, how can a judge reasonably know when it is appropriate to take the custody of a child away from her parents, or when it is safe to return the child back again? How does a judge know which parent should have primary custody of a child? Is a mother truly in fear of the child's—or even her own—being injured by the father, or vice versa, or is the complaining parent cunningly planting false stories in order to get what he or she wants? Is one parent simply using the situation in an attempt to punish the other?

Of course, a judge can always keep from making a wrong call in returning a child to her parents by never agreeing to do so, or by always giving custody to the parent levying the grievances, which is most often the mother. But I hope you will agree that this is not a proper response. When it comes down to it, these momentous decisions must be made by someone, and no one is institutionally in a better position to make them than those people in the black robes. We can seek the guidance and advice of counselors and other professionals, but the ultimate decisions must be ours.

The History of Juvenile Court Calendars

From the Colonial Period, through the gaining of our country's independence, and until the end of the 1800s, infants—those below seven years of age—were not considered to be able to form a criminal intent. So they were exempted from prosecution and punishment. However, anyone at seven or older was considered to be a "miniature adult." As such, children about that age could be forced to stand trial and, if convicted, sentenced to prison or even death. Systems of this kind had been in effect in many parts of Western Civilization since the *Twelve Tables of Roman Law* of the fifth century BCE (see page 11). The places of incarceration in most jurisdictions were changed by the 1850s, such that juveniles were held in facilities separate from adults, but otherwise this system for juveniles generally remained in place until the passage of the Juvenile Court Act of 1899 in the state of Illinois. The passage of this statute resulted in the establishment by Cook County, Illinois, of the first Juvenile Court in our country.

By the year 1910, thirty-two states had followed the lead of Illinois in this regard, and by the year 1925, only two states had *not* done so. All of these states used the justification of the doctrine of *parens patriae*. That doctrine declared that the State, as the parent, has the right and responsibility to intervene early in the lives of children in trouble during their formative years in an attempt to turn delinquents into productive citizens instead of punishing them like adults. The focus of the courts was mainly upon the offender, instead of upon the offense.

THE SIGNIFICANT WORK
OF JUVENILE AND FAMILY COURTS

In a great number of Juvenile and Family Court cases, many of the parties are angry, and they act as though the courts are significantly meddling in their personal lives—which, in many ways, we are! Nevertheless, I agree with the words of my esteemed colleague, Judge Leonard P. Edwards of the Superior Court in San Jose, California, regarding the truly important work that goes on in these courts:

I believe the work of our Juvenile and Family Court judges is critical to the future of our nation. That is a bold claim, but let me explain. Judges in the Juvenile Court are charged with keeping children safe; restoring families; finding permanency for children; and holding youth, families, and service providers accountable. Every day hundreds of judges make thousands of decisions regarding children in crisis. We decide whether a child should be removed from parental care, whether a child has committed a delinquent act, whether a child should be committed to the state for correction, whether parental rights should be terminated. When parenting fails, when informal community responses are inadequate, our Juvenile and Family Courts provide the state's official intervention in the most serious cases involving children and families. We are the legal equivalent of an emergency room in the medical profession. We intervene in crises and figure out the best response on a case-by-case, individualized basis. In addition, we have to get off of the bench and work in the community. We have to convene child- and family-serving agencies, schools, and the community around the problems facing our most vulnerable and troubled children. We have to ask these agencies and the community to work together to support our efforts so that the orders we make on the bench can be fulfilled. We have to be the champions of collaboration.

Many of these roles are not traditional for a judge. Yet for Juvenile Court judges they are essential if the work of the court is to be successful and if court orders will be carried out. The role of the Juvenile Court judge is unlike any other. In the traditional judicial role, deciding a legal issue may complete the judge's task; however, in deciding the future of a child or family member, the Juvenile Court judge must, in addition to making a legal decision, be prepared to take on the role of an administrator, a collaborator, a convener, and an advocate.[1]

Accordingly, considerable discretion and authority was given to the Juvenile Court judges in these "benevolent courts," and they had a lot of control regarding how to handle the individual cases. This resulted in the court hearings' being traditionally less formal, the "due process" protections' being less necessary, and the sentencings' being more creative. It was deemed that the courts could best determine how and why the juvenile had come to the attention of the authorities, and how the "best interests of the child" could be pursued. As a result, "The blindfold was purposefully removed from the eyes of 'justice' so that the total picture of the child's past experiences and existing circumstances could be judicially perceived and weighed against the projected outcomes of alternative courses of legal intervention."[2]

This practice continued until the 1950s and 1960s, when many people began to raise questions about the ability of the Juvenile Courts to succeed in their goal of rehabilitating delinquent youth. Some of these concerns came from people who felt that the majority of the subjects were simply already hardened criminals. According to those people, punishment was the only appropriate response. In contrast, others were concerned that the system was being increasingly used to institutionalize the subjects indefinitely in the name of "treatment," even for minor offenses.

Beginning in the 1960s, these concerns gave rise to United States Supreme Court decisions that afforded more of the Constitutional protections that adults enjoyed to the juvenile subjects. This changed perspective in turn resulted in more formal hearings, the appointment of lawyers, the invocation of rights against self-incrimination, more formal notice of the charges against the defendants and their ability to question the witnesses against them, and proof "beyond a reasonable doubt" instead of by a "preponderance of the evidence." In addition, Congress also stepped more into the picture by passing the Juvenile Delinquency Prevention and Control Act of 1968, which recommended that children who were then being charged with non-criminal or status offenses, such as truancy, incorrigibility, general disobedience, and being a runaway, should be taken out of the courts and dealt with through schools and community-based programs.

As the 1980s arrived, the emphasis in juvenile justice swung back much more in favor of "law and order" punishment at the expense of rehabilitation. Some states passed laws that gave prosecutors the discretion to file certain juvenile offenses directly in the adult courts; other states made that decision automatic, depending upon the type of offense; and some states required juveniles who were convicted for certain offenses to face mandatory minimum sentences. This trend continued through the 1990s and beyond. From 1992 through 1997, legislatures in forty-seven states and the District of Columbia passed laws that made their juvenile justice systems more punitive. In addition, the minimum age at which a juvenile could be sent to adult prison also continued to decrease. In fact, by the year 2007, seventy-three Americans were serving life sentences for offenses they committed at thirteen or fourteen years of age. No other country in the world follows such a practice.[3]

So in many ways the juvenile justice system has returned to the way it was before 1899. This should not be too surprising, because in our attempts to protect ourselves from crime and keep us safe there will always be a stressful relationship between punishment and rehabilitation. In my view, we must maintain a keen awareness of the strengths and weaknesses of both approaches, and adopt the best of both to the particular cases that are presented. Of course, that is not easy, and the political and practical tensions will always be with us. But particularly with our children, it is our responsibility to take whatever time and energy is necessary in an effort to achieve the best results possible in each and every case.

There are two specific areas of juvenile court: delinquency and dependency. Each of these warrants separate discussion. Therefore, this section is sub-divided into these two parts. You will notice that the usual format has changed a little, but you will still find both basic information and advice under each of these sections.

The Delinquency Calendar

Regardless of one's personal philosophy of juvenile justice, the juvenile delinquency calendar is an area in which judges are in a position to deflect or otherwise head off significant future problems with our young people. In these calendars, judges are frequently called upon to decide whether or not a young person has a reasonable chance of living a normal and productive life. That is the reason why, in most jurisdictions, the Juvenile Court judges are still given appreciable latitude in fashioning orders to rehabilitate juvenile offenders and are given authority to do everything reasonably necessary to accomplish the desired goals.

But regrettably in today's world some of the young people are so hardened in their outlook, and their offenses are so brutal and callous, that there is no reasonable alternative other than to send them off to "juvenile prison." It would not be an exaggeration to say that some of these young people talk about their involvement in murders in exactly the same way that other youths talk about their girlfriends or basketball games.[4]

Sending a young person to confinement is a hard decision to make, but we have only so many resources, and they are often better spent upon young people who are not so deeply immersed in such a cycle of dispassionate violence. That being said, in large numbers of cases juvenile delinquents can be managed through special programs and therefore be able to stay at home and have hope for a promising future. I offer advice on this and many other "delinquency" issues below.

Consider Establishing Stay-at-Home Programs

I will pass along to you some thoughts by Dr. Herbert Schreier, the Chief of Child Psychiatry at Children's Hospital in Oakland, California: "Kids will commit fewer crimes when sent home even to an abusing environment, than if they are sent to jail after juvenile detention. They do even better if they are given remedial school work and receive extra help in overcoming their deficits."[5] Obviously, the decision to send a juvenile to confinement or to a behavior rehabilitation program depends upon the background and prognosis of the child, as well as the nature of the offense committed. But I believe judges should be extra cautious before choosing the radical act of sending a minor to "juvenile prison."

In cases for which it seems logical to do so, judges should consider viable alternatives to prison. One of these is what Santa Cruz County in California calls their "Luna Evening Center" program, through which the offending minors are able to stay at home and continue with their schooling. But for five nights per week, plus another day of community service, the minors are assigned chores; receive mental health and drug counseling; have access to resume-writing classes, computer classes, and tutors for their schoolwork; meditate; eat dinner with probation officers; and have time for play at the ping pong or foosball tables. This program not only allows the youths a more normal after-school life, but it also gives them an excuse not to hang out with gang members and people involved in the drug scene.[6] If your county does not have a similar program, perhaps you could help to start one.

Use Screening Processes to Catch Treatable Problems

One way our Juvenile Court system can further reduce the offenses being committed by juveniles is to screen all minors the very first time they enter the system in order to determine whether there are any specific problem areas that need to be addressed. It is relatively easy and inexpensive to screen young people for substance abuse, hearing and vision problems, dyslexia, poor grades, truancy problems, family dysfunctions, and similar matters, and we are foolish not to do so. "Lost children" almost always become lost adults, and the earlier these conditions can be diagnosed, the earlier we can address present problems and head off future ones.

For example, some children who are dyslexic but undiagnosed end up thinking they are stupid. Then these children move to the back of the classroom, do not pay attention, and soon get into trouble. But once the children and their parents understand that dyslexia is a medical condition that has remedies, good things begin to happen. Another thing that is different but truly a detectable red flag that should trigger prevention and intervention efforts is the propensity of some children to be involved in cruelty to animals. These acts are widely seen as symptoms of future violent behavior, and they should be taken quite seriously.

Juvenile delinquents soon can become senior delinquents. But imagine the positive benefits that can be reaped by a juvenile justice system that detects, addresses, and heads off problems at an early stage. The primary indicator that judges should reference before deciding upon how to deal with young offenders is how they are doing in school. No matter what the problem, if a child's grades are acceptably high, the child is probably doing all right. But if they are low, the child—and often even his entire family—needs immediate attention and a change in course.

There are other types of screening processes that are tremendously useful as well. Several important studies have shown that approximately 8 percent of all juvenile offenders commit about *half* of all juvenile offenses. Fortunately, these "8 percenters" can be detected by a screening process to determine if they have three or more of the following four profile factors: 1) significant family problems, such as abuse, neglect, lack of parental supervision or control, or family members involved in criminal activity; 2) significant problems at school, such as truancy, failing more than one class course, or a recent suspension or expulsion; 3) a pattern of alcohol or other drug usage; and 4) delinquent peers, chronic runaway patterns, or a history of theft-related activities. Resources should be expended upon the juveniles found to have at least three of those factors, *and also upon their families*, in an effort to turn the situation around before it becomes hopeless in a practical sense. In addition, society should not wait for the juvenile's siblings to develop those same patterns of criminal behavior before appropriate actions are taken, and we in the juvenile courts can lead the charge for this action.[7]

So the old maxim, "A stitch in time saves nine," is an understatement when it comes to problems with children. If a child on the delinquency calendars could be screened at the earliest opportunity for these various behaviors and conditions before the Juvenile Court judge begins to sentence the minor for a criminal offense, the judge would have the answers to an entire laundry list of questions about that child's physical, mental, and social conditions, and that judge would be able to act accordingly. In my view, this will reduce the number of times in the future that we say, "If only we could have been able to reach this child sooner," and it will materially decrease continuing criminal and anti-social conduct in our young people.

Give "Booster Shots," When Needed, to Juveniles and to Parents

To the degree that there is an "answer" to criminal juvenile behavior—in addition to the ideal of a proper home, role models, access to a good education, and the like—teaching individual responsibility and offering incentives are the keys to the court system's response. One way to use incentives properly is to adopt the approach of what I call a "booster shot" of shock therapy. For example, a judicial friend of mine was involved in a Juvenile Court hearing in which the parents were making multiple excuses for the delinquent conduct of their child. My friend simply declared a recess in the proceedings, asked the minor to come with him, and told the parents he would be back in twenty minutes. He walked over to Juvenile Hall with the child in tow. When they arrived, my friend asked the personnel to open empty cell number 14, and then he calmly said to the minor, "This is where you are going to spend the weekend. I'll see you on Monday morning." The laws of most jurisdictions still permit judges to act promptly in the best interests of the child, and I strongly recommend that we use our judicial discretion and authority to do just that.

In addition, we can and often must use these opportunities to teach and encourage the parents to "parent." Many parents try to be friends of their children instead of parents. So judges must convince them that if they do not enforce curfews and bedtimes for their children, the courts will do it for them. Or if they do not monitor and even control who their children "hang out with," the courts will be forced to remove their children from that environment. Therefore, judges can use these opportunities to coach parents on raising disciplined and healthy children.

Another way to utilize incentives presents itself when children who are under the jurisdiction of the court system have been suspended from school. What kind of incentive can the court provide in order to get these youngsters to see the value of school? *In all cases,* children should be required to *earn* their way back into their school. How? By adopting the military approach of providing each child in our care with discipline, motivation, and a cause. Why? Because we must treat young people as if they are human and help motivate them to work toward a productive future. And if they are forced to earn their way back to school they will be more likely to appreciate it, and less likely to take it for granted.

I once heard a story about a conversation between a basketball coach and one of his players. The coach asked the player, "What is it with you and all of these failures in school? Is it ignorance or is it apathy?" The player responded, "Coach, I don't know and I don't care." Unless we can help our children to see that school is important and a privilege, we will all be wasting our time insisting that our children spend their time there.

Of course, if we force children who do not want to be in school to be there, they will not learn anything positive, and they will also spend most of their efforts to ensure that no one else has the opportunity to learn anything either. So instead we should come up with alternative activities, such as technical schools or even full-time employment for those not willing or able to progress in a traditional school setting.

Socrates was quoted as saying, "Before there is wisdom there is wonder." To that thought I add that before there can be wonder, there must be exposure to an alternative lifestyle and motivation in order to succeed. This is where our juvenile justice system must concentrate its efforts and resources, because today we are losing too many of our young people to ignorance, apathy, crime, and incarceration. And this is a preventable tragedy.

Monitor the Court System Itself

Juvenile Court judges must also use their positions to oversee the Juvenile Court system itself. For example, it is my experience that few Juvenile Court judges have ever taken the time to visit the facilities to which they send the juvenile delinquent subjects. That can be a serious mistake, and for several reasons. For one thing, as a matter of practicality, judges cannot make the best decision in a particular case unless they have an understanding of what their resources are like. Having firsthand knowledge about the correctional facilities will greatly assist in that regard.

In addition, if the facilities are in need of improvement, maintenance, or repair, who is in a better position to ensure that they are as good as they can be than the judge? One way for that to be done is to take a camera with you on your visits. If the mattresses are shoddy, the faucets have mold, or the facilities are in disrepair, a picture shown to the appropriate supervising agencies should be all you need in your call for action and improvement.

Implement "Story Time"

The staff at the Juvenile Hall in Orange County, California, say that probably the most emotional time occurs at "lights out" at the end of the day. That is the time at which the young people get despondent because of their situations, and that results in more misbehavior and increased tension levels. One way we have combated this problem, at least for the girls' wing, is to have adult volunteers come to the facility at "lights out" and read a short story over the intercom—followed by saying "goodnight" to each girl in the facility *by name*. This program, called "Story Time," has noticeably reduced the tension levels at the facility and seems to be appreciated genuinely by everyone concerned. I recommend the program to you.

The Dependency Calendar

When should the state take custody of children who have been abused or neglected by their parents or legal guardians? And once that has happened, when is an appropriate time to give the custody back, if ever? Fortunately the laws of most states furnish some guidelines about what questions should be asked in these areas, and what best can be done.

For example, in California's Juvenile Court we have quite a good statutory system to help us decide when it is appropriate to return the custody of a child to the parents. For the first year, which can be stretched to eighteen months, we focus our attempts upon "family reconciliation." That means we try to do everything that is necessary to bring the custody of the child back to one or both parents. We focus upon the parents' interests, as long as they would not be harmful to the child. However, as my friend, the late Justice Henry Moore of the California Court of Appeal, used to say, "There is only so long that a child should be forced to wait for his parents to grow up." So after this twelve- to eighteen-month period has elapsed, the focus switches to acting solely in the best interests of the child. This may still mean returning the child to the parents, or it may mean the child should be adopted by others, placed in foster care, or put into a group home. In the latter cases, sometimes the parent(s) can have visitation rights, *if* that would be in the child's best interest.

Nevertheless, the laws cannot in and of themselves answer the critical questions of when to remove a child from the parents' home or when to return custody of the child to the parents. Only an individual struggle with each case, assisted by all of the wisdom and insights a judge can muster, will help that judge with those decisions. In this struggle, though, try to be aware that some social workers can get bureaucratic and tend to remove children from their parents just to justify their own position in the bureaucracy. Or they might remove a child from the home because "we have always done it this way in the past." That is not at all to say that every social worker does not take these issues seriously, but the judge is the ultimate decision-maker in these critically important matters and must be aware of all of the circumstances.

One of the biggest assets a judge has in trying to do the right thing in these cases is the national group that calls itself "CASA," or Court Appointed Special Advocates. These people are volunteers who undergo vigorous training and certification. Then they are assigned to one or more abused or neglected children so that they can get to know them and their situations. It is the function of the advocates to make recommendations to the court as to the proper course to follow from the child's perspective. As I have said numbers of times publicly, these volunteers and their organization are "made of gold," and as a Juvenile Court judge, I put great weight upon their recommendations.[8]

Clearly, the juvenile dependency calendar judges carry a tremendous amount of responsibility. As such, the following advice is intended to offer unconditional support and a few helpful suggestions to those who fulfill or desire to fulfill this difficult task.

Listen to the Children

Judges should do more sitting back and listening to the subject children. Most of the time the children want to talk about what is going on, particularly at home. Often what they have to say is not good. Of course, judges have many important decisions to make, but in my view it is usually the children themselves who will best provide us with the insights to make them most effectively. So understand that many children will not be time conscious, and it may take a while before they will "open up." Be patient and—always with someone else in the room for your protection—get to know them. Give them a meaningful chance to provide you with information. With time they will often let you know if they are fearful of or being abused by a parent, whether they are eating regularly, or other serious issues.

Ultimately, a judge in Juvenile Court will have a fair amount of discretion to formulate a plan to keep children in or return them to the custody of their parents. But that ability is for naught unless she obtains insightful information. Frequently the children will provide that information, if the judge simply listens and gives them the chance.

Utilize Juvenile Dependency Mediation Programs

Frequently programs run by private professional juvenile dependency mediators will help parents who want to learn and who are not "fighting the system" to make progress. If your jurisdiction does not have such a program, try to establish one. It adds another level of assistance and support.

Encourage Proper Parenting Skills

Without exception, efforts toward the goal of family re-unification should be sincere and dedicated, because we, as a government, are not well situated to raise children successfully. Ideally children should be raised by their parents, and it is my experience that most people have the desire to be good parents and to take their parental responsibilities seriously. (Sometimes, of course, the parent is put in jail and options are limited. See the inset "When Single Mothers Are Sent to Jail, What Happens to the Children?" on pages 118 and 119.) To further the goal of family re-unification, judges should help the parents address the issues that are holding them back. That might mean enrolling the parents in anger management classes, parenting skills seminars, alcohol or other drug abuse programs, or even simple household skills lessons.

As an example, I once heard that a social worker removed some children from the household of a single mother because several windows were broken in the house, which caused the children to be cold and exposed to the elements. When the judge heard about the problem, she ordered the social worker not to fix the windows herself, but instead to show the mother how to clean out the glass from the old windows, measure the space, go to the store and buy replacement glass and some putty, and then install the new windows. After the mother fixed the windows, custody of the children was promptly and appropriately returned to her. If we can empower parents to be problem-solvers, the children will benefit.

Classes for parents—especially single fathers—can be truly effective in helping them to improve their parenting skills. Not only can these fathers be shown how their own behavior is transmitted to their children, but they can also be helped to focus effectively, often for the first time, upon their relationships with their children and other important people in their lives. For example, after just one session's concentration on what kind of woman they would like the mother of their children to be, some of the men in a particular program changed their focus and found wonderfully, mutually supportive women as partners. And this beneficially has changed their lives and those of their children forever.[9]

While I was working on these calendars, I also strongly encouraged parents, grandparents, and other guardians to turn off the television and to read to the younger children. In this regard, I myself handed out dozens of copies of Dr. Seuss' book *Fox in Sox,* which is my favorite children's book for reading aloud. It is fun, challenging, endearing, and silly. So not only will it be an entertaining activity and a great bonding experience for the children and their guardians, but it will also encourage the children to read. This is critically important because reading problems in school have been associated closely with a downward spiral of behavioral and anti-social problems, which then leads to low self-esteem, isolation, and dropping out of school. So it is very important to motivate parents and children to read together. It will really pay off for everyone.

WHEN SINGLE MOTHERS ARE SENT TO JAIL, WHAT HAPPENS TO THE CHILDREN?

I would like to share with you a problem area that most people are not aware of, and that is the number of single mothers who are in prison for non-violent offenses. For example, a full 80 percent of women in prison in California are mothers, and the vast majority of them are the sole caregivers to their children. Moreover, 60 percent of all women in prison are there for non-violent offenses.[1]

When I served as a judge on the Abused and Neglected Children's Calendar in Juvenile Court, I would have the following factual scenario brought to my courtroom about once every four weeks. A woman—let us take, for example, a single mother with two children—would make a bad decision. Namely, she would hook up with the wrong boyfriend. The boyfriend would be selling drugs, and basically the woman would be aware of it. Then one fine day the boyfriend would say, "Tell you what, Helen, if you will take this package across town and give it to Charlie, I'll give you $500." She would actually know the package contained drugs, but $500 would pay for half of her month's rent, and she really needed the money. So this woman would agree to do the task, and she would get caught, arrested, charged, convicted, and sentenced to five years in prison—which, under today's system, is not an unreasonable sentence for transporting something like 4 ounces of cocaine.

But when our efforts at re-unification are not successful within the twelve-to eighteen-month period, judges should understand that, as a practical matter, mostly it is not difficult to find adoptive parents for younger children. It is also amazingly possible for older children, or even several children in the same family, to be placed with adoptive parents. In one case I was working on, county officials were able to find adoptive parents for a sibling set of *five* children. It took a little time, and they were from out-of-state. But it actually did occur.

So I agree with Judge Len Edwards that Juvenile Court judging is the most important judging in the country, because it deals so directly with the future of so many children *and* adults. It is true that calendars that handle children who act like hardened criminals and people who are neglecting or otherwise abusing children can get through one's defenses. In response, when I was on these calendars, I had to figure out ways to keep myself from becoming jaded. So I actually took trips to the local zoo during my lunchtime so that I could sit back and watch a few happy children being treated well by their parents! But the tough stuff is

---

But ask yourself this question: When the mother is incarcerated, what happens to her children? Well, that is an easy question to answer, because under these circumstances she has legally abandoned her children. Now I would have a woman in a jail jumpsuit and handcuffs in my courtroom, and I would tell her the brutal truth, which is that she is not functionally going to be a part of her children's lives for the next five years. With that realization, her eyes would begin to get cloudy. Then I would look at her and tell her the rest of the brutal truth, which is that unless she is really lucky and has either a close personal friend or a family member who is both willing and able to take custody of her children, they are probably going to be adopted by someone else by the time she gets out of prison. So then she would break out in tears—wouldn't you?

But if that human issue is not enough to move certain people, I can reduce even the unemotional to tears when I reveal how the taxpayer is involved. For the first year it is going to cost the county upwards of $5,000 per month per child to keep her in a group home until she can be adopted, which is about $60,000 per child times two children (in our example). Then, add the incarceration costs for the mother, which run about $25,000. So we taxpayers are going to be spending approximately $145,000 for the first year physically to separate a mother from her children. In my view, this is obscene, both humanly and financially. Yet this is a common occurrence in every state of our country. I leave this issue with you by asserting that there must be a better way!

worth it, and the successes, when we see them, are deeply and permanently gratifying. As Judge Michael Nash of the Los Angeles Superior Court said, "I think
being in Juvenile Court has changed or brought out a part of me that cares more
about people and has given me a greater understanding of human foibles and
weaknesses, myself included."[10] The experience will change you as a person.

FAMILY COURT

Family Law deals with marital dissolution cases, and these cases often present
people in times of great vulnerability. Some of these cases can quickly get out of
hand, because this is a place where the law and emotions intersect and, often,
emotions prevail. At the very least, the cases that are litigated present partners
who were in a "beautiful mistake" during which "forever after" lasted well short
of a lifetime. Or as Christopher Morley was quoted as saying, "The trouble with
wedlock is that there's not enough wed and too much lock."[11]

The Basics of the Family Court Calendar

Call it what you will—Family Court, Divorce Court, or Centers for Marital Dissolution—this calendar involves the coming apart of the family unit. That means
that the marriage relationship must be addressed, along with custody and support issues for all minor children, possible spousal support, and a division of
property and other assets. It also can include claims to future property like earnings, royalties, or rents.

     In many states the decisions made by judges on spousal support issues have
been seen as so inconsistent that legislatures have passed laws that attempt to
resolve them by using various formulas. Therefore, the judge and the attorneys
can often "plug in the numbers" to figure out in advance if there will be any
spousal support and, if so, how much and for how long. But do not be fooled.
There is no substitute for human beings focussing upon individual problems and
attempting to work out a proper set of decisions. So, notwithstanding the legislative efforts, we still need judicial decision-makers in this important area, and that
is always likely to be so.

Advice for the Family Court Judge

Given the dynamics of family court circumstances, most experienced judges tol-
erate a little bit of attorney posturing to satisfy the clients, while still trying to get
to the core of the disputes. Ideally attorneys can and should keep their emotions
under control, and judges should help as much as possible in that effort. Actually, much of this posturing could be eliminated if counsel could only keep their
clients' expectations within reason. Among other things, attorneys could do this
by negating what most parties in a marital dissolution seem to feel: "What's
mine is mine, and what's yours is ours." But when counsel do not negate that
attitude, very difficult situations can be left to be resolved by the judges. So let

me pass along some tips that I have learned over the years about how to handle situations like this.

Use a Little Humor to Temper Over-Earnest Attorneys

It is my experience that on some occasions the attorneys in these cases can be a bigger problem than the spouses are, which is to say that some counsel figuratively pour gasoline upon the litigation fire. The majority of counsel do not fit this pattern, but it does happen. Sometimes they actually do this in a selfish and even scurrilous attempt to generate more legal fees. Other times they are simply trying to carry out their client's perceived wishes by "being tough," because they are acting under the express or at least implied threat that if they aren't tough enough, they will be fired by their clients. In fact, I have known of times when family law judges have seriously considered professional mediation for the *attorneys* to resolve *their* differences!

So what to do? Try a little humor. For example, a judicial colleague of mine gave me an example of how he handled a situation in which two "bull-elk" male attorneys were arguing hotly and heavily with one another. My friend simply waited patiently past the point where the attorneys subconsciously expected the Court to yell at them to stop. When they paused to see if my friend was paying attention (not unlike children fighting to show off), my judge friend said, "You know, you two must never marry." They both laughed, and one of them said, "Oh, Mr. X knows I love him."

Help Parties Identify Healthy Goals and Maintain Respect

From the very first, encourage the parties and attorneys to try to articulate what their final goals are in these various matters. Hopefully one of the main goals is to inflict as little pain and suffering upon the parties' children as possible. Another would be to get the parties through this difficult and emotional time as well and quickly as possible—without spending all of their money along the way. Of course, the ultimate goal should be to put this behind them and get on productively with their lives.

In my view, the most effective tool for reducing the stress level and identifying and pursuing goals is to refer the parties to specifically trained mediators. Many studies have shown that judicial orders after contested litigation are not nearly as effective over time as mediated agreements,[12] so I recommend that professional mediation be utilized as much as possible. This is usually done outside the formal court system.

But let us assume the ex-couple decides against or is unsuccessful in professional mediation and the trial continues. What happens next? In trying to reduce atmospheres of hate and remorse, I believe the best thing judges can do at the beginning of the proceedings, to the degree that they are able, is simply to make time to listen. Let the parties talk and get things off their chest. It is therapeutic, and often the parties will feel—just by this experience alone—that they have been able to tell someone in authority just how much of a "jerk" their spouses are and this can serve for them to feel that they had "their day in court." Then they can get on with the property distribution and other requirements.

When presiding over a Family Law trial, I once began by telling the following story: There was a wealthy man who told his wife, as her birthday was approaching, that she could have any present that she wanted—a new car of her choice, a new house, an around-the-world cruise . . . anything. The wife thought for a moment, and then she said: "I want a divorce." The husband quickly responded to her, "Well, I wasn't thinking of spending quite that much money." Sometimes that story can demonstrate just how expensive in both money and emotion a marital dissolution can be.

After lightly but poignantly jesting about how much money divorce trials can cost, I continue with my "universal truths discussion." So next I remind the two litigants who have children that, although I certainly cannot effectively order a divorcing husband and wife to go back and love each other, I can and will order them to treat each other professionally, especially in front of their children. Even though the ex-couple may no longer love each other, and even though they may be on their way to be living separate lives, they will always have one critically important thing in common with each other—they will always be the parents of children whom they love. As such, I remind the parents that they can show the love that they have for their children by *never* speaking in an unflattering way about any of the children's other family members within the hearing of any of the children. This includes the other parent, the grandparents, and anyone else for whom the children love or care. Literally every time a parent talks down a family member in the presence of the children, that parent is hurting those children. In addition, what the children eventually think of their parents when they are adults will be largely determined by what the parents do now. Except for extreme situations like severe child abuse or substance abuse, the thing that harms children most is their parents' inability to co-parent—that is, to work with one another in a business-like way to promote the children's best interest.

Similarly, judges should encourage the parents to be hesitant to make their children repeatedly travel long distances for visitation. If the out-of-town parent wants to have short periods of visitation, which are good things, that parent should do the traveling, not the children. My personal opinion is that so-called "joint custody" of children, in which the children live half of the time in the household of one parent and the other half in the household of the other parent, is often wonderful for the parents but *terrible for the children*. Children need stability, and that means they have only one home. They can and should visit the other parent, but again, they must have only one home.

Once we have established the goal or goals in the case, we should begin to gather information. What are the obstacles that stand in the way of accomplishing the desired goals? Does any of the parties have a problem with alcohol or other drugs? Anger management? Medical issues? Neglect or other child abuse? Encroaching mental disabilities? Lack of resources? Work schedules? Is there a friend or relative who has the confidence of both sides who can be used as an intermediary? These issues cannot be resolved or the resources utilized unless they have been first identified.

At this point, judges really do become social workers and mediators. Get used to it! In fact, in my view if this is not a concept that makes a person comfortable, that person has no business being a judge on most of our calendars. The best judges care for and about people and should always try to make the overall situation better. They are not simply dealing with files to be pushed through the system, they are dealing with important human issues that are crying out to be addressed. If we can get each of the parties to buy into the goals, then we can get everyone on the same side of the issue and can work together in an attempt to obtain a just and reasonable resolution. As an aside, for a comment on what to do if you identify problems such as tax evasion, see the inset "Do the Right Thing and Report Offense to the Proper Authorities" below.

Remind the Litigants That, One Way or the Other, Decisions Will Be Made

In reality, most of the time there are no "solutions" to the problems that confront us, no matter how hard we seek them. Perfection is simply not available. But there are "resolutions" for the problems. That means that there are ways to reduce or minimize the damages, increase or maximize the benefits, and allow the parties to get on more effectively with their lives.

But by the end of the preliminaries, the parties should know that if they cannot work their problems out themselves, decisions will still be made and orders will be entered. It is just that the parties themselves will lose the ability to have

DO THE RIGHT THING AND REPORT OFFENSES TO THE PROPER AUTHORITIES

Given the animosity and emotion of many litigants in Family Law cases, often the evidence will disclose income tax shenanigans or other irregularities. If that happens, I recommend you write a letter to the appropriate government agency and cite the record of the potential offenses. Although in the times I have done this I have never heard that there has been any follow-up investigation, I believe that when a judicial officer ignores evidence of an offense, her behavior is tantamount to condoning it.

any particular say in the outcome. The judge can and will divide up jewelry, automobiles, acreage, and even pots and pans quite easily. It may not be fair in the eyes of the parties, but it will be done. The same is true for issues of the custody and support of children. Judges will do their best, but they probably cannot make key decisions concerning children as well as loving, caring, experienced, and insightful parents.

So one way or the other, decisions will be made. Then, of course, the judge will move on to the next case. But the parties, on the other hand, will be forced to live with the results.

The Family Law judges must be prepared to put on their "hard hats" to protect themselves along the way. Many times, the fear, frustration, and rage of one or more of the parties will result in some ugly situations. Large numbers of insults and accusations may be leveled back and forth, and judges should not be surprised to find that much of the litigation can actually be driven by revenge. In fact, in one such case the matter got so extreme that neither party appreciated the irony when they had one final blow-up over who would get the custody of their wedding pictures! But in the end Family Court judges are significantly affecting the lives of the parties involved, and there is nothing more admirable than aiming to establish peace and resolution between fellow human beings during their times of need.

PROBATE COURT

One day in the judges' lunchroom I was talking to a colleague who strongly suggested that I ask to be assigned to the Probate Court calendar. It has everything, he said, including criminal, civil, juvenile, mental health, elder law, and adoption issues. It also can oversee the settlement of civil cases for minors, including the amounts of money to be spent for medical care and for attorney's fees, and the possibility of requiring "structured settlements" for the minors' funds so that they will be cared for through their college years or beyond.

I found that my colleague was right, that sitting on a Probate calendar was a great assignment. One reason was the gratification of the work. But another was that this type of court is often blessed with a small and collegial group of attorneys who are, for the most part, really knowledgeable about this area and pleasurable to work with. So I am glad I took his advice and requested this assignment, and now I will share with you some of the most valuable lessons I learned in this role. This section will focus on the general Probate Court calendar, which deals with the results of death, division of estates, and guardianship of the aged or disabled. As suggested above, often a jurisdiction's Probate Court also oversees cases regarding the mentally challenged, as well as adoption cases, but these two specialized calendars will be discussed in Chapter 5.

The Basics of the General Probate Court Calendar

As just touched upon, the Probate Court calendar is one of varied issues and responsibilities. It can truly stimulate the intellect and satisfy the heart. Fortunately, many probate situations involve people who have integrity, but the cases in which heirs and descendants do the decent thing and carry out their responsibilities honestly are not particularly called to the attention of the trial judge. Instead, they are routinely approved on the "consent calendar," which means the decisions made in them are not the subject of any objections, and so they are approved without much review. Unfortunately though, all too often the attraction of "free money" can give rise to endless bickering. And these are the cases you will see as a Probate Court judge. Overall, the mandate of this calendar was best described by one of Orange County's stars, legal research attorney Linda Martinez: "We in the probate department try our best to follow the law and the wishes of the deceased for the proper distribution of their property, and to use all available resources to establish and maintain a safety net and protective environment for cases involving children, the elderly and disabled adults."

The approach of settling Probate Court cases by seeking common goals usually works quite well if there is still a common bond among the litigants. But the judges are often faced with irreconcilable attempts by one or more of the parties who try to get a "larger piece of the pie." These are the cases in which "the wheels come off the bus," and they can require an inordinate amount of judicial time.

Just like in Family Law cases in which one spouse sometimes tries to hide or shield assets or falsify information so she can emerge from the case with more of the assets than the other party, similar problems often arise in Probate Court. Now that the parents or even "Old Uncle Edgar" are deceased, one beneficiary tries to get more of the assets because of simple greed, from some form of attempt to "even the score" for long-held grievances, or even to perform outright theft! Probate Court judges also frequently see some variation of "Daddy always loved you best, but now is the time for payback."

Of course, as mentioned previously, probate law can be about more than estates. Probate Court judges face different problems when dealing with the placement of the ill, elderly, and mentally disabled. It is often the case that family relations or long-term friends are put in legal charge of aging or mentally disabled people, their finances, and their belongings. In the court system, the people who are placed in charge are referred to as *conservators*. Most often they are family members, but they can also be private professionals. As can be imagined, those who do not have the best interest of the aged or disabled person in mind can often easily take financial advantage of the situation if not monitored. This is an area in which the Probate Court judge and the judicial system in general must be extra vigilant.

Advice for the Probate Court Judge

Naturally, virtually all of the advice set forth so far for trial court judges will apply to Probate Court calendars as well. But there are some unique areas of the law that will appear on this calendar because the relationships of the parties to each other are often different than in other types of cases—mostly because they are receiving money and other assets without regard to issues of liability, fault, or breach of contract. Accordingly, this calendar can require different approaches and skills from the trial judges.

Emphasize the Costs When Parties Do Not Want to Find Agreement

The classic situation for failure in trying to get beneficiaries to work together instead of squandering large amounts of the assets on attorney's fees is found where we have the children of the deceased by his first wife contesting the claims of the deceased's second wife. Often the second wife is about the same age as the children, and they have never gotten along with the "golddigger." These situations can be brutal, and there often is not much that can be done about them except to plod forward and remind the parties of the costs they will expend if they decide to fight it out to the bitter end.

In cases that involve self-serving beneficiaries who want to take too much of the cake, the most workable approach is simply to point out to the litigants that their present course of action is gratuitously expensive. One way I do this is to say to the parties that I anticipate that each attorney charges more than $22 per hour (wink, wink), and that there is no particular reason why the parties should send the attorneys' children to college as a result of this case. In addition, it is helpful to emphasize that they themselves are in a better position to settle their disputes than the judge could possibly be. The judge is not personally familiar with the deceased or with her connection to the various items of her estate. Of course, the judge can *become* familiar with the estate and, one way or the other, decisions will be made. But if the feuding beneficiaries decide they want to try to resolve all their disputes as well as possible themselves, the judge can make suggestions, and this will probably allow everyone to get a better, quicker, and much less expensive resolution.

One effective approach for a settlement is for one party to divide the assets up as equitably as she can and then to allow the other party to choose either one group of assets or the other. This method works quite well if we are addressing merely the commercial value of the assets. But it usually is not effective for emotional items to which commercial value does not so much apply. Another approach that works quite well when there are larger numbers of beneficiaries is for all of them to put a value on the assets and then hold an "auction" for them; the ones "buying" more assets logically will pay off the others in cash or credits from their share of the rest of the estate.

Arrange for Legal Research Attorneys to Help with Paperwork

As we have discussed throughout this book, courts around our nation are increasingly making efforts not to play "hide the ball" and instead to be more user-friendly. That is particularly true in many of the nation's Probate Courts. Typically these courts require numbers of steps to be taken and many forms to be completed as one proceeds from filing a case to its completion. Many Probate Courts employ highly competent legal research attorneys who will contact the counsel for the parties in advance of their court hearings and tell them if there are any defects in the forms or other papers. Therefore the errors and oversights can be corrected by the time of the hearing or the hearing can be postponed without a needless appearance. If your court does not provide this service, I recommend you implement it. Virtually everyone will appreciate these efforts.

Protect the Dignity of the Elderly and Vulnerable as Much as Possible

When dealing with the sensitive issue of deciding where an aged or vulnerable person should live, judges should try to resist or delay as long as possible the moving of that person from her own home. Many times when people are forced out of their homes, they in effect feel that their lives are over. Instead, judges should try to arrange for homecare, or even live-in homecare. That often can be appreciably less expensive than an assisted-living home, and if "ready money" is not available, the parties can look into a reverse mortgage to pay for the help. Most of the time, even though these expenses can diminish the eventual size of the estate to be distributed to the beneficiaries, if the beneficiaries care for the subject they will agree to the homecare. And if they do not, the Court should often step in and require it anyway.

Another way to support elderly subjects is to try to find a way for their family members and friends to be able to spend as much "quality time" with them as possible, unless particular contacts would be unduly disruptive. Seeing oneself deteriorating or slowing down is truly a cause for depression, but few things counteract that depression as much as continued good times with caring family members and friends.

Finally there is an additional effort judges can make in this area in order to help the aged or vulnerable person under discussion to be a little more comfortable. Try as often as possible for the person's pet dog, cat, or canary to continue to live with her. Pets are wonderful therapy and emotional ties to the past, and not having regular access to these animals can be psychologically devastating.

Arrange for Careful Monitoring of Conservators

Another recommendation in the area of general Probate calendars is that judges should arrange for the conservators of the estates and persons of the elderly and mentally disabled to be carefully monitored and audited—whether they are closely related by blood or they are working privately on contract. In many places around the country, the savings and other assets of these vulnerable people have been plundered within our court system. Since judges are in charge of that system, I believe the ultimate responsibility to ensure that this malfeasance is kept to an absolute minimum belongs to us.

In all honesty, Probate Court was one of the most enjoyable calendars on which I have ever served. The reason is a mixture of the "court team approach" with the highly competent and respected legal research attorneys, the relatively small and collegial group of probate attorneys with whom we dealt on a regular basis, and the wide variety of issues that always seemed to make these cases more interesting. So I say to you: Try it. I think you'll like it.

CONCLUSION

As has become clear, the calendars for Juvenile, Family, and Probate Courts deal directly with domestic relationships at a time when the parties are frequently angry, vulnerable, legitimately scared about the future, or downright greedy for an increased inheritance. Judges on these calendars are required to be firm but understanding, decisive but deliberative, and "no nonsense" but sensitive to the human condition. In other words, these judges are frequently called upon to preside over the impossible.

It can be done, but you will have to continue to be impervious to occasional personal insults and to remember that there probably will be no "solution" for most of the problems, only imperfect "resolutions." Yet when the victories come, and they will come, I promise that you will feel an extra amount of personal gratification because you were able to help your fellow human beings during some difficult times to get on with their lives productively. And I think you will agree with me that this can be a pretty good feeling.

Chapter 5

Additional Important Judicial Calendars

"Justice does not depend upon legal dialects so much as upon the atmosphere of the courtroom, and that in the end depends primarily upon the judge."[1]

—JUDGE LEARNED HAND

There is a temptation for people who are not familiar with court operations and the significant work that they do to consider the "important" calendars to be Criminal and Civil. Such people also consider the remaining calendars to be kind of "mop up" and not really mainstream. But now that you have reviewed the previous chapter about Juvenile, Family, and Probate Courts, you know differently. The same is true with the remaining calendars that most larger state courts have, which are Mental Health, Adoptions, and of course, Court Administration.

As you are about to read, the Mental Health, Adoptions, and Court Administration calendars are unique and demanding in their own ways. As a result, a judge sitting on any of these calendars needs to be a "people person." After all, the Mental Health and Adoptions calendars demand an additional amount of patience, compassion, and understanding, while Court Administration requires lots of budget work, sometimes endless meetings, and catering to a variety of "judicial egos." Therefore, I acknowledge that the specific calendars under discussion in this chapter are not for everybody. They call for a different atmosphere, and that is derived from you as the judge. So if this work is not for you, it will show. But if you fit the mold, I guarantee that you will derive a truly special fulfillment from sitting on these calendars. I believe that if people saw how most of our courts around the nation deal with such difficult and sensitive situations as those that arise in these calendars, they would agree, for the most part, that our justice system is generally doing a job of which we can all be proud.

MENTAL HEALTH COURT

Mental Health cases are a hybrid. The respondents are not accused of having done anything wrong. Instead, it is feared they are not able to take care of their own needs for food, clothing, and shelter, even with the assistance of their own individual "support systems." In such situations, the local governments bring proceedings to have the subjects found to be "gravely disabled," or in a similar legal condition, and placed upon a conservatorship of their person, their estate, or both. But before this can occur, the respondents are entitled to have a trial before a jury or a judge, as they choose.

The Basics of Mental Health Calendars

The finding of grave disability or similar legal condition cannot be established unless the jury or judge finds this determination by a standard of "beyond a reasonable doubt." That enables the courts, whenever reasonably possible, to keep people from the extreme but sometimes necessary measure of being placed upon conservatorships and having their individual liberties reduced. If the respondents are able to function even modestly well on their own, in my view they deserve the opportunity to do so. It is a major affront and intrusion into their lives and their liberty to be placed on a conservatorship. So even if the respondents stand a fair chance of being cold or hungry for a couple of days out on their own, most judges and participants in the mental health system believe this to be a reasonable risk. Of course, if there is a material threat of their really hurting themselves or others, that is a different story.

Accordingly, as I often said when I was on the Mental Health calendar, we are all on the same side of this issue. If the subjects have a reasonable chance to provide for themselves in the world, all people on the case should work together to maximize the subjects' chances of independent living. If they cannot, it is certainly not in their interest, or anyone else's, to have them live without the appropriate and necessary supervision and assistance. So on those occasions when I encountered friction among counsel, I would call them all into chambers and remind them that we all had the same goal: to do what was in the best interest of the subject.

Throughout this process, all concerned parties including the judges must bear in mind that the "substance" they are dealing with here is people and their future. They must not fall for the "shadow" of simply medicating the subjects' symptoms and warehousing them to keep them out of sight and out of mind. All efforts should also be made throughout these proceedings to treat the subjects as gently as possible. That means, for example, that concerted efforts should be put forth to find compassionate and understanding bailiffs to transport the subjects from their various facilities to the courthouses and back. And the courts should see to it that those officers are dressed in civilian clothes instead of uniforms while doing so. Issues such as these, which might seem small to the uninformed, are actually extremely important when it comes to the human dignity of these fragile people.

With regard to the trials or hearings themselves, counsel for the government have the obligation to present evidence about the subjects' background, how they have been living, and how they would function in the world using all support systems reasonably available to them. These resources include their own financial capabilities, the assistance of family and friends, and services that are available through public institutions and private philanthropic organizations. Then counsel for the government also must present a convincing expert opinion that the individual subject is gravely disabled. Thereafter, just like in a criminal trial, the subject has the right but not the obligation to call other witnesses and to testify about his background, resources, abilities, and conditions. Ultimately a decision is made by the jury or judge, and in most jurisdictions the subjects are statutorily entitled to these hearings once every year.

Often these trials can present truly sad situations. For example, sometimes a person who was looking forward to his yearly hearing—and has dressed himself in a rather bizarre outfit for it—comes in and testifies passionately about how this time he really believes he will be able to live without a conservatorship. But when that is not the court's decision and he begins to come to the realization that unless some new medication is developed that will turn things around he will probably never again be able to be on his own, he begins to cry. And to be honest with you, there have been occasions when I have gotten tears in my eyes right along with such subjects.

But the finding of grave disability is only one of the important questions to be decided by the court. All attempts must also be made for the mentally disabled person to live as independently and with as few restrictions as possible, even when on a conservatorship. For example, if subjects would likely fare well enough in board-and-care facilities or some other type of assisted living facility, they should not be confined in a lock-down facility. In other words, the least restrictive environment in which they will be able to be safe and cared for is where they should be placed. If they are able to be productive and hold some form of job, this should be strongly encouraged. In addition, the conservatees should be allowed to see their friends and family as often as reasonably possible, and even have daytime and/or overnight excursions with their supporters, as long as this would not jeopardize anyone's health or safety.

Unfortunately as we have already discussed, in most jurisdictions the largest "treatment" center for people with mental illnesses is the local county jail. In almost any jail, the reality is that, at any one time, probably somewhere between 10 and 25 percent of all of the inmates are on psychotropic medications. In today's world, this is not particularly surprising. If a mentally ill person is found urinating in front of a downtown business, the owners logically call the police. On the first occasion, the police frequently give the person a warning and take him to a local shelter, if one is available. But if the situation repeats itself, the police, for the most part, have no alternative other than to take that person to jail. The case sometimes reaches a Mental Health calendar judge from there, but most of the time it does not. So in my view, we as a society must do better.

The sooner we bring these mentally disabled people into a system that can effectively assess and address their needs, the sooner and more likely we will be able to break the downward cycle of anti-social conduct and deterioration—for the benefit of us all. But just getting the mentally disabled people into this system is obviously not enough. They must also receive appropriate treatment while there. Under our laws, if people's liberties are being restricted they are entitled to receive *actual treatment* that at least presents the legitimate hope of progress. And this treatment should be implemented as soon as possible, because the longer a person is institutionalized, the less of a likelihood there will be that the person will ever be able to adjust successfully back into mainstream society.

Accordingly, on those occasions in which a judge finds subjects that are simply being "warehoused" without reasonable attempts at treating them, my view is that it is the responsibility of the judge to step in and change the status quo. Judges are the "gatekeepers" of the system, which means they are the neutral judicial officers who oversee the mental health system. They are responsible to use all reasonable efforts to keep the intrusions and abuses of the system to an absolute minimum, as well as the efforts for positive treatment and results to a maximum. I am proud to say that on several occasions while on this calendar I used my authority to conduct reviews and even pursue reorganizations of the system that have done just that.

Another problem that is occasionally faced on the Mental Health calendar is one in which people—frequently parents—determine that a medical procedure is inappropriate for their child due to their religious beliefs. If that occurs, and the medical professionals on the case determine that the withholding of that treatment could be life-threatening to the child, a petition can be filed on the Mental Health calendar to bring the issue of whether or not such medical intervention procedures can be administered to the child without the consent of the parents.

Similar issues are also brought to this calendar when some members of the family of a terminally ill patient want "heroic measures" that will keep the patient's heart beating to be taken or continued, and others do not. Candidly, there is nothing in law school or a judicial college that can really prepare a judge to make decisions of these kinds. But if we listen carefully and thoughtfully, and if we derive guidance from statutes, the case law, and our natural common sense and compassion as best we can, no one in our society is in a better position to make these difficult and emotional calls than we are. And once the decisions are made, all we can do is hope that people will understand that we are simply doing the best we can under highly difficult circumstances.

Advice for the Mental Health Court Judge

There is nothing you have ever done professionally that will be like serving on the Mental Health calendar. Normally it is not one of the most intellectually challenging calendars, but it is one of the most human ones. It requires some of our most patient, sympathetic, and understanding judicial officers to make the system work. If you are one of those, you will love this assignment.

Let the Subject Talk

I have always found it to be insightful in Mental Health Court trials simply to let the subject talk if he chooses to do so. Sometimes he will begin quite rationally and coherently, but within a short time he will claim that he is Bill Gates, that he owns the local baseball team, that he is a prominent religious leader, or that he is even involved in extraterrestrial travel. As such, the decision of whether or not to assign a conservatorship usually works itself out one way or another within a fairly short period of time. So taking the time to listen and observe is well worth your while. For a related point on listening and not interrupting, see the inset "Do Not Stop the Flow—It Does Not Matter" below.

Do Not Close Your Mind to Medicine

Although I am certainly not an expert in the area of psychotropic medicines for the mentally disabled, I have seen some miraculous changes in people when they have begun to take or have resumed the taking of some of these medications. Here is an example. Probably the only time that I ever felt fearful of being attacked while on the bench occurred when I was presiding over a hearing to determine if a young man should be ordered involuntarily to resume the taking of his "meds." The evidence showed that he was a professional tennis instructor from another county who had been prescribed certain medications, but for whatever reason he had stopped taking them. Soon thereafter he had been found by

---

DO NOT STOP THE FLOW—IT DOESN'T MATTER

I have been in a hearing in which the subject was talking about having visited some distant planet, which he proceeded to name. At that point, the court reporter interrupted the subject and asked him to repeat the name. No! Interrupting is counterproductive in this situation. In the worst case scenario, it could lead to a bad reaction on the subject's part. In the best case scenario, it could simply result in a big waste of time, especially if the subject decides to elaborate. While it may seem like I am emphasizing a small point here, I think it is important to focus upon.

the police in our county while publicly acting in a truly bizarre fashion. This type of conduct continued during his testimony in my court, and with little difficulty after all of the evidence had been taken, I ordered that he be forced, if necessary, to resume the taking of his prescription psychotropic medications.

Less than a week later we had another hearing to see if he was stabilized sufficiently such that he could be released to go home. The change in him was monumental. He was conversant and cogent and acknowledged that he had deteriorated because he had forgotten to take his meds, which he knew he should take. We were soon talking about his life and his future, as well as joking about the game of tennis and the unlikelihood of my ever winning Wimbledon.

I bring this case up because, on occasion, I have heard people talking about the inappropriateness of forcing people to take psychotropic medications. I agree that there can be some abuses in situations of this kind, and I myself have seen subjects who have simply been over-medicated by their doctors so that they would not present as many problems to the staff at the clinics. But I have also seen literally hundreds of people who would have had to have been permanently institutionalized but for the medications they had been prescribed. And sometimes I myself had to force them at least initially to take the meds involuntarily. Obviously anything can be the subject of mistakes or even abuse, but my experience has shown me that some of these medications literally have been lifesavers and freedom-givers for large numbers of people. So I join thousands of others in being thankful for those pharmaceutical advances.

Remind Society We Need to Try Harder to Heal Hurt People

A judge cannot be on a Misdemeanor or Felony calendar for long without facing several cases involving obviously mentally disturbed people who are being prosecuted for what I call social misconduct offenses. These people are therefore faced with possible jail sentences that will only increase their likelihood of repeating those offenses. For example, while on a criminal assignment I had a case of a mentally disturbed man who was charged with the possession of a check that was stolen out of the mail. This person had been hanging around a church for a long time, so eventually the staff called the authorities. This resulted in a policeman's approaching and asking the man if he had any money on him. The man responded that, yes, he had this check in his pocket, and he produced the subject check as proof. It was clear to all of the members of the court system that the man had mental problems, and, since he had already served eighteen months in prison for a prior conviction of an identical type of offense, it was obvious that incarceration would not deter him. But our efforts to get him placed into the mental health system were unsuccessful because, as the mental health official told us, "We don't have the resources to take him."

All judges, particularly those on the Mental Health calendars, should use whatever persuasive powers they have to lobby for those people to be sent to

Mental Health calendars instead of Criminal calendars. A study showed that it cost about $3,000 to $4,000 to treat a person in an intensive treatment program in Richmond, Virginia, in 2000, as opposed to about $20,000 for incarceration.[2] Not only is jail the most expensive alternative in terms of dollars and cents, but it also can be quite emotionally expensive to these mentally fragile people. The better approach is to place as many of these people as possible into the mental health system and attempt to break the cycle of these offenses.

But in today's world, the irony is that we apparently do not have the tens of thousands of dollars to pursue the things that would actually help many mentally disabled people, yet without much thought we spend literally hundreds of thousands of dollars per year to keep them locked up. This is particularly shortsighted when dealing with those few mentally disabled people who tend to be violent toward others, because, as we understand in the criminal justice system, *hurt people hurt people.* So if society does not meaningfully attempt to heal the underlying problem instead of simply incarcerating the mentally disordered offenders, we will in effect be inflicting additional violence upon ourselves for years to come. There are many approaches to healing, and they are too numerous to explore here. But a brief comment on the power of meditation and mindfulness is offered in the inset "Promoting a Positive State of Mind" on page 135.

If your experience on this calendar is the same as mine, you will find that you have a large amount of power to do what you think is right under the law and facts of each case. In some situations you literally will be able to have people summarily confined, or people strapped down and involuntarily injected with psychotropic medications. Sometimes your decisions will cause people to be in a lockdown facility for a year, until they are entitled to a new hearing. And most of the time, as a practical matter, there are no appeals taken from your decisions. Take on this assignment if you wish, but please do so only if you are extremely patient and conscientious. If you do not have those qualifications, some dire injustices could be visited upon some pretty defenseless people.

ADOPTION COURT

If you want to be involved in something that will put a smile on your face, try performing three adoptions at the beginning of each workday. That will do it. In fact, it gets better if you make a nice ceremony out of the occasion. Of course, you and the court staff will have scrutinized each case in advance to be sure that all statutory requirements have been met. But then go forward and enjoy one of the true pleasures of the bench.

The Basics of Adoptions Calendars

Adoption Court is a wonderful place to work, as the judges partake in many heartwarming moments. Yet in reality, the Adoptions calendar does not just present fun and games. The judges and staff must be alert for problem areas that can arise at any time. For example, there are cases that involve the adoption by an elderly person of an adult. On occasion, these situations do legitimately occur with little or nothing to do with finances. But many such situations can also be used to manipulate an inheritance from the "adopting parent." Accordingly, judges should pay particular attention to ensure as much as possible that no one is being victimized in any adult adoptions.

There are additional special areas of concern in the Adoptions calendar. One that is unique to those jurisdictions that have not passed "same-sex adoptions" non-discrimination legislation is the proposed adoption of the natural child of a woman by her female partner, or the adoption of a man's natural child by his male partner. As I have noted throughout this book, it is not the position for judges to utilize their personal philosophies on these sometimes emotional sub-

---

PROMOTING A POSITIVE STATE OF MIND

On a side but related issue, let me say that the more one is exposed to issues involving mental health and human conduct—and many judges see plenty of this every day in court—the more one realizes that many people who come before the Court can use some help concerning "mindfulness." In that regard, there are an increasing number of mental health professionals—therapists, physicians, and hospital staff—who are focusing upon and modeling the positive sides of our human experiences. In doing this, they are emphasizing values and character strengths for others to see and adopting a contagious "attitude of gratitude."

Of course, all of the world's great religions have been preaching this course for centuries. But now more therapists, regardless of their or their patients' religious affiliations (or even the absence thereof), are becoming more "spiritually sensitive" and adopting the Buddhist and other similar messages of "slow down, meditate, and be mindful of each moment with each breath you take" in their efforts to "de-contaminate the mind."[1] Judges can take this lead and help parties who enter their courtroom by suggesting such positive practices, whether those judges are sitting on Criminal, Mental Health, or other calendars.

Without a doubt, judges must never *order* a person involuntarily to attend a religious-based institution for therapy or anything else because of the importance of the doctrine of the Separation of Church and State. But we should also understand that it is not only all right to accept people's *voluntary* participation in programs of this kind, even though they sometimes can be somewhat offbeat, but also we should be reasonably open to the ability of such programs to satisfy some counseling requirements and other conditions of probation.

jects. Instead, it is the judges' function to research and follow the laws of their jurisdictions. In most jurisdictions, the thrust of the laws for adoptions is to act in the "best interest of the child." I myself have had this situation arise about four or five times, and I give advice, based on experience, on page 138—see "Look at the Background and Facts, Not Gender."

One more issue presented to judges on the Adoptions calendars to take note of involves the adoption of children with even a small amount of Native American blood. The United States Government made a clear political decision when it passed the Indian Child Welfare Act, which provides that a child's particular tribe or tribes must be formally notified that an adoption of the child is being contemplated. Then any of the child's tribes are to state whether or not they are interested in tribal members' actually adopting the child themselves. This statute was necessitated by the recent history of Native American children's being taken into non-Native American homes and environments, resulting in a large decrease in the numbers of tribe members throughout the country. The Indian Child Welfare Act was passed in an attempt to stop or even reverse that process. Accordingly, if appropriate notice is not given to the tribe(s) and the child is adopted by non-Native American adults, the adoption stands a large chance of being voided. Obviously, this can result in huge emotional trauma both to the adopting parents and to the child himself, so all courts must be particularly aware of and be careful to follow the dictates of these federal statutes.

Advice for the Adoption Court Judge

The Adoption Court calendar offers some of the few situations in which almost everyone leaves the courtroom happy and satisfied. As a result, this can be a truly uplifting experience. But there are also a few special tips that I wish to pass along to you that will even increase the happy times and help you to avoid some occasional pitfalls.

Make Each Proceeding a Special Ceremony

Many times the adopting families, who often have been waiting a very long time for this moment, will bring balloons, hats, and streamers. They will treat this as the big occasion that it is. And there will be lots of cameras along with the smiles. My recommendation is to try to make each ceremony unique in some way, within your time restraints. One way is to stress a special fact in the procedure—something unique to that particular situation—to help the family know and appreciate that this is not simply a routine chore for you.

Here is a tip in that regard. In most jurisdictions it is required that the Court take some sworn testimony in an adoption proceeding, so do your best to make a big deal about swearing the witnesses, and pause so that the photographers can get lots of pictures while the people's hands are raised. In my court I also requested that the prospective grandparents raise their hands and take an oath along with the prospective parents, because, as I solemnly told them, "Grandparents have firm responsibilities in these matters as well." Then, after the parents had sworn to provide guidance and support for their child, I turned to the grandparents and made them swear that they would "spoil" the grandchild: "Of course the child may have a chocolate chip cookie before dinner," and the like. Almost always that approach was well received by everyone, and the grandparents readily agreed that they would be very good at spoiling the child. Next, I recommended that a picture be taken of the judge alone with the person to be adopted; then a picture of the judge, adoptee, and parents; and, finally, a big group picture.

When I first began on the Adoptions calendar, the judge that was departing recommended many of these things to me. He also recommended that I request the adopting parties to send me a copy of one or two of the pictures so that I could put them into a scrapbook of my adoptions. I have done that, and those scrapbooks are the source of some of my fondest memories of my time on the bench. In addition, since those occasions I have come across numbers of people for whom I had conducted adoption ceremonies. Frequently they have quoted to me almost exactly what we did in the ceremony that was special and told me how much it meant to them for all of these years. So that has added a great deal to my enjoyment as well.

Look at Background and Facts, Not at Gender

As mentioned previously, some jurisdictions have not passed non-discrimination laws when it comes to a same-sex couple's wanting to adopt a child. Sometimes this includes the situation in which one adult is the biological parent and the other is that parent's life partner. As one can imagine, if the laws do not instruct judges on how they must preside, judges could realistically rule by their own ethics. But in my view, judges must be very careful not to let their own cultural beliefs rule here. The decision must be based on providing the child with a safe and hospitable home.

I always simply looked at the facts and backgrounds of the parties so that I could act in the best interest of the child who was proposed to be adopted. The first thing I did was to determine if the prospective parent was mentally and financially competent to raise the child, and committed both to the child and to the natural parent. Next I asked myself what would happen in this particular situation if for some reason I were to decline to allow the adoption to go forward. Would the natural mother simply stop seeing her female partner and find a man to marry? Not very likely. Instead, the two women would almost certainly continue living together and raising the child, but without the formal commitment from the second woman that she was voluntarily seeking to undertake. So in the matters submitted to me, I determined in each case that the parties were capable and committed, and that it was in the child's best interest for the adoption to be finalized, and I signed the orders and performed the ceremonies. In addition, I have used the same approach in single-parent adoptions.

A large number of emotionally charged and human matters can be found in Adoption Court cases, and they are matters that can intimately touch the lives of the people who come before the Court. The judges must be patient and try to learn as much as possible about all of the sometimes subtle but important issues. They also must be aware of sometimes hidden problems and they should ask questions. Only then can judges both ethically decide on such sensitive issues and avoid some critical problems in the future. But let us not emphasize the struggles that can arise in Adoption Court without also focussing on the exciting and fulfilling work that judges accomplish when they legally pronounce someone as part of a new family, a new home, and a more secure life.

COURT ADMINISTRATION

Most courts in our country have steadily become larger, more complex, and more expensive. As a result, courts have needed an increasing number of judges and other skilled people to be involved with Court Administration calendars. I myself have always been grateful that my court has consistently been staffed with colleagues who were willing to become presiding and assistant presiding judges, because they virtually do nothing but administrative matters—for years. In fact, I seem to view this assignment in the same way that Wernher von Braun did when he said, "We can lick gravity, but sometimes the paperwork is overwhelming."[3]

It is estimated that the state courts conduct about 148,500 jury trials each year, with an additional 5,900 conducted in the federal courts. California state courts have the largest number of jury trials with about 16,000 per year; Vermont and Wyoming have the lowest number with about 125 each. Alaska has the highest number of jury trials per capita, with about 177 per 100,000 population, and Alabama has the lowest with about 15 per 100,000. To obtain enough jurors to try these cases, an estimated 31.8 million jury summonses are mailed each year to about 15 percent of the adult population, while about 1.5 million jurors are impaneled. Over the course of their lifetimes, a little more than one-third of all Americans are likely to be impaneled as trial jurors.[4] That takes a great amount of administrative organization, planning, and effort just in itself!

Since the judiciary is an entirely separate branch of government, the court system obviously has some large administrative duties and responsibilities for each individual judicial district and courthouse, both statewide and nationwide. Those duties and responsibilities not only involve judges, but they also often involve large numbers of administrative and clerical workers as well. So it is important that Court Administration judges, as well as others, develop and maintain solid relationships with the administrative personnel and treat them like the professionals that they are. If judges make it clear that they value the personnel's skills and talents, and that they do not intend to micromanage their work, those judges will help to further the smooth running of the courts. After all, since it is the job of the administrative personnel to keep the judges happy, we should appreciate and respect them for their efforts.

The concept of professional court administrators can be traced back to a famous discourse by Dean Roscoe Pound of the Harvard Law School, who in 1904 decried the popular dissatisfaction with the court system and recommended a more organized approach to its business. But it took until the early 1970s for a master's degree program in Court Administration to be established in our nation's universities, and for formal programs to be taught for middle management positions, supplemented by national conferences and journals for these professionals. Information about how each court is run administratively is now widely available on the Internet. If even a small part of that information were provided here, I am afraid that would create an unacceptable amount of verbiage. So instead I will simply furnish a short summary of the framework of judicial administrative responsibilities.

In the federal system, the Chief Justice of the United States has numbers of administrative responsibilities, and each Associate Justice also has administrative responsibilities for at least one of the twelve federal circuits. In addition, of course, each of the circuit or appellate courts has its own administrative system, as does each of the ninety-four judicial or trial court districts.

The state court systems basically function in the same fashion. The state's highest court—usually, but not always, called its supreme court—has, under its chief justice, overall administrative responsibilities for each of its courts. Each appellate court and trial court district, in turn, under its chief or presiding justice or judge, has its own individual responsibilities as well. As a result, all of the courts can have a natural tendency to become increasingly bureaucratic. This is exemplified by the fact that the very first receipt for supplies submitted by the first clerk of the California Supreme Court when it opened up for business back in 1850 was for "one bottle of black ink, three gross of Gillette's pens, and 24 sticks of red tape."[5]

Probably the most all-encompassing responsibility faced by all of those administrative entities is to plan, obtain approval for, and oversee their court's budgets. Not only is this a naturally difficult area for the courts, but it is a sensitive one as well, because the Judicial Branch of Government is entirely dependent upon the other two branches for its general funding. The benefit of this situation is that it tends to keep the courts from becoming too unrealistic in their decisions, but the drawback is that it can tend to make the courts' decisions too responsive to politics.

The following list of some of the administrative matters that most courts routinely address will probably not be surprising to those who have thought about it. But like many other things in this world, most of these activities go unnoticed. The administrative responsibilities include, but are not limited to, the education, continuing education, and training both for judicial officers as well as for court staff; procurement of supplies; management of human resources matters, including retirement and other benefits; labor negotiations; the creation and publishing of procedural rules; information technology services; fiscal operations; records retention, including electronic and physical storage; bench/bar and other community education, relations and outreach; video and telecommunications services; construction, repair, remodeling, and maintenance of the court facilities; after-hours duty assignments for such things as search and arrest warrants, bail, emergency protective orders, and writs; transportation of custodial prisoners; accounting services; jury services; lobbying efforts for pending legislation; legal research support for judges; the recruitment, selection, training, and supervision of clerks, bailiffs, administrative staff, court reporters, and interpreters; appellate procedures; the creation, organization, scheduling and staffing of court calendars; collection of fines and fees; the formation of contingency plans for natural disasters; services for families and children; mediation and other alternative dispute-resolution services; and crime victims' restitution and other services. There are also the increasingly difficult and complicated matters of court and courtroom security and safety. Many judges report that they have been threatened during the course of their work (mostly in Criminal and Family Law assignments), and security screeners are seizing increasingly large numbers of weapons at the entrances to courthouses, including guns, knives, razors, and mace.

Obviously the above information is only a partial list, but the scope of what is involved in setting up and administering a court system can be mind-boggling. And as technology progresses and problems continue to get more complicated, administrative demands will continue to increase. For example, as most jurisdictions attempt to evolve into "paperless courtrooms," even more administrative work will be required. The same need will occur as they try to make the courtrooms more computer-compatible for the presentation of evidence and the retrieval of case files by judges and litigants.

One of the particular things that is generally not realized by the public is that the only real powers that presiding judges usually have over the fellow judicial officers in their courts is the power to assign cases to them and to designate the courtroom in which they will sit. Now it is true that this can be a formidable power, especially in large jurisdictions where the outlying courthouses can be located a long distance from where an "offending" judge happens to live. But otherwise presiding judges are not in a position to review the work or even the ethics of their fellow judges, or to make appellate decisions about it. For that reason, presiding judges are often referred to as "First Among Equals."

Nevertheless, presiding judges often receive complaints about the decisions or demeanor of their peers. They invariably respond by explaining the system to the inquirer. For example, the judge will confirm there is a difference between a judge's making a decision or ruling with which the complainant disagrees and a judge's being involved in an ethical violation. But if an ethical violation is possibly involved, in most cases the presiding judges are themselves ethically required to refer the complainant to the appropriate governmental agency.

As a result of the reality of all this never-ending administrative responsibility, whenever judges in my jurisdiction announce that they wish to run for presiding or assistant presiding judge, or even request to be the supervising judge of a particular department, I try to go out of my way to thank them and wish them good health. After all, neither I nor most of my judicial colleagues became judges so that we could become bureaucrats and spend most of our waking hours involved in meetings, financial planning, and assuaging various egos—judicial and otherwise. If some of my fellow judges would not take on these duties voluntarily, I might be forced to do so myself out of a sense of necessity, or at least obligation. And heaven help me from that fate.

CONCLUSION

Now that we have discussed, over the course of several chapters, some of the basic calendars in our courts, I hope that you will want to be involved with each in some way over the course of your career. Or at least I hope you will desire to be involved with many of them. Judges are blessed with the excitement of being able to "change jobs without changing jobs."

So I finish this section by saying that life is short, and so is your judicial career. Therefore, I strongly recommend you sit on a number of different calendars. Not only will this be more interesting for you, but it will also make you a more knowledgeable, complete, and effective judicial officer.

Chapter 6

Trials, from Start to Finish

"Judges must beware of hard constructions and strained inferences,
for there is no worse torture than the torture of laws."[1]

—SIR FRANCIS BACON

In the past several chapters, we have explored various court calendars in
detail, reviewing both the basic responsibilities that come with the assignments and recommending suggestions on how to deal with the associated challenges. But now is time to enter the judge's chambers and the courtroom itself,
and to discuss the actual trial experience. This chapter provides information on
the judge's role as a case travels through its pre-trial, trial, and post-trial stages.

PRE-TRIAL MATTERS

Since less than 5 percent of all civil and criminal cases filed normally go to trial,
pre-trial matters are where most of the judicial contact is found. By design, cases
are filed in order to call to the attention of the other side that there are problems
and that the prosecutors or plaintiffs are serious about pursuing them. Once that
occurs, both sides formally come together—sometimes in the courtroom, sometimes not—to attempt to resolve, or at least to conclude, their disputes in some
fashion. This section explores various elements of this pre-trial stage, from general pointers to information on specific practices and procedures.

Initial Suggestions

Pre-trial matters involve crucial information and instruction sessions that result
either in the settlement of a case or at least in the defining of the issues in the dispute. But whether pre-trial occurrences are a way to settle a dispute before it is
officially argued in a courtroom or simply the initial stages in a long process,
there are some important things a judge should think about in overseeing them.

Therefore, I recommend judges bear in mind several general issues during the pre-trial stage that, if followed, will help to treat those involved in the pre-trial matters with respect, fairness, and dignity, while at the same time moving the matters expeditiously toward a resolution.

Understand That Court Processes Are Unfamiliar to Many Litigants

Remember that many of the people who enter the courtroom are unfamiliar with the judicial setting and procedures. Therefore, the court staff must treat those people with understanding and assistance by providing extra explanations and definitions of legal terms. Consider the following example. A defendant, representing himself in a criminal matter, was in a particular court for his arraignment. Several people were ahead of him, so he had to wait. He seemingly listened intently while others came forward, each entering a plea of not guilty and having the matter set for a "D&R," or a Disposition and Re-Setting. When his turn came, the defendant under discussion politely came forward, entered his plea of not guilty, and asked for a "D&C," which, of course, is a gynecological procedure. (Fortunately he did not ask for immediate sentencing!)

Similarly there was a defendant who came into court representing himself on a civil matter and discovered that he already had a judgment entered against him by default, because he had not formally appeared in the case. When the judge asked him if he wanted a "stay of execution" of the judgment, the defendant thought he himself was going to be executed, and he fainted! From these somewhat humorous but also poignant examples, the need for a judge's patience, compassion, and guidance becomes evident.

Remember the Way It Used to Feel

Once one becomes a judge, it is easy to forget what it was like to be an attorney. Attorneys manage more than one case at a given time, and they often legitimately are required to travel to several courthouses, depositions, or client meetings on the same day. Within reason, judges should give them some understanding and some slack. For example, judges should mostly be understanding if the attorneys request "second call" on a calendar, or even if they have a substitute attorney appear at a status conference who is not entirely familiar with the case.

Do Not Forget the Original Intentions Behind Our Statutes

I try always to bear in mind the well-known saying of Aeschylus, which dates back to 458 BCE: "Wrong must not win by technicalities."[2] In the legal profession there can often be a tendency to get so intensely wrapped up in procedures and precedents that judges can lose sight of what is really happening. That does not at all mean that we should not enforce the laws and procedures, but we should do so with a comprehension of what the framers of the statutes intended the results to be.

So what happens if a plaintiff seems to have a viable case but is representing herself and has already failed to state a cause of action in her pleadings once or twice? A good judge would refer her to a public counsel or the bar association so that she can get some prudent legal advice before her case is dismissed for pleadings deficiencies. Ultimately, judges are not in the business or playing "Procedural Gotcha"; they are in the business of doing justice.

Become Familiar with Likely Defenses

Judges should become familiar with the rationale for the main affirmative defenses that will come before them in civil cases. Some of these are the Statute of Limitations, Statute of Frauds, Lack of Standing, and the Doctrines of Pre-Emption, Laches, and Unclean Hands. It is difficult to apply these potential "death penalty" defenses prudently if the judge does not understand the political and practical reasons why they were created and the problems they were designed to address.

Publish Your Guidelines

All judges have a special way of conducting their courtrooms, and that is fine. But it is easier for everyone concerned if the judge's guidelines are published and provided to the litigants at their first appearance in court. Some of my guidelines, for example, are that litigants are to mark all of the potential exhibits with numbers instead of letters, and that counsel are not to get closer to the jury than the podium during voir dire, opening statements, or closing arguments. So if they want to use the easel during their presentations, they should have the bailiff help them move it to the podium before they begin.

But judges should also bear in mind that, hard as it may be to believe, theirs is not the only courtroom in the world. It is difficult for counsel to prepare for and try cases in each judge's separate world, as well as to be knowledgeable of each judge's idiosyncrasies. Therefore, if and when you are publishing your own guidelines, try to keep your own "local" rules to a minimum, and be understanding and forgiving when things do not go exactly as you procedurally might wish.

Be Meticulous and Prudent Regarding Search and Arrest Warrants

The issuance of search and arrest warrants are critical stages of pre-trial criminal proceedings, and they are too often dealt with in a sloppy fashion by law enforcement officers, prosecutors, and even judges. Remember, there probably is no way to correct a mistake that is made with a search or arrest warrant, so the challenge to do it right the first time is especially applicable with warrants. As discussed in Chapter 2, when making the decision of whether or not a warrant is justified, judges must remember that they cannot consider or act upon anything unless it is actually written in the declaration, affidavit, or sworn document that is presented to them. So if information is missing, there are two avenues that can be taken. Either the document should be returned with the recommendation that the officer come back when the missing information is included, or, if the officer can swear to the information, it can be added by hand to the document and initialed by both the officer and the judge.

The reviewing authorities either at trial or on appeal must be able to understand what was considered by the issuing magistrate of a warrant, and what was not. The best way for this to be done is for the police officer to number the pages "1 of 12, 2 of 12," and so on. Frequently, the warrants consist of a cover page and a number of police reports. So it would be virtually impossible for anyone to know with any confidence what was and was not reviewed by the judge unless the pages were numbered in this fashion.

Finally, search warrants should be issued with great prudence. Judges must understand that if law enforcement officers are given unlimited powers to seize the records, files, and computers of an ongoing business, that has effectively given the officers the power to close the business down. Under some circumstances that may be appropriate, but judges should first explore viable options to this radical and potentially far-reaching result.

Case Management / Trial-Setting Conferences

Now that we have discussed several general pointers for the pre-trial stage, let us examine more closely specific elements of pre-trial matters. We begin with the case management conference, also referred to as the trial-setting conference. It is the first conference between all parties and the judge, and it involves things like setting a trial date and a settlement conference date. This meeting can also include a discussion of potential discovery problems.

The first specific issue to determine at this stage is whether or not the judge assigned to the trial will be officiating over the case management/trial-setting conferences herself. If the judge is not going to officiate and instead the conference will be handled by the clerk, the conferences probably should be done by mail. This will save the litigants the expense of paying attorneys for about three hours of their time to attend personally.

What happens when the trial judge *is* the officiating authority? Then the case management/trial-setting conferences are probably worth doing in person. Much of the following material in this section proves why face-to-face conferences can be so beneficial. I believe that if the conferences are run correctly, they can be a truly effective part of the litigation process. But they should be brief, and all efforts should be made for them to start on time, so counsel can schedule accordingly and move on to their next appearances. I offer some suggestions for how to "streamline" these conferences a little later on in this section.

Conducting case management/trial-setting hearings in person is useful for humanizing the process, because often this is the first time opposing counsel actually meet each other. At the very least, counsel are less inclined to act arrogantly or inappropriately in the discovery stage after they have actually met and conversed. I have also had some success in ordering counsel to walk back to the parking lot together and not to part company until at least one of them has brought up the word "settlement." So, as stressed above, these early conferences can be useful.

In addition, since all parties are represented at this conference, and counsel can often reach their clients with their cellular telephones and obtain their consent on important matters during the conference, counsel are likely to be able to stipulate to many things that are short of full settlement of the trial. For example, counsel can decide upon things like jointly hiring a neutral accountant, mechanic, appraiser, or design engineer to address some of the facts in their dispute, or they might even agree to submit the case to binding arbitration. While counsel play a large role at this stage of the case, so does the judge. The following guidelines offer even more discussions about the judge's role.

Ask the Right Questions

In case management/trial-setting conferences, the very first question I ask is one that calls for the parties to start providing productive, straightforward information: "What can the Court do to assist you other than giving you a settlement conference and trial date?" As a result of this direct question, I have sometimes been able to short-circuit many situations that otherwise would have taken a great deal more time and expense, such as discovery disputes, consolidation of actions, discovery cut-off dates, and scheduling of motions and Demurrers. In certain circumstances, that initial question has even led to partial or entire settlements of the cases themselves. Often the question also leads to reminding the parties that they might be able to obtain important information by using devices like a Bill of Particulars instead of time-consuming Demurrers or Interrogatories. Any enhancement of focus on the disputes themselves and suggestions for how to streamline the handling of them helps to keep expenses down and to promote a dialogue among the parties so that they can resolve or at least prepare the case more expeditiously.

Sometimes during the case management/trial-setting conferences, counsel will complain at length about how they are being abused by the opposition, mostly in discovery matters, and no one seems to want to budge in her position at this time. In those circumstances, I call upon something I learned when I went "police car riding" while I was still in law school. On the occasion when the officer received a call to go to someone's house for a disturbance of some kind, the police officer would listen for a short while, and then ask, "What is it that you are asking me to do?" In the conferences under discussion, I believe that this same approach is helpful. With the understanding that there are many things that the Court cannot do unless presented with a formal motion and time for a formal response, the question, "What is it that you are requesting the Court to do right now?" will provide practical focus to everyone concerned. Thus, I commend it to you.

Try to Avoid Continuances of Trial Dates

With regard to setting the trial date, I tell counsel that I can give them any reasonable date that they want, but the odds are good that they will be forced to stick to that date once it is set. And since the trial attorneys are actually present at the conference (or are supposed to be), subsequent excuses intended to change the trial date in the weeks after it has been set—for example, they had a vacation planned or another trial set for that date—are usually to no avail. Continuances of trial dates are often good for the attorneys but most often not good for the parties themselves, so they should be avoided. This is yet another reason why I believe that face-to-face case management conferences are helpful to all concerned.

I once had a plaintiff's attorney request a continuance of the trial because *his own expert* had just been deposed and he had learned some useful information. The request was denied. As the defense counsel later told me, when he left my courtroom and told the plaintiff's counsel he would see him next Monday for trial, the plaintiff's counsel said, "No, I'm not coming." And indeed he did not show. Basically, the plaintiff's attorney was just using the continuance as one last try to force the settlement of a claim that had no merit. So often continuances can be counterproductive, wasteful, and expensive.

Law and Motion Proceedings

Throughout the litigation process—from the filing of the complaints up to the beginning of the trial—motions, applications, and petitions can be brought by the litigants and heard on the court's Law and Motion calendar. This part of the pre-trial stage can include Demurrers to the sufficiency of the complaints, motions to compel arbitration, motions for a change of venue, motions for summary judgment, and many more. But probably half of the motions filed are discovery disputes, such as motions to compel further answers to Interrogatories, independent medical examinations for the plaintiff by the defendant's expert doctor, or the taking of a deposition. And, of course, most of these motions are accompanied by requests that the opposing side be sanctioned for its "abuses" and "unreasonable behavior."

Discovery disputes are often the bane of trial judges and frequently make them want to travel back to the days when attorneys simply showed up for trial without having received any advance information from the other side at all. In fact, in some ways the discovery rules have resulted in enormously higher litigation expenses for all sides without that much benefit. Nevertheless, in many ways the discovery laws have also been helpful because they provide information to each side, which promotes settlement of the cases and reduces the chances of "trial by ambush." Moreover, from all indications, discovery rules are here to stay, so trial judges must accept the fact that they are part of the calendar.

There are official pleadings that must be filed in order to initiate discovery disputes and other Law and Motion proceedings. Most jurisdictions have page limitations that apply to these documents. I offer some recommendations suggesting brevity of these documents in the section titled "Adhere to Page Limits" (page 151). Keeping discovery dispute documents brief will certainly help judges and their staffs make progress in this sometimes tedious process.

Notwithstanding some of the discovery disputes, many Law and Motion matters can be fun. In fact, in my view Law and Motion usually presents judges with the purest form of judging. Some disputes involve truly interesting and important issues that are litigated by bright and well-educated attorneys. The issues often are not easy, but it is a delight to test and otherwise throw back and forth possible results in this legal crucible, and to be a part of the addressing and resolving of the problems. When really complicated matters arise, judges should try to have their clerks or research attorneys flag the matters and provide feedback as early as possible so that the judges can spend some extra time working on those difficulties and otherwise digesting them.

Sometimes judges can be presented with quite a few Law and Motion arguments for the same case. How do they know which ones should be argued and which ones simply should be submitted based upon the briefs? For the answer that works best for you, see the inset "Assessing Yourself: Are You Visual or Oral?" on the following page .

During oral arguments for Law and Motion matters, some judges will drop into the discussion one of the more minor cases in the pleadings and either comment or ask a question about it. This does not necessarily move the argument forward, but it is used by the judge as a device to make counsel believe that the judge is completely familiar with even the smaller details of the pleadings. I personally do not believe in "bluff and bluster" because it is not intellectually honest, and it also can come back to bite the judge on occasion. But some judges do it with a certain amount of regularity because they believe it promotes a feeling of confidence among the litigants and increases the preparation of the attorneys for the hearing. For more on my personal preferences and suggestions, see the advice sections below.

Issue a Tentative Decision as Soon as Possible

In all Law and Motion matters, when it is possible a judge should issue a tentative decision as early as possible, hopefully on the Internet. This will allow counsel to ponder the judge's tentative rulings and be better able to address their resulting comments. And remember, these are only tentative rulings—judges should not consider themselves legally or emotionally bound to stick with tentative rulings. Not only does the practice of issuing tentative decisions help all parties involved to focus more upon the pivotal issues of the case, but it also saves time in the arguments themselves, because the "winning" sides need not say anything unless they want "to talk the judges out of their tentative."

Discuss, Do Not Confront

I have almost always found it to be helpful—as an attorney *and* a judge, as well as in my private life—to approach matters as a discussion instead of a confrontation. The way I manage Law and Motion arguments is no exception. In other words, instead of saying or implying, "I think you are wrong or mistaken about that," or "That case does not stand for that proposition," I try to use words such as, "I have thought about what you suggested, but doesn't this other analysis get us closer to the right result under the law?"

Similarly, just as it is often the purpose of all plaintiff's attorneys or moving parties on a motion to simplify the facts under the law, and it is the purpose of defense or opposing attorneys to show how the facts are quite a bit more complicated, it is the task of the judge continually to be aware of both possibilities and take them into account. So oral arguments give me the opportunity to ask the plaintiff's counsel to discuss with me why the case is not more complicated, and they give me the opportunity to ask the defense counsel to discuss with me why

ASSESSING YOURSELF—ARE YOU VISUAL OR ORAL?

Not all jurisdictions require oral arguments to be heard on all Law and Motion matters. So how do judges know how many arguments to hear? When and where do they draw the line? That depends on how much they will benefit from these arguments. It is the nature of some human beings to feel more comfortable and prepared after simply reading the briefs, while others naturally are more comfortable making decisions after also hearing oral arguments.

Try to determine if you are a "visual" person or an "oral" person. I tend to be more oral, which means that, although I work hard to be prepared on the pleadings, being able to listen to arguments, ask questions, and hear responses about the issues really helps me reach a conclusion within my comfort level. Therefore, I almost always hear arguments on the issues presented to me, and I try not to hesitate to change my tentative rulings if persuaded that they are not as accurate as they should have been.

On the other hand, judges who are more visual often schedule fewer arguments. But those judges should be aware that, on some occasions, the parties and counsel will feel that they may not be getting "justice" unless a traditional argument before the Court is allowed to take place.

it is not more simple. All of this usually helps reduce the level of "heat" and increase the amount of light on the subject.

Adhere to Page Limits

As discussed earlier, Law and Motion matters involve the filing of formal documents. Some jurisdictions impose page-number restrictions on these documents in order to keep the case moving in a timely fashion. I recommend as a usual practice that you adhere to these restrictions if you have them.

When the issue of overly lengthy documents comes up, there are several ways you can deal with it. One is to remind the parties that a pleading in Law and Motion is called a "brief" for a reason. Another tactic is to remind counsel that the Court and its staff have only so much time. So as a practical matter, counsel should be made to understand that the more pages that are submitted, the less time that will be spent per page on their pleadings. This usually gives them a reality check and convinces the attorneys that they should do their best to cut back on their wordiness.

Do Not Waste Time on Unimportant Details

In most jurisdictions the pleadings in civil cases are not actually read to a jury. So if they contain surplus information, are argumentative, or are not as precise as they could be, what difference does it make? If the defense is on notice of what the claim is, that is sufficient and the parties should move on.

Except for Trial Dates and Post-Arbitration Review Hearings, Let Counsel Set the Dates for Their Court Appearances

As stated previously, frequently a continuance of the trial date is good for counsel but not for the parties. And counsel often want to continue post-arbitration review hearings because they were not diligent enough to follow the Court's schedule. For such situations, I require specific Court approval for those dates to be changed. Otherwise, I recommend counsel be allowed to stipulate to the dates of all other court appearances.

Assert Your Authority When Counsel Get Unreasonable

It is unreasonable for attorneys to pursue discovery disputes for cases that simply do not justify the time and cost. I have a suggestion regarding the very first thing a trial judge should do when a discovery dispute shows its face for a small case: Call that case first on the calendar, hold up the file, and state that it is a matter that involves only $7,500, or whatever amount, so the case does not justify yet another motion to compel. Then order counsel to go outside in the hallway, telephone their clients, and try to settle the case—now! At the end of the calendar, speak to the counsel again. It is surprising how many of these cases will be settled within an hour. Try it with feeling. It works.

As for those cases in which one attorney is bickering in writing about the other attorney, I recommend that the judge invoke what my father called the "One Growl Rule." On the first occasion that one attorney calls the opposing attorney a name, I stop reading that pleading, and I instruct my legal research attorneys to do the same. If this rule is announced in open court, it will probably have a big effect both upon all counsel for that particular case, and also upon the other counsel who are waiting for their cases to be called. I know this rule is effective when judges stick to it.

Impose Sanctions Wisely

The word "sanctions" is an unpleasant word. Unfortunately, it is sometimes necessary. In my career, I have tried to order sanctions sparingly, and almost never when the losing side has had a rational position. But when judges find that sanctions are appropriate, they should not hesitate to impose them. In the first place, I believe that an unreasonable party should pay the other side's costs caused by that behavior, and secondly, this action will deter future conduct of this kind both in this case and with counsel on other cases that happen to be listening. But if they are used, instead of using the term "sanctions," try using the term "cost redistribution."

There are also certain rules of thumb that most experienced judges apply before they allow this reimbursement. For example, before a party is awarded costs for a discovery dispute, counsel for that party is required to show the court that she actually sent a letter to the opposing counsel setting forth the problem and suggesting a reasonable resolution. If no such letter has been sent, no reimbursement should be issued. Also, most judges understand that it is unprofessional to schedule depositions without making provisions for them to be convenient for the schedules of all other counsel and the proposed deponent. Without such efforts, no reimbursement for a missed deposition should be given. Do all jurisdictions have rules requiring such attempts? No. But I believe that all professionals have a right to expect that such courtesies will be employed. Certainly, all counsel in my cases quickly hear that these courtesies are required. So now counsel comply with those requirements almost without fail.

Be Kind to the Clerks

Finally, it is a good thing to remember that when judges have called and addressed the last motion and leave the bench, often with a sense of relief and accomplishment, the paperwork is only just beginning for the clerks. A little judicial understanding of that fact is appropriate and will be appreciated! In addition, reminding your clerk that you are always available to discuss how the issues can best be described and resolved in the Minutes Order is not only a kindness, but it will also help to make your court records much clearer.

Non-Binding Arbitration

Many courts have programs to which they refer certain types of cases for short non-binding arbitration proceedings. These can include cases for slip and fall, automobile collisions, and even assault and battery. The statistics in our courts in Orange County, California, show that about 70 percent of civil automobile collision cases that are referred to our program of non-binding arbitration are voluntarily settled and never come back to court for trial. As a result, this program is a truly useful means to resolve those cases.

Schedule Post-Arbitration Review Hearings Wisely

When I order cases to non-binding arbitration, I give them a firm date by which the arbitration is to be completed, and also a date about three weeks thereafter for a post-arbitration review hearing. This gives the arbitrator time to render a decision and the parties the chance to digest it before returning to court. Then if the case has not yet settled, encourage them to talk about settlement but also give them a trial date within about three months so that the issues and incentives will remain fresh. In my experience, setting that early trial date will probably result in the settlement of the case.

Make Careless Parties Pay

Sometimes, albeit rarely, it becomes clear that one side has not taken the court order for non-binding arbitration seriously. Perhaps they do not appear at the arbitration, or perhaps they do not produce evidence or ask any questions in the proceedings. What should the judge do in those situations?

In my view, there is no reason why the parties cannot be ordered to repeat the arbitration process. Go back and do it all again. But importantly, the recalcitrant party should be ordered to pay for the costs that the performing party incurred as a result of the repetition. When this condition is made clear *prior to* the original non-binding arbitration conference, disrespect and carelessness rarely occur.

The Management of Possible Problems

As a trial attorney, I always hoped to have strong and professional counsel on the other side of my case. I also hoped for parties who were more interested in dispute resolution, and less interested in drama and doing unnecessary damage. This would make everything go more smoothly and a good result much easier to obtain. As a trial judge, I have the same hopes, and for the same reasons. But there are inevitably those occasional, dreaded uncivil attorneys or problem cases that find their way to court. I have found certain techniques to be effective in dealing with such people/cases, and they are addressed in this section.

Quickly Identify Problem Attorneys, Parties, and Cases

You should try to find out as quickly as possible who is being the unreasonable party, and then order full "cost redistributions" (or sanctions) every time their inappropriate actions are called to your attention. This will deter the party from wasting time and being counterproductive. If pressed, you can also do things like ordering the depositions for these cases to be held in your jury room. That way any problems can be addressed immediately and without additional expense to the parties.

There is an additional technique that is mostly appropriate for out-of-town depositions, and it should be used only sparingly. It involves judges' providing authority for telephone calls to be made directly to their chambers during the middle of problem depositions. This allows for the arguments to be presented and for the rulings to be made immediately, without requiring a recess of the depositions and the filing of motions. If this procedure is adopted in your court, I further recommend that you, as the judge, use a speakerphone in your chambers and have the court reporter present so that she can take down everything that transpires.

On occasion judges will have problem cases that will constantly appear on their Law and Motion and Ex Parte (or "emergency") calendars. In such situations, there are often motions to compel discovery, complete with whining and requests for sanctions ad nauseam. Sometimes you simply must face these cases when they rear their ugly heads. But when it is possible, as the date for the trial gets nearer, I recommend the extraordinary approach of having all counsel come into your courtroom or even chambers with a court reporter present. Once there, instruct them to go over each and every discovery problem that remains. Listen to the requests, get a response, and rule decisively on each dispute as it is raised. In this way, you can order specific Interrogatories to be answered without objection, others to be modified and answered no later than a specific time, and still others to be withdrawn, or a deposition to be taken on a specific date and time. Furthermore, as trial approaches, do not forget that a Saturday deposition is a viable option.

But when the approach of gathering the parties together one last time at the pre-trial stage is used, you must make it clear that if the parties do not raise a particular discovery issue at this session, it is waived. This procedure will accomplish a number of beneficial purposes. First, it will resolve all remaining problems without the further expenditure of time for counsel or the Court. Second, it will save the Court lots of time on the Law and Motion and the Ex Parte calendars. Third, it will avoid a compromise of the trial date that has been set. Finally, it can avoid formal discovery motions and hearings, which will save the parties thousands of dollars in attorney's fees. On the few occasions when I have employed this approach, it has worked famously well.

Clarify That Default Prove-Up Hearings Are Still Trials

As you know, when defendants fail to respond after being formally served with a summons and complaint, defaults can be entered against them. Do not forget that hearings held in response to the default are actual trials in which the rules of evidence and burdens of proof still apply. Similarly, the damages awarded still must be caused by the actionable conduct of the defendants, and attorney's fees also should still be reasonable. In other words, just because the defendant has defaulted does not mean that plaintiffs are relieved of the requirement to prove each element of their cases by admissible evidence.

Use Available Tools

Numbers of tools are available for trial judges, who should not hesitate to use them. For example, as long as a complaint puts the defendant on reasonable notification of viable causes of action, try not to sustain a Demurrer or preliminary objection to the pleading unless there is a reasonable likelihood that an entire cause of action or claim for punitive damages can be eliminated. Demurrers and similar motions are mostly effective in increasing the costs of litigation, but seldom helpful in moving the cases forward, particularly since the allegations themselves are almost never read to the jury. Instead, suggest the defendants utilize a request for a Bill of Particulars if they want more information. This allows the case to move forward without loss of information or accountability.

Another tool for the judge to use productively is the request for an offer of proof. An offer of proof can help you decide how to rule on a motion or other request. For example, in deciding whether or not to allow leave to amend a complaint after sustaining a Demurrer, ask the plaintiff's attorney for an offer of proof of what she would allege if you were to give her the opportunity. Not only does that give a fair chance to the plaintiff, but it also gives you the opportunity to decide if the plaintiff can actually allege a viable cause of action or not. In addition, it gives the court of appeal some additional information to act upon if your ruling is appealed.

Set Mandatory Settlement Conferences

Not only do I believe judges should set mandatory settlement conferences, but I also believe such conferences should be set at the earliest opportunity at which a given case has a reasonable chance of settling. As mentioned earlier, most cases do not have to go all the way to trial; they often have the potential to be settled much earlier.

For about a year I set settlement conferences before I actually set my cases for trial, with the hope that the cases would settle early and save the parties lots of attorney's fees and costs. But I soon found out that many cases were not ready to settle for numbers of reasons, so the settlement conferences were not productive. One reason is that many people really do not seem to take their cases seriously until the trial date has actually been set and is fast approaching. Another reason is that they have not yet learned enough information about the strengths and weaknesses of all sides' cases. As a result, now I try to set my trial dates at the earliest reasonable opportunity, which is normally about a month before the trial date. That way counsel feel their feet are "in the fire," much of the important discovery has been taken, and the information about strengths and weaknesses has been obtained.

Nevertheless, there still are significant numbers of cases that will benefit from my original approach of establishing settlement conferences earlier. I try to be perceptive in setting those cases accordingly. Of course, settlement conferences are part of the pre-trial process, but they are such an important and multifaceted part that much of Chapter 7 is devoted to them.

During the pre-trial phase of the trial process, the courts can really be involved in a public service for the litigants. By being aware, diligent, and perceptive—by being an active but constructive part of the process—judges can move cases onward toward settlement or trial with reduced mental, physical, and monetary costs to the litigants. That is what good and experienced judges seek to do. And by using the approaches suggested for the pre-trial phase, that is what I believe we judges can regularly obtain.

TRIAL MATTERS

Trials do not just happen. They take a great deal of preparation and effort on the part of many people. But in the final analysis, they are orchestrated by the trial judge, and that is not an easy thing to do effectively. This section attempts to provide a concise as well as general discussion about the important stages of a trial, and offers what I hope you will find to be additional useful trial tips and treasures. To cover the material on trials most efficiently, I have veered from the usual format and placed most of the applicable advice in one large section after the stages of trial have been explored. Finally, I set forth some practical realities about a judge's contempt powers and the restrictions upon their usage.

Pre-Trial Conference

The pre-trial conference is an informal conference in chambers with all trial counsel, and it takes place immediately before the trial commences. This conference can be used to exchange witness lists, exhibit lists, jury instructions and verdict forms; to discuss trial procedures, such as sensitive questions counsel wish the judge to ask of the jury during the voir dire process; to address taking witnesses out of order and/or other scheduling matters; and, of course, to make one final attempt at settling the case. If the case does not settle, the judge is about to embark upon a unique experience, because each and every trial is different. Each is a living and breathing thing that has never existed before and never will again. And the judge will preside over its life.

In Limine Motions

In limine motions are the last clarifying motions before trial. The term literally translates to mean "at the very beginning." These motions are mostly heard after the pre-trial conference and just before trial. They are often brought in an attempt to exclude unduly prejudicial evidence from being presented to the jury or otherwise to avoid the wasting of time once the trial has begun. Unfortunately, many of these motions are simply a waste of time in themselves—to the extent that one of my colleagues on the bench always referred to in limine motions as "the last billable event before trial."

Trial judges should request that in limine motions be filed in writing and served upon opposing counsel at least on the day before the trial is scheduled to begin. That way, the judges can be prepared to deal with them effectively. It will also give opposing counsel an opportunity to be prepared before the motions are heard and the rulings placed on the record. Another related and helpful practice is to inquire during pre-trial conferences if there are any oral motions in limine that can be addressed, and to ask if there are any undisputed facts that can be the subject of stipulations or agreements by counsel. Although judges never have the authority to *order* parties to stipulate to anything, judges can certainly strongly recommend the parties do so if a matter is not in dispute. This will save everyone time and allow more focus to be placed upon the matters that *are* in dispute.

Pre-trial or in limine motions sometimes can be helpful in more precisely framing the issues for trial, shortening the trial, or at least reducing the time that the jury will need to wait outside while some last minute and "unforeseeable" issue is being discussed between the Court and counsel. The motions can also be helpful in educating the trial judge about more complicated issues that will arise as the trial progresses. Probably many of the rulings on the in limine motions will be deferred until some time during the trial, but at least the judge can begin to contemplate and research those issues.

Jury Voir Dire

The general translation of the term *voir dire* in Norman French is "to speak the truth." The translation in modern French is "to see and to say." But one way or the other, the term, sometimes phrased as *jury voir dire,* is used in the law to describe the process of attempting to select a fair, neutral, and impartial jury by determining each juror's ability and competency to serve. Of course, if all of the parties have waived or given up their right to have a jury, the voir dire phase of the trial is unnecessary.

Most of the time, judges do the initial voir dire, with counsel doing some follow-up questioning. But in most federal courts and some state courts the voir

dire is done by the judge alone, after she has received some requests from counsel. I detail my own voir dire agenda later in this section, offering step-by-step
instructions on how to narrow down potential jurors until a solid, fair jury panel
is found.

Unfortunately, the legal profession has become so competitive these days
that, as a practical matter, some attorneys do not want a "fair trial." Instead, they
desire—or even need—to win. So they do not want twelve unbiased jurors; they
actually want twelve jurors who are biased in their favor. Similarly, many attorneys do not hope for the truth to come out in trial but actually aim to suppress
it. And jury voir dire is a pivotal place in their attempts to put this plan into
action. Sometimes these attempts are subtle, and sometimes they are not. It
depends upon counsel, and it depends upon how strictly the rules are enforced
by the judge.

If in the process of selection the judge runs out of jurors in the jury box, the
clerk is instructed to call enough additional jurors to refill the box, and the selection procedure is repeated. After the questioning by counsel, and after either all
sides have passed on any challenges for cause or the challenges have been ruled
upon, each counsel may exercise up to a certain number of peremptory challenges. No reasons need be given for these challenges, unless they raise constitutional issues such as the exclusions' being based upon race, national origin, or
religion.

In my view, however, the issue of peremptory challenges is truly an inexact
science. Many attorneys and professional jury advisor services believe they can
spot potential jurors who would be harmful to one side's case, and that may well
sometimes be true. And there also are probably some general peremptory challenge guidelines that counsel can follow to their benefit. But otherwise, I think
any people who say they can tell with any kind of certainty about what a particular juror will do with a case is probably fantasizing.

As an example, years ago I was prosecuting a case in federal court before
Judge Lawrence T. Lydick. We were in his chambers after the taking of evidence
had been completed and were discussing the upcoming jury instructions. During this discussion, the judge surprised me by saying that he really thought we
were wasting our time because the jury was going to hang, and that he could
pick out which juror would hang them up. I thought to myself, "What did I miss,
and how could he know that?" Well, sure enough, the jury did hang at eleven to
one for conviction. After the jury was excused, I spoke to some of them and tried
to learn what had happened. The jury told me that there was one juror who simply had made up his mind for "not guilty" and refused to talk about it. In fact,
the situation got so heated that when a fellow juror tried more forcefully to get
the first juror at least to discuss his reasons, the first juror threatened to throw the
second one out the window! About a week later I was walking over to the cafeteria and I saw Judge Lydick. I reminded him what had happened, and I asked

him what I had missed. He responded, "Well, as a matter of fact, the juror that I thought would hang the jury was the one that was threatened to be thrown out the window." In other words, no one has perfect vision in this area.

It is good for a judge to have a standard protocol when it comes to the voir dire stage of the trial. I recommend that the judge begin the proceedings by having the parties and their counsel stand and face the jury as an entire group. Then the judge can introduce them and ask the jurors if they have known any of these people for any reason prior to that introduction.

Next, in a criminal case, I suggest the judge paraphrase the charges in the complaint and tell the jury that the defendant has denied the charges such that the matter needs to be submitted to them for possible resolution. In a civil case, instead of paraphrasing the causes of action or giving a "joint statement of the case" that has been agreed upon by all counsel, I recommend the judge give each counsel no more than three minutes to give a short statement to the jury as a group concerning what the case is about. I have found this procedure gives the jurors a "feel" for the case and can, in turn, change the jurors' outlook from one of resignation to one of actual interest in sitting on the case.

In my own protocol, I then provide the jurors with an anticipated trial time schedule and ask them whether they feel that a judge ordering them to be present for the anticipated length of the trial would, in light of either their personal or professional lives, be an unreasonable thing to do. That will allow the jurors to become "time qualified" without going through the time-consuming process of calling each of them forward and only then being forced to excuse them if they are not reasonably available.

Over the years, I have also learned to be more easygoing in asking counsel for a stipulation that jurors be excused for time problems. In most jurisdictions judges do not have the authority to excuse jurors themselves unless they are granting one of counsel's challenges for cause. Short of that, the jurors can be excused only by stipulation of the parties. But the truth is that if they are not excused for time difficulties, almost all of the jurors who really do not want to serve will come up with some strange reason or other as to why they could not be fair, neutral, or impartial. That way, eventually they will be excused anyway. So now I just excuse them earlier without the extra waste of time. But if it is a close call, I give the jurors a choice of either staying for our trial or going back to the jury commissioner and rescheduling their service for another date.

Finally, before having the clerk call the individual potential jurors forward to take their seats in the jury box, I recommend that they be asked if any of them has any problems understanding or communicating in the English language. Moreover, I suggest asking if, for any reason at all, they have difficulties sitting, thinking, or being able to hear, understand, retain, and act upon the evidence in the case. These questions give the jurors an opportunity to bring forth issues that could potentially cause problems with their service to the court.

Once these issues have been addressed, I describe to the jury panel the procedure that will be followed during the trial. That means I briefly describe the voir dire process and the reason for it; what an opening statement is; the process of calling witnesses and the procedures for questions to be asked of them and possible objections to be raised; and what "closing arguments by counsel" are. I also tell them that after closing arguments I will instruct them in the law and remind them that they must apply that law to the case. Then and only then will they be able to retire and begin to deliberate and otherwise discuss the case amongst themselves. I have found this short explanation to be helpful for jurors to understand the process they are about to enter.

I further recommend that the "six pack" method of jury selection be utilized. This means that the first twelve jurors will be called forward, sitting in the order in which they were called. Then an additional number are called to fill in the remaining seats of the jury box, plus an additional six chairs that have been placed in front of the jury box—hence the name "six pack." Once that has been done the judge asks questions to the prospective jurors. The areas for questioning are numerous and are frequently set forth in the court rules for different jurisdictions. In my questioning, I tell the prospective jurors that I know they will all do their best to be fair, neutral, and impartial. But if one of them has a family member or a friend who is one of the participants in the trial, obviously that juror would be considering information that others do not have, plus the whole litigation would have the appearance of unfairness. So that juror should not sit on this jury. Similarly, if this case involves allegations of, for example, driving under the influence of alcohol (and then I assure them that it does not), if one had a relative or close personal friend who was killed by a drinking driver, even though that juror would do her best to be fair, neutral, and impartial, it certainly would be possible that this highly emotional experience would creep into that juror's thought processes. As a result, it would be better for that juror to find some tax case or breach of contract action to sit on instead. At the least, those questions communicate to the jury panel what we are trying to accomplish.

Other matters that judges must discuss with jurors are whether they have any familiarity with the witnesses that are expected to testify or at least be mentioned in the case; whether they have any past experience as a juror; whether they would be able to follow the law that the judge provided to them, to the exclusion of any other law they may have heard of; and whether they have any background in the subject of litigation, such as employment in the insurance field, prior auto collisions, familiarity with a particular type of medical procedure, or an unfavorable experience with a building contractor. The jurors should also be reminded that in this trial they should search for the appropriate outcome under the facts and the applicable law, in addition to using their common sense in understanding how the real world operates. Therefore, the point should be made that the trial is not intended to be a personality or competency contest among the lawyers, because the facts and the law should be considered in reaching the verdict, not the relative skills or attractiveness of the attorneys.

Then comes the hard part: asking questions that stand a reasonable chance of ferreting out potential biases of jurors. Virtually all of the time, if one simply asks members of the jury panel if they can be fair, neutral, and impartial even though one of the parties is, for example, a felon, a transsexual, an illegal immigrant, or someone who does not speak English, the answer will be, "Yes, of course." A more effective technique is to avoid buzzwords like "bias," "prejudice," or "ethnic," and instead focus upon specific feelings and opinions from which bias could reasonably be inferred. So instead of asking potential jurors if they can be fair even if it is shown that a party is an illegal immigrant, I recommend you say something like, "Many Americans feel that illegal immigrants take advantage of our system without doing their part to contribute to it. Does anyone here feel that way?" Or "Does anyone feel that illegal immigrants should not have the same right to a lawsuit, protection under American law, or the right to recover damages that a legal citizen has?" Asking questions in this fashion will more often lead to genuine issues of possible bias.

In addition, frequently each case will have its own problems or particular area of inquiry. If police officers are likely to testify, will the jurors assess the officers' credibility using the same "yard stick" as they would use for any other witness? If there are particular medical or legal issues in the case, do any of the potential jurors have any medical or legal background (as opposed to, as I often joke, an illegal background)? And then the judge should be sure the jurors understand they are to receive the evidence during the trial and not from their background information or any other source.

I also try to address emotional issues head-on. For example, if the plaintiff or victims suffered serious injuries from the incident, I acknowledge that fact at the beginning and state that they are fully entitled to our sympathy, concern, and best wishes. But the issue of whether or not those injuries were legally caused by the defendant—and if so, to what extent—must be decided without being affected by that sympathy. So I remind the jurors that this is their duty under our laws, and I ask them if they will be able to carry out that duty, or will they instead be better suited to sit on a different type of case? Thus, in effect, I ask them that if they were a transmission in an automobile, would they be in neutral?

In concluding my questioning of the jurors, I go through three final areas. First, in the jury's presence, I instruct all of the counsel, parties, and their witnesses to treat the jurors "as if they were a plate glass window in a department store." What does that mean? It means that we have close quarters in the courthouse, and so the jurors are likely to see some of the participants in areas such as the hallways, the court cafeteria, and the parking lots. But the participants are to "look right through them," as if they were a department store window, and they are to give no indication that they know them whatsoever. They are not to smile, nod, or say as much as "good morning." And the jurors are to treat the participants in the same fashion. The reason for this order I hope is obvious to them: There is not to be *any* exchange of information in any way, or even the *appearance* of such an exchange. Then I instruct them that they can be upset with me about this order if they wish, because it is my order. But they should not hold it against any of the participants. I follow up by asking, "Does any of this give you a problem?"

Secondly, I go around the jury panel and ask the members to provide four pieces of information for us: their name; in what city they reside; who resides in their household, including parents, children, boarders, roommates, and even pets; and then their occupation if they work outside the home, as well as the occupations of everyone else who resides in their household. I have found that this lets all of us see if the potential jurors are good at following directions. In addition, by getting each juror to talk a little bit, counsel can get a feel for them as individuals. These questions also occasionally disclose jurisdictional problems, such as the fact that a juror has recently moved out of our county, or that a juror does not understand English well enough to respond to questions like these.

Finally, I ask if there is anyone on the jury panel who simply does not want to be with us. Because if that is true, we do not want them either, since they probably would not be concentrating upon the evidence and would not be a thoughtful and conscientious juror. If I get any responses, although by that time I rarely do, I ask that those jurors be excused and allow them to slink out of my courtroom.

At this point, I open up the floor to the counsel. It is appropriate for counsel to ask their questions, since, as I tell the jury panel, counsel are skilled and knowledgeable about the case and have their own insights into it. But counsel know that they are to stay within some time constraints, and they know not to repeat what I have already asked. I have found that these comments tend to hold counsel to a cleaner set of questions. Although the formal purpose of jury voir dire is to assist counsel in more intelligently exercising their peremptory challenges and their challenges for cause, all trial counsel—to a greater or lesser degree—will also try to use the opportunity to attempt to ingratiate themselves to the jury, educate them in the facts favorable to their case, instruct them as to the favorable law, and predispose them toward their side. Try, within reason, to keep that from occurring.

Preparation of the Jury for Trial

There are steps involved when it comes to preparing the jury officially for trial: the swearing in of the jury and the pre-instructing of the jury. Swearing in the jury is a critically important stage of the trial because if the judge does not cause it to be done, it is jurisdictional. The case will almost certainly have to be retried.

It is becoming increasingly popular for judges in most jurisdictions to give the jurors some pre-instructions about their duties once the jury is sworn but before opening statements. Examples of these are not to visit the scene of the incident(s); not to have any contact whatsoever with any of the parties, witnesses, or counsel except in open court; not to conduct any form of investigation or research whatsoever of the facts or the law; and not to discuss the case in any fashion with anyone else in the world, including their cats, dogs, and parakeets, until they have been authorized to do so. In addition, the jurors are instructed about the various types of evidence and burdens of proof that will apply. They are also told that they will be furnished with notepads and pencils to take notes, but they are reminded not to allow their note-taking to distract them from other testimony and not to use their notes as exhibits during their deliberations. It makes sense to pre-instruct the juries in these matters, because it not only helps to give the jurors some early guidelines, but it also can help to avoid future problems.

Opening Statements

Many attorneys, judges, and legal commentators feel that, other than the issue of the credibility of important witnesses, the opening statement is the most important aspect of the trial when it comes to convincing the jury. That is my belief as well. Skilled attorneys will use this opportunity to tell the jury about what they *anticipate* the evidence at the trial will be, which means they will tell a story that allows the jurors to see the case through their clients' eyes. Another way to look at this stage of the trial is to see the opening statement as a trailer or preview of a movie. If you find that metaphor helpful, you could then see the presentation of evidence as the movie itself and the closing argument as the critique of the movie.

If an opening statement is done well it can be a beautiful thing to behold. But it is not a time for counsel to "ingratiate themselves" to the jury by showing them how nice they are, or for counsel to try to precondition the jury in favor of their clients, or to instruct the jury as to the law. Although judges should be vigilant at this time to keep the opening statements on track, unless the comments are egregious, normally the judge should wait for an objection from opposing counsel before interfering.

I personally feel that opening statements are so important that if the parties have waived jury and are presenting the case to me alone, I solicit the giving of an opening statement even though I have already read the trial briefs. It allows me to ask clarifying questions and get a more defined overview of each side's position.

Parenthetically, if by this point an attorney has not articulated and established a viable theory of the case, she will probably be in real trouble. As an illustration, in one of my jury trials based upon allegations of bad faith practices by an insurance company, that company's attorney's expressed theory was that there was an exclusion in the policy that negated coverage. But when it became clear from the first witness, who was the insurance agent for the insurance company, that there was no such exclusion, the only real issue remaining to be determined in the case was the amount of punitive damages to be awarded against that insurance company.

Accordingly, one of the most important things litigators can do to be successful is to formulate theories of their cases. Of course, there can be more than one theory for a given case, and the theories can certainly be modified as the preparation for trial progresses. But everything litigators do on one of their cases must be done—or not done—with that theory in mind. In other words, an attorney's theory of the case is the main thing in litigation, and, as in the rest of life, "The main thing is to keep the main thing the main thing."

Presentation of the Evidence

Since the prosecution in a criminal case and the plaintiff in a civil case have the burden of proof, that party is required to go forward first with its presentation of evidence. When witnesses are called to the stand, the judge should be sure that they are sworn in and that they give the complete spelling and pronunciation of their names. It also generally sets a nice tone for the judge to greet the witnesses and thank them for being available to the court. (But try to remember not to do that for a defendant in a criminal case.) The judge should also make the swearing in of a witness a serious occurrence.

Once that tone has been set, the judge should ask the counsel by name if she wishes to proceed. Then the judge can sit back and listen, unless there is an objection that calls for a ruling or the witness is speaking too softly. If the latter is the case, it is sometimes appropriate for the judge to ask the juror who is farthest away from the witness if she is able to hear the witness well enough. These touches help to make the courtroom a less forbidding place, so that the participants feel more comfortable and are able to focus upon the important business at hand. Otherwise, a judge should try to follow the reminder that a judicial colleague of mine places upon his bench: "Mind Open—Mouth Closed."

During the trial, the judge has the right to ask clarifying questions of the witnesses. That is true in both criminal and civil trials, in jury and non-jury trials. But a troubling issue remains: When is it appropriate for judges to ask questions, and what types of questions should they ask? After all, as mentioned previously, a judge should try to remain rather quiet.

The easiest issues are clarifying questions. For example, when a witness gives a date, the judge can ask which year the witness is talking about, whether the reported time was "AM" or "PM," or whether the intruder entered the house itself or only the garden. But otherwise the judge should try not to ask a substantive question in a jury trial, unless it appears that the trial testimony would be truly misleading to the jury without that question's being asked. As another of my colleagues puts it, "With a judge, most of the time, less is more."

In contrast, in regard to a non-jury trial or when taking testimony on a motion, my view is that a judge should be more vocal. In these situations, I will usually ask only clarifying questions until each counsel has had an opportunity to examine the witness, and then I will ask more probative or substantive questions if I am still unclear about what happened. The reason for the difference is that in a non-jury case or on a legal motion, the judge is the fact-finder. Therefore, judges should not only be able to solicit information that will make the evidence clearer so that justice can be done, but in many jurisdictions they actually also have a duty to do so.[3]

After all attorneys have questioned a witness, the original counsel has an opportunity for "re-direct." Only questions responsive to those raised by the other side are allowed. No new avenues of examination, or those "outside the scope" of the cross-examination, are allowed unless counsel moves the Court to "re-open" the questioning. These rules generally allow the trial to keep moving forward.

Finally, if witnesses who have already testified in the trial are recalled to the stand, remember that they do not have to be re-sworn. But in every case, the judge must remind those witnesses on the record that they are still under oath, ask if they understand that fact, and get an audible affirmative response for the record.

As an aside, there are certainly times when a witness has been on the stand for what I view as an excessive period of time. So when all counsel finally say they are finished with their questioning, I say to the witness, "You may now step down, and leave quickly before they change their minds!" The jurors seem to like this, and it makes a point to the attorneys.

Closing Arguments

Some judges schedule closing arguments before they instruct the jury, and some reverse the order. It is simply a matter of judicial preference. But closing arguments are the time for counsel not only to tell the jurors what they believe the evidence has been, but also to argue the significance of that evidence, particularly in light of what they expect the instructions of law to be. In other words, skilled attorneys will show the jurors how their version of the facts is the truth. During the closing arguments, judges should protect the jurors from counsel's getting too close to the jury or doing things like pounding their hands on the jury box. In addition, sometimes the judge should remind counsel to "stay within the evidence" if counsel begin to "testify" about things for which there was no colorable evidence. But otherwise, judges should let the arguments take their course without interruption.

Since the prosecution in a criminal matter, or the plaintiff in a civil matter, has the burden of proof, that party is also allowed to have both the first and the last arguments to the jury. This last argument is called "rebuttal," and it allows counsel to respond to the arguments that were raised by the defense in its closing. But judges should be attentive not to allow those counsel to raise new issues for which defense counsel would not have an opportunity to respond. In other words, the rules do not allow for "sandbagging."

Instructions for the Jury

This is a difficult part of the trial. Most of the instructions given by the judge to the jury are "tried and true," but they can also be deeply boring. Judges must read them so that the instructions are legally correct, but they should also try to read them with various vocal inflections so that they make some sense and keep the attention of the jury. Unfortunately, "this ain't easy." But disputed jury instructions are the biggest reason for reversals on appeal, and time and care must be taken to make sure that they are as accurately prepared and presented as possible.

Let us first discuss the preparation of the instructions and how the final instructions are decided upon. I recommend that the requested jury instructions—and the proposed jury verdict forms—actually be received by the Court from each counsel *before* the trial actually begins. I further suggest that counsel be ordered to meet together on some evening after court is concluded, or no later than a certain date, to go through each instruction together in an attempt to agree upon which ones should be given. Then counsel should meet with the judge and go over each and every word of each proposed instruction. If there are additional issues, or the status of the presentation of evidence is still unclear, a paper clip should be put on the unresolved instruction, and the judge and counsel should come back to it at a later time. After the presentation of the testimony has been concluded, the judge should go on the record with all counsel—but outside the presence of the jury—and make a clear statement of which instructions the Court is going to give, including specific amendments and in which order. The record should also contain a list of which instructions or parts of instructions counsel have objected to. Finally, each counsel should be given an opportunity to make a record of whatever objections they may have. Even at that time, judges should consider the objections and not hesitate to change their rulings if they are convinced that the instructions could be made more appropriate.

Next, the jurors hear the instructions. Increasingly, judges are able to input the instructions into their computer programs and then provide a clean copy to each counsel and juror so that they can follow along while the instructions are being read. This seems to increase the jurors' understanding of the instructions, and also their interest level. So I recommend the practice.

I further suggest that, after the reading of the instructions is concluded and the jury has retired, the judge ask each counsel on the record, "Are there any objections to the instructions as read?" This will allow the Court to hear and address at the earliest opportunity any instructions that were promised and somehow omitted, or errors that were made in the reading. The Court, therefore, has the opportunity to correct the error. This will also often stop counsel from later successfully bringing up any problems on appeal that should have been addressed when they were more curable.

Jury Deliberations

I have found that in cases that submit more than a few questions to the jurors for their decisions, it is helpful to provide a copy of the verdict form to each juror. But I obtain the agreement of all counsel on the record before I do so. Otherwise, the period of time in which the jury deliberates is the most awkward time of the trial. Getting twelve people to decide when to go to lunch together is difficult enough. So getting jurors to agree upon a verdict with sometimes emotionally complicated and confusing facts and legal situations is no easy task. The thing for a judge to be truly careful about, however, is to make the jurors feel that they are not being hurried and to address with *extreme* care all questions that they ask during their deliberations. Please see the inset "When the Judge Alone Deliberates" on the following page, for information on non-jury trials at this point in the process.

Return of the Verdict

When the jury returns from its deliberations, the judge should ask the foreperson of the jury if the jurors have reached a verdict, and, if so, to hand the verdict forms to the bailiff. The bailiff will, in turn, hand the forms to the judge. Then the judge should look at the verdict forms *carefully and precisely* for any defects or inconsistencies whatsoever. All of the following must be checked: whether all the applicable verdict forms have been signed and dated by the foreperson; whether any signed verdict forms are inconsistent with each other—for example, there should not be a signed form for both "guilty" and "not guilty" for the same charge; and whether all of the required lines on the verdict forms have been filled in and the mathematics on the damages are correct and consistent (if there is a verdict on a civil case for the plaintiff). If all appears in order, tradition seems to dictate that the judge often gives the verdict forms to the clerk to be read out loud for the record.

As best as I can determine, even though most clerks prefer not to read the verdicts, this procedure is traditionally followed. Otherwise it would appear that the Court itself was adopting the proposed verdict. Of course, the verdict form itself should list only the parties that still remain in the case. All "John Does" should be eliminated, and the form must not contain the names of the attorneys who drafted it or any other extraneous materials.

Once the verdict has been read, the judge should ask the entire jury if what was read is their actual verdict: "So say you all?" If the response is in the affirmative, the judge should ask if any counsel wish the jury to be polled. If that is

---

WHEN THE JUDGE ALONE DELIBERATES

In non-jury trials it is obviously the responsibility of the judge to decide upon the verdict. So how does a judge go about the process of making the decision? The answer, in my view, is that judges should be in the *process* of making up their minds as they go along, but they must always be receptive to additional evidence that might refine their decisions or even change them. So not only should judges instruct juries to be receptive to evidence regardless of the time in the trial in which it is received, but they must also heed that important advice themselves.

Most judges, like most jurors, begin formulating their decisions from the very beginning of the trial—probably during opening statements, and certainly by the completion of the testimony of the first witness. In doing so, they should be on the lookout for "the little things" that demonstrate the state of mind of the important participants who can help clarify facts of the case. In addition, referring to sample jury instructions can help a judge to focus upon whether every element of the charge or cause of action has been proved to the necessary degree.

Although continuing to be receptive to new evidence, toward the end of the trial judges should start to sketch out the nature of their thoughts—including issues of credibility and amounts of damages, if appropriate. Thus, they can relate those tentative thoughts to counsel before they make their closing arguments. I have used this procedure for years, and I have found that this results both in a verdict that is more "battle tested," and also in more satisfaction for the attorneys, since this way they can confront head on what are perceived to be the weaker areas of their cases before the final decisions are made. Under all circumstances, judges should take the time they need in order to provide a thoughtful, practical, and workable judgment that can be easily understood and effectively enforced. "You lose because I say so" is not an appropriate explanation, and the parties are entitled to understand all of the important bases for the verdict.

---

requested, the verdict is read count by count, or issue by issue, and each juror should be asked individually on the record if he or she voted with what is perceived to be the stated verdict. The verdicts in criminal cases must be unanimous, and in civil cases in most jurisdictions they must be decided upon by at least 75 percent of the jurors. Increasingly, judges are requesting the foreperson of the jury to write the vote count for each question on the verdict form, instead of simply checking "yes" or "no" to the questions asked. To some degree, this practice in and of itself automatically polls the jury.

Closing of the Trial

If the verdict forms are all in order, the judge should thank the jurors, compliment counsel when appropriate, and give some closing instructions to the jurors. Those instructions can include that the jurors may now talk to anyone they choose about the case, including counsel and the parties. But if they prefer not to do so, the participants will certainly respect their wishes. In high publicity cases, increasingly jurors are told that, based upon statute, they are prohibited from selling any articles or interviews about the trial for a minimum of six months.

Frequently judges will, at this time, also state to the jurors that our system of justice is probably the most expensive, laborious, and time-consuming system ever devised—but it is also the best. They often also further say that they hope the jurors have felt a sense of contribution and gratification at having been involved in the judicial process. Then jurors should once again be thanked for their service, and, in most jurisdictions, excused from further service for a set period of time.

Some judges invite the jurors back into the judge's chambers. This is not a commonly recommended practice, yet I have found that it is appreciated by the jurors and I do it regularly. But it must be made clear that the purpose of this gathering is for the jurors to tell the judge how those of us in the profession can make the jury system work better and afford a more efficient usage of time. Judges are normally prohibited from a discussion with the jurors about the case itself, as well as from telling the jurors whether they agree or disagree with the jury's verdict. The answer to those questions is always, "That is what you decided, so that was the right result." Thereafter, many judges cause a letter on their court stationary to be sent to each juror, again expressing appreciation for carrying out their civic responsibilities. I have found those letters to be well received by the jurors.

Incidentally, with greater frequency in truly horrendous cases, the courts are providing individual psychological counseling for the jurors who request it. *This occurs only after all of the jury's work has been completed.* These courts understand that a very small number of cases can be so graphic that those jurors being exposed to them could benefit from counseling. I believe this is an appropriate thing to do, and I recommend this to your courts as well.

Signing of the Judgment

The trial is not completed in a civil case in most jurisdictions until the trial judge has signed the judgment. Trial judges may prepare the judgment if they so choose. But my recommendation is that the judge instruct counsel for one of the prevailing parties to prepare one document of judgment that addresses the final results for all parties in the case. It should include any judgments by default and should be lodged with the court within a week after the verdict is returned, with actual service of the proposed judgment to the other side at the same time.

Then, even if it is not statutorily required, trial judges should hold the proposed judgments at least for several court days after their receipt in order to give the other parties an opportunity to provide any objections that they may have to it. Special care then must be taken by trial judges to be sure that the judgments they sign are accurate in every respect, and that all parties and counts or causes of action that remain in the case are accounted for. Judges have been very careful throughout their trials up until this point, so they should try to finish it off correctly!

Powers of Contempt of Court

Just like some people feel that something is unconstitutional if a judge does not like it, others feel that judges may use their "powers of contempt" if a judge is simply displeased about something that happens in court. In truth, "contempt of court" is normally seen as a systemic failure, and judges are trained to use those powers only as a last resort.

Instead of holding someone in contempt, alternatives should almost always be explored. The most utilized alternative is to declare a recess to allow both the judge and the other participants to calm down. Another alternative is to ignore the violation if it is reasonably feasible to do so. That is to say that, as Seneca suggests, "It is often better not to see an insult than to avenge it."[4] Other reasonable options are to give the offending person an opportunity to explain her actions, or for the judge to accept an apology. Yet another is to set the matter for an "order to show cause" hearing regarding sanctions instead of pursuing contempt procedures, and then let the subjects know that if they have made a "voluntary" contribution to the county home for abused children or a similar public institution, you will take the order to show cause hearing off calendar.

But judges also have an affirmative obligation to preserve the integrity of the judiciary and the judicial process. So on rare occasions the invoking of the powers of contempt of court is unavoidable because it is the only appropriate course to take. If that is the case, judges should not be timid in doing so.

If a possible contempt of court situation presents itself, the first thing judges must do is to decide if it is a direct contempt or an indirect contempt. Direct contempt occurs when an act that impugns the integrity of the court is committed in the immediate view and presence of the Court. If someone, in any way, has to tell the judge about the contemptuous act, it is not direct contempt of court. The only exception to that rule in most jurisdictions is if a person makes contemptuous statements in documents that are filed with the court.

Examples of contemptuous acts are disorderly or insolent behavior toward a judge while court is being held, or acts that tend to interrupt the due course of a trial or other judicial proceeding; breach of the peace, boisterous conduct, or violent disturbances that also tend to interrupt the due course of a trial or other judicial proceeding; willful neglect or violation of a duty of certain people, including an attorney; abuse of the process or proceedings of the court; disobedience of a lawful judgment, order, or process of a court; any unlawful interference with the process or proceedings of a court; disobedience of a duly served court subpoena; or a witness's refusal to be sworn or answer questions. In summary, judges are vested with the duty and responsibility of running their courtrooms appropriately, efficiently, and under the law. That law provides powers to those judges to sanction immediately anyone who unreasonably impedes that process.

If the contempt is direct, judges must cite it immediately *on the record*, but they should *always* excuse the jury before addressing these matters. Judges must specifically describe the act on the record and state that it was carried out in the immediate view and presence of the Court. Then they must give the person cited an opportunity to explain or apologize, and the judge should state on the record that the explanation or apology has been weighed and considered. The burden of proof for contempt is "beyond a reasonable doubt."

In cases in which contempt powers are used, I recommend that judges contemplate a stay of execution of the sentence—which is mandated in some jurisdictions if the person cited is an attorney—thus giving both the person cited and also the judge the opportunity to exercise "sober second thoughts." And if the citation still stands, judges usually must document the matter with a signed order that contains specific explanations of what occurred, what actions were taken, and what alternatives were considered.

Every contemptuous act that is not performed within the immediate view and presence of the judge is an indirect contempt. But those acts can only be relayed to the judge by another judicial officer—which includes a referee, commissioner, or court reporter—from a deposition. In indirect contempt proceedings, the person cited is entitled to reasonable notice and a hearing. Otherwise, the procedures are the same as outlined above. Also, in any situation in which the original judges decided that they were too "personally embroiled" in the matter to be fair and impartial, the matters would normally be assigned as an indirect contempt proceeding before a different judge.

The punishments for contempt of court vary among the jurisdictions, but they most often include short periods of incarceration and/or fines. In California, the maximum sentence is five days in jail and/or a $1,000 fine. But sometimes judges get creative, and, depending upon the circumstances, unusual orders of contempt have been upheld on appeal. For example, after a trial an attorney was found by the court to have been involved in the fabrication of false sworn testimony. In addition to being ordered to pay all fees and costs for all defendants and the defendants' employers, as well as being ordered to pay sizeable sanctions to the court, the attorney was also ordered to post prominently the court's findings of facts and conclusions of law on his law firm website for a minimum of one year. He was further required to use the same font and size as he had used to publicize the original complaint. Obviously, only an egregious case would warrant such action, and judges should be sure to be prudent when ordering such sanctions.

As you can see, using a judge's powers of contempt is an extreme act. And it also can be cumbersome and a nuisance. But when left with no other viable alternatives, judges should not shy away from using this authority if the integrity of the judiciary and the judicial process has been demeaned or placed under attack.

Trial Tips and Treasures

A while ago I had a dream that two of my friends and I had climbed up a rope to the top of a four-story building that was covered by vines. We were then trying to decide how to get down. The problem was that our rope was quite frayed by that time, and the vines were not strong enough to handle our weight. Nevertheless, one of my friends slowly started down using the frayed rope that eventually broke and dropped him into about 5 feet of water. He was not hurt, but we knew that he was just lucky. Then it was my turn, and I tried to find a few ways to get down, none of which looked very promising. I was in such a quandary about my predicament that I began to wake up. As I came to full consciousness, the answer came to me: "Oh, come on, Jim, just take the stairs."

I see my dream as a metaphor for the process of deciding trials. To be honest, as some cases have begun I have been at a loss to know how I—or anybody else—would ever be able to decide them. But then I consciously have told myself, "Come on, Jim, just be patient. Listen to and question the evidence, and eventually things will begin to become clear." And every time I maintained patience and made sure to be alert and attentive, and just like waking from my dream I have been able to "find the stairs" and get back down to the ground.

In those situations, two thoughts have always brought me consolation. The first is that *some* human being must make a decision on the case, no matter how difficult that decision might be, and no one is really in a better position to make it than a judge like me. So I tell myself to go ahead and do the best I can, and probably my best will be good enough. And if by chance it is not, there will be some justices on the court of appeal with much more time to think, ponder, and research the matter—as well as receive the help of several highly trained staff attorneys—who can correct my mistakes. The second thought is that if a judge is patient, listens, asks questions, and follows the evidence, almost unfailingly the issues and the answers will become apparent as the case unfolds.

But make no mistake, being in the judge's seat can be a major source of pressure. In fact, it calls to my attention a story that my father used to tell (I am sure with poetic license) about himself. Just before he took the bench in court for the very first time, his bailiff, who was completely new as well, came up to him and asked what kind of an opening my father would like to have as he entered the courtroom and took the bench. My father responded that the standard opening would be appropriate: "All rise! In the presence of the flag of this country, and recognizing the principles for which it stands, the United States District Court is now in session, the Honorable William P. Gray, Judge, presiding. God save this Honorable Court!" Over the next few minutes, my father saw his new bailiff rehearsing his lines in preparation for the big moment. But when the time came and my father entered the courtroom, his bailiff blanched and stammered out, "Here he comes. Here he comes! God save the United States!" Although this is a humorous example of what judges sometimes think about themselves but hope no one else says, the truth is that all judges sometimes have the feeling that they will not be the optimal judge for the situation presented.

So here are some trial tips and treasures that I have found over the years to be of assistance. Of course, they are only recommendations, and some things work for some circumstances and not for others. I also acknowledge that some of my advice is certainly "old school," but I think it is still quite applicable.

Start on Time

If, at 10:15 AM, you declare that court will be in recess until 10:30 AM, and if all parties or jurors are not back by that latter time, you should simply have the bailiff bring in those who are present and wait in open court for the rest to return. When the latecomers arrive, they will often mumble something about being sorry for their tardiness. But the situation probably never will arise again, for they just received a reasonable dose of silent reproach. Moreover, everyone will appreciate the punctuality in the future.

Be in Charge, but Maintain Judicial Dignity

It is widely known in the legal profession that there is always one person in charge during every trial—and it is not necessarily the judge. That is why you must make sure that it *is* you who is in charge in your courtroom. A stronger, dramatic personality will step into the place of authority if the judge does not fill that position. It is my experience that once you as the judge set the tone and the participants realize that the rules are going to be followed, all parties will settle down and have a more pleasant experience trying their case within the rules. But if they feel they can gain an advantage by being able to take charge themselves, the situation will continually be stressful.

In some ways judges are a lot like teachers and parents; if they establish control at the beginning, those in their charge will not press them so much in the future because it is understood that rules and boundaries will be enforced. And once within their proper boundaries, counsel can be creative and prosper. If judges set reasonable rules, ensure that people are aware of them, and then enforce them with an even and gentle hand—backed up with a more forceful one, if necessary—issues will tend greatly to be decided upon the merits instead of the personalities of the players.

In addition to exhibiting an authoritative and wise persona, you should make it clear that your courtroom remains justly neutral. For example, if attorneys are wearing jewelry or other symbols that would obviously tend to pander to the jurors—whether they be religious symbols or crests for the United Way, the Red Cross or a Masonic lodge—instruct them to conceal or remove such jewelry. This will reaffirm to all participants that neutrality always prevails in the courtroom.

Part of remaining in charge is knowing how to deal with various approaches by counsel. It is well known in the legal profession that most attorneys are either "lovers" or "fighters." The corporate attorneys are usually considered to be the lovers, because they are always trying to reach an accommodation so that the deal can be completed. The litigators are the fighters, because they are in an antagonistic arena and must appear to be tough. Judges can be both lovers *and* fighters. But they first must show that, if necessary, they can be tough and fight with the best of them. Once this is established, love can be in the air, so to speak.

I have already established the importance of a judge's remaining in charge of the courtroom. Now I would like to add that you, as the judge, should maintain judicial dignity throughout the entire process. At all times, show the counsel, the parties, and the general public that you are ethical, professional, practical, and prepared. Moreover, make it clear that you expect the same from them. By doing so, your courtroom will be a much happier, productive, and professional place to do the business of justice.

What simple but powerful techniques can you use to maintain dignity in the courtroom? On those occasions when things begin to get out of hand because people are getting angry or are interrupting each other, you can simply but firmly say "Stop!" and make sure that everybody does so. Then regroup by calmly but firmly reminding the witnesses and counsel not to interrupt each other, not to argue with each other, or whatever would be appropriate for the moment. Hollywood would have judges maintain order by pounding a gavel. But neither I nor any judge I know even has a gavel on the bench. In fact, the only time I have ever used one was at a peer court in a high school!

Another good technique is not to allow two attorneys for the same party to question, cross-examine, or make objections during the testimony of the same witness. If you let both of them participate, you can easily lose control of the proceeding. Instead, for those cases in which more than one counsel represents the same party, let everyone know that the first counsel who asks a question of a witness or interposes an objection is the *only* counsel who will speak during the entire testimony of that witness.

While on the subject of counsel's questioning witnesses, I have another suggestion to make. You should clearly assert that counsel are required to state all of their objections to a particular question at the same time. Allowing attorneys to practice the "Well, if that objection didn't work, how about this one?" approach is not a productive way for judges to control trials.

Also be careful to curtail "speaking objections" during the testimony of a witness. These explanations of one's position are often inappropriate and even unprofessional attempts to argue a case to the jury, or even to coach a witness. They can take many forms, such as when counsel says that she has "absolutely no objection" to a particular exhibit's being received into evidence. Another example, given by Judge Irving Younger, involves a judge's asking counsel if he wished to cross-examine a witness who had just decimated his case. The counsel responded, "Oh no, Your Honor. He didn't hurt us none." Be diligent in curtailing inappropriate and unprofessional comments like these because if you are not, things can quickly get out of control.

I believe that during a jury trial the judge should allow counsel to approach the witness only with the permission of the Court. Then the judge should be sure counsel retreat once her purpose has been accomplished. Allowing the counsel to linger and manipulate the situation passes control into that counselor's hands. As the judge, you should always be the one who directs counsel's proximity to the witness.

Finally, I suggest that you not allow any attorney to offer to stipulate to anything within the hearing of the jury. This type of "good guy" gamesmanship is inappropriate and should not be allowed. In fact, sometimes it can actually be grounds for a mistrial.

Let Attorneys Try Their Cases Largely Without Judicial Interference

Effective judges keep their interruptions of counsel in front of the jury to a minimum unless there is truly a reason to do otherwise. Bear in mind that counsel probably know a great deal more about the case than the judge does. They most likely also have a plan about how to present it, and they probably have discussed that plan with their clients. So counsel should reasonably be given the ability to carry out their plan. Nevertheless, if there is a reason to interrupt, and it is not appropriate to excuse the jury before doing so, do not hesitate. Then the business should be handled quickly and firmly. But then let it go!

If and when you preside over a trial, remind yourself that it is not your job to do the attorneys' work for them. If attorneys want to hurt themselves in their cross-examinations by clarifying the opposing party's story to their own detriment, let them. What attorneys do with the facts is their business. But what is done with the law is the business of the judge, because once the legal rulings are made, they belong to the judge, not counsel. So you will want to do whatever research is necessary so that you can be correct on the law. Otherwise your rulings stand a good chance of being reversed on appeal regardless of whether it was agreed upon by all counsel or not.

Impress Upon Your Staff Always to Be Professional and Courteous, but Not Overly Friendly

Imagine being a party who watches the bailiff or court clerk shake hands with, or even hug, the attorney on the opposing side. Understand that many litigants will attempt to impress their clients or the jury with how well received they are by the court staff. And that can breed resentment and even bitterness, if not more serious problems. Therefore, all court staff should be instructed to be pleasant but certainly not affectionate or familiar with anyone participating in the case.

Remain Open to Settlement

Most cases settle, and the trial that you are working on at a given moment can settle as well. For most situations, settlement is still in the best interest of everyone—except, sometimes, the attorneys. So even if the trial is about to start, or even if it has already started, there still are chances to settle the case. Of course, judges should never imply in any way that if one or more of the parties is determined to go to trial, it will be held against them in any fashion.

Help Your Memory Regarding Names

Jurors, witnesses, parties, counsel, and people in general appreciate having their names pronounced correctly. So when you first have contact with those who will be participating in the trial, ask them how to pronounce their names and then write down their names phonetically. During the "heat of the trial," it is common not to be able immediately to retrieve the name of an attorney or party in the case. So it is a great idea for you as the judge to paste a piece of paper on your bench and put, in large letters, the phonetically-spelled names of the parties and the attorneys on it. I promise this will reduce the stress of the moment and will make your courtroom a more professional and comfortable place. By having a reminder of the pronunciation of each name, you will continue to give participants respect, and they will appreciate it.

As an aside, it continually amazes me when, after I have helped them by making it a special point to ask for the correct pronunciation of a juror's name, counsel pronounce it incorrectly during their voir dire questioning of the same juror. Little things count, and not enough people heed the importance of details like that.

Be Sure All Participants Are Addressed Appropriately and Express Themselves Appropriately

All adult participants—with the exception of you, the judge—should be addressed and referred to only by their last names. This maintains a professional and neutral environment. You should address yourself as "the Court," and gently encourage counsel to do so as well. Technically, it is not you as a person who is saying something or issuing an order, it is your office. Moreover, gently encourage counsel to rise when addressing the Court out of a respect for the office, unless they are making an objection of only a few words.

Participants can certainly be inappropriate with words, but they can also be inappropriate with gestures, expressions, and the like. You should not allow counsel, parties, or even onlookers to show any unreasonable facial expressions of agreement, disagreement, incredulity, or the like during your proceedings. Similarly, if you ever see an attorney, party, or onlooker trying to communicate with a witness or juror by winking, nodding, frowning, or appearing puzzled, call this to the attention of all counsel, but outside the presence of the jury. Then take all necessary steps to curtail it.

There are a few more rules of etiquette that are helpful to propose at this point. I recommend that a judge require counsel to address their comments to the Court, and not to each other. In addition, a criminal defendant and the associated counsel should be required to stand and face the jury when the verdict is read, and also thereafter on those occasions in which the Court imposes a sentence.

Avoid Risky (and Risqué) Humor

Humor from a judge can be wonderful, but it can also be damaging. We have already stressed that judges live in a fishbowl. Any humor in front of a jury, or counsel for that matter, that is seen as even slightly derogatory (of anybody or almost anything), off-color, or just a little bit out of place might not only fall flat, but it also can actually launch an ethical inquiry.

For example, even though the following joke was forwarded to me by my wonderful wife and I think it is cute, in my view this type of joke is *not* one that a judge should tell on the bench, or even in public: The owner of a golf course was confused about paying an invoice, so he decided to ask his secretary for some mathematical assistance. "You graduated from the State University, and I need some help. If I were to give you $20,000, minus 14 percent, how much would you take off?" The secretary thought for a moment, and then replied, "Everything but my earrings." While it might cause a chuckle among some listeners, this type of joke, in my opinion, is clearly unprofessional. Although it probably would not actually offend many people, it would disappoint them. Therefore, a judge must be supersensitive when it comes to humor.

Putting those landmines aside, jurors always appreciate good, tasteful, and *appropriate* attempts at humor. For example, I pass along to you a joke I will frequently tell during voir dire, when I ask jurors about their household members, including pets: "Ms. Jones, do you know the difference between a dog and a cat? A dog looks up at its owner and says, 'You love me, you feed me, you pet me; you must be God.' Given the same circumstances, a cat looks up at its owner and says, 'You love me, you feed me, you pet me; I must be God.'" This story has been "test marketed," and it works for me.

Obtain Early Copies of Helpful Lists and Forms

You should insist that each counsel provide a copy of a witness list and an exhibit list for you, your clerk, your court reporter, and opposing counsel. The trial will go much more smoothly if this occurs. I use the lists for various purposes: to ask jurors during voir dire if they are familiar with any of the potential witnesses; to keep handy notes about the order and date of the testimony of each witness; and to record the marking and receipt of each exhibit into evidence, as well as the name of the witness who laid the foundation for it.

In addition, the jury instructions are matters that many counsel naively leave for the last minute, but they are enormously important. As suggested previously, if you insist that they be provided at the beginning of the trial, you and all counsel can begin to consider them more completely. I also request that counsel provide the proposed verdict forms ahead of time for the same reasons. Everyone knows that all of these things are subject to modification as the trial progresses, but it is good to have a foundation from which to work. And, always, care should be taken to ensure that the verdicts are in proper form, the questions are numbered correctly, the instructions about how the jury is to proceed are correct, and that they do not have the name on them of the counsel who prepared them.

Support the "Law of the Case"

Children often play one parent against the other. The appropriate approach of each parent should be to support the other. As a good friend of mine used to say, regarding his role as a father, "I am a couple." This teamwork approach is appropriate between judges as well with regard to prior rulings by another judge on the same case. Within reason, once a ruling is made, it is the law of the case and should be honored.

Use Smaller Juries, When Possible

In most jurisdictions, the laws require that at least 75 percent of the jurors be in favor of a judgment in a civil case. But there is no reason that the parties cannot stipulate to a total of eight jurors on the jury instead of the more traditional twelve. Six of eight is the same percentage as nine of twelve. The parties will get the same decision with the smaller number as the larger, and it will take less time and will cost everyone less money to use a smaller jury. So a judge should encourage the parties to stipulate to the smaller jury if that is an option.

Use a Formal Opening Each Morning

When a jury is present for the trial, I recommend you have your bailiff give a formal opening each day. My bailiff gives the following: "Everyone please rise. In the presence of the flag of our country, emblem of the Constitution, and remembering the principles for which it stands, Department 9 of the Orange County Superior Court is now in session, the Honorable James P. Gray, Judge, presiding." Why do I do this? I think it helps me and everyone else to focus upon the tasks at hand. A moment ago we may have been joking or informally addressing various matters, but now we are officially at work on professional and important tasks.

In addition, I have developed the habit of nodding at the flag when my bailiff talks about recognizing the principles for which it stands. I think that all of us occasionally need a reminder of those principles. A formal opening and a visible acknowledgement of the flag trigger those reminders for me and probably for others.

Be Creative with "The Admonition"

In most jurisdictions, at every recess the judge is required to remind jurors not to discuss the matter with anyone else in the world, to keep an open mind all the way until they have heard the tentative thoughts of their fellow jurors during their deliberations, and to come back to court at the stated time. These instructions are "the admonition." But this admonition can get boring. When my father was serving as a judge, he used to ask individual jurors to assist him with the admonition. This helped to turn the process into a fun ritual.

I have followed my father's lead in my courtroom and have had some fun with it. For example, during one somewhat lengthy trial, I asked one of the jurors to assist in giving the admonition. When the time came to state it, all of the jurors chuckled, bent down, and then held up hand-printed cards that progressively set forth the admonition. Apparently, all of the jurors had gotten together to give me a little surprise, and we all enjoyed it. On another occasion, one of the jurors created a humorous poem that (amazingly enough) incorporated the admonition into its lyrics. Anything of a nature that is creative but still professional and constructive can be a healthy thing for morale and still live up to the legal responsibilities of the judge.

Keep the Trial Moving

I have stated it before, but this advice is worth reemphasizing: The trial must be kept moving at a reasonable pace. Some attorneys seem to feel that a trial is a dumping ground for every fact and document that was uncovered during discovery. If you as the judge are experiencing that situation, ask for an *offer of proof* outside the presence of the jury. Then show counsel, in applicable circumstances, how this line of questioning is either unnecessary or that it has already been covered. This problem can also be addressed by reminding counsel that it is quite unlikely that a jury will even think about, much less discuss or consider, any document that is not mentioned by them in their closing arguments.

Another method of keeping the trial moving is to tell counsel during the pretrial conference that you want to let them try their own case. But add that if you feel too much time is being taken during the trial, you will ask the question,

"About how much more time do you anticipate your questions will take for this witness, Ms. Smith?" That signifies that if they do not pick up the pace voluntarily, you will do it for them.

Be Courteous About Time

Yes, you are eager to get the trial finished so you can start the next one, or read your Law and Motion matters, or tend to any other number of waiting tasks. But the jury, the attorneys and parties, and the court staff—especially the court reporter—need a break! A conscientious and compassionate judge does not forget to call a fifteen-minute recess every morning, and another fifteen-minute recess every afternoon. Everyone will appreciate it.

And while we are on the subject of time management, there is another point to be made. You will occasionally find that a trial is in danger of going beyond the estimated length. In such a case, ask your staff, counsel, and the jurors if they would mind starting the trial a little earlier the next morning, taking a shorter lunch break, or even staying a little later in order to finish the trial on time. This is a considerate thing to do, and under some circumstances it could actually prevent the declaration of a mistrial because the jurors were not left with enough time for their deliberations. The request to start, end, or resume earlier can also be applied when it would help the scheduling for a professional expert or out-of-state witness.

Be Considerate of Jurors

There are certain approaches a judge can take in order to demonstrate additional care and respect for the jury members. Within reason, conscientious judges try to recess their jury trials before daylight ends so that jurors can get back to their cars before it is dark. This highlights a safety issue that should be considered during the winter season.

Also, considerate judges try to recess early on special days such as Halloween and the day before Thanksgiving. Thus the jurors, parties, counsel, and staff can be back with their families at a reasonable time on these important occasions. Going the extra mile when it comes to kindness will rightfully earn you the reputation of a caring and conscientious judge.

Consider Allowing Jurors to Ask Questions of Witnesses

On occasion, juries have returned verdicts based upon erroneous information that could have been easily corrected if only they had been able to ask questions of witnesses. So I recommend that jurors be allowed to ask questions during a trial. The best way for this to be done is for jurors to get the judge's or the bailiff's attention toward the end of the questioning of a witness *and then write out their question*. The question can be shown to all counsel, who can adopt it into their own questionings as they feel appropriate. Many judges make provisions for a procedure of this kind and then attempt to discourage its utilization because it can be overdone. But the jurors should know that if they really have a question they think should be asked, there is a procedure in place for that to be done.

Be Decisive Concerning Evidentiary Objections

When there is an objection to a question during the trial, you must just rule on it. Simply do the best that you can. What is the alternative—to take the matter under submission and get back to counsel next Thursday? If you need more time to think about the ruling, you can ask that the question be rephrased. I do not recommend that approach, but it will buy you some time if you are desperate.

Another way of buying some time is to state, "The objection is overruled," instead of simply saying, "Overruled" or "Sustained." Just the few extra words in the suggested phrase can give you a little more time to decide upon your ruling. And you should not worry that you are in danger of eliminating a very important issue by sustaining an objection. If the issue is *that* important, the attorneys will come back to it by asking a slightly different question. The important part is that you respond to the objection in a timely manner.

Keep It Simple in Regard to Hearsay Objections

When it comes down to it, hearsay objections are not that difficult. The basis for all hearsay objections, and most of the hearsay exceptions, is reliability. If the hearsay statement has a strong chance of being reliable, it probably will be admissible. If not, it probably should be excluded. If you keep this point in mind, your rulings will be easier to make.

Discourage Sidebar Conferences

Sometimes sidebar conferences with counsel—which occur outside the hearing of the jury—are necessary. But they are often overused. I advise you to tell your jurors that you will attempt to keep sidebars to a minimum, but that when they occur, the jurors should not attempt to listen. Instead, the jurors are welcome to stand up, move around, and talk to their neighbors about anything that does not concern the trial. Then warn counsel not to take advantage of the sidebar process, because if they start to do so, you will be forced to try to guess if the conference is really necessary or not. And nobody wants guesswork at a trial that is requiring so much time and energy.

Make a Good Record

Some of the things that trial judges can do to ensure that the system works as well as it can is to cause the best possible record to be made of the proceedings. That means that you should always allow counsel to make a record of their positions, whether those positions are on objections, motions, jury instructions, or anything else. In the first place, that is the way justice is done—it is only fair for counsel to be able to document their positions on important issues. And in the second place, as a judge I would much prefer to be reversed for something that I actually did than something that I did not do. Would you not feel the same way? So when you issue a ruling, try to imagine an appellate judge reading your words on a transcript.

Another example of how to make a good record has to do with jury voir dire. If you ask whether any prospective juror knows any of the witnesses and no one raises her hand, there is no record of that fact unless you literally say something like, "I see no response." A good and effective judge is aware of verbally documenting what is happening in the courtroom. Furthermore, on those occasions during which someone with the same last name as you is a party to a case or is even mentioned during testimony, it is a good idea to state that—to the best of your knowledge—you are not related to and do not even know the person. This will not only put the minds of the parties at rest, but it will also make a clear record if there is ever an appeal of the case.

Making a clear record also performs a kindness to those good folks on the courts of appeal. Imagine reading a transcript and trying to understand what happened at a trial during which a witness looked at a diagram and testified that she first looked in "here," and then followed the burglar around from "here" into "there." Judges who know the frustrations of reading such records probably never allow that type of testimony in their courtroom. Instead they will have the witness testify in words exactly where she went, or whatever details apply.

The most noteworthy occasion in my experience in which a judge made a clear record occurred when I was a federal prosecutor in Los Angeles. I was appearing before Judge Irving Hill, who was taking the guilty plea of a defendant. The man was already serving a life sentence before he escaped from prison and committed numbers of bank robberies that I was then prosecuting him for. Somehow Judge Hill said something that rubbed the defendant the wrong way when he was attempting to enter a plea of guilty to some of the charges. As a result, the defendant threw the pen he had been holding onto the counsel table, whereupon it broke into numbers of pieces. He then took a step toward Judge Hill and called him a "Nazi"—but not without first modifying that term with a hardened piece of profanity. Judge Hill did not miss a beat. He declared, for the record, that the defendant "took a step, no two steps, toward the Court, *with fire in his eyes,* and said what the record will reflect he said."

At that point, Judge Hill took a recess in the proceedings, during which the defense attorney actually allowed me to talk to his client in his presence. I convinced the client that all we wanted was to document these additional offenses because there really was nothing more that could be done to him. When court reconvened, although Judge Hill was literally surrounded by marshals, the plea went forward without a hitch. But this will always stand out in my mind as an amazing example of a judge's making a clear record of the proceedings.

Take Good Notes

A judge's notes almost unfailingly can prove useful as the trial goes along. The most important contribution note-taking will make is that it will keep you aware of what is happening, so your mind has less of a tendency to wander. But notes can also be helpful with regard to motions to strike testimony, asked and answered objections, records of exhibits, cumulative testimony, and a multitude of other things that arise during a trial.

In order to be effective at note-taking, try to develop your own shorthand for names of the participants and words that are commonly used in trial. Over the years, I have developed my own shorthand notes, and they are set forth in Appendix 1 (see page 301). Feel free to adopt any of my contractions or symbols you find to be useful, but I do strongly recommend that you develop your own.

Finally, making notes regarding the time when a counsel's jury voir dire, opening statements, direct and cross-examinations, and closing arguments actually begin and end will help to keep the trial moving. The notes will keep you aware of how long different proceedings have been lasting. Such notes also remind you to hold counsel to agreed-upon time constraints. Moreover, keeping notes on the witness list concerning the date the witnesses began their testimonies and in what order they testified, plus dog-earing the trial notes in a long case when each witness begins her testimony, will allow you to find your notes on each witness more quickly. So notes can definitely be a part of your artistry.

In Extreme Cases, Use a "Chess Clock"

If all else fails and counsel are simply droning on to the extent that if you do not do something the trial will go on forever, strongly consider giving each side a certain total amount of time to present its case. That includes direct and cross-examinations and closing arguments. And keep track of that time! This is an extreme measure, but if the circumstances warrant it and you have given proper notice to all of the parties, I recommend you use this practice as a last resort.

Ask, If You Do Not Know

There is no need to reinvent the wheel. If you do not know the answer to a question, ask the attorneys on the case to get the answer for you. Judges are in a remarkable position: Truly intelligent attorneys are paid good money to answer their questions. So use them! Or if it is not appropriate to ask the attorneys, ask a fellow judge. It is perfectly ethical for a judge to "compare notes" with a fellow judge and get legal advice, as long as the trial judge is the only one who eventually makes the final decision. So do not be proud; if you need help, ask for it.

But in that regard, I give you a note of caution: In most jurisdictions it is inappropriate and actually unethical for a judge even to discuss any legal matter that has not yet resulted in a final judgment. And that includes discussing the matter with her spouse, child, friend, or students in a classroom. So be careful!

Keep Clear Protocols Regarding Exhibits and Evidence

If you allow witnesses to address anything other than the actual marked exhibits, your record is likely to be a mess, and things could really be confusing on a possible appeal. Sometimes copies of exhibits are different from originals, and if it is unclear on the record what the witness was actually looking at, the case actually could be reversed.

Similarly, and for the same reason, do not allow a *part* of an exhibit to be received into evidence. If that is what counsel is requesting, physically require counsel to remove the remainder of the exhibit after obtaining a stipulation on the record from all other counsel. Or you can also ask counsel to mark what they want as a new exhibit, and then move that into evidence.

Finally, it is really difficult to resurrect the testimony about whether the proper foundation was laid for an exhibit three trial days ago. Try to avoid this problem by encouraging counsel to move their exhibits into evidence while the evidence is fresh in everybody's mind. That also avoids the necessity of bringing back a witness from out of state to ask a foundational question that could have been asked before. This way, everyone comes out ahead.

Discuss Eyewitness Identification Issues

I do not consider myself to be particularly good at eyewitness identification. So sometimes when witnesses are making an eyewitness identification, I explain my feelings about myself to the witnesses and ask them if they consider themselves to be particularly good at making these identifications or not. I think this is a neutral question that can help the witnesses and also help the jury.

Listen for Clues Concerning Witness Credibility

You cannot actually *know* if witnesses are telling the truth or not. In fact, I will go so far as to say that some thoroughly honest people perspire or twitch while testifying, or have beady eyes. On the other hand, there are others who are liars even though they look completely comfortable and self-assured. There are some indications that may help you in your decision-making on these issues of credibility. Ask yourself, "Does what the witness is saying fundamentally make sense?" I know this sounds logical, but force yourself to take a step back and ask yourself the question anyway.

Other clues can be found in whether or not the witnesses are consistent in their testimony, and whether they appear to be rehearsed. Have the witnesses exaggerated anything they have testified about? Or have they inappropriately become angry? Anger often can hide a lack of substance.

Consider Locking Your Courtroom Doors During Jury Instructions

We have already discussed how difficult it can be to make the jury instructions "come alive." That process is directly hindered when the jury or you as the judge are distracted by people's coming into and going out of the courtroom. One way to counteract this distraction is to lock the courtroom doors during the giving of jury instructions. Have your bailiff inform the people in the audience that if they choose to stay, they are obligated to stay until all of the instructions have been completed.

Include the Phrase "Please All Rise When the Jury Retires"

Once the jury instructions have been concluded and the jurors are told that they may go out with the bailiff to begin their deliberations, consider ordering everyone in the courtroom to rise while the jury retires. This emphasizes the importance of the jury's task and makes the members of the jury feel appreciated. It also gives additional respect to the jury as an institution.

Be Extremely Careful with Jury Issues

We live in a professionally technical world, and problems with juries can often end up in a mistrial. One problem can be avoided if you instruct your bailiff not to have any interplay with the jury during their deliberations about *anything* other than scheduling and providing water or coffee (or similar matters of that kind). Then tell the jurors that this rule is in effect. If it is determined after the trial that your jury asked your bailiff any kind of a substantive question and the bailiff answered it in *any* fashion, that determination can lead straight to a mistrial, particularly if it is discovered after the verdict has been rendered and the jury has been excused. The losing side will be sure to insist that this was the very question that caused a wrong result in the verdict.

Other problems arise when the wrong trial exhibits are submitted to the jury—either some that were not admitted into evidence at all, or some that were provided to the jury that had been improperly redacted or modified. The best prevention for this problem is to require all counsel to review all exhibits before they are made available to the jury during their deliberations, and to put on the record that they have done so.

It takes forewarning and anticipation to avoid problems because they can rear their ugly heads under the most unanticipated circumstances. For example, when I was a federal prosecutor on a bank robbery case, we selected a jury one day and were scheduled to begin testimony for the trial the next day. When the appointed hour came the next morning, defendant Hillman (not his real name) was not present. Hillman's attorney excused himself, called his client, and then reported to the Court that the defendant had apparently told his family he was coming to court and had left home in plenty of time. We waited all morning. Finally the judge said that we could be excused for lunch, and that if the defendant did not appear when we returned, the judge would issue a bench warrant for his arrest and declare a mistrial. At that point, the jury, my witnesses, and counsel (including me) were excused. Almost immediately my bank teller witnesses came running back into the courtroom saying, "There he is! There he is!"

It seems that when Hillman had been walking into the courtroom that morning, the bailiff had asked him if he was on the Hillman jury. Since the defendant's name was Hillman, he had simply said yes, whereupon he had been directed into the court's jury waiting room. And that was where he had spent the entire morning. I spoke with some of the jurors later and asked them what had happened all morning in the jury room. They said they had thought it was a bit unusual, and that there had been an awkward silence the entire time. Naturally, a mistrial was declared, since the defendant had had improper contact with the jurors. But since the defense had been based upon issues of identity and my tellers had immediately identified him, the defendant ended up pleading guilty. I give this example only for the reason that no one can anticipate what can go wrong with jury issues, so the best we can do is to stay on our toes.

Jury questions posed while the jury is deliberating are also an area that is fraught with peril. Second only to jury instructions, jury questions are *the* area of the trial that will most likely result in a reversal of the verdict. Nevertheless, a jury is entitled to have answers to its questions. So what can be done? In my view, the judge should first listen to the question, think about the question, and then answer *only* the question that was asked. If you volunteer answers to questions that were not asked, you are inviting boatloads of trouble. Be as straightforward in the answer as you can be, while still answering the question. And never should a jury question be answered without the full involvement of all counsel. If you can, try to get a consensus among all trial counsel about how a question should be answered and put their agreement or their objections on the record.

Secondly, much of the time the jury's questions during deliberation can be answered by one or more of the instructions that have already been given. If that is the case, simply call that instruction to the attention of the jury. Otherwise, my advice in this area is not to be too creative.

Understand That the Laws Are There to Help Judges Decide Cases

Once, several weeks after a non-jury civil case had been submitted to him, I heard a judge make the comment, "I don't know what to do. I am hung." Such a statement does not particularly inspire confidence in the judiciary, but the judge had actually answered his own problem. By law, the plaintiff has the burden of proving that there is evidence on the record that is sufficient to convince the judge that the plaintiff should prevail. If the plaintiff has not met that burden and the fact-finder is "hung," then the plaintiff loses.

Laws like these have evolved over the centuries by the toil of wise and learned people who were dedicated to the concept of justice. They are not to be feared or seen as intimidating. Instead, they are there to help and guide us all.

Listen to a Set of Judge Irving Younger Lectures on Evidence

The late Judge Irving Younger from New York is the best teacher on evidence I have ever encountered, and his recorded lectures will make questions on evidence come alive. I strongly recommend you obtain and listen carefully to his lectures. I myself listened to a series of these tapes decades ago, and his teachings and examples are still with me. I know it will be the same for you.

If You Have Not Already, Take a Judicial Class on Economics

Many of a judge's decisions should be affected at least in part by considerations involving "the invisible hand" of economics, as described long ago by economist Adam Smith. The law generally intends that those who are in a position to avoid or reduce harm are to be liable for that harm when it occurs. As a result, when a judge makes decisions that shield those people, companies, or other entities from that liability, to some degree those decisions will be responsible for failing to prevent similar avoidable harm in the future. Of course, that does not mean that judges should impose those outcomes when the law or facts do not provide for them.[5]

Trust Your Instincts but Avoid Overconfidence

Balance the truism, "If a proposed ruling is not in keeping with your instincts, look at the issue again," with the one that states, "If you are certain about an issue, look at it again." Quite a while ago I took a judicial class on legal fact-finding and decision-making. During the class the instructor showed us a video of some nurses who were told that, on some occasions during the course of their professional lives, they would be called upon affirmatively to lie to some of their patients. For example, if someone was severely injured and would be harmed by learning the truth about the death of a loved one, the nurse sometimes would be forced to lie in order to protect the health of the patient.

In the film we were watching, each nurse was shown two videos. One of the videos presented an extremely tranquil setting with lakes, blue sky, and butterflies. The second documented the bloodiest operation that could be imagined. Each nurse was instructed to describe the tranquil scene regardless of which video she was watching at the time.

The students in the fact-finding and decision-making class, including me, were then shown a separate video of the nurses as they described the tranquil scene they saw. But we could not see which video the nurse was actually watching. All we knew was that the nurses were lying in one of their two descriptions. We were told to try to determine which time each nurse was telling the truth and which time the nurse was lying. Many judges did not do well in determining when the nurses were lying.

Of course, the purpose of the exercise was to show judges that they should not be so confident in their abilities to differentiate honest testimony from dishonest testimony. I have always retained that, as I consider it good advice. And I pass it along to you.

Give Tentative Decisions to Counsel Before They Make Their Final Arguments in Non-Jury Cases and in Law and Motion Matters

As was discussed earlier, I have found that good attorneys appreciate knowing where they stand before they present the judge with their final argument. So in non-jury cases and Law and Motion matters, present to counsel what you consider to be the failings of the potentially losing parties, and then let them give you their best shot to change your mind. On occasion they may be able to change the result by raising evidence or case law you had not considered sufficiently. If nothing else, at least you will be more confident in your ruling after you have heard them argue their case fully under those circumstances. And in addition, counsel will at least be satisfied that they were able to confront their weaker points directly before the "hammer fell."

Remain Attentive at All Times

Try as you might to keep yourself primed and interested in the trials before you, some matters can be downright boring. Nevertheless, it is a judge's responsibility to follow along with those matters and to issue legal and meaningful decisions in them. Among other things, sometimes issues can arise from nowhere with amazing quickness that will require your full concentration, such as warnings to witnesses about their Fifth Amendment rights against self-incrimination; explanations to jurors about how to consider deposition testimony or Interrogatory responses; requests for witnesses to explain the definition of various terms being used in their testimony; instructions for the jury that they can consider certain evidence only for a limited purpose; or sua sponte instructions that judges are required to give to the jury without a request from counsel, and sometimes in spite of an objection to it. So push yourself to be attentive and on top of what is happening in your courtroom at all times. And if for some reason you start to lose your focus, call a short recess.

Make Haste Slowly

One of the most capable and successful generals and administrators in the history of mankind was Caesar Augustus, who was the Emperor of Rome from 27 BCE to 14 CE. He attributed much of his success to following the credo: "Make haste slowly." UCLA Basketball Coach Johnny Wooden employed a similar motto when he instructed his basketball players, "Be quick, but don't hurry."

I believe judges should adopt this type of credo in presiding over their trials. The purpose of a trial, of course, is to get a just and fair judgment under the facts and the law. But it is also a goal to try to move the case along with as little expenditure of time and resources as reasonably possible. Judges who follow this approach will best reconcile these two goals, which can sometimes seem to be in conflict.

Rule as Carefully and Concisely as You Can, and Then Move On

In many cases, people will credit themselves with being brilliant if they win their trial, and they will think the judge was dense, slow, or biased against them for external reasons if they lose. Such is life. So once you have done your best and you have decided the case, simply move on. Second-guessing yourself is counterproductive. That does not mean that judges should not learn from their mistakes, but if you dwell on past decisions, they can eat you alive.

So that concludes our journey through a trial and some tips and insights into how to preside over it effectively. Of course, you will want to develop your own style and approach, but I hope that you can begin by learning from my experiences and observations. Serving as a trial judge can be a fascinating and gratifying experience and, honestly, I would enjoy doing it all over again with you.

POST-TRIAL MATTERS

For attorneys, there is almost never any prompt closure of a lawsuit, unless the parties have reached a settlement. After a trial often comes an appeal, an attempt to find the losing party's assets to pay the judgment, and more. An attorney could even have further work to collect her fees. But that is not true for a trial judge. A few final duties are required of the judge, as described below, and then the job is done. And what happens if, according to one party, the case was unfairly adjudicated? Of course, as mentioned above, the case could be appealed, a process that is discussed in this section. But then an appellate court judge would inherit the issues and start a review of the case. The trial judge would not be involved.

The Trial Judge's Final Duties

Once the verdict has been announced and issued, judges should finalize their notes and sign the judgments. Occasionally they will hear a post-trial motion for a new trial or a motion disputing the fees and costs of the prevailing party. They also occasionally have to oversee a proceeding for the defendant/debtors to give testimony to the plaintiff/creditors about what assets they have. But other than those issues, the job of the trial judge is over when the judgment is signed.

The Appellate Court System

For several reasons, in most cases appeals are not pursued. In the first place, most cases are settled. Second, many of the cases that do not settle are simply not worth the expense, delays, and risks of an adverse appellate judgment. But if an appeal is taken, the subject issues will normally be addressed quite fully and carefully.

The life of an appellate court justice is quite different from that of a trial court judge. Other than listening to oral arguments once or twice per month, appellate judges mostly work in their chambers, at home, or anywhere else there is a computer and a fax line. They read briefs, memoranda, and cases, and they prepare drafts of opinions. It is an intellectual life, mostly without the appellate court judges' seeing or having much personal contact with anyone except their staff and their fellow justices. Justice David G. Sills of the Court of Appeal in Santa Ana, California, explained the position well when he said, "You are practicing pure law here. You don't have clients. You don't have to worry about billable hours. . . . If you wanted to be where the action is, you should be a lawyer."[6]

Where the trial judges, for the most part, act by themselves (even if they have a staff) and often have literally hundreds of decisions to make every day—many of which are made without much advance notice—the appellate justices have more time to ponder, analyze, and deliberate. They also usually have a staff or pool of research attorneys to assist them in reviewing and working up their cases. In addition, the parties involved in each case will have had the opportunity to focus upon and research the individual issues much more carefully and fully, and will have fully briefed these issues before the appellate staff even thinks about considering them.

Otherwise, the appellate judges attempt to make their decisions the same way that trial judges do, except that almost universally they are limited to the evidence as it was already presented in trial. They also understand that some appeals are pursued for many reasons other than justice, as implied by a long-discussed memorandum in a law firm that declared, "Justice Prevailed—Appeal Immediately." Nevertheless, the courts of appeal are a bulwark to guarantee as much as possible that our laws are followed and our rights are protected. And certainly they sometimes unearth true injustices and set them right.

As a practical matter in appealed cases, the trial judge's reputation within the appellate court may affect the outcome in close cases. (This has been confirmed to me privately by two sitting appellate court justices.) That is to say, each trial court judge has, in one way or the other, earned a reputation with the appellate court. If that reputation is solid—that is, if the appellate justices have reviewed that judge's work in a number of other cases and it has always been reasonable, organized, well-documented, and the like—more weight will be given by the appellate courts to that judge's exercise of discretion. And, of course, the reverse is also true.

This actually should not be a surprise. If one thinks about it, this is the way most things work in a practical society. If you have worked with someone who is professional, reliable, and thoughtful, you are much more likely to rely upon that person's work without as much scrutiny as you would a person's work whose reputation is not as strong. So sometimes the recommendations of sophis-

ticated attorneys to their clients as to whether or not to appeal a case are affected by the reputation of the trial judge.

The benefits of an appellate court life are that the judges are more independent and more in charge of their own time. Also, they may dress more casually,
except on oral argument days. They get to be challenged by doctrines and evolving concepts, and they can derive a great deal of gratification in creating well-
thought-out and well-written opinions on tough issues—opinions that will help
to guide others in the future in similar or analogous situations. To add to the benefits, in some states appellate court judges are not up for reelection as often as
trial judges, and many of the elections are often for retention, so they don't have
a candidate running against them. Finally, the pay and the prestige of the office
are higher.

The downside of the position for many is that appellate justices are isolated
and shielded from much human contact. To some degree they must be involved
in politics within the court; their ideas and resolutions will not prevail unless
they can get a majority of votes on their appellate panel (although the ability of
appellate judges to write and publish dissenting opinions has markedly contributed to our pursuit for justice). And lastly, to a certain extent, they are the
"rightful prey" in the commentary of law school professors who are certain that
they are much brighter than the appellate judges will ever be.

In summary, the appellate courts are a different world. The job is more intellectual and less people-oriented. Many judges who have gone on to appellate
assignments have regretted having done so for the downsides discussed. But if
you feel that this job would fit your personality and your abilities, you can have
a truly rewarding life on the appellate courts.

As has become evident, each phase of the litigation process has its own rhythms
and insights, and the post-trial phase is no exception. Here the trial court must do
everything reasonable to make sure the final judgment is clear, concise, and
understandable so that, if there is an appeal, the parties, the public, and the appellate judges can determine what happened during the trial, what the result was,
and why. And even at these late stages of the proceedings, productive efforts can
still be made for the voluntary settlement of the dispute by the parties.

CONCLUSION

So now we have completed our discussion of trial matters from start to finish.
Those who are involved in this process know that trials and trial-related matters
are filled with nuances and contradictions, bright lines and compromises, harsh
reality and emotions. But that is natural to the process, because we are dealing
with real people and their real disputes.

Accordingly, we need the people who wear the judicial robe, who manage
and oversee this process, to be mature, organized, and knowledgeable general-

ists. This takes art and responsibility—but it certainly can be done. Of course, much of the time it would be wiser of the litigants to resolve their disputes by settlement, because then they would still have a voice in the outcome. So considering the critical importance of that area, we will now turn our attention to settlement issues.

Chapter 7

Skills and Strategies
for Settlement Conferences
and Sentence Negotiations

"What really settles cases is patience, waiting to figure out what the secret, hidden agenda is. You have to be a good listener; that's sort of our stock in trade."[1]

—JUDGE DAVID B. MOON, JR., JUDGE OF THE SUPERIOR COURT,
SAN DIEGO, CALIFORNIA

The skills that will bring the best results in settling disputes are huge topics of discussion. Numbers of books have already been written about this subject alone. If you desire to get into the topic at any great depth, I recommend you read as many of those books as possible in order to pick up pointers that might work for you. My personal favorite is *Getting to Yes: Negotiating Agreement Without Giving In,* by Roger Fisher, William Ury, and Bruce Patton of the Harvard Negotiation Project.[2] The book sets up a great framework to maximize the chances of settlement of court disputes—or any other disputes that people might be facing.

At the outset, it is crucial to understand that there is an important difference between a mediation and an arbitration. Each of these requires separate types of skills. A *mediation* is what judges and others do during settlement conferences. It is an attempt at settlement in which the opposing sides voluntarily try to find and agree upon a resolution of their dispute. Therefore, in a mediation the parties maintain control over the destiny of their dispute. In contrast, an *arbitration* is similar to a trial. Witnesses are called upon to testify, legal arguments are made, and a verdict is rendered, but all of these are accomplished outside of court. Thus in an arbitration, the parties give control of the dispute to someone else. So as the saying goes, "As a mediator I generally make two friends, but as an arbitrator I generally make one temporary friend and one permanent enemy."

This chapter intends to cover the nuances of mediations, since most of the points previously raised about trials also apply to arbitration.

Some people naturally have better negotiation skills than others do. This point was brought home to me when I read a story that Ulysses S. Grant told about himself in his personal memoirs. When he was eight years old he saw a colt that he very much wanted to purchase. Grant's father offered the owner $20 for the colt, which was as much as the father thought it was worth. But the owner wanted $25 and would not budge off that price. The young Grant was so heart-broken that he would not get the horse that eventually his father relented and agreed to buy the colt. But the parent instructed his son first to offer $20 once again. If that did not work, he should offer the owner $22.50. And only if the second offer was not accepted should he offer the full $25. Young Grant went to the owner and said that his father told him he should again offer the $20, but if the owner would not take it he would offer $22.50, and only if that was not accepted would he pay the whole $25.[3] Guess what the final purchase price was for the colt!

Many people, including judges, start out with the same level of negotiation skills as did the young U.S. Grant. But with time, effort, patience, diligence, perseverance, and attention, all people can improve and add to the skills they have. This chapter will offer some applicable advice to get you started on becoming an effective mediator.

Later in the chapter, we will cover the related topic of the negotiation of criminal sentences. Judges are often called upon to oversee agreements that would make a defendant's sentence lighter in return for a plea of guilty, assuming this would still be consistent with justice. It is not difficult to imagine why this type of negotiation can employ the same type of tactics that a negotiation of compensation or damages would use. The overarching qualities needed are persuasiveness, persistence, and the ability calmly to assure the parties that a settlement or negotiation of sentence will be a reasonable and practical resolution.

RESOLVING CIVIL DISPUTES

As they should with any other aspect of a judicial career, judges should try to be responsible artists in their settlement efforts. Each judge should not only develop his own style, but he should also be flexible enough to adjust his approach to each individual case. As suggested above, the art of procuring settlements can be learned over time. One of the lessons that will become clear is that when it comes to settlement discussions, the right answer at the wrong time can actually be the wrong answer. So a judge needs to develop a sense of "when" things should happen, as well as "how" they should happen—in addition, of course, to "why" they should happen. Some cases will respond well to a judge who expresses concern and understanding. Others need a firm and seemingly almost inflexible hand. Sometimes it works for the settling judge to give recommendations about settlement figures toward the end of the negotiations; sometimes it does not. But seldom should judges take a position about settlement figures at the beginning or even in the middle of the discussions.

And sometimes what the judge does simply will not work. In fact, if and when you serve as a judge there will be occasions when you will be like the man who came upon a desperate friend. The friend was depressed and frustrated because he had a skunk under his house and did not know how to get rid of it. The man recommended that his friend should first find the skunk's point of entry and then put a path of breadcrumbs leading from that point away from the house. The friend liked the suggestion and said he would follow it. A week later the advice-giver saw his friend, who looked even more agitated than before. When the advisor asked what happened, the homeowner said that now he had two skunks under his house!

When you are not successful with your approach on a case, do not give up, because if you keep trying you will be amazed how often you can still turn it around and *ultimately* be successful. Yes, all of this takes work, perseverance, insights, and experience. But I have no doubt that once you start being successful, you will agree with me that resolving disputes is among the most gratifying work in which any person can engage. Along those lines, one experience that will always live with me concerned a lady who broke down in tears after I helped her husband and her to settle a difficult, emotional, and never-ending case. She told me, "I have been praying for a judge like you."

Pitfalls to Avoid

It is true that in negotiating civil settlements (and criminal sentences), certain approaches work well for some but not for others. It is also true that there are some things that *do not work at all for anybody*. I call such things "pitfalls." In the following paragraphs, we will identify some pitfalls and discuss how you can either avoid or manage them in your settlement conferences. I acknowledge that by the time you find yourself in some of these positions, it may be too late to manage them optimally. Yet it should be helpful to be aware of them nonetheless.

A Critical Participant Is Not Personally Present

If you do not require the parties, in addition to the actual trial attorneys, to be physically present at the settlement conference, you will have seriously reduced your chances of settling the case. Remember, it is the parties who actually have the decision-making power to agree to a settlement. If the people in control—whether they be the president of the corporation, the entire city council, the insurance adjuster with the ultimate say, or anyone else—are not personally present, the case is far less likely to be resolved.

That is not to say that you should be unreasonable. If the attorneys can convince you in advance that, for example, the authorized insurance agent who resides out of town will be in his office with "the telephone sown onto the sleeve of his jacket" until he is released by the court, you can excuse his personal presence for the first session and see what happens. But if you later determine that his presence would have materially increased the odds of settling the case, I recommend you continue the conference and order him personally to be present at the next one.

If a person with settlement authority is not present—and has not, by prior agreement, been given permission to be available by telephone or otherwise absent—*do not abandon the effort*. Still go forward, and only "get tough" if you subsequently determine that the case was close enough that the absence of that person was a likely cause of the lack of resolution. In fact, here is a good tactic to use at the end of an unproductive session due to a key player's absence. State that you are going to enforce the local rules and have another settlement conference in two weeks or so. Explain that the absent party who was not officially excused from attending this current session is *ordered* personally to be present at the next conference. Furthermore, he is required to pay the extra fees and costs of the party who actually complied with the rules, because that party will now be forced to attend a second session. Probably half of the time the case will settle after taking this firm but reasonable approach. Frequently the parties who are ordered to pay the sanctions all of a sudden become more reasonable in their efforts to settle the case in order both to keep from having to appear and to keep from paying the other side's expenses. So by the time the two weeks have passed, you will often hear that the case "settled on its own."

On a side note, make sure that all parties and their counsel understand from the outset that they will be required to stay for the full morning or afternoon of the settlement conference. In fact, they should be aware that they might even need to stay longer if it is thought that extra time will produce a settlement. That will assist the resolution of the cases in numbers of different ways.

Attorneys Are Overselling Their Cases

One of the worst things that attorneys can do is to oversell a case to their clients or potential clients. If that occurs, even if the attorneys work hard thereafter or just get lucky and achieve a good settlement—or even a good verdict— most of the time their clients will still not be satisfied. If you find this to be the case, dropping the hint at the appropriate time privately to the offending attorney that his legal fees could/should be reduced in order to make the settlement happen is frequently an effective idea.

One or More of the Parties Are Using "Poisonous" Words

Words or terms such as "liar," "cheat," "bad faith," or, in an extreme case, "slime-ball," used in the presence and aimed in the direction of the other side almost always move the case backwards. The same goes for allowing an attorney to say he will offer a particular amount of money only as a "nuisance value" settlement. Inflammatory words and phrasing should be intentionally and strictly avoided. If they are used, the judge should interrupt immediately and demand this practice cease. Normally that will end the problem.

Parties Are Spending More Money on the Case Than It Is Worth

It is really hard to settle a case for $30,000, even if that is all it is worth, if the parties have already invested $40,000 in fees and costs. In these situations, help the parties to understand that the spending will probably continue to get only worse from here, so they should focus upon trying to cut their losses and not throw more good money after bad. This first should be done through the attorneys. But if that is not enough, I frequently have had success by gathering all of the attorneys and parties together either in chambers or in the courtroom. Then I confront the problem directly by saying that if this is a business dispute the parties will probably be better off even arbitrarily choosing a figure and settling their case, because I know their attorneys are charging them "more than $22 per hour," and it will get only worse from here.

A Case That Previously Settled Is Now "Unsettled"

One of the hardest types of cases to settle is one that has already settled and then, for some reason, has been upset because one of the parties has backed away before it was finalized. At this point, nerves are frayed and resentments are building. Even if the balking party eventually agrees to the original settlement terms, the other sides are going to say that they have been unnecessarily forced to incur more expenses. The best approach is to acknowledge candidly that these cases are much more difficult to settle and then see if all sides can make some adjustments. Those adjustments could take the form of a slight allowance from the party that backed away from the original settlement, or a recognition that there was an additional issue that had not been fully considered when forming the original agreement and now must be addressed.

The Dynamics That Drive the Case Have Not Been Clearly Identified

Sometimes it is hard to discern the factors that are motivating the parties to push for a full trial of a case. Discovering those factors is key to its successful settlement. Some of those possible "driving forces" are discussed below.

Emotion. When I speak with parties, I frequently tell them that if the case involves a business decision, I have a fair amount of experience in the area and have some thoughts that may help them. But if the case is based upon emotion— which is perfectly all right—there really is not much I can do for them. After all, in an emotionally driven case, the issue really cannot be quantified. Either way, parties with competeing emotional interests are fully entitled to go to trial if they wish, as long as they understand that it will probably be expensive. They should also understand that they will be giving up the ability to have much of a say in the outcome. Reminding them of these factors often puts the case back on track toward a resolution.

Family disputes. "Mother always liked you best, but now I'm going to get you." Family disputes involve so much unseen history that it is difficult for a judge to know what angle to take. Sometimes asking the feuding family to see the dispute through their parents' eyes—"Your parents would have tears in their eyes if they knew about this litigation"—might help. At other times, that approach would be a disaster. So first get the advice of the attorneys.

Another possibility is to get the parties to go to lunch together, along with their counsel, and then come back in the afternoon in order to pursue the settlement conference. Again, sometimes that strategy can help, and sometimes it can be counterproductive. But these approaches are worth a try if the situation does not look too fragile or dangerous. Sometimes family members who are arguing just need a third party to take the reins and guide them in the direction of the conversation. This "forced" communication, if you will, might provide the impetus for resolution. And there is no feeling in the world like seeing two brothers who have not spoken to each other in years return to court with tears in their eyes, give each other a hug, and wonder why they had spent so long in resentment.

Company politics. In some cases, the key decision-maker in the company made a mistake that led to the lawsuit. Therefore, some way must be found to soften the blow or diffuse it into some form of plausible mistake that "could have been made by anybody under the circumstances." I put the previous phrase in quotations to highlight the approach or attitude that is best taken. If the judge can help the parties to see the mistake in that light—that this could have happened to anybody—often the decision-maker of the defendant company will have "political cover" and will allow the case to be settled. If the situation is not seen in that light, the decision-makers will probably take the case to trial, because if they lose, they can always blame the "stupid jury" or the "stupid judge," or even their "stupid attorney."

Saving Face. In some closely-knit cultures, to settle is to be *seen as agreeing* that you lost a case. In and of itself, that can justify going to trial and actually losing. But there are ways to appease those who need to save face or honor. Once I settled a case involving a matter of principle by suggesting that the defendant make a "voluntary" contribution to our county's abused children's home in full settlement of the case. By this settlement the plaintiff was able to be publicly exonerated and the defendant was able to save face by just making a donation to help abused children.

Years later, leaders from that community still tell me how brilliant that settlement approach was because it allowed both parties to be exonerated.

Need for someone to listen. A surprisingly high number of cases can be settled if someone in authority, such as a judge, simply listens and shows reasonable understanding and sympathy. Sometimes after the expense and anxieties of litigation have begun to dull the pleasure of inflicting pain upon the opposing party, the only real thing that is left is the serious need to "vent." If catharsis is the parties' driving force, you can anticipate serious progress to be made in resolving the case after that venting has taken its course. And even when venting does not settle a case outright, it often brings settlement goals a great deal closer. So in cases that come close to settling but do not, judges failing to make themselves available to listen can actually be the only reason that the cases go to trial.

Desire for a simple apology. Several years ago I read an enlightening newspaper article about an insurance company and medical doctors it insured. The article reported that once the insurance company allowed its medical doctor insureds simply to apologize to potential plaintiffs when the results of their efforts were not as good as they might have been, the number of lawsuits that were filed was significantly reduced. The article claimed that the clear, sincere apologies made a big difference. In my view, judges can sometimes successfully use this approach in settling those cases that have already been filed by having the defendants give a "heartfelt apology" on the record in open court. That does not mean that the defendants even necessarily have to agree that they were at fault. But it does mean that they are sorry for the problem and the unsatisfactory results.

Moreover, I once settled a case involving the writing of a racial epithet by some children on the plaintiff family's garage door. A primary part of the settlement was an apology by both the offending children and their parents. But as a further part of the settlement, I, as the trial judge, was required to be persuaded that the apologies were "heartfelt."

On some occasions I myself have apologized that society—or the governmental agency, or whoever—could have allowed the harm under discussion to have occurred. And that expression alone significantly moved the cases toward settlement. At other times, I have given what I call a "conditional apology." For example, I say that if the offending party—the police officer, desk clerk, or whoever—had unknowingly done something that unnecessarily caused hurt feelings, I was sure that he apologized for that action. Then I follow up with a stern, "Isn't that right, Officer (or clerk or mechanic)?" Usually, the offending party nods some form of agreement. So do not underestimate the value and impact of an apology of at least some honest form at settlement conferences. Failing to explore these possible apologies can be a pitfall that hinders settlement.

Lack of preparation. As discussed earlier, when I first conducted settlement conferences, I held them before a trial date had yet been set. This was done in an effort to save the parties some needless litigation expenses. But I soon found that postponing the setting of a trial date often did not work. The reason for this failure could be either practical or cynical. The practical reason would be that the parties have not yet had an opportunity to learn enough about their own case and the case of their opponent. The cynical reason would be that the attorneys have not gotten paid enough money from the case yet. But I learned that, one way or the other, if the parties are not prepared and trial is not imminent, most cases stand a poor chance of being settled. Accordingly, I believe it is a good idea, in a majority of cases, to set a trial date and then schedule a settlement conference for about thirty days before trial.

The general exceptions to that rule are cases involving the dissolution of business partnerships and neighbor disputes. In partnership cases it is usually clear to all that the parties must be separated as quickly as possible in order for the business to survive. In disputes involving neighbors, since the situation affects their homelife, mostly people want the dispute to be resolved as quickly as possible. So with those cases I still set a trial date, but I often set a settlement conference for a time much earlier than normal.

A plaintiff must get at least some money. Let us consider that you are trying to settle a personal injury case that is weak for the plaintiff, and it is on a contingency with the plaintiff's attorney. In such a situation, it often can be in the plaintiff's *attorney's* best interest to settle the case for a low amount of money, simply to get back some of the costs involved. But unless the plaintiff himself can get something, he will have no incentive to agree to the settlement. This is true because, at that point, going to trial will usually not cost the plaintiff anything except a little time. Moreover, if he loses he may be judgment proof or have no discoverable resources to cover the costs sought against him by the other side. So one way or the other, unless it can be structured for the plaintiff to walk away with at least something tangible in his pocket, the case will not settle.

I hope the discussion of the various motivating factors that drive cases forward has helped you see where settlement is possible and where it is unlikely. Closely examining everything from the emotional level of a case all the way to the plaintiff's requirement to gain at least some money from the settlement agreement will help you know what settlement skills to flex.

Judges Take "Failure to Settle" Personally and Will Not Accept That Settlement Is Not Possible

On some occasions, settlement is doomed. For numbers of reasons some cases simply will not settle, and the judges on these cases should not take it personally or demand countless additional conferences. Some cases actually involve legitimate or emotional disputes that simply need a full and final hearing in order to satisfy the parties. In my view, very few of the cases filed fall into this category. Of course judges should never automatically accept the attorneys' conclusion that this case simply must go to trial. But judges should try to recognize quickly the disputes that will not settle and keep from wasting too much time on trying to settle them. If you do decide a case truly will not come to settlement, then disband the settlement effort and move on to a more productive usage of your time.

One way of determining whether a case can be settled is to ask the parties if they want to resolve this case "today" or not. If the answer is yes, then follow that up by asking the defendants if they are willing to pay "at least some amount of money" in order to settle the case today. In that regard, telling the defense attorneys to come back with "no offer" is preferable to coming back with an unreasonably small one.

The threat of future multiple plaintiffs can present a situation that makes settlement almost impossible. For example, consider the following scenario: A defendant is faced with possible multiple similarly-placed plaintiffs in the future, and you currently have the first case or "test case." If the defendant's side feels that the case is possibly defensible, they may *have to go* to trial. After all, if they settle the case the rest of the plaintiffs will pursue their actions against them as well, and a precedent will be set. So this is going to be a tough one to settle. In fact, the case simply *cannot* settle unless either the plaintiff agrees to dismiss it for a waiver of fees and costs, which does not happen too often, or the case could settle for a low enough amount that the defendant would be willing to pay the same amount to all of the future parties. (And by the way, anyone who thinks that a "confidentiality order" will have any effect upon the word getting out to other potential plaintiffs is virtually dreaming.) Unless it fits one of those categories, this type of case is one you might sometimes just have to allow to go to trial without wasting too much time or effort at a settlement conference.

Yet another situation that makes settlement extra difficult is when the case involves emotions that would result in one or more of the parties' ruing the day that they settled it. For some reason, plaintiffs in these cases want to have the opportunity to cross-examine that "miserable excuse for a human being," and want to see him sweat. They desire to retaliate against him by inflicting pain in open court, or they are controlled by the "thousands for defense but not one penny for tribute" mindset. These types of emotional findings can control the result. In such cases, I normally look straight at the party and tell them that they *should* go to trial. I acknowledge that they are entitled to do so, and that is what we are here for, as long as they understand that they will probably be sending their attorney's children to college for their efforts. On a positive note, there have been occasions when, after we have gone through this approach and accept that

trial is inevitable, realities begin to creep into the minds of the parties and productive settlement discussions soon begin!

PROACTIVE SETTLEMENT APPROACHES THAT WORK

Let us leave the tricky context of pitfalls behind and now look at settlement skills
from a different perspective. I would like to share with you some of the proactive strategies I have learned over the years that have helped me settle numbers
of cases, including many cases that *supposedly* simply could never be settled. I
hope you find these tips useful. But just as players must develop their own
unique batting stances in baseball, you will have to develop your own style and
approach to negotiating and settling cases. So find the pointers that appeal to
your personality and your approach to judging, then make them yours and "win
one for the Gipper."

Never Betray Confidences, and Always Tell the Truth

A judge's reputation—just like that of an attorney—is critical. If a judge is not
fully truthful, even on one occasion, that word will get out, and it will be much
more difficult for that judge to do his job effectively for many years to come. To
reinforce that thought, guess what attorneys talk about when they go out to
lunch together: judges. And one misstep will be talked about for years. (On the
heels of that sobering thought, however, I ask attorneys to guess what judges talk
about when *they* go to lunch together.)

I am not suggesting that judges or counsel must reveal everything they
know. Settlement conferences are a lot like the game of bridge—only a dummy
puts all of his cards on the table—and somewhat overstressing certain strengths
or weaknesses of a party's case is not being untruthful. But when you as a judge
say something, everyone must be able to count upon it as being the truth. Similarly, if a judge allows any information that was given in confidence to "slip out"
to the other party, that judge will seriously undercut his future effectiveness. As
a result, if I have any confusion at all about what information can or cannot be
provided, I either keep it completely to myself or I ask the attorneys who provided the information to articulate what they feel is appropriate to say in everyone's
presence.

Encourage the Attorneys to Get You,
As the Judge, to Work for Them

If the attorneys are having problems, encourage them—either collectively or
individually—to let you know. Make yourself available to help them address any
and all problems that would hold up settlement. What are a few examples of
such problems? Well, attorneys might have "client control problems," need the
deposition of a witness, or have to deal with significant liens on the case. Maybe
emotion is controlling the case and they are at a loss about how to bring reason

back into the situation. Together, the judge and the attorneys can try to overcome problems that are unnecessarily driving the case further toward trial. So be sure the attorneys are aware that they can come to you and that you will assist them. It can only help everyone concerned.

In a similar fashion, on those occasions in which attorneys tell you privately that they have a "smoking gun" that the other side is unaware of, and that the evidence is not subject to change—such as a document, physical object, or "sub rosa" (clandestinely taken) video—it is helpful to get that information out on the table. But I tell counsel that I will do so *only* with their express agreement. For example, I once had a wrongful termination case based upon an alleged atmosphere of sexual harassment. The defense counsel had copied the e-mail traffic of the plaintiff/former employee. This material showed that this atmosphere had not only *not offended* the plaintiff, but also that she had affirmatively joined in it and often even initiated it. I knew that the attorney could barely contain himself in anticipation of having some fun with this material at trial, but I was able to convince him to reveal the plaintiff's messages to plaintiff's attorney. After he did so, the case was dismissed within half an hour, with the saving of a great deal of time and expense to everyone.

So tell counsel that if they have a "smoking gun" that will control the outcome of the matter to please give it to you as the judge, so you can help to "beat the other side up with it." They certainly are not required to disclose this to you or the opposing side, but mostly saving these things for trial simply wastes everyone's time. Furthermore, sometimes that party's evidence or case law is not as persuasive as they think, and they can become more interested in settlement when they face that reality.

Work to Settle Your Own Cases

It is a natural part of a judge's profession to reflect on some things and not on others. A good judge knows what material to consider heavily in a case and what material is not applicable. Settlement negotiations are no exception to this rule. As a result, I have always openly participated in the settlement conferences of my own cases. I believe the actual judge on the case is in a far better position to resolve it, and I personally feel that I can resolve my cases better than anyone else can.

Nevertheless, I take steps to assure counsel and the parties that I have "an extremely short memory," and that absolutely *nothing* that happens in settlement discussions will affect how the trial is held in any fashion or what the eventual verdict will be. I also have a procedure for those who do not wish me to be involved in the settlement negotiations to request an alternate judge before the settlement conference date arrives. But working on the settlement of my own cases does not make me at all uncomfortable, and I have never really had a reason to believe that the litigants have had much of a problem with it either.

Set the Right Frame of Mind

At a settlement conference, the first thing to do once I have all of the trial counsel present in my chambers is to try to put them in the right frame of mind for a settlement. (I always have the parties, except for insurance adjusters, wait outside, and I deal only with the attorneys.) I do this because I want to try to put them at ease. Generally, I stand up and introduce myself to the attorneys and adjusters as they come into chambers, and I say their names while I shake their hands. I also try to employ a little small talk, or even a quick bit of humor. For example, just when counsel are sitting down, I sometimes joke that considering my job and some of the cases I have seen, I often sleep like a baby—that is to say, I go to sleep for a few hours and then wake up screaming.

In situations where I deem it appropriate, I next mention my view that often we will have failed in our duties as professionals if the case has to go to trial. That is true because settlement is often the best thing for everyone, and that includes the parties as well as society. Most of the time, it is even the best thing for the attorneys as well, because at least one side is going to have a far less unhappy client if they settle. Furthermore, the attorneys should remind their clients that if they do not settle, they literally give up the ability to have a "say" in the outcome of the matter. The juries or the judges certainly can make decisions on the cases, but most of the time they not will be able to do so with nearly as much insight as the parties themselves.

Further, of course, the participants should not have to be reminded that litigation is expensive. If there is an attorney's fees provision for the side that ultimately prevails, that could be ruinously expensive for the loser. That does not even address the cost and the time delays of an appeal, if the case comes to that. And even though these comments are discussed with the attorneys, I tell them I am assuming these realities have already been discussed with the parties.

Use the "Three-Minute Drill"

As a matter of procedure, allow each side's attorney to have at least three minutes to talk at the beginning of the session without being interrupted in order to present his view of the issues in the case. Usually counsel for plaintiff should go first. While this is going on, the judge should be *listening*. If you are not good at listening, you should do everything reasonably in your power to get better at it. And if you still are not good at it, then I venture to say that you are in the wrong assignment.

Using the "three-minute drill" does not mean that you cannot ask short clarifying questions during the attorney's explanation. As an example, clarify exactly to whom pronouns are referring. If counsel says "she" or "they" did a particular thing, request clarification so you can be certain which people are being discussed. After all, clarity is critical. At a later time during the session, you should ask some of the hard questions raised by the facts and law. Judges should not put the attorneys into a "this is the way it is" mode at the beginning. Instead, simply ask for more information and clarification.

Later in the conference you can make some suggestions and even imply, by your questions, where you feel the strengths and weaknesses of the matter reside for both sides. Most of the time the attorneys will report your perceptions accurately back to their clients. Finally, bear in mind that sometimes the parties almost literally will see this settlement conference as their "day in court." That being accomplished, they will settle the matter and go away more or less satisfied that a fair hearing has been provided to them.

Keep Control

Do not allow counsel or the parties to interrupt each other or to interrupt you. It is of paramount importance that you are—and are seen as being—the person in charge. Both the parties and their counsel will accept that situation as long as they also have an opportunity to be heard without interruption.

Discover Each Side's Goals

Ask counsel or the parties themselves, on those infrequent occasions when you speak to them and their attorneys without the other side's being present, what their actual goals are for settlement. As we have discussed, sometimes the goals can be the desire to hear an apology, saving face, personal vindication, or simply feeling they have had their day in court. Spend some time on this, because often the goals are not (just) money.

Be Cognizant of the Human Aspect of Your Cases

I almost always tell the parties involved in neighbor disputes that their situation is much worse than a business dispute, because, as discussed above, it affects where they live. Litigation does not tend to make for more peace at home, so the parties should try extra hard to work out their problems in order to regain more harmony where they live. Of course, that is often even truer in disputes among family members.

Similarly, if you are dealing with a wrongful death case, often you, as a judge, can be a source of comfort by extending appropriate condolences to the surviving family members. You can start by telling them that judges mostly deal with money issues in these matters, but you know that money will not bring back their loved one, and you are truly sorry for their loss. In addition, you can say that in the settlement sessions when only the attorneys were present, there were numbers of comments made by all of the sides concerning what a good person the deceased had been, and that all of the participants were universally sorry about the tragic result. (Naturally, be sure that you are telling the truth. But I am confident you get the idea, and there is always some way to convey such a message truthfully.)

Choose Someone to Break the Ice

There is no fixed rule about who should give the first offer or the first demand at a settlement conference. But I usually begin by asking counsel for each of the parties if their clients want to settle the case today. Then I say that settlement is unlikely with just an apology, so we will need some money to change hands from one party to another. So are the defendants (or cross-defendants) prepared to offer at least *some* amount of money to the other side in order to settle the case?

Since it is the plaintiff's burden, I usually request the plaintiff give his demand first, particularly since the plaintiff is dealing with "unreal" money, while the defendant is dealing with the actual stuff. The rationale is to tell the plaintiff's counsel, in the hearing of the defense counsel, that we need a *reasonable* demand in order to get back a meaningful offer to settle. So if they need to take a short break for the plaintiff's counsel to consult with plaintiff, go ahead and allow it. Then, once I have obtained that "settlement zone" demand from the plaintiff's side, I try to get the defendant's offer into that zone as well.

Suggest a Neutral Accountant or Other Expert

Many disputes dealing with business or finances are generated because of either a lack of financial information or a distrust about the source of that information. Frequently these cases can be moved toward resolution if all of the parties will agree jointly to hire and pay for a neutral accountant as a court expert. Then both sides can provide financial information to the expert—as well as copies of that information to the opposing side—along with their views of its genuineness and relevance. But no one can communicate with the expert except in writing, with a copy given to the other side. The expert can then report back to the parties about the results and, hopefully, a settlement will be reached. If the case actually goes to trial, the expert can also be called by whichever side wishes to do so. This same approach can be used for other types of experts as well.

Find Common Ground on Which the Parties Can Stand

Sometimes it works that parties can settle for future business services or products instead of the present payment of money. When they can agree to some sort of compromise like that, I say they have reached "common ground." We already discussed this for Small Claims Court cases, but the technique can work equally well for any business disputes. An example of common ground in a business matter could be for the parties to work out an arrangement for credit from the defendant to the plaintiff for future business transactions. This can consist of virtually anything from providing a number of "platinum" detailings for plaintiff's on a car at the defendant's car wash like in our Small Claims case, to $10,000 of credit at the defendant's printing shop. In a wrongful termination case, common ground could mean the defendant would rehire the plaintiff, with some adjustments to provide for his attorney's fees and benefits. Frequently, this can be worth far more to a plaintiff than a much larger monetary award.

Many times if the case goes to trial the parties lose the opportunity of pursuing some important remedies. For example, I helped to settle a major Catholic priest/child sexual molestation case by prohibiting the parties from discussing money at all. Instead I had the plaintiff and his counsel draft a list of institutional changes they would propose to be utilized in the two defendant Catholic dioceses that would materially reduce the chances of this hideous conduct's re-occurring. After they presented a list of ten proposals, I had the defendants take some time and respond to each of the items. The defendants' response was that they agreed with all ten points, and they even added another one of their own to the list! After several sessions, both sides had so much invested in the institutional reforms that, later, when I made a suggestion about the amount of money to be involved, they all accepted that amount without much further discussion, and that bitter case was resolved. This example clearly illustrates how the parties in many civil cases can actually lose the ability to develop many worthwhile remedies if they go to trial.

Uncover and Focus upon That "Certain Something" That Will Get the Attention of the Jury

When parties in personal injury cases are unrealistic in their demands or offers to settle their cases, I try when I am speaking to them privately to call to their attention certain pieces of evidence that will probably get the attention of the jury. Of course, the classic example involves the parties themselves. An injured child is almost always a sympathetic plaintiff, although some are more sympathetic than others. But as a practical matter, in those cases you should assess how a jury will feel emotionally toward the plaintiff. Similarly, an unsympathetic defendant will also enter into the analysis. For example, if a physician comes across as conceited or uncaring, that can be a factor to stress in your settlement discussions.

Further examples are presented if plaintiffs have photographs showing substantial damage to the vehicles in an automobile collision case. In those situations, remind defense counsel that this will probably add to the recovery awarded by the jury. Or if they do not have pictures, I remind plaintiff's counsel that lack of photographs will probably subtract from the recovery amount. The possession of x-ray or MRI reports showing some physical injury—or the absence thereof—in a malpractice case is likely to result in similar outcomes.

Yet another example is one I stressed to defense counsel and his insurance adjuster. It occurred when a plaintiff subjected herself to three adjustments of her coccyx, or tailbone, which she said had been injured by defendant's negligence.

The adjustments had to be done through her rectum. I reminded both of them that no one would undergo that procedure unless she was actually in pain, and the jury would understand that. The defendant increased his offer with that realization in mind, and the case settled.

Be Aware of the Psychological Impact of Numbers

Numbers themselves can have psychological consequences. For example, a case that would almost never settle at $50,000 will often settle as $48,750. Why is that? Defendants often psychologically see $50,000 as a big number, but something even slightly below that can seem acceptable. On the other hand, numbers that do not contain as many zeroes often sound like higher numbers to plaintiffs, or they—unlike defendants—might focus upon the fact that $48,750 is almost the same as $50,000 anyway. Psychology is not my field, but I can tell you that for whatever reason, adjusting the numbers even slightly often works.

Be a Devil's Advocate

At the appropriate time, it is advisable to ask counsel for the parties about specific vulnerabilities of their cases. You can do this either in front of counsel for the other side or privately, depending upon the circumstances. A judge asking a neutral but appropriate "hard" question will often force the parties to be more realistic. In addition, sometimes counsel privately tell you they agree that they have these problems and ask you to have a similar discussion with them while their parties are present. Asking these hard questions in a forthright but neutral manner can be an effective settlement tool by forcing the parties to face reality.

Take a Break to Review the Bidding

Sometimes when the discussions begin to get polarized or off track, I stop them by saying words such as, "Okay, let's see. Here is how I understand the story so far." And then I provide a summary of where we are. I have found this to be useful both in helping everyone to focus upon the important points and also by letting everyone know that I know there is still more to the story. Frequently this little break is helpful.

If All Else Fails, Give the Parties a Number for Settlement

Judges' opinions differ on this issue, but I have had a great deal of success in using a particular technique toward the end of the settlement conferences. When I feel the parties are becoming firm in their negotiations, and I believe the chances to continue to "inch forward" to a settlement are small, I tell the plaintiff that I will not ask him to accept a nickel less than a particularly stated amount of money. Then I tell the defendant that I will not ask him to pay a nickel more than the same amount. In other words, the negotiations are now over. Then I urge the attorneys to go out, talk with their clients, and come back with either a "yes" or a "no." I also tell each side that they cannot hurt themselves by this procedure, because unless both sides say yes to the proposed number, I will never tell one side what the other side's answer was, and I will forget the discussion. This approach, which is sometimes called a "mediator's offer," has worked quite well for me.

In a Close Civil Situation, Consider Flipping a Coin

This piece of advice applies to civil cases only. On some occasions involving smaller cases, and in others in which the parties have deadlocked for some reason just a short breath away from settlement, I have actually settled cases by a flip of a coin. In doing this I remind each side how close we are to a resolution and ask them if they are "sporting spirits." If they are, we go forward. But first you must put all of the terms of the agreement completely on the record in open court. Get the full consent of all of the parties and their counsel that if the coin toss is heads, the case will settle for $71,250, and if it is tails, the case will settle for $72,500—or whatever amount applies. Then and only then, on the record, have your bailiff or someone flip the coin, and have it land and stay upon the table.

Of course, you must be prudent with this strategy. Provide in advance on the record that if the coin does not stay on the table, it will be re-tossed. You must think of every possible argument against the stipulation and eliminate it in advance. If you flip the coin before getting everything on the record, I assure you that the losing party will object and claim that there was a misunderstanding. I bring up this subject with some hesitation, but there is nothing wrong with settling by stipulation in the right case, with unanimous and formal agreements.

Even in Complicated Cases, Do Not Give Up Hope for Settlement

In some cases—such as those involving landlords for mobile home parks and their tenants, for example—numbers of seemingly never-ending disputes can arise. As a result, one or more of the parties eventually "simply have enough" and want to go to trial out of exasperation. If this occurs at your settlement conferences, do not be convinced that the opportunity to avoid a full trial is hopeless. There still can be another option.

Suggest that the parties contractually provide for a specific procedure that must be followed as a condition precedent to the filing of any future lawsuit. That procedure can also include any future clients of the plaintiff's attorney because the plaintiff's attorneys can bind themselves to the agreement as well. This procedure will usually include a requirement for all of the principals to meet "face to face" for a discussion of the future problems. It can also require a mediation or non-binding arbitration among the parties before a complaint can be filed in court. Frequently, that can be enough to persuade all parties to settle the subject dispute.

Consider Using Advisory Juries

During a regular trial, a jury can be consulted for non-binding "advice" on decisions about equitable issues to be decided by the Court. In addition, sometimes judges have found that impaneling an "advisory jury" can be a successful tactic in settling long civil cases. That means that with almost no voir dire, a jury of twelve is quickly impaneled, opening statements are given about what numbers of witnesses would say—even if they will not actually testify—and then one or two of the important witnesses on each side are called upon briefly to testify about the high points of the case. Next, short closing arguments are given and the jury is briefly instructed, mostly about the elements of the critical causes of action. At this point, the jury retires and decides upon a verdict. But this verdict is only advisory. After the verdict is given, counsel and the parties can speak with the jurors and get their feedback.

The whole process should take less than a day, but it allows the parties to present their main witnesses and their issues in order to see how a jury responds to them. I am not recommending that an advisory jury be used in every case. But for some it has been a most productive use of a trial day, because it allows counsel for the parties to get a flavor of what would and would not impress a neutral jury about their case. So it has often helped an otherwise long and expensive dispute to be settled expeditiously.

Be Prudent and Careful When Talking to the Parties Before Trial

When I talk with the parties to a civil lawsuit, it is always after I have first exhausted my efforts with counsel alone. Moreover, it is often only with all of the parties present either in open court or in my chambers, and it is *always* in the presence of their individual counsel. In addition, I try to avoid seeing the parties separately in chambers if we have a court trial scheduled instead of a trial with a jury.

But I think these individual conferences can be helpful for many of the reasons already stated in other sections of this book. Parties often feel that just by attending the settlement conferences they "get things off their chest" and "have their day in court." They also hear about the facts of life in trial litigation: expense, possible time delays in appeals, and the loss of their ability to have any say in the outcome of their dispute. As I have mentioned previously, I also make sure to tell them that whatever happens in the settlement conference will have absolutely no bearing upon how the case is tried. Then before listening to their comments, I tell them that it is not at all my position to try to talk them out of going to trial, because it does not really matter to me. If I do not try their case, I will try someone else's.

While on the subject of talking to parties, I have another suggestion. Whenever I can truthfully compliment counsel in the presence of their clients, I always try to do so. Frequently this can be done by saying that the counsel are really making me work and "I have the scars to prove it," because they keep bringing up so many things in support of their case, or something of that nature. It can be hard to be an attorney, and if I can make things easier for a deserving attorney I try to do so.

Be Optimistic and Persistent About Settlement

Make no mistake, settlements can be difficult, and they almost always take a lot of work. One of the pointers in *Getting to Yes,* mentioned in this chapter's introduction, is that only one person can get mad at any one time. To that I add that it can almost never be the judge. You as the judge must always be even-tempered, and you must also show by your statements, actions, and optimism that settlement can be achieved.

When others are angry, I recommend at the appropriate time you say something to the following effect: "I understand how you feel, but may we get back to the settlement discussion?" Recognizing the angry party's emotions will at least satisfy the party to a certain degree. Yet asserting your authority and maintaining a productive agenda will remind all who are involved that there is no time to waste. If you are serious about it, this approach usually works. Finally, remember that there is no such thing as a "bottom line" for any of the parties. The only real bottom line is an enforceable settlement agreement.

Get the Settlement Agreement Finalized on the Record

Once the settlement is reached, be sure either to put it on the record in open court with the court reporter present, or to cause a writing to be prepared—it can simply be handwritten on the spot if necessary. The settlement record or writing should set forth all of the material terms of the agreement. And if it is a writing, *it should be signed by all parties and their counsel.* In many jurisdictions, no settlement is effective unless this procedure is followed.

You as a judge are not doing the parties any favors if the settlement you reach in the case falls apart, is ambiguous, or later gives rise to additional litigation. So before going on the record or in writing, anticipate, address, and resolve any problem head on. That means you must be strictly careful about possible ambiguities in your settlement agreements. For example, there can be a world of difference between the terms "identical" and "equivalent." You never want your settlement to result in future litigation!

Also, in some states there is a statutory provision that a party will retain claims against another settling party if those claims are unknown and not reasonably capable of being ascertained at the time. But this provision can be given up or waived. Before you go on the record to finalize the settlement, ask the attorneys if their parties wish to waive this provision of law. Most of the time this is in the best interest of everyone. The parties probably wish to settle all matters and get on with their lives, "free from the shadow" of the opposing sides. So ask them if that is what they wish to do, and then if so put that additional term of the settlement on the record as well. And remember to clarify on the record that, except as otherwise stated, each side bears its own fees and costs. Otherwise further misunderstandings might arise.

Be Aware of Tax Consequences

One of the largest but sometimes hidden problem areas can be the tax consequences of a proposed settlement. For example, in a wrongful termination case, the plaintiff's lost wages would generally be taxable, but compensation for the personal injuries involved—such as slander and emotional distress—would not be. If the situation is complicated, consider recommending that the parties get competent tax advice before the settlement is finalized.

But the parties should always understand that although they might agree to characterize the settlement proceeds in a particular manner for tax purposes, no one present can actually control the governmental taxation agencies. That realization should be stated in open court, and the parties should declare their understanding of it on the record. Thus, if the tax results later do not work out to their satisfaction, the underlying agreement of the settlement still does not get set aside.

Have a Plan for Formalizing Settlement When a Party Has an Excused Absence

When you have settled a case in which a party is not physically present in the courtroom but has been officially excused, there is no reason in my view why that party's consent to that settlement still cannot be procured. Simply place that party on a speakerphone during the settlement proceedings in open court, with the court reporter present. Be sure to explain on the record to the party on the telephone that if he does not hear and understand everything that is said, he must interrupt and request it to be re-stated. Further explain that otherwise you will infer that he has heard and understood everything that was said.

Then, as you would do with all of the other parties and their counsel, ask the telephonic party individually if he heard the recitation of the proposed settlement agreement. Also ask if he has any questions he wishes to ask either his counsel or the Court. Lastly, if he does not have any questions, ask if he expressly agrees to the settlement as stated.

Know How to Cope with Difficult Personalities

The best thing I can do to prepare you for dealing with difficult people is to refer you to the book *Coping With Difficult People,* by Robert M. Bramson, PhD.[4] Bramson divides difficult people into six general categories: hostile-aggressives, complainers, super-agreeables, negativists, know-it-all experts, and indecisives. Each type requires a different response from the mediator during the settlement conference and is briefly summarized below.

The Hostile-Aggressive. Just from the title, you can begin to visualize this personality type—the tension, the raw emotion. This personality can be further broken down into a number of types. One type of hostile-aggressive person openly attacks, insults, and throws tantrums—both in response to ideas or suggestions that displease him and also in the direction of the person who presents them. The best way to respond to this type of hostile-aggressive is to stand up to him without fighting and give him time to run out of steam. Once he has calmed down, state your neutral views, feelings, and perceptions forcefully, while maintaining eye contact but without arguing with or attacking the attacker.

The second type of hostile-aggressive is one who does not attack directly but instead engages in "guerilla tactics" by using snide or under-the-breath comments, as well as not particularly funny jokes. One way to respond to such a person is to address him directly by saying things such as, "That sounded like you are insulting us. Did you mean it that way?" Another response is to ask the rest of the group if they see the particular problem in the same way. The benefit of these approaches is that we can address the hostile people's behavior without demeaning their negotiating positions, so we will not interfere with the substance of the issues at hand.

The Complainer. This is the person who finds fault with everything and expects someone in charge (namely you) to do something about it. The best way to respond to a complainer is first to listen to his complaints. This will both give you some information about what the problems are or may be, and it will also allow the complainer to work off some steam. Then acknowledge what he is saying by paraphrasing his complaints. By doing so, you show the complainer that you are listening and that you take him seriously.

But do not apologize to the complainer, even if you believe the complaints may be true. That will allow him to conclude that he is entitled to more in the settlement than is reasonable. Instead, continue to lay out the facts of the situation at hand and press on to a resolution. If the situation persists, you can at least ask the complainer, "How do you want this settlement conference to end?"

The Super-Agreeable. This is the person who tends to tell you everything you want to hear but will not necessarily be able to follow through. According to Dr. Bramson, the super-agreeable actually agrees with you in order to receive your approval. The best response is not to allow such a person to make statements that are unrealistic. Moreover, instead of addressing things that are not working, focus upon things that actually are working pretty well but could be improved with the super-agreeable's help. Cases that involve non-monetary resolutions or getting answers to still unresolved questions of fact can frequently furnish opportunities for a super-agreeable to "invest" in a resolution of the dispute.

The Negativist. According to the negativist, any tasks that are not in his hands will surely fail. The best response is to suggest that there are some alternatives that are at least worth a try. Also, make optimistic but realistic statements about similar problems that have been successfully dealt with in this manner by you or others in the past.

The Know-It-All Expert. This type of person often does know a great deal, but he has little regard for the possible knowledge or expertise of others. In these matters the mediator must be fully prepared. If you show ignorance, the know-it-all expert will undercut your authority by simply not dealing with you any longer. The best response is to listen diligently, paraphrase points of the "expert's" presentations back to him, and then raise anything that is missing as a question that must be addressed. If you are seen as taking him on directly—that is, challenging his knowledge—you may quickly find yourself to be in an unresolvable mess.

The Indecisive. This is the person who avoids facing the issues or simply cannot make up his mind. In many ways, according to Dr. Bramson, indecisive people simply try to stall things out long enough to the point that the need for a decision simply disappears. The best response is to examine the facts and prioritize the alternative solutions, which will limit the number of alternatives the indecisive person will have to agonize over. Then give as much support as you can to the best of the alternative resolutions.

The examination of the various personality types above will help you develop an expertise in dealing with the public. Recognizing a personality type and having a few strategies up your sleeve for dealing with each one should improve your people skills and help you to arrive at a settlement more quickly and efficiently than you otherwise would.

Consider Structured Settlements for Minors and Incompetents

If a minor or an incompetent is involved in a fairly large settlement, substantial thought should be given to requiring a structured settlement of the proceeds that would provide for that plaintiff for life, or at least through the college years. On several occasions, I have refused to approve a settlement of the case unless and until a structured settlement was procured. There have been situations in which the parents of a minor or the conservator of an incompetent has felt that his integrity is being questioned by utilizing a structured settlement, but I recommend in larger cases that this virtually always be done anyway. Otherwise the settlement proceeds could be spent on a fancy home for the parents "that the minor will live in," or a fancy car to "drive the conservatee to his physical therapy appointments." Structured settlements will ensure the plaintiff's future, and that is what the courts must protect.

Find Creative but Fair Ways to Divide Up Property

Sometimes disputes center around a division of real or personal property. If the emotional value of the property is not a particular factor, frequently a good approach in a two-party dispute is to have one side divide the property into two equal parts and then let the other side pick which pile he wants. Another way is to have the parties conduct an auction, with the highest bidder "purchasing" the property. A third way that frequently works well for personal property like jewelry or furniture is to allow one side to pick the first item, then the second party to choose the second and third items, and thereafter to alternate.

I once had a Probate Court case in which all three parties were bickering without end about the distribution of some jewelry. So I had the trustee bring the jewelry into the courtroom and, with their prior agreement, I allowed the parties to choose in the order of "one, two, three; three, two, one." Quickly no one wanted to choose anymore because, when it came down to it, the jewelry was not really worth very much. All they had truly wanted to do was argue about it. Creative ways of handling property distribution can actually bring some main issues to the forefront.

Do Not Allow the Discussion of How a Party Arrived at a Particular Monetary Amount

After the settlement conference has gone along for a while and the various sides have explained and calculated what the reasonable damages should be, I recommend that the parties simply deal in numeric demands and offers without giving their calculations about how they actually arrived at those numbers. I suggest this because frequently if the parties give the underlying reasons for their calculations, that can sidetrack the negotiations. Then the settlement becomes a matter of whether the lost wages should be $30,000 or $35,000, or whether the lost profits were $60,000 instead of $70,000, or whether the interest should be at 7 percent or 10 percent—you get the picture. Tell the parties that, at the end, they can each privately calculate their figures however they wish, but they should not explain the calculations to the other side. Just discuss the bottom line amount.

Consider Making a Defendant Who Is at Fault for Intentional Misconduct Pay Some Compensation Out of Pocket

If you are working on a case involving both the negligence and intentional conduct of a defendant with insurance coverage, there is no reason why the defendant himself cannot contribute some money to the settlement as well. Damages for intentional misconduct, much less punitive damages, are not covered by insurance, and insurance companies are well within their rights to refuse coverage for them. But the companies are still on the hook for damages due to negligence and for financing the defense of the case. So as the negotiations proceed, if the amount from insurance is not enough to settle the case, you can still reasonably look to the defendant for a personal contribution, if the case involves allegations of that person's intentional actions.

Make Requests of Counsel

It is the ethical duty of counsel to pass along all of the demands and offers that the other side makes for the possible resolution of cases. In addition, as a judge I also request counsel to pass along to their clients any observations or recommendations that I make. Finally, I also ask if counsel will recommend that we settle the case at the amount I have mentioned, because this places some heat on the counsel.

Of course, the attorneys can give whatever *advice* to their clients that they feel is appropriate. But if I can convince counsel to adopt my recommendations, I know we are getting close to a settlement. If they oppose my suggestions, the case probably will not settle at that number—or maybe not at all.

Confirm the Plaintiffs Know That a Settlement Means No Future Compensation Beyond What Is Agreed Upon

You should remind all plaintiffs on the record that even in the unpleasant event that their injuries or damages get worse in the future for any reason, they will have no further recourse against the settling defendants. Then it is crucial to ask if they understand this fact and still agree to the settlement. Remember, we are not operating a railroad and are not trying to push anything past unsuspecting people. It is our desire and intent that everything be clear and that there be no surprises. But we also are seeking finality, and we want to be clear about that as well.

Employ a "Terror Clause"

Use what I affectionately call a "terror clause" in the proposed settlement of some of your cases. For example, the judge proposes that the case under discussion will be officially settled for a judgment to be entered in favor of the plaintiff and against the defendant for $50,000. But if the defendant pays $35,000 no later than a specified date, or adheres to a specified payment plan for that amount, then once that money has been paid in a timely manner and in full, the case is dismissed and the defendant receives several benefits: a "discount for cash"; a judgment that will never be filed; and a dismissal of the case. If the payments are not made in a timely fashion, the judgment will be entered for the original amount, minus any monies that actually were paid.

Through this strategy everyone wins. Plaintiffs feel like they have won because they are receiving actual money instead of just a judgment. But if they are forced to pursue the judgment because the defendants do not fulfill their end of the agreement, the larger judgment amount originally proposed (minus any amounts the defendant has already paid) makes it more worth their while. On the other hand, defendants get the opportunity to settle the case at a discount, so they see themselves as coming out ahead as well.

In addition, my experience tells me that psychologically the plaintiffs tend to focus upon the higher amount and the defendants tend to focus upon the lower amount. So each side has that added inclination to feel "victorious" about the settlement agreement. The only concern with this procedure is that it must be seen and understood to be a discount for cash, *not* unliquidated damages or usury.

Pursue Alternative Avenues to Resolution

One sometimes successful alternative approach to settlement is for the parties to pursue a binding arbitration with a private arbitrator. Sometimes that arbitration can have "a floor and a ceiling." That means that the parties will have formally agreed, often without telling the arbitrator, that no matter how low or how high the award is after arbitration, the parties agree that it will not be less than one amount or higher than another.

Other alternative approaches to settlement are to utilize what is known as "baseball arbitration," which was first employed in addressing salary disputes for professional baseball players. First, each party publishes to the arbitrator and to each other a particular amount of money. Then after listening to the evidence, the arbitrator must choose either one amount or the other—whichever he feels is the closest to reasonable based upon the evidence. Baseball arbitration has two beneficial results. To begin with, it procures a final decision. Moreover, often once the two sides start publishing their "final" amounts, they continue to get ever closer to each other and the cases often settle without the actual arbitration hearing's taking place.

Do Not Be Too Quick to Cancel the Trial Date

Be careful about vacating a trial date unless and until there is a final written agreement signed by all counsel and the parties, or the settlement is placed on the record by all of them in open court. A more formal agreement can always be prepared and signed later, but having a less complicated one that sets forth all of the material terms and is signed by all parties and their attorneys should effectively end the litigation. This will significantly reduce the chances of the settlement's falling apart due to a change of heart, the discover of new facts, or even the lack of recollection about what the exact terms of the settlement were.

This brings up the related point of sticking to the original trial date even if the parties tell you the case is settled. Let it loom close by until the written and signed agreement is finalized. That keeps everyone's feet to the fire in procuring the final agreement. Nevertheless, some circumstances can present good reasons to change the protocol a little. For example, consider a situation in which the full city council that needs to approve the settlement is not scheduled to convene until after the trial date. It would be reasonable to continue the trial date for that short period of time to allow that consent to be procured.

Know That Open Courtrooms Settle Cases

Frequently the arguments of the opposing parties start to sound a little more convincing, and the party's own arguments a little less invulnerable, when the jury panel has been called or is actually waiting in the hallway outside the courtroom. To an appreciable degree, that is also true if the judge is available to start a trial but has three trials in his courtroom that are all ready. If you find yourself in such a situation, be sly and do not tell anyone which trial you actually will start. When the trial is literally seen as about to begin, or when it becomes evident that a particular case *might* be the first one taken, that is the time many of the cases settle. So the more open courtrooms that appear to be ready to try the cases, the more the cases will settle. And when the case does go to settlement at the last minute due to the reality check of the jury's presence, be sure to have your bailiff explain to the jury panel that their presence materially helped to settle the case.

Effective Phrases to Use

Finally, here are some subtle (and some not so subtle) comments that I have made to counsel and sometimes their clients over the years. The use of these comments has yielded a successful outcome in my attempts to resolve disputes through settlement conferences, because sometimes a couple of good words is all it takes to get the details rolling into place.

"Plaintiffs often lose but, of course, so do defendants."

This thought can be communicated effectively, either orally or by placing recent copies of Jury Verdict Reports from legal newspapers conveniently on counsel table and making them available for anyone to see on the settlement conference days. In addition, privately reminding attorneys and parties about risks that are particular to their upcoming trial is often effective. Finally, tell parties the truth, which is that many plaintiffs have been upset for the rest of their lifetimes that they "left good money on the table" and instead took the risks of going to trial.

"Control your future."

In telling the parties to control their own future, you are essentially asking them, "Do you really want to leave the decision in this important case up to twelve jurors from off the street?" For example, I tell them about an actual transcript from a criminal trial in which a juror was asked, as a part of an attorney's voir dire: "Would you be able to participate in an endeavor in which the final and ultimate result might be the demise of the aforementioned, and that due to a lethal injection?" The juror answered, "I guess I could on a weekend." Do you want to leave your fate up to people like this?

"Whatever actually happened in this matter is irrelevant."

I know this phrase sounds strange. In fact it might even sound irreverent. But the parties must understand that, when it comes to a trial, the only thing that matters is what can be *proved* to have happened by admissible evidence. If one or more of the parties realize the practical truth that the case will look differently—and less convincing—through a neutral stranger's eyes (based upon the evidence presented, regardless of what actually happened), the chance for settlement will increase.

"Get within 15 percent of 'fair.'"

Tell the parties that if we are able to get our settlement within 15 percent of "fair," we will have done a good job. Life is uncertain and litigation is expensive. So getting within 15 percent of a "fair" result often works out better than actually going to trial.

"Give me a plain-old, standard vanilla verdict."

Formulas can often be helpful in settling civil cases. One formula that has been helpful to me is to ask the plaintiff's counsel what he believes would be a plain-old, standard vanilla verdict if plaintiff were to recover—not a "home run," and not a "strike-out," but just a routine "ground-rule double." Most of the time, counsel will give me a fairly reasonable estimate, but sometimes I modify it. Then I try to use that figure, but it must be discounted by the chances that the plaintiff will get a judgment at all. For example, if a plain vanilla judgment would be for $100,000, but the plaintiff only has a 70-percent chance of getting that judgment, the reasonable settlement value of the case would be about $70,000.

If we are dealing with a negligence case, I also ask what a likely percentage the jury would find of comparative negligence that would be attributed to the plaintiff, and then discount the amount a second time by that figure. For example, if the comparative negligence would be about 20 percent, the final settlement value of the case in the above example would be about $56,000. The same approach can be used for offsets in a business dispute. Obviously this is an inexact approach, but I have found success with it on more occasions that I can recall, because it helps to quantify a subjective situation. Therefore, I recommend it to you.

So you are now armed with the awareness of settlement conference pitfalls. The more you are familiar with what could go wrong, the more you can move things along in the right direction. You have also received numbers of pieces of advice on effective settlement strategies and have collected some helpful phrases that you can use to nudge a case toward resolution. Now you can apply these new insights to yet another aspect of "judging." How? Read on.

DECIDING HOW INVOLVED TO BE IN CRIMINAL SENTENCING NEGOTIATIONS

As a practical matter, it is common for a defendant in a criminal case to ask for a reduced sentence in exchange for a plea of guilty to some or all of the offenses. This is commonly known as a *plea bargain.* How involved should judges actually be in these negotiations?

Arguments for and Against the Judge's Involvement

One big argument in favor of a judge's active participation in negotiating sentences is that unless a vast majority of cases are resolved in some fashion by a plea of guilty, the number of cases that go to trial will literally swamp the system. Of course, all criminal defense attorneys understand this reality and continually threaten to "bring the system to a stop" by taking all cases to trial. So, like with everything else, it is frequently the function of a judge to participate in the process and to strike a fair balance.

To some appreciable degree that argument is counteracted by the fact that Rule 11 of the *Federal Rules of Criminal Procedure* has for years prohibited *federal* judges from being involved with these negotiations, and yet the federal courts continue to function. It is further countered by the concern that if a defendant is seen as declining the Court's "reasonable offer" in a non-federal case, and then that defendant goes to trial and is convicted, the judge could be upset by the defendant's original decision and ultimately increase the punishment due to the perceived "insult."

In the final analysis, the decision whether to be active or passive in jurisdictions where this judicial involvement is allowed is left up to the individual judges. I myself have always taken a fairly active negotiating role in both criminal and civil cases. Yet I do not do so until after firmly promising the litigants that absolutely nothing that takes place in the settlement negotiations will have any effect upon the trial or the ultimate outcome whatsoever. And I mean it. Nevertheless, all judges will simply have to find their own comfort level on this issue.

Reasons to Be Extra Prudent in Negotiating Sentences

Even if the prosecutor and the defense counsel work out and agree upon a sentence without the judge's participation, once the plea is taken and the matter is completed, that sentence usually belongs entirely to the judge. After all, the judge is responsible for determining if that negotiated sentence is appropriate. So judges are well advised to become aware of all of the facts and circumstances of each offense, as well as the background and record of each defendant. That way judges can assure themselves that the agreed-upon sentences are fair and just.

Of course, in this process if the prosecutors say the magic words that they have "problems of proof," then any resolution they have worked out should pretty much be accepted. Just be careful that the court record reflects that the prosecutors stated that they had problems proving their case. Therefore, if there ever is a question about the result in the future, it will not appear that you as the judge "gave away the store."

Also be aware that in the real world prosecutors will sometimes try to use the judges as "fall guys." They do so in cases that they have trouble proving or in which they have overcharged the offenses but politically do not want to appear to be "backing down." So they prefer to have the formal decision and accountability for their problems come from the Court. In fact I have often had prosecutors tell me privately in my chambers that they agreed with my proposed sentence but would rather leave it to me. In a lot of ways that is all right because judges are not supposed to be political and are supposed to do the right things for the right reasons. If the situation is explained to me up front and I agree with the resolution, I do not hesitate to make the call. Nevertheless, there have been several occasions in which I have refused a plea agreement reached by both the prosecutor and the defense counsel and signed by them. Why? Because I did not believe that the sentences were strict enough, and there did not appear to be any problems in proving the allegations in trial.

In most jurisdictions, it is required by law that the record reflect that all defendants were fully advised about their constitutional rights at the time of their arraignment, or on other occasions in which they subsequently decided to enter a plea of guilty. This is an important aspect of the law, for, as mentioned previously, we do not "run a railroad" in our courts. Not only do defendants have rights under our constitutions, but also we want to be sure that they understand their rights before waiving them and pleading guilty. These rights normally include their right to have a trial by jury within a specific period of time after their arraignment; to be represented by an attorney at each critical stage of the proceeding; and that if they cannot afford an attorney, to be appointed one to represent them at no charge or at a reduced charge based upon their ability to pay. In addition, they have the right to confront all witnesses that testify against them; to testify themselves in their own behalf or to remain silent, knowing that they cannot be forced to give evidence against themselves; and to use the court's subpoena powers to bring in additional witnesses or evidence to present in their own behalf. Also, in many jurisdictions the defendants are told that if they are not a citizen of this country, a conviction of any of these offenses could lead to their possible deportation, exclusion from admission to the country, or denial of naturalization. Making sure the defendants are fully aware of their rights will keep your professional record clean and, even more importantly, let you rest secure in the knowledge that you are a person of justice.

My intention behind this short but important section on a judge's involvement in sentence negotiations highlights some key issues to consider when it comes to settlement skills of all kinds. Similarly, the information under "Procuring Settlements" will be useful in sentence negotiations as well. Fundamentally all of these various skills are transferable from one calendar to another, but I thought that passing along a few insights about civil and then criminal calendars would be helpful as well.

CONCLUSION

At this point we have addressed the history of judging, the nuts and bolts of most judicial calendars, trial issues from start to finish, and some settlement techniques. So is this professional position for you? Would you enjoy it and be an effective judge? Would you fit the lifestyle, and would it fit you? Will you be able to function well within the ethical restrictions of the position? These are the issues we are about to address in Part II.

PART II

Living the Life of an Effective Judge
From Obtaining the Title to Handling the Attention and Responsibilities

You might now feel as though you already have enough information either to continue your judicial career more effectively or to get it started. But when it comes to a profession that touches so many lives, there is always room for more information. Part II of *Wearing the Robe* offers additional practical advice for judges who want to breathe new life into their service and for attorneys who are considering careers as judges.

We will begin with the general pros and cons of serving as a judge, as well as a discussion of the important topic of Judicial Ethics. Then we will move into the traits and talents of the most effective judges. I have noted certain qualities that the best judges consistently possess, and I hope that shining a spotlight on these qualities will assist you. In addition, and importantly enough, no discussion on "wearing the robe" would be complete without an exploration of the public side of the position—from community involvement to media attention. So the final chapter of Part II dives into the "fishbowl" of judicial life. Lastly, please take a look at the Conclusion of this book for my own further hopes and visions for our ever-evolving judicial system. Perhaps the discussion will help us all to continue to do our part to provide the people of our country both with justice itself and with an appreciation of our judicial system as a whole.

Chapter 8

How to Become a Judge—
And Why You Would Want To
Under the Ethical Restrictions

"I love my job. The idea of going back to private practice
doesn't appeal to me."[1]

—ROBERT N. BLOCK, CHIEF U.S. MAGISTRATE JUDGE,
LOS ANGELES, CALIFORNIA

Now that we have focused upon numbers of details about judicial calendars and accumulated practical advice on everything from pre-trial to trial to settlement, try answering the following questions. Are *you* meant to be a judge? Would you enjoy the work and the position of authority? Would you be *good* at it and provide a meaningful service, particularly under the ethical restrictions? These are questions that most lawyers have asked themselves on more than one occasion, and many of those lawyers answer all of these questions with a resounding, "Yes!"

If *your* answer is yes, what should you do? Well, the first thing to do is to look at the formal requirements for the jurisdiction in which you are interested. If that jurisdiction is federal and you wish to become a United States District Judge, the qualifications are quite simple and straightforward: Be appointed by the President and confirmed by the Senate. Nothing else.[2] It is not formally required that you be an attorney, or even a United States citizen. Believe it or not, it is not even necessary to have reached your eighteenth birthday! Of course, realistically a President is simply not likely to appoint, or the Senate likely to confirm, someone who is not in the field of law, is not a citizen, or is under eighteen. But again, these qualifications are not *required* to obtain the position. Similarly, the qualification for becoming a United States Magistrate Judge or Bankruptcy Judge is to be appointed by the District Court judges in that district. That is all.

With regard to the qualifications in the various states and the District of Columbia, they are quite diverse. A chart of some of the requirements for each state is easily obtained on the Internet, through a search for "Judicial Selection" and the name of the state in which you are interested in pursuing the position of judge. A summary of the judicial selection process in those jurisdictions is included in Appendix 2 (see page 303). But if you are *really* interested in becoming a judge, I recommend that you obtain a complete list of the official qualifications from your state government, because the chart furnishes only a summary, and the qualifications and procedures can change.

In deciding whether you want to become a judge, however, you must consider the benefits and drawbacks of the position, and how they would impact upon you. Of course, most of these have already been addressed in one way or another throughout this book, but in this chapter I provide a short recap of some of the pros and the cons. Then I will provide more details on the actual process of becoming a judge. Finally, I have included a section on Judicial Ethics in this chapter because, if you are considering becoming a judge, it is important for you to know some of the ethical requirements that you must meet, and whether you would be comfortable within that context.

THE BENEFITS OF BEING A JUDGE

For the most part, judges are in position to make their own unique contributions to society on a regular basis and to lead truly interesting, varied, and gratifying professional lives along the way. A judge enjoys an increased ability to participate in community activities in general, and her daily work can be quite a bit more interesting than that of most attorneys. Think of it this way: How many interesting situations does a typical active attorney get involved with in the course of a year? At the most, maybe seven or eight? But a judge usually gets that many in a week, if not more. As my colleague Judge Michael Brenner put it, "If you like people, and I do, where is there a better place to be than the courthouse? Everything washes up on the shore here at the courthouse—everybody's dispute, and everybody's odd business deal." What a treat, how interesting, and what an educational stimulation! But dealing with interesting issues is just one of the many benefits of being a judge. Consider some other benefits.

Fulfillment of a Higher Calling

A judge is in a position to do what is right, under the facts and the law. In addition, a judge is in a position to show all concerned that justice is being done. And by doing this, a judge can be an inspiration to others. In the overall scheme of things, it is hard to ask for more than that.

More Control over Your Own Schedule

Imagine a world without time sheets, where you have some element of control over your work schedule, where you do not have to go out and seek business or pay the overhead, and where you have more time for family and other endeavors. That world can be yours as a judge. It is not that you will not be busy at work, because you surely will be. But in most jurisdictions the workload takes into account that a tired or overstressed judge is not in a position to seek and oversee the pursuit of justice in a calm manner. So "unwinding" time is programmed into the schedule of a judge. And when a vacation is scheduled, you can actually take it.

Good Benefits and Retirement Prospects

It is simple, but true: Judges usually have good benefits. Most jurisdictions provide a generous system of medical and dental benefits for their judges. In addition, for the most part judges will be able to retire when they still have years of productive life ahead of them. And when most judges retire, they also normally will have numbers of viable and even exciting choices regarding what to do next. Consider a couple of examples: private judging; sitting on assignment and earning per diem pay; going back to the practice of law; engaging in charitable work or other non-monetary pursuits; or simply drawing your retirement pay and reading, traveling, and/or sleeping until noon, if that is attractive to you.

A Great Investiture Ceremony and at Least Some Respect

Everyone should be lucky enough to have an investiture ceremony, which basically is a formal enrobing ceremony at which people tell you, your family, and your friends how wonderful you are and what a terrific judge you will surely be. In other words, it is a memorial service for you while you are still alive to enjoy it. In addition, and without trying to be at all stuffy about it, there is a certain amount of prestige that accompanies the position of a judge. And that can be a nice thing.

Lots of Support

An increasing number of measures are being taken to protect, support, and aid judges both in their work and in their personal lives. For example, more formal governmental efforts are being undertaken to protect the safety of judges and their families. This is a great relief because, although Criminal and Family Law assignments usually are the ones that generate the most threats of harm to judges, any calendar brings with it the potential for violence to occur against a judge.

In addition, most jurisdictions have confidential programs available—including toll-free hotlines—for judges who are stressed and in need. These programs offer support regarding everything from ethical struggles concerning a case to alcohol or other drug abuse issues that are linked with the anxiety that can accompany a high-profile career. Finally, there are more casual, mainstream ways judges receive support, such as being given the ability to pursue exercise programs and athletic activities during their lunchtimes.

Opportunities to Keep Learning

For most people, being a judge satisfies the challenge posed by Hall of Fame UCLA Basketball Coach Johnny Wooden: "Live for education like you will live forever, and live for life like you will die tomorrow." There are abundant opportunities for learning and countless gratifying experiences to be found in being a judge, even in places where you would never look for them. This brings pleasure to life, making it a satisfying adventure. As an example, as a judge you will have numbers of intelligent attorneys working with you who are paid big money to do nothing but answer your questions. In fact, usually their only response to you will be, "Do you want the answer orally or in writing?" This luxury should not be abused, but it is an interesting position to have. Use the opportunity to enhance your own knowledge and appreciate the various personalities around you.

I have certainly not exhausted all the wonderful things about being a judge. Instead, I have simply highlighted some of the most striking benefits. I hope these "perks" have whetted your appetite and encouraged you to pursue more information about becoming a judge. But it would not be fair and complete if I did not provide a few warnings as well. So please read on.

THE DRAWBACKS OF BEING A JUDGE

Of course, as with any professional position, there are "cons" to living the life of a judge. Some have to do with the public nature of the position: The more prominent of a leader you are, the more demands that are placed on your own behavior, freedoms, and the like. Others have to do with the stresses that are often involved with being a decision-maker regarding other people's lives. But let us look at a few of the drawbacks that being a judge can present.

Lower Pay and Being "On Duty"

While judges are often highly respected, they are not necessarily well paid. Usually, the pay for judicial officers is not nearly as much as that which is received by many of the attorneys who appear before them. In fact, many first-year lawyers with large law firms make a higher salary than most judges. So that can be a trade-off, especially if you were previously involved in a very lucrative legal field such as a large private practice or corporate law.

Moreover, the lower salary does not leave you immune to after-hours duty. I am not contradicting the "pro" mentioned previously—that you can actually plan a vacation and take it. But there are some decisions that cannot be delegated to non-judicial officers, such as issuing search and arrest warrants and injunctions, as well as some questions in setting bail. So almost all judges will be required to have duty on certain nights, weekends, and holidays. The frequency of those assignments will normally be determined both by the number of judicial officers in your court and by your presiding judge.

A Sense of Isolation

Longer hours and solitary work can make a judge feel quite isolated as well. As my father was told by a friend when he was first appointed to the federal bench, "Because of your new position, people you care about will have a tendency to take a step back, and people you do not care about will have a tendency to take two steps forward." Sometimes life can be awkward for judges and their families. Because of your standing in society, people will tend not to invite you and even your family to certain social functions, and on occasion you will run into people whom you have sentenced to probation—for example, a box-boy at the market. In addition, there will be times when you or your family will be asked what you do for a living. If people are uncomfortable with the legal system or defensive about a past event in their lives, the answer that you are a judge can tend to stop the conversation, or even simply lead to a more awkward situation.

Increased Risk of Danger

Because of their visibility, judges and their families find that life can become a little more dangerous. Unfortunately in some jurisdictions it is possible to put a judge's name into a website and actually see a satellite picture of that judge's home and neighborhood. So if disgruntled litigants really want to find and do harm to a judge, they are increasingly able to do so.

Too Many People Watching Your Every Move

"Judge not, that ye be not judged."[3] It is often said that every defective character trait one has is magnified ten-fold when that person becomes a judge. If you are inherently impatient, intolerant of others and their idiosyncrasies, prone to drink alcohol too much at times, likely to tell off-color or "insensitive" stories, previously involved in less than above-board financial or social activities, or anything along any of those lines, the likelihood that those traits will be discovered and publicly held up for criticism is high. This can bring down upon you the wrath of the biblical phrase quoted above. So stand advised that you will want either to be "squeaky clean" or tough-skinned if you pursue the position of judge.

High Stress

Being a judge can subject you to chronic and continual stress. Judges deal with people, their emotions, and their problems on a regular basis. And yet they are the only ones who simply cannot lose control of themselves. If you are a person who has trouble dealing with stressful situations, or a person who is not able to "pull the trigger" and make hard decisions at the appropriate time, you probably should not become a judicial officer. Therefore, being able healthfully to manage anxiety is a key trait of the good and effective judge.

Exposure to Upsetting Issues and Personalities

Being continually exposed to life's seediness is not an uncommon position for a judge to be in. Prepare yourself, because a judge continually deals with discouraging conduct and regularly sees the low value some "people" attach to human life. In addition, judges can be repeatedly subjected to extremely upsetting cases. These can involve graphic details concerning the murders or untimely deaths of people, including young children, and/or injuries resulting from any number of causes, such as evil intent, negligence, or innocent accident. As a good and human person, you will *never* get accustomed to the violent or tragic content of some of the cases that come before you.

Tough Competition

In the majority of jurisdictions judges are involved in elections or at least in reelections. In actuality, most judges are never challenged in their elections. But if the *idea* of being contested and forced to run for reelection on your record (or even off it) turns your stomach, the profession of judge is likely not for you. In addition, if asking people you know and you do not know for campaign contributions is something you simply cannot face, you might want to look for another line of work.

Furthermore, judicial elections are getting ever more political, and costing larger amounts of money. And the funding is mostly contributed by political parties and special interest groups like the business community, lawyers, and labor organizations.[4] Then, of course, after the election judges are required to be immune from even considering any special treatment for the people or organizations that helped them to obtain or retain their office. If you are not made of the "sterner stuff" that allows you completely to resist this pressure, you should not be in a judicial position.

Many judges have been forced to face the dilemma of deciding controversial cases at the same time that they are facing a reelection campaign. As former California Supreme Court Justice Otto Kaus said about this situation, "You cannot forget the fact that you have a crocodile in your bathtub. You keep wondering whether you're letting yourself be influenced, and you do not know. You do not know yourself that well."[5]

We judges must withstand any influence in our decisions and orders from any source except the facts, the law, and our common sense. This institutional reality was expressed by Justice James D. Ward of the Court of Appeal in Riverside, California, when he said, "We have no 'telephone justice' here—the situation in the communist world when, after hearing the evidence in a case, a judge phones the local party boss to ask how the case should be decided."[6] So judges are not in a position to "dodge" controversial decisions like legislators can, or to be affected by the dictates of politics in any fashion. If you do not see yourself being able to "do justice" in those situations under pressure, you should probably reconsider your desire to become a judicial officer.

Reduction of Judicial Immunity

There is increasing talk all around the country of reducing judicial immunity for a judge's actions and rulings.[7] That reduction would mean a judge could be sued for unpopular decisions or even for a party's "dissatisfaction." In addition to being a direct and serious threat to judicial independence, reducing judicial immunity could be ruinous financially for judges. With this realization, more jurisdictions are procuring judicial malpractice insurance for judges in the event that either litigation is brought against them or they are forced to respond to formal charges for ethical improprieties.

Loss of General Freedoms

There is a definite loss of constitutional freedoms for judicial officers in that judges are restricted in a number of ways. They are limited in what they can discuss in public. They are also held to restrictions regarding raising money, involving themselves in non-judicial elections, deciding the amount of money they can donate per year to political candidates or parties, and earning extra money in most other forms of employment. Furthermore, they are increasingly prohibited from being a member of clubs or other organizations that are perceived to be discriminating against people because of their race, gender, or background, and many of their finances and those of their spouses are required to be open for public inspection. Another restriction to consider is that in every state except Georgia and California, sitting judges who wish to run for a non-judicial office must resign their positions in order to do so.

A judge's own access to the courts can be restricted as well. As a practical matter, it is often so awkward for a judge to bring a lawsuit against anyone that judges mostly refrain from doing so. At the very least, the case will be sent to a neighboring county to be tried because all of the judge's colleagues will recuse themselves. At best it is an embarrassing situation in which to be involved.

Lack of Opportunity for Self-Defense

There will be times in which your integrity as a judge, and even as a human being, will be criticized, and mostly you will not be able to respond. Many litigators and parties may think and say that you are really a great judge, until you rule against them. Then they can become deeply and publicly personal, if not vicious. This situation can be even more pronounced in small communities, where many rural people still seem to think the judge has the power to decide the case the "right" way, instead of following the statutes and the case law.

And that is just for openers. On some occasions disgruntled parties to an unsuccessful lawsuit will simply make things up about you. For example, according to one judge from Sacramento who was the subject of a recall election for an unpopular decision he made in a high-publicity case, sometimes judges must "be prepared for the 'big lie.' If you want to stop cross-dressing men from going into women's restrooms, if you believe the age of consent for sex should be lowered to fourteen for girls and boys, you need to recall me. I didn't realize I made all these decisions!"[8]

Most of the time judges cannot respond to such comments or criticisms. Instead they must rely upon bar associations and groups like the American Board of Trial Advocates for a public explanation, response, or defense. This can be a frustrating part of judicial life.

After reading the downside of being a judge, you might feel a bit overwhelmed or discouraged. That is not my goal or intention. Instead I simply want to raise your awareness of the tougher side of the profession so that you will not get blindsided by it. If you are aware of the challenges in a judge's life yet still feel motivated to pursue becoming a judge, then you can be confident that you are making a great life decision by pursuing a judgeship.

IMPORTANT STEPS TO TAKE TOWARD BECOMING A JUDGE

If you have thought about all of the above and still wish to pursue your dream to become a judge, how should you go about it? Well, that is an easy question to answer: There is no magic pathway. The particular president, governor, or other appointing agency will have individual procedures. And it is a fact of life that almost all of the people who do not know what happens say a lot about it, while the ones who do know usually keep silent.

But I think it is safe to say that those who aspire to an appointment to the bench fall into two categories: the appointed and the disappointed—and the second group is almost always much larger than the first. Of course, the common response from those who have been successful is that the appointments are made on merit. Those who are not successful say that the appointments are based upon politics, or they describe a judge as a person who went to all of the right fundraisers for the governor. The fact is that probably both sides are somewhat correct in their descriptions.

Nevertheless, one thing you should keep in mind throughout this process is that the politicians who are making these appointments not only do not want to be embarrassed by them, but they also actually want to derive a benefit from them. As such, they want to appoint people who both do not have "skeletons in their closet" and who are generally recognized in their communities as people of integrity and leadership. Accordingly, there are some things you can do to increase your chances of separating yourself from the pack and obtaining a judicial appointment. Although the possession of these qualifications will certainly not ensure success in the appointment process, or the election process either, the absence of them will almost certainly ensure failure.

Establish Your Integrity

First and foremost, be well-known in your community as an attorney and a person of integrity. Few things impress appointing authorities as much as comments from opposing counsel that the people under consideration are people of their word, and people of integrity. As a result, if you have had any disciplinary problems with your state bar, or you have a reputation that is shaky, you will probably not be successful in the appointment process.

Accrue Practical Trial Experience

Judges preside over trials, and they simply must have more than a casual understanding of how trials should effectively be run. For many attorneys in large law firms this can be a significant obstacle in obtaining a judicial appointment. Large firms pay good money and attract good people, but they normally do not offer junior attorneys much actual trial experience. So those attorneys who have prior experience as prosecutors or in a public defender's office or legal service office before going to the large law firm have a real advantage over those who do not.

Be a Well-Rounded Person

Read, observe, travel, and involve yourself in things that would naturally broaden your perspectives of the world around you. This will give you a better understanding of and rapport with people. And importantly, be well-rounded in your legal practice as well. It is a common criticism that judicial applicants have practical experience in only one specialized area, or that all they really care about is money. Obviously, no lawyers can specialize in every area of the law, and those who try will run an unacceptably high risk of committing legal malpractice. But there are some things that a person can do in order to broaden her legal base, such as the following suggestions.

Volunteer to Serve As a Judge Pro Tem, or Temporary Judge

Practical experience, as much as anything, will be taken seriously by the people who are making appointments or recommendations about them. Most courts are open to and appreciative of free judicial labor. Not only can you help by "giving back" to our professions, but doing so can help by "giving back" to you.

Involve Yourself in Pro Bono Work

When you do pro bono work as an attorney, you volunteer your professional time to take on a case for someone who could not otherwise afford legal counsel.

As long as you are careful and do a competent job, this can be done outside your normal field of professional work. Demonstrating a concern for others and a social consciousness, as well as rounding out your professional experience level, will all be of material help in your application for becoming a judge.

Work in a Different Field for a Little While

Take time away from your present job and work for a while in another area of the law. Many offices in the criminal justice field have programs at which good people can work for a couple of months and then go back to their original positions.[9] Similarly, many civil legal service offices are overjoyed to take prosecutors or defense attorneys for a short time while they are on an unpaid leave of absence from their criminal justice assignments. Not only will such changes help you in your judicial application process, but also they are bound to help you to be a better attorney in your specialty once you return to it.

Become a Teacher

Teach legal classes in colleges, law schools, or even schools for paralegals or legal secretaries. People who teach others are widely respected as being highly knowledgeable, as well as highly dedicated to the cause of justice. Having teaching experience also demonstrates that you have the ability to work with various personalities, to organize material well, and to be an effective public speaker.

Keep Up on the Latest

One of the best ways to remain well-rounded is to become knowledgeable about computers and computer research. People today are increasingly seen as not being "educated" if they are not proficient in the use of computers. If you can show a mastery over a certain bit of modern technology, you will be sure to impress many staff members.

Also, keep yourself current in all areas of law in the "advance sheets" of recent appellate decisions. This is an important and reliable way you can obtain and maintain a sophistication in the practice of law, as well as keep your legal instincts finely honed.

Be Involved in the Activities of Your Local Bar Association

In my view, this is a good recommendation for all attorneys, regardless of their judicial aspirations. The possibilities of contributions to your local bar association are many. For example, you could become involved in continuing education, charitable work, mentoring children, and bench-bar activities. For those with hopes for a judgeship, being active in the organized bar will help you to get the support of the professional community that you will need.

Join Philanthropic Community Service Activities

Appointing authorities, and communities in general, want to have judges who are interested in the public good and who display solid community values. So being involved with organizations such as the Red Cross, YMCA, religious institutions, and service clubs will help in your application. The same goes for participation in local community theater and even mock trials with local high schools, colleges, and law schools.

Get Political

To some degree, be involved in political activities. Since you will be dealing with people involved in the political process, it will help you to know some of those individuals and to be familiar with their issues. In addition, elective officeholders score extra points in the judicial application process because they are seen as having already passed the "acceptability test" by having been elected and therefore accepted by their local community. The largest boost would probably go to a person who had been elected to a position in government, but it would also be helpful to have been elected president of one's Rotary Club, political action committee, or the like. Even working on a political campaign will help in that regard.

Being well-rounded enriches both your professional and your private life. It will certainly make you a more desirable candidate by highlighting how much you enjoy working with others and how well you perform in multiple tasks. Appointing authorities are naturally partial to people who exhibit a healthy and successful balance of activities in their lives.

Prove You Will Make the Appointing Authority Proud

Show the appointing authority that you stand for something that is beneficial to her legacy. Presidents, governors, and other appointing authorities do not want to appoint people about whom it can be said, "He could walk into an empty room and blend right in." Instead, they want to appoint strong leaders who will bring lasting credit to the person who appointed them.

Link Yourself with a Minority Cause

In some way, show that you are a part of one or more minority groups. Today, political officeholders are legitimately concerned about being seen as sensitive to minorities. Since everyone is in a minority in some way—be it racial, religious, some form of disability, background activity, or some type of unusual hurdle to be overcome—without exaggerating or puffing about it, try to accent that involvement. Speaking a language in addition to English can also help in that regard.

Associate Yourself with Law Enforcement

Show your involvement in or at least connection with some "law enforcement" work. In most political climates this is of significant help. As such, any involvement in the military by you or even your family members, your work as a prosecutor or even police cadet, or your support from your local police or firefighter's association will be seen as a definite plus for your application.

Be Conscientious Regarding the Application Form

First you need to get a copy of the appropriate application form. Do this if you are even the slightest bit interested in becoming a judge, and then review and discuss it with other people who have experience in the process. Application forms can be quite complicated and sophisticated, and they should not be filled out and returned without quite a bit of thought and effort. So give yourself the time you need and the benefit of counsel from others who have insights so that you can avoid the pitfalls of emphasizing philosophical points that are in conflict with the appointing authority or forgetting to mention one of your attributes. Once you obtain the correct form and review what's needed—on your own and with knowledgeable others—do your best with it and then follow the suggestions offered below.

Maintain Honesty

Remember throughout your application to be honest and forthright about any negative items or character traits that might be disclosed in background investigations. This would include any citations for professional misconduct, traffic violations, allegations of domestic violence, or other negatives of that kind. You can and should put all of these matters in their "best light," but if you are seen as concealing any of your problem areas, you can probably forget about being appointed to any judicial office.

Have Multiple People Assess Your Draft

Submit drafts of your finished application to people whom you respect and who will keep your confidences. These efforts cannot help but increase your chances of success. Not only will your reviewers give you substantive suggestions, but they will serve as proofreaders as well. And all the details—especially including grammar, spelling, and punctuation—are important.

Leave Humor Aside

One of the judges on our court tells the story that when his former law partner filled out a questionnaire about the judge's appointment, the partner included numerous compliments, but ended by remarking, "But he doesn't know how to go to his left." The concluding statement was meant to be a humorous comment about my friend's inability to drive to his left while playing basketball. But unfortunately that comment resulted in concern among numbers of liberal-leaning confidants of the governor about the applicant's sensitivity to political issues. The lesson in this story is that the judicial application is a serious process that basically has no room for humor.

Get Letters of Recommendation from Respectable People

Letters of recommendation can be of considerable importance. Therefore, be sure to request them from people whom the appointing authority will respect. These people can include local politicians, judges, business and religious leaders, union officials, and others in positions of admirable responsibility. Presidents and governors want to appoint judges who will reflect well upon them years after they have left office, and thus they will respond favorably to people from all walks of life who have positions of respect and acceptance in the community.

Request each letter by calling the selected people and personally asking if they would agree to write on your behalf. Then carefully gage the response. You do not want people to write letters for you *unless they are truly enthusiastic about your candidacy.* If you have many letters that "damn you with faint praise," or, even worse, are accompanied by a yellow "post-it" saying to take this recommendation with a "grain of salt," it can be lethal for your appointment.

The judicial appointment application might sound like a daunting task. Certainly, the process should be pursued with great attention and meticulousness. But if you take it seriously and carefully, and heed the above pointers, you should feel confident by the time you submit your application. Moreover, you will have the peace of mind that you did your very best job. Now the rest will be in the appointing authority's hands. So you should put it aside and go on with your business, because often this process can take a frustratingly long time.

Campaign Effectively

With regard to winning a judicial seat by election, many of the issues outlined in this section on becoming a judge will apply. But in addition, you will have to be prepared to spend a fair amount of money—yours or somebody else's—and time. Probably the most important thing you can spend your money on (after getting qualified for the ballot) is a ballot statement, which is published in the election information distributed by your state elections commission—if, indeed, your state commission uses that protocol. Secondly, short brochures about your qualifications will also help, with emphasis on your ties to law enforcement groups. If you know politicians who have groups of precinct walkers who would agree to distribute your brochures along with theirs, that would be a huge plus. You will also want to speak with as many local groups as possible, and attend their functions.

But remember, you will be governed in your election campaign by the same ethical standards as a judge. That means, among other things, that you cannot promise "more convictions" or "longer sentences for criminals" or "more defense verdicts in civil cases," or anything similar. If you do that, you will probably lose your seat before you are even sworn in to fill it. For more on judicial ethics, see the section that begins below.

Hopefully these recommendations will increase the chances that you will be appointed or elected to the bench. But even if you are not successful in that effort, following these recommendations almost certainly will increase the success, satisfaction, and enjoyment of your professional and personal life. So, one way or the other, you will certainly come out ahead.

A DISCUSSION OF JUDICIAL ETHICS

Judicial ethics are a critically important area to consider as you make a final decision on whether or not to pursue a judicial career. The weight of ethical standards that is placed upon and expected of judges is significant. It is hard to believe that anyone would undertake the duties and responsibilities of a judge while also harboring the advance desire to commit some kind of ethical violations or involve herself in any kind of ethical improprieties. This is particularly true since judges come from a caring profession that routinely donates millions of dollars every year, in money and time, to providing legal representation to people who could otherwise not afford it.

Put simply, I am proud of the legal profession. As a result, I personally do not tell or even laugh at lawyer jokes because I believe they demean our profession. And as the foremost representatives of the legal profession, I assure you that judges expressly do *not* abide by the credo, "On even days we are to be arbitrary, and on the odd days capricious."

So why do we hear with surprising frequency that judges are involved with ethical problems? In my view, the answer to that question is that ethical issues and rules are all-pervasive and sometimes difficult to spot, and life sometimes can be complicated beyond imagination. Of course, although we all try to take steps to conceal this fact, judges actually are human too: Sometimes they make mistakes and sometimes they even violate the law. Now obviously some ethical mandates are straightforward, such as not issuing rulings based upon friendship or a desire for one side of an argument to prevail. Clearly, a judge is not allowed to "fix" traffic tickets for friends or in exchange for the receipt of "special favors." And judges are expected never to solicit donations for their reelection campaigns from lawyers who are trying their cases before them, nor can they give out gift coupons for gasoline or coffee to potential voters,[10] or make any public comments that could be construed as favoring any particular non-judicial candidates in an election campaign.

But other ethical violations are not so obvious. And some actions that would seem to be violations as a practical matter simply are not. For example, how could a judge from Iowa ever sit on a criminal case entitled *People of the State of Iowa v. John Jones*? Could not the judge technically be considered a party to the lawsuit? So sometimes ethical questions can be complex or even obtuse and difficult to discern.

The Canons of Ethics

Today, many omissions and commissions of judicial officers are regulated by various canons of ethics. The American Bar Association (ABA) has promulgated a series of five canons as a model code of judicial conduct, and every one of our fifty states has its own canons as well, many of which have adopted those of the ABA in whole or in major part. Judge David Rothman of the Los Angeles Superior Court explained the canons in this way: "The Code of Judicial Ethics . . . represents an attempt by those who sit in judgment of the lives of others to set out the 'moral principles' and 'values' governing their solemn task. It is not just a set of rules. It embodies those principles that our system of justice articulates as essential ingredients to preserve the rule of law."[11]

In most jurisdictions, the canons apply to all people who occupy any type of judicial office or who carry out judicial functions at all, whether they are full-time or part-time judges, magistrates, commissioners, justices of the peace, special masters, or referees. They even often apply to candidates who are simply running for a judicial office.

In the *federal* system, censures for improprieties of trial judges can come from the courts of appeal, but anything more severe must come from Congress in formal impeachment hearings. In most *state* jurisdictions, most allegations of ethical lapses by judges are brought by specific state administrative agencies and can result in sanctions. Those sanctions can include private or public admonishments, public censure, and even suspension or removal from office. In fact, between 1980 and the end of 2005, approximately 336 state judges were removed from office nationwide. In addition, 12 judges were removed from office in 2006; 11 resigned or retired in lieu of discipline pursuant to agreements with judicial commissions that were made public; 1 judge was required to retire; and an additional 116 judges were publicly sanctioned for their ethical misconduct.[12] In this regard, however, it is critical to keep in mind the distinction between legal errors (which can be corrected on appeal) and ethical transgressions, the latter of which are basically violations of a group of moral principles or set of values. Only ethical violations can subject a judge to disciplinary sanctions.

The canons of ethics, by their terms, address matters that help judges to uphold the integrity and independence of the judiciary, to avoid improprieties— and even the *appearance* of improprieties—and to help us to perform our duties impartially and diligently. They also require judges in their private lives to act in a manner that minimizes the risk of conflicts with their judicial obligations, and otherwise to reduce the possibility of bringing discredit upon their offices. Accordingly, we now have many rules strictly limiting and putting prohibitions upon judges' abilities to accept gifts, which include the receipt of honoraria for speaking appearances. Judges are also prohibited from communicating with attorneys or parties about their cases without all other parties' being present, and from failing to acknowledge, support, and uphold the constitutional and statutory rights of all people who appear before them in court. Judges must recuse themselves in appropriate circumstances and make appropriate and timely disclosures about personal things that might even appear to affect their impartiality. For example, judges are forbidden to act without proper authority, particularly with regard to the exercising of their contempt powers; to make improper comments involving sexual conduct or other demeaning comments about or in the presence of court staff or others; and to fail to discharge their judicial or administrative duties appropriately and without inappropriate delay. In addition, most state judicial advisory committees recommend that a judge recuse herself from cases being handled by an attorney who is running against that judge in the next election. But the judges have no duty to recuse themselves in response to threatening telephone messages, because that would allow people to manipulate the system.

Another thing for which judges are sometimes disciplined is the mistreating or disparaging of attorneys or parties, particularly those parties who are not represented by attorneys. Further examples representative of this problem are public statements by judges saying that an attorney should have learned this or that in law school, telling an attorney who was born in Ecuador that he should "lose" his accent, and ordering an attorney to confess her mistakes to the jury. Disciplinary action can also be launched against a judge for the mistreatment of court staff. In fact, virtually any time judges engage in sarcastic, disparaging, belittling, or discourteous remarks on or off the bench, they can be considered to have committed an ethical impropriety. (In other words, I am proud to say that anyone on the bench acting like television's "Judge Judy" would be quickly vulnerable to ethical investigation and discipline in the real world. What a great thing it is to be involved in a profession that takes ethical issues so seriously!)

Just like defendants in the criminal justice system, judges who are found to have misled the disciplinary commission that is involved in the investigation of their conduct, or who have previously been disciplined for other inappropriate conduct, will see those matters considered to be factors in aggravation that could subject them to additional or more severe discipline. Similarly, if judges engage in conduct that demeans judicial proceedings, even if they are acting in good faith, they would be subject to discipline. For example, on one occasion a judge was disciplined for telling prospective jurors that if they harbored a racial bias but did not wish to admit it, they had permission to lie and to make up some other reason to be excused from jury service. A judge condoning a violation of the law by directing jurors to violate their oath is a sanctionable act, regardless of the judge's beliefs or intent.

Subtle Ethical Quandaries and Challenges

Most of the above-discussed ethical issues probably seem straightforward and logical. But some of the situations that judges face in both their professional and their personal lives are simply not that clear. In fact, there are entire books written to provide guidance for judges in ethical matters—not just regarding disciplinary matters, but to advise and counsel judges about complex and subtle issues.[13] For example, judges are frequently requested to write letters of recommendation for people seeking untold numbers of positions. When is such a letter appropriate, and when is it not? What do you think?

Well, different states treat these matters differently, so prudent judges simply must become familiar with the ethical canons of their particular jurisdictions. But in most of them it usually is considered appropriate for judges to write letters of recommendation for people who are seeking *judicial* positions, or even to endorse candidates who are running for them.[14] In contrast, it is not appropriate to write letters for people seeking any non-judicial positions. Accordingly, it would not be appropriate for a judge to write a letter of recommendation on behalf of an attorney applying for a life insurance policy, or for or against a person involved in a disciplinary proceeding, or for a person a judge knows who is applying for an alien labor certification.[15] On the other hand, most jurisdictions consider it appropriate to write letters of recommendation for college applicants or for someone who is being considered for an award, as long as the judge actually knows the person and the letter is not simply a character reference.

With regard to various administrative proceedings or investigations, most states allow judges to submit information and conclusions, but only if *expressly* requested by the administrative organization itself.[16] Similarly, it is inappropriate for judges *voluntarily* to testify at any court proceedings, except when they are parties thereto, and they can do so only if they receive a court subpoena *requiring* their appearance.[17]

But once again, it should be stressed that each jurisdiction makes its own rulings. So in Maryland a judge may serve as a director of a non-profit corporation formed to solicit funds from the community to provide incentives for drug court participants, as long as the judge's participation does not itself involve active or even passive fundraising activity. But in Colorado whether a judge may sit on a board of directors of a homeowners' association will be determined on a case by case basis. In New York a judge may not establish a legal defense fund to pay his own legal expenses for allegations of his ethical improprieties. In Arkansas a judge may not write a letter on behalf of his lifelong friend—at the request of the friend's attorney—to a judge who is sentencing that friend. Yet in Kentucky a judge may write a letter urging members of the bar to donate some time to pro bono work. And in Kansas a judge may attend open houses sponsored by law firms if they are open to practicing attorneys and friends of the firm, but she may not accept an invitation from a law firm to play a complimentary round of golf.[18] When it comes down to reality, it is overwhelming to think about all of the ethical decisions that have been made in each locale.

In summary, the common thread I find that links most of these ethical rules together is the desire to maintain the respect, dignity, and integrity of the judiciary. Accordingly, the main intention is to keep judges from using their positions to promote any particular cause except justice. This last issue can bring up some sensitive situations for judges, because as a natural result of the respect for a judge's neutral and authoritative position in society, many people will try to use that respect for their own goals. So, with the exception of assessing those seeking to obtain judicial positions and the fairly neutral act of recommending students to be accepted to different schools, judges are usually not allowed to use their offices to further their own or other people's private goals.

The Disallowance of Charity Fundraising

Continuing our discussion of judicial ethics, let us look at something that frustrates a lot of people. Judges are not ethically allowed in most jurisdictions to use their names or positions to raise money for any cause whatsoever, except judicial elections. That means that judges cannot even take part in boosting certain charities that seem inarguably noble. Okay, most people understand that judges should not be involved in raising money for partisan elections (even if the candidate happens to be the judge's spouse), but why cannot a judge "help society" by raising money for a non-partisan and humanitarian effort? There are numbers of worthy causes in the world, from boys and girls clubs to feeding the hungry, and from disaster relief to saving the environment. The answer is the same as the one provided in previous discussions: Judges must use their positions only to promote justice and not to further their own or other people's goals. What some people see as philanthropic others see as political—it is simply not possible to draw any meaningful line separating one from the other. If you think about it, for good reason it is seen as unfair for judges to use the dignity of their positions to give assistance for "your" noble project at the expense of "mine." Thus, the line has been drawn, and it disallows judges from using the prestige of their offices to raise money for anything except judicial elections. In my view, this is rightly so.

The Effects on Personal Details and Professional Practice

The rules of judicial ethics also can extend far into judges' personal lives. In most jurisdictions, judges must disclose their personal assets, including real property ownership, stocks, and securities holdings every year, as well as those of their spouses, so that the public at large can be assured that judges are not personally profiting by the decisions they make on the bench. In addition, of course, if judges have an ownership interest of more than a small amount—frequently set at $1,500—in one of the litigants in a case before them, they must recuse themselves from the case. And even smaller amounts must formally be disclosed to the parties at the earliest opportunity.

Further, judges in most jurisdictions are prohibited from practicing law in any fashion. Hopefully the reason for that rule is obvious. Aside from the problem of judges' being seen as advocates for a particular party or cause, or using the prestige of their positions to get favorable treatment for their clients, if a person gets a legal opinion from a practicing judge, that person seemingly would be justified in relying upon it as established law. Why? "Because a judge said so." That circumstance would simply be inconsistent with a fair, neutral, and impartial judiciary, as well as the orderly administration of justice.

But the previously discussed situation can bring some inherent problems. Since judges are professionals in the law and judges are not precluded from having friends, often those friends or other acquaintances will seek legal advice from judges as a favor. What are judges to do when their friends are in need and seek such advice? It can be awkward, but the only thing that judges can do is listen and sympathize as much as they can, remind their friends that judges are not allowed to practice law, and then recommend strongly that their friends get an attorney to advise them.

Of course, there can be some exceptions to those rules. For example, if the advice being requested is only a description of which government agency might have jurisdiction over the friend's problem, a judge can comment. If the question can be answered with an explanation of the jurisdictional limits between a small claims or limited jurisdictional court, or what procedure one should follow to file some documents in court, or even other procedural information that anyone could learn from the clerk's office, a judge can give some directions. But judges must always be scrupulously careful not to give legal advice. For example, if judges are being asked how to file an appeal from a trial court judgment, they could reasonably respond. But if judges give information about the time limits within which the appeal must be filed, that would be legal advice and is therefore prohibited. Why? Because if the person relied upon that advice and it was incorrect, the person would have a reasonable argument that she relied upon a judge, so the information must have been correct and her late filing should be excused.

During the time I was a federal prosecutor in Los Angeles in the mid-1970s, it was commonplace for bailiffs and other staff members to run errands for the judges. A judge would routinely have a staff member shop for a present for the judge's family member; get the judge's shoes shined, or car washed and filled up with gas; balance the judge's personal checkbook; or even send out invitations for an upcoming private party at the judge's house. But those days are over, and judges today that give these tasks even to supposedly willing staff members frequently face charges of ethical improprieties.

Similarly, most attorneys who practiced in those days had their "horror stories" about things that some judges routinely said or did without any ethical repercussions whatsoever. On one occasion, I was in federal court for a sentencing hearing for two female defendants of Mexican descent who were being held in custody. When the time came, the judge looked at his bailiff and said, "Well, bring in the Taco Bells." On another occasion I personally saw that same judge looking at a *Playboy* magazine while on the bench. Fortunately, if those things were to happen today, in most jurisdictions the judge would quickly be held accountable. Since the time of those incidents, the American Bar Association has promulgated those canons discussed on page 239, and they have made a sizeable difference.

It is also considered to be unethical for judges to use their positions to obtain special treatment for themselves. For example, judges are not allowed to let the police know about their position when stopped for traffic violations, or to make dinner reservations when using their title as a judge, because each of those instances would convey the expectation that a judge expects to receive some form of extra consideration. In addition, any violations of the law, such as driving under the influence of alcohol or other drugs, spousal abuse, income tax violations, or the failure to pay outstanding traffic tickets, are considered to be ethical improprieties.

Judges know when they seek the office that in doing so they are voluntarily giving up some of their personal freedoms. And rightfully so. Most of the time the reasons for the rules governing judges' behavior are apparent and appropriate. Consider that judges in most jurisdictions are prohibited from obtaining any government property for personal use whatsoever. Even if property is no longer needed and is being discarded, neither judges nor, in most jurisdictions, any other government employees are allowed to remove it from the trashcans and take it home. Similarly if property is being auctioned off, judges are not allowed even to bid on it. But upon reflection, the reasons for those rules become obvious. Since judges and other public employees are in a position to decide what public property is "excess" and what is not, there can be a temptation to discard even useful items, which the judges could then obtain for a cost below fair value or even for free. It is far better to draw a clear line and assure the public in general that its interests are being protected.

And not only do ethical canons require judges to refrain from certain conduct, but they can also require judges affirmatively to take certain actions. For example, in many jurisdictions judges are ethically *required* to report attorneys and even themselves to the appropriate ethical watchdog agencies if either is involved, or even being investigated for involvement in, certain forms of misconduct.

It is also important to understand that not only do these watchdog organizations seek to discipline judges, but many of them are also there to provide help to them as well. For example, since some of these ethical issues can pose difficult problems, most jurisdictions have established telephone hotlines for judges to call for advice and other assistance—and that not only includes ethical conduct, but it also includes help with drug and alcohol dependency, depression and similar problems.[19]

Of course, not all acts that reduce the respect of the judiciary and the judicial process can be the subject of a formal ethical inquiry. If a judge takes the bench with his robes open or with an open collar and no tie, or if she has the sleeves of her robe casually rolled up, those actions might tend to demean the integrity of the bench, but there would probably be no formal action taken against that judge. In addition, I have personally formed the opinion that it is simply not appropriate for a judge speaking in public to use even the most mundane swear words like "hell" or "damn," not because in this day and age those words actually offend many people, but because people are simply disappointed in judges when they "lower themselves" by using that form of language. There are and should be limits to *formal* controls over judges' actions, but we should be aware of and abide by the informal as well.

So as a bottom line, the ethical rules are based upon attempts to assure the public that judges are and remain fair, neutral, and impartial, and to safeguard the dignity and integrity of our System of Justice. That means that if there would be even the appearance of impropriety in one of your actions, do not do it. Or if you would be embarrassed to read about any of your actions on the front page of your local newspaper, rethink what you are about to do. In other words, show anyone concerned that in all of your actions, you are a professional and worthy of being called "The Honorable." In addition, you will also yourself be judged not only by what you say, but also by what you write in your e-mail messages. Along those lines, remember that the "e" in e-mail stands for "evidence," because it will never go away.

Without question, it is difficult to live up to all of these standards. But as Thomas Jefferson said, "When a man assumes a public trust, he should consider himself as public property." Does that mean that this mandate will intrude to some degree upon your personal freedoms? Without question the answer is yes. But for the respect of the judiciary, for the cause of people's believing that they are receiving justice from a fair and neutral magistrate, and for the honor of serving in this capacity, I say that the intrusion is a truly small price to pay.

As we have discussed, many formal efforts are appropriately being taken around the country to convince the public that judges are being held to the high standards that the public should expect. I am proud to say that judges are increasingly diligent in their attempts to be worthy of those high expectations. As a result, even though the actions of judges are sometimes held up for minute or even petty scrutiny, overall I believe that this is a good thing, and that we are passing the test.

CONCLUSION

We have discussed some reasons why you would, or would not, want to become a judge, and how you could do so. Many of the reasons for your pursuit of a judicial position would be personal. But many, such as whether you could perform within the ethical constraints of this high-visibility profession, would be practical as well. In the case that you are blessed to obtain a judicial position, I would like to point out to you some of the traits I have observed in some of the best and most effective judges. So please read on.

Chapter 9

The Attributes of
Good and Effective Judges

"The strength of your character
does not depend upon the weakness of others."
—Martin B. Weinberg, Esq., Newport Beach, California

Mark Twain once said, "Always do right. You will gratify some, and astound the rest." The job of a judge is meant for a person who strives to do what is right, and to do it for the right reasons. Judges are in a position to be respected, but not necessarily to be liked. In fact, I actually believe that if you hear people say things such as, "Everybody likes Judge Jones," Judge Jones is probably in some ways not doing his job. In truth, judges are there to do the right things under the facts and the law of the case, which often means that they are in the "dissatisfaction distribution" business. Accordingly, a judge's chambers and courtroom are not places for politics or egos, or for those who develop a case of what is called "robitis," which occurs when judges take themselves too seriously.

I think most judges want, in their own way, to be a part of the government envisioned by George Washington and described in his "Thanksgiving Proclamation," which was delivered in New York on October 3, 1789. They desire to help "to render our National Government a blessing to all the people by constantly being a Government of wise, just and constitutional laws, discreetly and faithfully executed and obeyed; . . . and generally to grant unto all mankind such a degree of temporal prosperity as He alone knows to be best." In other words, most judges want to be missionaries for the cause of justice.

But there is a contrary feeling, as symbolized by British television personalities David Frost and Anthony Jay, who were once quoted as saying, "This is what is to be remembered about the law: Beneath that cold, harsh, impersonal exterior there beats a cold, harsh, impersonal heart."[1] Unfortunately, that comment all too often can be true; the System of Justice *can* sometimes be cold, impersonal, and harsh. Even people who are remorseful and want to comply with their obligations can get beaten up by our System of Justice. As such, it is up to the judges to take each case and decision seriously, to listen, and to be thoughtful, decisive, and fair. We also must explain our decisions and blend the necessity of individual responsibility with appropriate compassion.

To counteract the perception of Frost and Jay, judges must develop the ability to be calm and understanding under all circumstances. As stated frequently in these pages, judges are the only ones who can never lose their tempers. They must also learn where to look for answers and how to be educable. Then they will be good and effective judges. This chapter further elaborates on the qualities and practices of the best judges. It discusses real-life responsibilities that these servants of justice always bear in mind, as well as the winning character traits and most effective courtroom approaches that they have mastered.

BASIC RESPONSIBILITIES THE BEST JUDGES BEAR IN MIND

Judges are historically recognized as keepers of wisdom. But preliminarily, I must acknowledge that some of the wisdom of judges is a façade. By law, judges must wear a judicial robe, which sets them apart from others; their chairs are to be elevated above all others in the courtroom; and they are to be addressed with a title of respect, such as "Your Honor." To this I add the old, humorous story that there are three traits that good judges should possess: patience, so that they can appear to be listening; gray hair, so that they can appear to be wise; and hemorrhoids, in order to generate that look of concern. These ceremonial and visual elements are meant to generate respect and standing so that judges can do their jobs. In effect, they cloak judges in an aura of wisdom and invincibility.

But obviously, there is a great deal more to being a judge—and a good and effective judge at that. In fact, in my view, in order to live up to our responsibilities, judges are obligated to carry out the following six general duties:

1. To provide justice under the facts and the law, using common sense and all the wisdom that they can command.

2. To provide the appearance of justice, so that both the litigants and their counsel believe that they are receiving justice.

3. To provide justice as expeditiously as possible. In so many ways, justice delayed really can become justice denied.

4. To keep expenses under control as much as possible for both the litigants and the public in general.

5. To live a public and personal life within the ethics of the profession, which means that judges must at all times be true to their word and otherwise uphold the integrity of the judiciary.

6. To help to educate the public about our system of government and its Judicial Branch, and to strive to make improvements in our government when necessary.

The best judges always keep these responsibilities in mind. They are governed by them in every court case and promote them at every event. But of course, in carrying out these duties, judges need all of the assistance society can provide them.

Then there are additional guidelines that the best judges also keep in mind. The System of Justice must work to keep the marketplace of ideas open, so that our society can continue to be vibrant and successful. That means confirming that minority peoples and viewpoints are appropriately protected, and that just causes are heard fully and on their merits. The finest of judges will always be mindful of this as well.

In fact, if you think about it, the Judicial Branch of Government is the only one designed to protect the rights and interests of people, positions, and viewpoints that are in the minority—despite political powerlessness and even unpopularity at times. The Executive and Legislative Branches of Government always tend to favor those in the majority, because that is where the votes are found. But for the court system to work, justice must be available and procured for everyone, no matter what the parties' religion, gender, race or background, or whether they are politically or economically weak or strong. This goal is so fundamental to our System of Justice that the words "Equal Justice Under Law" are carved in marble above the entrance of the United States Supreme Court Building in Washington, DC.

So how can the goal of true justice be successfully pursued? Not by judges' doing what they individually happen to think is best, because that can be fickle, and it provides almost no consistency or foreseeability. Instead, justice must be based upon the Rule of Law, which comes from our federal and state constitutions and statutes. Why is this so important? Because this is the only approach that protects all of us. People must understand that circumstances can change, and that any of us can be placed in a minority position at any moment, and thus in need of protection from the majority.

For example, it was President Franklin D. Roosevelt, whom I happen to admire, who gave us the following inspirational words, which have since then been carved into the granite blocks at the FDR Memorial in Washington, DC: "We must scrupulously guard the civil rights and civil liberties of all citizens, whatever their background. We must remember that any oppression, any injustice, any hatred, is a wedge designed to attack our civilization." Those are lofty words, yet they were spoken by the same man who himself ordered thousands of Japanese-Americans into "relocation camps" during the emotional days that followed the bombing of Pearl Harbor and the beginning of World War II. We need institutions to protect us against the rule of individual people, no matter who they may be or what exalted doctrines they happen to articulate. That is why we must continue to abide by one of our founding principles and be a "Nation of Laws, not of Men." A neutral, effective, and independent judiciary is our primary hope that this Rule of Law instead of the rule of men may continue. On this, all judges must be firm.

For those of us old enough to remember, back in the 1950s, Walt Disney's episodes of *Davy Crockett,* starring Fess Parker, took the country by storm. In those shows, at least as Disney would have us believe, Davy's credo that governed his actions was, "Be Sure You're Right, Then Go Ahead." As corny as it may seem, I think this is the credo judges should follow. We are uniquely positioned to put this approach into action. Be patient, learn the facts, and research the applicable law until you are in a position to understand it. Then, once you are sure you are right, and the result is consistent with your instincts, go ahead and issue your ruling, regardless of what the political consequences might be. It is not a judge's job to be politically correct, or even to be popular; it is a judge's job to do justice under the Rule of Law.

ADMIRABLE TRAITS THE BEST JUDGES DISPLAY

Allow me to set forth some views and perceptions about the attributes of good and effective judges as they attempt to live up to the ideals just expressed. I base these opinions and observations upon my years of experience on the bench and as an attorney. Of course, these are just my own views, but it would surprise me if they were not shared by an overwhelming majority of my colleagues.

Professionalism

Appearances and attitudes count, and that goes from how you present yourself to what you put on your desk. Many people would be surprised at the numbers of ways that the impartiality of judges can be questioned by attorneys and their clients. For example, did you ever think you could make a negative impression based on the type of law magazine you have on your desk? If a plaintiff's attorney in a civil case happens to see a magazine on your desk that is published by the defense bar, it will often be taken as a cause for concern. Of course, judges cannot control who sends them what things in the mail. And the truth is that you would probably have another similar magazine somewhere on your desk that was published by the plaintiffs' bar. But most of the time people react quickly and make snap judgements. That is not to say that judges should stop accepting mail, but they should be aware of the potential problem area caused by what is visible on their desks and at least keep certain items out of sight.

Similarly, if a judge asks a question of a witness simply because the subject is personally interesting that could be seen as inappropriately enhancing the credibility of the witness in the eyes of the jury. Or if a judge smiles more freely at one party for any reason whatsoever, the other side will certainly read something negative into the reaction. Of course, it is very difficult to anticipate all of the ways that a judge could unintentionally offend or concern a party, and we simply cannot cover all those ways here. But we can safely say that the best judges always do their best to maintain a professional appearance and attitude. That includes, among other things, treating all parties decently and equally, keeping visible office space tidy and impartial, and displaying only appropriate emotional reactions.

Authenticity

It is okay to be yourself. In this book, we have gone through lots of things that make it sound like judges must always be careful of what they do and say, never lose their tempers, and the like. This makes it sound like being a judge is not a job for a human being. Well, being a good and effective judge means that you try to be careful about all of those things while not taking yourself too seriously, but it does not mean that you cannot be yourself. It has taken me quite a few years to learn that fact, but it is true. Judges have a lot going for them; otherwise they would not have obtained a judicial position in the first place. You will be—or are—the same. So you should not try to be something you are not; just try on the bench to be the best "you" that you can be, all the while being guided by the ideals and ethical standards we have discussed.

So, *at the appropriate times,* it is okay to use humor, if it comes naturally to your personality and will not demean the present atmosphere of the courtroom. Or, if you feel it is called for, you might speak firmly to a defendant, witness, or party who is acting inappropriately—as long as you never lose control of yourself. Perhaps you will get off the bench and congratulate a defendant in a report-back situation who is doing especially well on her drug treatment program, or give condolences to a victim who has suffered a big loss and is still in need of comfort from someone in authority, as long as that would not be seen by the parties as taking sides in a dispute. You might even allow yourself to show pain in some of those truly human tragedies that are unfolding in your courtroom.

This is not to say that judges should become all "touchy feely," because, in practice, these circumstances are rare. But they do arise, and when they do, you *can* respond in a way that fits your personal style. Judges often deal with intensely human situations, and it is okay for them to show (in appropriate ways) that they are human too. This view was further brought home to me when, in preparation for writing this book, I requested that some court staff members voluntarily give me their thoughts about things judges did or did not do that were appreciated. One of the court processing specialists responded to me as follows:

> I think it is awesome when I happen to be in a courtroom, and the Judge is sentencing someone, and the Judge gives that person advice or encour-

agement. It rids me of the notion that all Judges are just mean machines out to crush all criminals. I know Judges must get angry sometimes, and they hear the same old excuses day in and day out, but, when I hear those words from the Judges, it just reminds me that I should not be biased when helping a customer at the window, regardless of what they are charged with. It reminds me to treat them the way I would want to be treated.

Punctuality

Years ago, my father and I sang together in a church choir, and we had a director who never started our rehearsals on time. When my father recommended to him that he start the rehearsal at exactly the time that he said he would start, the director's response was that he really could not, because only half of the choir members were there on time. So Dad explained that if the director would start on time, people would get the message and would be there on time in the future. The director took his advice. Not only did it work but, after just a few rehearsals, it also resulted in our being able to end the rehearsals on time as well, which everyone appreciated.

This lesson applies to our courts. Judges should make particular efforts to start and end when they say they will. If, as a judge, you make it a point to be punctual, things will mostly work quite well. And everyone, including your staff and the attorneys, will be appreciative.

Good Listening Skills

Listening is the art and ability to understand and respond effectively to oral communication. It is not easy, and in fact it sometimes is not a natural thing to do. But the best judges have mastered the skills of listening. Just remember that it is hard to learn when you are talking, so good and effective judges minimize distractions, maintain their attentiveness, and develop their listening skills as a habit. In other words, the opposite of talking is not waiting to talk, and pretending to listen is not the same thing as listening.

Also keep in mind, as we have said throughout this book, that justice is both a result as well as a process. When people leave a courtroom, particularly those who were not successful in their legal pursuits, they at least want to feel that they have been able to explain their position. A judge who listens intently will make the parties feel heard and, at a minimum, somewhat satisfied. Judges must also understand that their own efforts to listen well can be highly therapeutic for certain parties.

Courtesy

Good and effective judges are courteous to all. That does not mean they are "pushovers" or that they are not in control. It means that they have established a calm and a "judicial eloquence" that converts the courtroom into a temple of justice.

Judges are seen as having enormous power, but good and effective judges underplay it. Not only does being courteous to all litigants, attorneys, witnesses, jurors, and staff make a courtroom a much more pleasant place in which to be, but also people will then be able to focus better upon the matters at hand. That, in turn, allows the judges to do their jobs better. Thus, justice is served.

Patience

The demeanor of the bench officer almost always controls the tension level in the courtroom. Therefore, judges should be understanding of all of the various people that come into their courtrooms. Many of those people can be under a great deal of stress, and if a judge is irritated on top of that, the chance of a just result's being obtained is seriously diminished.

In addition, to be effective, judges must also learn to be patient in their decision-making. One thing that keeps me mindful of that goal is the old saying, "There is nothing as embarrassing as jumping to a conclusion that isn't there." I recommend that you keep that saying in mind as well.

Truly adept judges are also patient with non-English speakers. Let us face it, English is a difficult language. The court environment is stressful enough as it is. Now imagine a person who does not have a good command of English trying to communicate effectively in a language in which "slim chance" and "fat chance" mean the same thing, but "wise man" and "wise guy" are opposites. It is hard to be proficient in a language in which there is no egg in an eggplant, no ham in a hamburger, and neither a pine nor an apple in a pineapple! So try to put yourself in the place of litigants who do not speak or understand English well. This really can be a "due process of law" issue, because people can lose their homes, cars, jobs, and even their children in court without ever understanding why. Therefore, judges should be aware of the difficulties of our language and patient with people who are struggling with them.

Self-Trust

If a tentative decision conflicts with your instincts, would you give the decision some further thought? If so, you—like the most conscientious judges—trust yourself and your instincts. That does not mean that the best judges never make a decision or ruling that conflicts with their instincts. But they consider their feelings of discomfort to be a "red flag" indicating that the contemplated decision may not be appropriate.

Of course, "gut feelings" must be balanced with updated information. So it is important for judges to keep their legal instincts well honed by being familiar with the law cited to them on each case and being current on the advance sheets of recent cases. But with education and experience comes confidence in oneself, and thus the most effective judges know that their inner voice is always worth listening to.

Consistency Without Dogmatism

In their hearts, litigants and their counsel really want consistency and fairness, and nothing more. They should be able legitimately to formulate the belief and expectation that if they are right on a certain point, and they have the good fortune to be in your court, they will prevail on that point. Accordingly, a good and effective judge will simply convey the question to counsel, "Tell me why, as a matter of law, I should rule in your favor," or "Tell me why, as a matter of law, I should deny the opposing party's motion. Point me to the evidence and the law." Then that judge listens and waits to be reminded or even educated on what the law is, instead of dogmatically showing off how smart and learned he is. Not only will the parties be more respectful of the judge, but also legal mistakes will be less likely to occur.

Time Management and Verbal Control

Shakespeare's Hamlet said, "But break, my heart, for I must hold my tongue."[2] Of course, Hamlet was not stating this for the same reasons as a trial court judge might. But the sentiment works well in this context. As difficult as it can be, judges must learn to walk the fine line between being quiet and allowing attorneys to try their own cases on the one hand, and maintaining control in their courtroom and moving the cases along at a reasonable pace on the other hand.

"Do we really need to go on this long with this witness?" "Is this issue really so important?" These are questions that judges must continually ask themselves. A good and effective judge will learn how politely to refocus a rambling witness or attorney, for example, and keep the proceedings going forward. But otherwise, as long as the trial is moving along at a pace consistent with a fair trial on each side, good judges will normally hold their tongues and not interfere with the attorneys as they present their cases. Attorneys have spent lots of time preparing their cases for trial, and judges should let them use their knowledge and material to the best of their abilities, even though it is in the judges' nature as former attorneys to intercede.

Humility

Good and effective judges are aware of their own biases. Human beings, including judges, naturally have prejudices. That is not a crime, but it is something to be aware of. For example, one of my biases is that I tend naturally to distrust people who talk quickly. Being aware of this bias, I try not to let it sway my judicial decisions.

If judges feel that they cannot overcome their biases on particular matters, they should recuse themselves from cases that would be affected by those biases. It is more respectable to remove yourself from a situation than falsely to make it appear that a bias is not there. You do not want that worry to burden your conscience.

Broad-Range Vision

Good and effective judges see the forest as well as the trees. I heard a story once that illustrates this trait—or a lack thereof. In response to a rumor at a manufacturing plant that a particular worker was pilfering some equipment, the plant put on an extra security detail to watch him. Every evening the security officers watched while the man pushed a wheelbarrow full of sawdust waste out the gates of the plant. Each time the security personnel sifted carefully through the sawdust to try to determine what the man was taking, but always without results. Finally, long after the man had retired, one of the security personnel saw the former suspect at a bar, and struck up a conversation with him. After a few drinks the security guard broke down and revealed that they knew the man was stealing something, but they could not figure out what it was. The man laughed and said, "It was wheelbarrows."

Judges should always try to be cognizant of what is really going on in their courtroom. In other words, hopefully they will see the wheelbarrows instead of just the sawdust. There once was an unusual case involving an Asian woman who was charged with the misdemeanor battery of her husband. It seems that an American man had met her, divorced his first wife, and then married the woman under discussion. Thereafter, he treated her as a virtual slave, making her paint houses all day long, while keeping the money for himself. One day she had had enough and slapped him, which gave rise to the battery charge. The district attorney wanted her to plead guilty to the charge and take anger management classes. But when the judge heard about what had really happened, he told her that her only problem was that she had not gotten angry long before this and convinced the prosecutor to dismiss the charges. So if judges can monitor the big picture in addition to the details, they are much more likely to make statements and decisions that achieve the right result.

Dignified Firmness

It is important for judges to establish rules in their own courtrooms and then enforce them with as much dignity and understanding as they can. Of course, all judges must generally insist that the rules of evidence be followed and that all attorneys talk to the judge instead of to each other. But judges also have their own pet peeves regarding things that happen in the courtroom, and they are entitled to address these as well. One of mine is when counsel sit or lean on the bar that separates the working part of the courtroom from the seats for the audience. Another is when counsel get so close to the jury that they "look down their gullets" during their opening statements or closing arguments. In the courtroom rules that I distribute before a case, I try to set forth a small number of "local" rules that will be followed so that everyone will be on the same page.

It is only fair to everyone that a judge put down his various rules in his own court's procedures. Then the most effective judges responsibly enforce their rules, at least within reason. Trial participants can adjust to the rules and then work effectively within them. Attorneys, like virtually everyone else in the world, get frustrated by *not* being informed what the rules are and by inconsistent enforcement.

Civility

Civility is more than just a word, and successful judges know that. They let it be known through their demeanor and even their words when necessary that they expect and demand that all participants in the courtroom will be civil and courteous to the staff, to the Court, to the witnesses, and to each other. In turn, the trial participants can expect the same thing from the judge. Of course, the best judges hold themselves as examples of the standards they expect and demand from others. So if you want to be a "civil" trial court judge, strive for people to discuss you like they did a well-known and respected trial attorney in my community, where people often remarked, "Those who laugh at lawyer jokes never knew Joe McNeil."

Decisiveness

The ability to "pull the trigger" is definitely an attribute of the good and effective judge. Study, preparation, contemplation, and extra thought are all good things, but sometimes a judge simply must get on with it and issue a ruling. For example, imagine a judge is in trial and there is an objection to a question that calls for speculation. It does not help anyone if the judge takes the matter under submission and announces his ruling next week. He must just rule! This can also be true with regard to more complicated matters.

Deliberation is certainly a good thing, but within a reasonable time a judge has to make a decision. As Judge Irving Younger used to say during some of his legal lectures, "Eventually a judge has to jump, and hope there is water in the pool." Decisiveness takes courage, inner strength, and self-trust. That is why it is an attribute of the *most effective* judges.

Humor

I have discussed the power of humor—when appropriate—a number of times throughout this book. Unlike television court dramas, real court proceedings can often be slow and even boring. Throwing in an occasional quip or light comment can truly be helpful in keeping the jury's attention and good spirits engaged.

Of course, the most important ingredient in a sense of humor is knowing when something would be funny. There are obviously numerous times when humor would simply not be appropriate, and one must be rigorously careful not to say anything that could be considered offensive. But as long as guidelines like these are honored, a little well-placed humor that flows from the bench can strike a proper balance, both maintaining the dignity of the proceedings and offering a bit of relief for everyone. And the jurors will thank you for it.

Flexibility

The most successful people know when to roll with the punches. Judges are no exception. The only thing that is predictable about what will happen in court is that it is not normally predictable. So good and effective judges understand that reality. They simply apply themselves to problems when they arise so they can respond to them and resolve them as best they can.

For example, there was a hearing in a criminal matter during which a court interpreter was sitting between two Spanish-speaking defendants. About forty-five minutes into the hearing, one of the defense counsel finally spoke up and said that his client was deaf in one ear and had not heard more than half of the interpreted testimony. I think everyone would agree that it would be hard to anticipate such a problem. Nevertheless, if problems are ignored in this sensitive business, these can be easy issues on appeal, and if not addressed, probably everything will have to be done over again. So instead, the best thing to do is to stop the proceedings, analyze the problem, get advice and agreement from counsel for a resolution, and confront the issue head on.

In the sample case discussed above, the judge immediately stopped the proceedings, verified on the record that the subject defendant could hear perfectly well out of the other ear, asked the interpreter to sit on the side of the defendant's good ear, and then asked the reporter to go back and read what had transpired so far with the assistance of the interpreter. All sides agreed to this procedure on the record, and after an hour's delay, the court went on to finish the hearing. The important thing is not to ignore the problems and hope they will go away, but instead to recognize and deal immediately and directly on the record with whatever unforeseen problems may be presented.

Respectfulness

There is no question that one of the highest qualities of effective judges is their ability to be conscious of and respectful toward people who are standing up for what they believe is right. Judges may agree or disagree with these litigants, but they know that all of those people deserve extra time, consideration, explanations, and respect. Many times judges are the representatives and spokespeople for society, and they must try to be sure that honest feelings and actions are treated with appropriate consideration and respect.

In addition, although judges deal with important issues almost every day, the best judges remember that each of the issues they address is important to somebody, and therefore worthy of a judge's care. An attorney once told me a story about arguing an important issue in an important case late in the afternoon. The judge made the comment, "Counsel, you have spoiled my glass of chardonnay with my wife for the evening," whereupon the attorney's client spoke into his ear, "My company is at stake, please keep fighting for me." Although the judge's comment seemingly was made out of weariness or even exasperation, hearing about it made me shudder. It simply lacks respect for the process.

We have contemplated a number of truly admirable general qualities that good and effective judges possess. These qualities have ranged from punctuality to patience, and from flexibility to firmness. The list of traits may seem a bit overwhelming to accomplish, but the truth is that these qualities develop more strongly over time and with diligence and experience. I am confident that you can rise to the occasion during courtroom procedures and be recognized as a top-notch judge.

STRATEGIES THE BEST JUDGES EMPLOY

Throughout many of the earlier chapters of this book, I have offered advice that I have collected and developed over my years as a judge. Sometimes the advice pertained to serving on a particular judicial calendar. At other times, it was geared toward a particular segment of the trial process, or even the development of a particular specialty. But below we have something a little different. I have selected just a few strategies generally practiced by the most effective judges, but they are not specific to any one calendar, pursuit, or stage of trial. Some repetition of material from earlier in the book does occur. But this section offers an easy-to-consult body of advice for people who want to improve their roles and reputations as judges. I hope you find it to be helpful.

Check Up on Yourself

We have discussed humility as one of the traits of a good and effective judge. This strategy is related to being humble and willing to critique one's own strengths and weaknesses. With some regularity, look at yourself from the point of view of a party, attorney, witness, or general observer who comes into your courtroom. Then go beyond that and read a transcript of one of your contested hearings. See if you live up to your own expectations. Are you the type of judge you think you are? Are your words as clear as you hoped they would be? Are your responses as respectful as you would like? Are your standards as high as you desire to set them? Sometimes this can be a shocking experience.

Another way to monitor your own strengths and weaknesses is to ask someone you respect to observe you while you are sitting on the bench. I expect that during the observation time you will be more attentive, professional, smart, and respectful, and that you will sit up a little straighter and even work a little harder than you normally would. Well, if that is the case, maybe you would find it productive to make believe that you are being observed by a professional and respected audience member each time you take the bench. Of course, in truth people actually are always watching you in such a way that you will want to be at your best, so I expect that you will find this advice useful.

Remember What It Was Like to Be a Practicing Attorney

Yes, what you are doing is important, and yes, it is important to maintain the sanctity of the Court. But as a fact of life, there are other important things going on in addition to what is happening in your own courtroom. Sometimes people do get stuck in traffic; sometimes minor, unforeseen emergencies do occur; sometimes appointments and other court appearances do run longer than expected. And it does not hurt to respond favorably to a "Rule One" request for a continuance, so that the attorneys can get paid before they commit to becoming the counsel of record on a criminal case.

In addition, always remember that since attorneys have nothing to sell but their time, either someone is paying for each appearance the attorneys make, or they are forced to work for free. Be aware and be thoughtful of that reality. For example, if you happen to be sick one day, do everything possible to have counsel and the parties notified in as timely a manner as possible so they do not appear in court without reason. And let it be known that attorneys are welcome to participate via speakerphone in your courtroom for the more routine appearances. This will reduce expenses and be of assistance to lots of people.

Also remember the stress that attorneys today have to face. Television law show character Perry Mason never had to wait for days or even hours for a courtroom to become available, but that happens regularly in real life and can cause client problems, witness availability problems, and economic problems for everybody. Sometimes those problems cannot be avoided, and judges should be understanding about them. I also try to keep in mind the story about an attorney who asked a judge if he could prepare the Order on a motion "so that my client will think I won." Of course, the answer was "No," but being an attorney can be a hard job filled with constantly stressful situations.

Finally, when I was a criminal defense attorney in the Navy, many times the factual situations were heavily weighted against my clients. Yet I *always* tried to do at least something to help them. On one occasion, I remember that all I was able to do was to help my client get his car out of impound. I believe most attorneys feel that way—they truly want to provide at least some help to their clients. The best judges remember what that was like, and they act accordingly.

Take Your Recesses

There are numbers of reasons to take recesses from trial. Jurors, witnesses, attorneys, court reporters, and even judges cannot effectively focus on the business at hand for hours at a time. People need to get up, walk around, and simply relax in order to give their "concentration" a break.

In addition, attorneys frequently need to talk to their secretaries, clients, and upcoming witnesses about lots of things. Court reporters need a recess in order to rest their fingers as well as their thoughts. Clerks and bailiffs need to be able to leave their stations and attend to other matters. And everybody needs to use the restroom. Furthermore, remember that not everybody in the courtroom will be as committed to finishing the trial quickly so that you can get started on the next case that has been waiting. So judges should always be mindful of the clock and take regular recesses.

Set a Standard of Excellence

Good and effective judges are diligent in their work and set the standard of excellence: no typographical errors, no grammatical errors, correct citation forms. Moreover, the cases cited stand for the proposition for which they were cited. And cases are distinguished honestly and realistically on the facts or the law. Rulings and judgments actually fit the context of the questions presented.

A standard of excellence means that even the little things will be done right. Postage stamps are straight on the envelopes that are mailed out in the judge's name. Papers are stapled neatly together. It is hard to demand professional excellence if the judge does not lead the charge. So if and when you serve as a judge, be sure you and your staff pay attention to the little things that can mean so much.

And do not forget that even a judge's appearance establishes important standards. We must maintain the dignity of the institution of the judiciary. Judges who take the bench with their robes in disarray, male judges who do not wear ties underneath their robes, and judges who read magazines while a trial is in session take away from the dignity of the court as an institution. I have also formed the opinion that judges should simply not use even the mildest forms of swearing when speaking in public, not because such language will necessarily shock most people, but because it will disappoint them.

It also degrades the judicial institution if judges allow people to come into their courtrooms while wearing shorts, having their shirts untucked, or otherwise being unsuitably dressed, chewing gum, drinking soft drinks or anything but water, and/or reading a newspaper while sitting in court. The best judges understand that respect for an institution can be a fragile thing, and we must continually treat that institution with respect, or we will lose it.

Offer Explanations

Many people simply are unfamiliar with court procedures and options. So the best judges make sure that everyone knows that "we are not running a railroad." They explain what is happening and what the various litigants' choices are, especially to people who are not represented by an attorney. That not only applies to confirming that litigants understand their constitutional rights at arraignment or at the taking of a guilty plea, but it also applies at every other time that a person may be unfamiliar with court procedures. For example, if, as a judge, your rules require you to impose "penalty assessments" along with criminal fines, be sure to explain that a fine of $100 plus penalty assessments will actually result in a total payment of $250—or whatever it is. Good and effective judges do not wait for defendants to go downstairs to the clerk's office with money in hand before they hear the news of the higher total amount.

Treat Staff Like Family

There is nothing as effective as judges who are "team builders" and "morale builders" in managing their courtrooms. Experienced judges commonly take their staff out to lunch to celebrate their individual birthdays and even the holidays. It is also truly appreciated when they are aware of the names of their staff's children.

In addition, I have found it quite helpful to ask each staff member with some regularity how things are going for them in my courtroom. This extends to assessing their relationships with fellow staff members. I also ask whether I am— or anyone else on staff is—doing anything that irritates them or makes their job more difficult. Also consider asking your staff if you or anyone else could do something that is not being done that would make their jobs less difficult or more enjoyable. If a judge monitors staff morale regularly and treats the staff like valued family, mostly because they really are, the courtroom will be a wonderful place to work. And the work accomplished there will be much more productive.

As a final matter on this subject, even though your court staff is your "family," for some reason one of your staff might not go with you when you change assignments. If that occurs, I believe it is disrespectful to your colleagues to offer that staff member a position back with you when you return if that person has a permanent position with another judge.

Happily Try All Cases That Are Sent to You

There is no such thing as an unimportant case, or a case that is "beneath" a judge. In the first place, judges are ethically required to try all cases referred to them by their presiding judges. In the second place, every case, and every decision in every case, will affect real people's lives. So each case is entitled to be treated with diligence, thought, interest, and professional care.

Set a Trial Date and Stick with It

We have emphasized this strategy in previous chapters, so by now you know how important it is. Continuances of trial dates are often quite convenient and helpful for the attorneys, but quite expensive and even harmful for the parties.

Good judges are reasonable in setting the initial trial date, but they let all counsel know that the date probably will not be changed unless someone gets "hit by a train." And they mean it. The main exceptions to that rule would be personal injury cases in which the plaintiff still has not stabilized medically, and situations in which one of the participants has become ill or has a "family emergency."

That said, all judges should be aware of the "statistics trap." Many courts publish statistics about the numbers of cases that each judge has and how long it has been since the cases were filed. Do not fall into the trap of giving too much consideration to those statistics. Instead, set the trial for the time that is appropriate for that particular case, try the case when appropriate, and let the statistics worry about themselves.

Only Issue Orders That Can Be Enforced

A judge's rulings must be clear, and there must be some reasonable means of having those rulings carried out under virtually all eventualities. Otherwise, the orders are ineffective and can actually put our system in disrepute. For example, it is perfectly appropriate in Juvenile Court to order a student to be on time and to attend all classes, but it is not any more enforceable to order the student to maintain a "B" average than it would be to order him to run a four-minute mile.

In addition, be familiar with various "summary sheets" that set forth the minimum and maximum sentences for various offenses and the various findings that must be made. Issuing "illegal sentences" does not further anyone's interests. Experienced judges know what orders can and cannot be effectively enforced, and they govern their pronouncements accordingly.

Be Aware of Your Staff's Professional Needs and Admirable Talents

Let us now discuss a few of the court staff positions and needs, starting with court clerks. When making rulings from the bench, conscientious judges remember that their clerks must prepare the minutes for the proceedings, even though they may not understand all of the legal issues. Therefore, in addition to being approachable to clerks on and off the bench, responsible judges will try to speak clearly, audibly, and slowly when making their rulings and orders.

On "volume" calendars such as Traffic and Small Claims, it is helpful for judges to write down on the calendar in shorthand what it is that they are ordering. That will assist the clerk later in recording the sentences accurately. Similarly, when judges do something out of procedure, it can be difficult for the clerk to fit the order into the court's reporting system. This will almost certainly require extra time for the clerk and the supervisor to accommodate the particular ruling. I am not suggesting that judges should not be "creative," but they should be aware that sometimes their creativity causes additional work, problems, and anguish for the staff.

Moreover, every judge should learn to read a court file and docket sheet. Much of what is in a court file and dockets is in "code," or "hidden" in standardized places. You will greatly increase your efficiency if you learn to "read the codes," and you will also increase your aura of approachability if you simply ask some of the clerks to explain the entries to you.

Next, there is the court reporter. Effective judges let their court reporters know that they expect the reporter to interrupt any speaker in court if he does not understand what is being said. The same is true when more than one person is talking at the same time. It is appropriate for judges to maintain order in this fashion, and judges should try to do so. But no one really knows what the reporter has or has not heard better than the reporter. So a good judge makes sure that the reporter knows that this is a team effort, and that he should not be bashful in asserting himself in the appropriate situations. In addition, try to ask your reporter to read back questions or answers during the trial as infrequently as possible because it slows down the pace of the trial. And your reporters uniformly do not like to do it.

On a criminal calendar it is often appropriate or necessary to take a person into custody. The bailiff becomes key here. For those occasions, careful judges will have worked out a code with their bailiffs that will tip them off and allow them to prepare for that action to be taken. My code is to express concern or sorrow that the person "has chosen to act" in a particular manner. When my bailiff hears me say those words, he gets into an advantageous position to take the person into custody. In addition to ensuring safety, this procedure will also facilitate the smooth operation of the courtroom. I assure you that if you, as a judge, follow this strategy, your bailiffs will appreciate the coded "heads up."

In a related issue, effective judges try to keep their bailiffs active. It is difficult for bailiffs to stay attentive while courts are in session. But vigilance is a part of their job, and they should help the judge continually to monitor the courtroom. Bailiffs assist in making sure jurors or people in the audience are not dozing, in helping feeble witnesses up to and down from the witness stand, in answering the telephone when the clerk is otherwise occupied, and much more. So they are a significant part of the courtroom happenings, and that is why the best judges pay attention to their needs.

There is another important role the bailiff can play that is often overlooked. Most judges are not particularly safety minded, so it is helpful to be briefed by someone who is trained in that important area. The most prepared judges cause this to happen. So if you want to be ready for anything that comes your way, have your bailiff give you and your staff a briefing about safety issues and the equipment in your courtroom to deal with them.

We also cannot forget to discuss the interpreters in our courtrooms. One of the hardest jobs in the courthouse to be done well is to interpret contemporaneously—that is, to interpret without requiring a pause in the discussion. But attentive judges assist these talented people by remembering to speak clearly, audibly, and slowly; admonishing witnesses to allow interpreters to complete their interpretations before they answer the questions; and instructing attorneys to avoid compound questions.

Judges can also be helpful by providing the interpreters with a copy of the jury instructions or documents that are being read during the proceedings. Finally, since it is the sworn duty of interpreters to state as exactly as they can what the witness has said, we must remember that it is inappropriate to get upset at interpreters when the testimony does not come out as "clean" or as understandable as desired.

Lastly, good and effective judges build a respectful relationship with court management professionals. Judges can be a mystery to the court administrative staff, even though it is the staff's job to keep judges happy. So if you want to be among the most effective judges, make every effort to take away the stratification between you, as the judge, and the court management professionals, by respecting their professional standing, expertise, and competence. Be sure to include them as a part of your team, because you will be miles ahead if you do.

Take Steps to Reduce "Judicial Intimidation"

No matter how friendly and approachable judges feel they are, because of the power they have their positions often carry with them an amazing amount of inherent intimidation—even for the general court staff. One effective way to moderate this problem is for judges to take the time to learn the names of court staff members, such as the runners from the clerk's office who deliver various files to and from the courtroom. Engaging in small talk with various court workers while together in the hallways or elevators is another fine way to establish a connection.

Some staff members have told me that I would be surprised how many runners actually arrange their lunch hours so that they can go into the courtrooms when the judges are not there, simply due to the fear they feel of the judges. If we take some of these "humanizing" steps, we should be able to reduce those instances almost to zero. Then there will be a much more secure, relaxed, and productive atmosphere within the courthouse. And all of these thoughts also apply to the court's custodial staff.

Use Gender-Neutral Terms

The words we use really do have an impact upon people, and not just the unduly sensitive. So try to use gender-neutral terms in all court correspondence and jury instructions. For example, use the words "foreperson," not "foreman"; "postal worker," not "postman"; "work-hours," not "man-hours"; "person to person," not "man to man." This will help you to establish and maintain an atmosphere in which gender discrimination is not tolerated in your court.

Be Prepared on Practical Things

What does it mean to be prepared on the practical things? It means that you have on your bench such easily verifiable things as calendars of past and future dates so you can take judicial notice of them during trials and management hearings. It also means that if, for example, your court is in a port city, you have a chart about the tides for the past or next few months or years.

These are some ways that judges can enhance their practicality. Another thought worth mentioning has to do with the size of the courtroom. Some judges have a chart on their bench that documents the dimensions of the courtroom. When a witness testifies that she was about as far away from the suspect as it is from the witness stand to the far wall, the judge can take judicial notice for the jury and the record as to the distance. These things seem simple, but they can convey organization and even sophistication to the parties. Plus, they help to move the case along smoothly, with fewer interruptions, and they make a better record.

Take Good Notes, and Retain Them

As stated earlier in this book, there are numbers of good reasons why good judges take notes and retain them. Taking notes tends to keep their minds from wandering during the course of a trial. It also helps them keep track of what exhibits have been marked and received into evidence, what the various witnesses have testified to, and many other useful details that judges should have at their fingertips during a trial. Further, judges who are able to take notes on their computers during trial will be able to provide verbatim quotes from testimony and argument for their Statements of Decision and other rulings.

Judges who are prepared and organized also know how helpful it is to accumulate notes on each case and to keep the entire body of notes close by until the end of the case. And if judges keep within reach their notes from their law and motion hearings, those notes will quickly remind them during a settlement conference what the case is about and where the strengths and weaknesses may lie. They will also help in determining the amount of "reasonable attorney's fees" to award to the prevailing party when a final judgment is rendered.

Take Responsibility for Your Name and Your Courtroom

Be careful of the use of signature stamps. The stamps can be convenient, but anything carrying your signature carries your review and approval along with it. So stand advised.

Another way effective judges take responsibility is by confessing errors if they indeed do make mistakes. Throughout my years as a judge it has almost astounded me how few files we misplace and how infrequently we confuse one case's ruling for another. But errors do happen from time to time. So when a mistake occurs, or when you have neglected to prepare for a particular motion, or when you simply have made a ruling that subsequently you see was not appropriate, simply face it, admit it, apologize for it, and correct it. Of course, you will not want to make the same mistake several times over, but people will understand and even appreciate a judge who admits to an honest mistake or oversight.

Always Allow Attorneys the Ability to Make a Record

Think of the various elements of a court case that could provoke strong agreement or disagreement: objections to evidence, jury instructions, rulings on a motion, offers of proof for potentially excluded testimony. All of these are areas in which the fair and impartial administration of justice cries out for the parties to be able to make a record of their agreements or disagreements with the rulings of the court. It is difficult for attorneys to be able to argue on appeal if they do not have a chance to make a record.

It is also difficult for the appellate courts to figure out what happened at the trial court level and decide the issues if there is not an adequate record. So fundamental fairness dictates that counsel have the appropriate opportunities to record their positions. The most effective judges know this and allow the proper time and attention to be given for this purpose.

Keep Current on Your Orders and Judgments

Most of the time it is a small task for judges to review and sign various orders and judgments that are lodged in their courts. These orders and judgments document their prior decisions and rulings. But that small task can sometimes make a major difference to the parties. So the best judges keep current in signing their orders and judgments, and this will almost always leave the impression that the courts are acting diligently and professionally.

In addition, of course, these documents represent the Court's final work product on various issues, and people will rely upon them. So you will want to be absolutely sure that all of your orders and judgments are precise and accurate, as well as timely.

Provide a Glossary for the Use of the Jury

In a complicated matter—such as a medical or legal malpractice case, or engineering breach of contract case—a number of technical terms are likely to be used. In order to help the listeners to follow the case adequately, the most concerned judges include in the handout on their court procedures the suggestion that counsel jointly prepare a glossary of the spelling and meaning of technical terms for the use of the jurors. Then they remind the attorneys actually to follow through with the glossary on those types of cases.

This type of attention to detail is truly what separates extraordinary judges from the rest. It shows organization, fosters a sense of trust in the judicial system, decreases confusion, and enables the jurors to understand and concentrate more effectively upon the evidence as it is presented.

Within Reason, Keep the Record Clear

There is a difference between a witness's testifying what he "would have done" and what he actually did do. This is just one example of how testimony can become unclear and confusing. The most effective judges make every effort to have trial testimony be as precise as possible. In turn, the case record also becomes clearer.

In addition, keep in mind that some questions inherently can cause ambiguous answers. For example, if an attorney asks, "Do you know if your fax identifier was working on August 28?" and the answer is "No," does the answer mean that the witness did not know, or that the fax identifier actually was not working? An attentive judge asks questions that will clear up the ambiguity. That will not only help the jury, but it will also help the record if the case goes on appeal.

Gently Discourage Attorneys from Thanking You for Your Rulings

It is the job of judges to issue rulings, set timetables, reduce expenses, and do justice. I, as a judge, do not feel we should be thanked simply for doing our job. In fact, allowing counsel to express verbal thanks is risky because it can be used by counsel to play games in front of the jury. For example, imagine that after a side bar conference one of the counsel returns to the lectern and thanks the Court, as if all of the rulings went in his favor. So, at worst, allowing the attorneys to thank the Court is patronizing and can be play acting, and at the best it is unnecessary—at least until the case is finally concluded and you are ready to adjourn.

But if and when you are in the position to receive a legitimate compliment after everything is said and done, simply say, "Thank you." Yes, as a judge you will receive a fair amount of "apple polishing." Take it for what it is worth, which often is not much. But do not allow yourself to get jaded. On some occasions you will receive genuine and heartfelt compliments. Learn to recognize when that happens, and when it does, simply give to the person an honest "thank you."

Give Deserved Compliments to Parties Concerning Their Choice of Attorneys

Judges should try hard not to reprimand attorneys in front of their clients, unless circumstances really demand that it be done. But when attorneys have worked hard and effectively for their clients, I believe that judges should compliment those attorneys within the hearing of their clients. For example, sometimes I do this after a case has settled, by confirming that the clients have chosen attorneys who have really worked hard for them.

Show the System's Appreciation

Like it or not, judges are *the* representatives of the judicial system. Judges should honor that reality, and use all appropriate opportunities to show the system's appreciation to those who contribute to it. Good and effective judges take the time to do so. That means that they thank non-party witnesses for taking the time to cooperate and appear in court. It also means that they thank the media who effectively contribute to the public's truthful understanding of the way the justice system operates. And it means they thank the jurors for being willing to serve as they have been called upon to do.

Finally, extending thanks to staff members for their efforts in keeping our system running smoothly will go a long way in keeping up morale in a sometimes burdensome job. For example, I once witnessed a clerk running after a traffic defendant to return some documents to him after he had inadvertently left them at her window. After she had accomplished her mission, I stopped her and thanked her for her efforts. Similarly, I once sent a letter of appreciation to two court clerks who consistently had been fully explaining the Small Claims Court procedures to the litigants, and I told them how much their efforts were appreciated. On numbers of occasions for years thereafter each of these clerks has commented to me how much both of them appreciated a judge's being aware of their efforts and extending his thanks for them. Expressing legitimate appreciation does not take much effort, but a judge's taking the time to do it is virtually always well received.

On the subject of letters, I try to send each juror a letter of appreciation for his service. This is a final touch of appreciation that jurors say they really appreciate. Judges can also use this gesture as an opportunity to ask the jurors for their suggestions about how the overall judicial process can be improved.

Invite Jurors into Chambers After the Trial

Some judges are concerned about inviting jurors into their chambers after a trial is over, but I do it regularly. During these visits I make it clear that I cannot discuss the case as such with them. In fact, I expressly decline their invitation to comment about their verdict, except to say that it was their verdict so, by definition, it is pretty much considered by law to be the correct result. But I do ask them for their feedback about how they were treated by everyone during their time with us. That includes the Jury Commissioner and her staff, my staff, me, and everyone else who took part in the trial.

In addition, I ask them for their suggestions about how we can make their time with us more pleasant, or less unpleasant, depending upon their points of view, and what we can do to help them understand the evidence better. (This is how the suggestion of providing them with a glossary arose, among other things.) And finally, jurors really appreciate the "personal touch" of being able to receive the thanks of the trial judge for their service. In short, I believe it is a fun and productive thing to do, but it must be done carefully.

Do Not Fear to Be Reversed

With regard to cases' being reversed on appeal, my wonderful father once said, "The court of appeal has a right to be wrong too." Obviously, trial judges should be mindful of the case law and the statutory law, and they should apply these laws to the facts of the case. But once that has been done, they cannot look over their shoulders and worry about what the court of appeal will do with their decisions.

Good and effective judges know that they have spent the necessary time and energy on the decision reached in a case. And it was as right as they could make it. So I recommend you let the appellate courts take care of themselves, and join me in taking comfort in my father's words.

Advise Your Presiding Judge of Anything Unusual

Judges should see themselves as a team, with the presiding judge as the captain. As such, inform your presiding judge of unusual difficulties or problems, particularly if they might become public issues or security problems. This will help everyone concerned, especially you!

Let Yourself Relax

First of all, take your vacations. I believe judges should follow this strategy in order to help themselves avoid burnout. As has been stated several times, judges are the only ones in the proceedings who simply cannot lose their tempers. They are also continually being watched and assessed by the public eye, and being under constant scrutiny can take its toll. So one big way in which judges can reduce the chances that they will burn out and lose their patience is to take all of their vacation time. Society has a vested interest in not "burning out" its judges. So I, for one, take my allotted vacations, and I strongly recommend that all judges do so.

There are additional ways for judges to practice relaxation and maintain their good health. One I like to encourage is meditation. In my view, there must be something to a practice that has been around for thousands of years. Meditation can be quietly satisfying and help to clear your mind of clutter. First, allow your mind to drift unharnessed by convention, and then you can quiet and focus it—on a candle flame, a mantra, or another focus tool. Ultimately, advanced meditators pass the need even to focus their quiet minds; they can simply let their minds "be."

I relied on periods of meditation to help me focus my mind enough to come up with numbers of concepts, thoughts, and examples for this book. Over the years, I have also used meditation to help me generate the calm and openness I needed to figure out approaches and resolutions for my trials and settlement conferences. I previously recommended that people who are incarcerated get involved in meditation because lots of options are not available to them, but I also recommend the approach to judges.

Generate Good Feelings and Good Memories

You never know the lasting effect your actions will have, for better or worse. When I think of the number of times people have called to my attention, years later, something that I did or my father did that had a lasting effect upon their lives, I am almost astounded. Most of the time it is something we might have considered small. For example, numbers of people have recalled times that my father made a simple—and, for a judge, common—ceremony of swearing in an attorney to practice in the federal court so personal and meaningful. Also, I have been reminded of adoption ceremonies over which I have presided. The participants expressed heartfelt appreciation, long after the fact, because I took a little bit of extra time to make the ceremony special. What a journey we are on, so make the "little things" special along the way!

In a similar vein, I once heard an interview with a famous football coach, several years after he had retired. When asked if there was anything he would have done differently, without hesitation he responded that if he could do it all over again, he would have fostered a better and more human relationship with his players. I think the same can be true for judges. Generating a professional but human and respectful relationship with your staff and the attorneys who practice before you can be the source of lasting gratification. Good and effective judges know that this is a priority, and savor it.

Be an Activist—in the Good Sense

I once heard a story about a judge who made the comment, "I was told not to get any ideas when I was first appointed to a judgeship, so I haven't had any for years." Judges should not just try their cases and draw their paychecks. The best judges are alert to opportunities to educate and even brag to the public about our judicial system. They are also alert to new situations and ideas that will help to improve that system.

If you want the justice system to be the best it can be, then become aware of the "Six Deadly Sins" *against* progressive thinking and constructive change:

1. "We've always done it that way!"

2. "That must have cost a fortune!"

3. "Let someone else do it."

4. "That doesn't concern me."

5. "We've done fine without it so far."

6. "If it's not broken, why fix it?"

For example, if our procedures are unnecessarily taking too long and thereby making people miss more time from their employment, actively work to improve the procedures. Or, if from information presented to you, it appears that anyone in the public sector has done either a really good job or a really poor job, or has done something unusually professional or unprofessional, once the matter is concluded consider writing a letter to the person's supervisor. The letter could simply offer a few accolades or call attention to the possibility of taking some corrective action. Judges must understand that the only way "the system" will work effectively is for all of us to *make* it work. In my view, that is being an "activist" judge in the good sense.

By now, you have accumulated a lot of advice. But the strategies above are broad and reasonable enough for all judges to apply to their positions. You might notice that many of the suggested strategies involve good people skills. That is because a judge's job is a public one. Any great judge will like to work with people, helping them to enhance their understanding of the world around them and the best standards to keep it running.

CONCLUSION

I will leave you with a final thought to wrap up this chapter. As a rule of thumb, if the public becomes familiar with the name of a judge as a result of a trial, it may well be that the judge did not do his job as well as he might have. Good and effective judges "call the balls and strikes," but otherwise try to blend in with the scenery. Most judges get noticed for ethical improprieties and people's dissatisfaction with the justice system. But if the judicial machinery is working as designed, the judges will mostly be anonymous. I hope this chapter has made that point clear.

Chapter 10

The Public Life of a Judge

"It is important for a judge to be actively involved in community organizations so as to prevent the formation of a jaundiced view of society that everyone is either dysfunctional or a criminal."

—John C. Lindstrom, Judge of the District Court, Willmar, Minnesota

In Chapter 8, we reviewed a number of the benefits that come along with being a judge. As we discussed, there are no attorney time sheets to fill out, numbers of paid holidays throughout the year, many weekends without being required to go to work, more time to spend with your family, and the ability to schedule vacations and actually rely upon those schedules! Therefore, it was pointed out that being a judge often allows you your private time. Fortunately that also allows you the time for some extracurricular activities. So why not savor the opportunity and get further involved in the world around you?

This chapter will provide a number of ideas for you to consider if you are looking to become more involved in your community. And I encourage judges to do so. You can take part in religious organizations or volunteer for the local high school's mock trial team. Judges who actively involve themselves in the community are usually well-respected and honored judicial officers who have made the most of their positions, education, and humanity.

Of course, it is one thing to *desire* to extend your public image, and a whole other thing to be thrust into the public eye—possibly unfavorably. So if you are assigned to a high-profile case, whether locally or nationally, you may profit from some other tips on how to conduct yourself. In fact, you may also require some tips on just how to keep your private life somewhat normal. Therefore, the second half of this chapter is dedicated to media issues that could present themselves in a judge's life. Even if it is hard to picture now, there is some chance you will be in the media spotlight—whether print, radio, television, or all three—at some point in your career. And it is best to be prepared.

EXTRACURRICULAR ACTIVITIES

If you want to use your lunch hours, evenings, vacations, and other periods of free time to golf, travel, or raise chickens, you will not need any further thoughts from me. Just go at it and enjoy it! But if you think about it, you can also use some of the available time to attend local meetings and functions at which you participate, learn, and blossom. Moreover, by partaking in community events you will be able to carry out one of a judge's ethical responsibilities: to educate the public about the justice system and the important role it plays in our society. You can do this by speaking at organizations such as service clubs, faith-based gatherings, boys and girls clubs, and universities. As long as you remember the most important rule of public speaking, which is to show that you believe what you are saying, you will be gratified at the role you will be able to play in this regard.

As a judge, you also will be a desirable candidate for acting as a director of various public interest groups, such as the YMCA, or you could be asked to serve on the Board of Trustees of a religious institution. Perhaps you will consider joining organizations like the Rotary Club or a speakers' group such as the World Affairs Council. Let us discuss some of the ways you can become an active, appreciated, and key member of your community. The possibilities are endless, but we can explore a few ideas.

Additional Judicial Work

If there is work to be done on your court cases, then you will want to do it. In fact, in my years as a judge, I have stayed late at work numbers of times, even until midnight, to prepare my Law and Motion calendar, finalize jury instructions with counsel, or nail down settlement agreements with counsel and their clients. You are certain to do the same. But after you have settled or tried your cases, after you are caught up on your work and in those times when there are no other matters pending, and after you have checked with your supervising and presiding judges and found that there are no other cases available to be tried at the moment, you will have some extra time at your disposal. Then is the opportunity to spend your time on *other* judicial matters, such as developing programs for those who are involved in court cases and need special help.

We have already touted the results of the efforts of dedicated and forward-thinking judges when we discussed some of the specialty courts such as Drug Courts, Homeless Outreach Courts, and Community Courts. Those calendars were mostly created and established by judges after they had completed their regular assignments. And you can help to establish additional effective judicial/societal responses to problems in other areas. Two that come to mind and still need to be addressed in many jurisdictions are the plight of many of our elderly people and the struggles of substance abusers and the mentally ill. Regarding the latter, there is much need for assistance in the criminal justice system so that it can be more receptive to and utilize new developments in the medical community for the diagnosis and treatment of drug addictions and mental disorders.

Because we have discussed the creativity and success of various specialty programs in Chapter 2, I will not take the space in this chapter to do so again. I simply refer you to Part I of this book, and Chapter 2 in particular, to be inspired by those judges who have designed these successful programs. Keeping a journal of your own ideas so that you can compile your thoughts into a proposal for action at a future time will be particularly helpful in this regard.

Teaching Opportunities

If and when you serve as a judge, not only will you be able to attend informative classes and seminars in your extra time—some of them even at government expense—but you will also have the opportunity to share some of your knowledge and insights by teaching some of them yourself. In fact, in most jurisdictions you are permitted to be paid for your educational efforts. These can include teaching at local colleges, universities, and law schools, as well as at various professional continuing education seminars and courses.

In addition, as a judge you will have more time to read, attend general education classes, and even write a book. In fact, I would never have had the time to write this book if I was still a practicing attorney. The point is that you will accumulate a great deal of knowledge that you can easily share through various aspects of teaching. Some of that knowledge you will have gained in the courtroom and some you will have gained from your own private studies, research, and brainstorming.

Of course, you will still want to surround yourself with people who will keep you from being "all full of yourself." (Having teenagers around helps a great deal in this regard!) Just because you have become a judicial officer does not mean that you know everything. In fact, when I sometimes start feeling this way, I try to remind myself of an introduction I once received as I was about to address a local service club concerning an important judicial matter. The introduction was, "I know you all want to hear the latest dope from the courthouse, so here's Judge Gray." Nevertheless, in many people's opinions these opportunities make the normal decrease of salary far worth it when one exchanges the practice of law for judicial robes. To have the opportunity to touch so many people with your knowledge and efforts is truly rewarding.

Furthermore, based upon your judicial experience, you will most likely be an effective and highly interesting teacher. Why? Because you have had a front row seat in addressing many problems regarding all walks of life. You will have seen what works and what does not. And you will be in a position to pass your wisdom and experience on to others who are thirsty for it. They will trust and admire you, so you will be looked up to as a leader. For more on teaching and the power of words, see the inset "Teaching the Playfulness and Power of Words" below.

American Inns of Court

As the story goes, former Chief Justice Warren Burger was so disappointed at the caliber of some of the legal representation before him in the U.S. Supreme Court that he and several other legal professionals patterned a new group after the old Inns of Court in England. In those British "temples," young barristers and solicitors learned their profession by, among other things, sharing meals and conversation with more experienced attorneys and judges. So Chief Justice Burger and others began the American Inns of Court, at which experienced "Master Benchers," mid-level "Barristers," and novice "Pupils" spend time together focusing upon legal excellence, civility, professionalism, and ethics.

Now there are more than 300 separate chapters of the American Inns of Court operating in the United States. As a judge you will be in demand, either to

---

TEACHING THE PLAYFULNESS AND POWER OF WORDS

If as a judge you become involved in teaching the younger members of our society, you will be able to do your part in showing your students that words actually mean something. One of the best ways to gain their attention is to start with humor. For example, get them chuckling by pointing out that when their airplane lands and an airline host states, "I would like to be the first to welcome you to Portland, Oregon," instead of saying he would *like* to welcome us to Portland, why doesn't he just do it? You can also help them to laugh at parking signs that proclaim, "No parking at any time—especially on Saturdays!" and greeting cards that promise, "You are the only one for me," in boxes of ten. Furthermore, you can instruct them to question signs such as the one at the entrance of a high school gymnasium that instructs, "Visit Our Snack Bar Inside," right under a sign that insists, "No Eating or Drinking in the Gym!" How about getting them to recognize that if everything is "urgent," nothing is urgent? This is exemplified by some airfreight businesses' pre-printing the words "Extremely Urgent" on all of their shipping boxes. You are likely to get your students to appreciate a funny t-shirt message I once saw, which was, "Recently I have read so much about the harmful effects of what we eat, what we drink, and what we breathe, that I have decided to give up reading."

start a new chapter in your area or to be an active participant and mentor in a chapter that has already been established. If you take part in the activities of these organizations, you will find this to be a most wonderful and productive use of some of your extra time.[1]

Judges' Associations, Judicial Councils, and Bench/Bar Committees

Groups such as judges' associations, judicial councils, and bench/bar committees provide a wealth of services to the judiciary, to the legal profession, and to the community in general. Many of the advances discussed earlier regarding community outreach, "Access to Justice" (see page 19), and other improvements in the administration of justice have come directly from these professional organizations in the legal community. In addition, they have contributed greatly to the process of heading off problems and misunderstandings in the legal community, and to the organizing of numbers of charitable activists for various causes. So I am convinced that your participation in them will bring you a great deal of gratification.

Obviously, a playful introduction to the power of words—and how we abuse that power—is a wonderful way to communicate the importance of the proper use of such a tool. But you will also be in a position to pass along some very serious messages to your students, including the fact that the mind thinks only in words. Therefore, the power of words cannot be overrated. Consider that if we do not understand the shades of meaning of words, we cannot understand important distinctions. For example, more than half of the dialects of all of the world's languages do not make a distinction between the word for "stranger" and the word for "enemy." So in those cultures, anyone who is a stranger to you is automatically your enemy.

Through your teaching opportunities you can also help students, as well as young attorneys, to understand and appropriately use words with various shades of meanings they choose to use in their pleadings and in their questioning of witnesses. For example, when describing two automobiles coming together, there are many words one can use: "accident," "collision," "touch," "crash," "bump," "tap," "hit," or "impact." These are just a few of the choices, and those choices can make a difference! So as a judge, you will have the time to help your students gain an appreciation for carefully selected words, and that in turn will sharpen up their thinking. What a gratification that can be, and what fun!

Moot Courts and Mock Trials

Most law schools have their own moot court programs, and many of them are involved in state or even nationwide competitions. As a judge, your involvement will be solicited and treasured by those schools and students. Moreover, you should have the time to participate in them.

In addition, in many parts of the country there are competitions for high school students called "mock trials." In these competitions, a factual scenario and some legal issues, mostly in criminal law, are provided to the high school teams. The various team members become prosecutors, defense attorneys, and witnesses. In those roles they present and argue a "trial" before real judges and real attorneys.

From my experience as a judge of mock trials in every year since I became a judge, I can tell you that the presentations these young people make can be truly inspiring. In fact, many of these students were more effective advocates in their high school competitions than I was when I was in law school. Actually, several of them even have been much more effective than some of the attorneys who have argued cases in my courtroom!

And what results! Many of these young people will never be the same because of their mock trial experiences. For the rest of their lives they will better understand the concept of complexity. They will also realize that often when a criminal defendant is "let off on a technicality," actually the defendant is released because our principles in upholding our constitutions and laws are actually considered more important than any individual case. In addition, the experience will make these students better voters, parents, and citizens. So everyone wins in our mock trial programs.[2]

Peer Court or Teen Court

Today there are numbers of different kinds of high school peer court or teen court programs in over thirty different states around the country. All of them address real but less-serious juvenile cases that are screened by probation offices or local prosecutors for possible diversion from the criminal justice system. That means that if the juvenile subjects successfully complete the sentences they are given, the underlying charges will thereafter be dismissed and the subjects will not have a criminal record for those offenses.

Some of the programs use high school "attorneys" to prosecute or defend the cases, and the guilt or innocence of the subjects is determined by high school juries, as well as the sentences if the subjects are "convicted." Other programs require the subjects first to acknowledge their culpability, and the peer court sessions focus only upon an appropriate sentence to be completed. These latter programs allow more time to address the actual choices that were made at the time by the subjects, and the effect that those choices had upon those subjects, their families, and their friends.

Some peer courts are held at courthouses and some are held at local high schools, but most often not the high school that the subject attends. Most of the programs of which I am aware have a high school jury that deliberates and then returns with a recommended sentence to a real judge, who tries to impose as much of that sentence as is practical. The sentences can involve virtually anything except incarceration or a fine. Most often they include community service, half of which is picking up trash in a park, and the other half of which is served at a fire station, boys and girls' club, or a comparable venue. Counseling and restitution are required as appropriate, and serving as a juror at a future peer court session is also frequently imposed.

Sometimes it is required that the subject's parents come to the hearing, and the student jurors ask questions of the parents. Frequently the jurors' questions show, to the astonishment of some parents, that the students actually *expect* the parents to parent. A sample question might be, "What do you mean that you didn't know your sixteen-year-old daughter was out with friends at 2 AM on a school night?" The students also expect the subjects to acknowledge their negative influence on others. They might ask a subject, "So you were smoking marijuana that evening, correct? And you said you have a younger sister. Don't you agree that you are a really important person in her life and that she really looks up to you? Well, do you want your sister to smoke marijuana? Because if she learns that you smoke marijuana, she probably will think it's the thing to do. Had you thought of that before?" The answer is usually along the lines of, "No, I guess you're right. I really had not thought about that before."

I have also found it effective to use these occasions to reinforce some of society's values that, in many ways, seem to have eroded. For example, before a male subject sits down, I naturally expect him to assist his mother first in taking her seat. And since this is a real court, it is entitled to the sanctity that accompanies it: no gum chewing; no talking to one's neighbors while court is in session; no untucked shirttails and the like. And sometimes I use the opportunity to try to make important points that most young people—whether the subject, the jury, or those in the audience—have not thought about before. For instance, I will stress, "There is no such thing as peer pressure. Each of us is the captain of our ship, and no one can make us do anything unless we agree." In addition, I often ask a subject who has acknowledged an offense of stealing, "Are you a thief? I know you stole a CD from the store on that date, but did your parents raise you to be a thief?" Then I use the discussion to make him come around to the following conclusion: "Yes, I did take something that didn't belong to me on that day, but I am not a thief, because *I am better than that!*"

The beauty of programs like these is that not only do they keep subjects from having juvenile records, but they also are successful in getting the subjects to start thinking about the choices they make, their actions, and the people whom they "hang around with." In other words, the judges tell the subjects, "You show me your friends, and I will show you your future." And the peer courts focus on the importance of getting a good education and learning some skills. Probably most of the jurors have already made the same mistakes that the subjects before them have acknowledged. The jurors, as well as the subjects, can learn very important lessons. If they shoplift an article from a convenience store or write graffiti on public property those acts might truly affect their ability to go to a good college or get a good entry-level job. Plus, they begin to realize that if they do something really good, the result has a beneficial effect upon their family and friends who love and care for them. But the reverse is also true; if they do something illegal, or even dumb, the result can have a substantially negative effect upon their family and friends, as well as themselves. So the choices they make— even now—will affect what they are going to do for the rest of their lives. In summary, just as sports teach physical discipline and balance, we try to teach mental discipline and balance.

You can be a major part of programs like these and have a material effect upon the future of young and impressionable people. "Teachable moments," as overseen by you as the judge, can do some big and positive things for the youth in your area, and for society in general. It is great to be a part of it.[3]

Volunteers in Parole (VIP) and Child Mentoring Programs

Groups like Volunteers in Parole and child mentoring programs are made up of concerned and dedicated people who want to provide a support system for both adults and teenagers who have just been released from their "correctional facilities," as well as for youths who are at risk because of a lack of responsible leadership or guidance. The fact is that *someone* will mentor our children; if we as parents, teachers, and basketball coaches do not do it, gang leaders, drug dealers, and even people like Charles Manson will. In effect, mentoring those who are recently released will be putting into play the advice of Plutarch, who recommended that we study noble people in order to improve our own thoughts, actions, and lives. Judges can serve as these types of role models.

Most of the mentoring participants in these types of programs are volunteers who do not have credentials in counseling and do not have a magic ability to procure jobs for the juveniles or parolees. All they do is make themselves available to listen and be a confidant to someone who is trying to start over or live a better life. And the mentors are remarkably successful in doing just that, as shown by the much smaller recidivism rate for those who have volunteer supporters and mentors than for those who do not.[4] I do not believe that it is a good idea for judges actually to be the volunteers that directly work with the clients, because that can be seen as a conflict of interest. But organizations like these need administrative assistance and a foundation in the community for support, and judges are singularly in a position to give programs like these the necessary credibility to be able to exist and even to thrive.[5]

Stay in School Programs

It is not an exaggeration to say that literally millions of young people all around the world would give virtually anything to have the opportunity to receive the education that is being offered for free to the children in this country. And it is a national disgrace that many of the children here are dropping out of school without so much as a high school degree. There are some programs around the country that simply send volunteers to speak to a classroom of students one day per week for six successive weeks, discussing with them the importance of staying in school and getting an education. Among other things that are shared with the students is a very interesting factual comparison. The average person who graduates only from elementary school earns an average of about $595,000 over the course of her entire lifetime. Yet the average person who graduates from high school almost doubles those lifetime earnings, which climb to about $1,105,000. And finally, the average lifetime earnings of people who graduate from college will be more than two and a half times the earnings of those with only a high school education. They earn about $2,846,000.

In summary, in the "Stay in School" programs we tell young people, as they are beginning their high school careers, what the numbers show: If they stay in school and earn their degrees, over the course of their lifetimes they will be paying themselves about $117.00 per hour for every hour they spent in a high school classroom.[6] Then we ask what jobs these youngsters can currently get that would pay them anywhere near that amount of money. Hopefully this cements in their minds the fact that they will be giving up those earnings forever by dropping out of school.

Moreover, it is important to ask who is counting upon these youths to get their education. Certainly (most of the time) their parents and their other family members, but also some people that they probably do not even know yet—namely their future wives or husbands. In addition, some people who are not even born yet are counting on them enormously so that they have a better chance in life—namely, of course, their eventual children. So we can help to spread the word that by making the decision to stay in school, these young people can materially increase their ability to have good and interesting jobs and to make more money and be able to have nicer houses and cars, take vacations, and support their families. In addition, they can prevent being held back from advancing in their jobs, even if they are otherwise qualified, because often they will not be promoted unless they have a certain educational degree.

Dropping out of school is a choice and a decision, and the young people might as well be aware of the effect that this decision will have not only upon their own lives but also upon the lives of those who are counting on them. As a judge, you can impress this message upon these young people as much as or more than anyone else whom they will ever encounter if you take part in the "Stay in School" programs.

Official Welcoming Presentations for New Jurors

Most courts have a welcome and introduction presentation each morning for new jury panelists who are reporting for duty. This is a great opportunity for a judge to provide a warm and personable presence and thus allow the judicial system to make a great impression. As a judge, you can welcome the new panelists, invigorate them about their ability to contribute to our critically important justice system, and express appreciation for each juror's willingness to serve. We ask so much from our jurors, and this presentation gives us an opportunity to show that their service is genuinely appreciated.

Police Academy Classes

Some people feel that it is not ethically appropriate for a judge to teach classes to police departments about such procedures as search and seizure because that could be seen as showing partisanship toward the prosecution instead of the defense. But I have never encountered any such comments about a judge's addressing police academy classes and instilling in the cadets a sense of the importance of their upcoming duties and responsibilities. In addition, the judge can then provide the cadets with basic information about how the courts actually operate and what participant performs what function.

In fact, it helps to talk with the cadets about how judges and police share the same goals. The way I put it, "Back the Badge" means that *all* of us in the justice system should always tell the truth—on the witness stand, in our official and non-official comments, and in our written reports. We should treat people with respect and dignity, certainly including those who are in our custody. We should use our positions of authority to reduce tension levels in society instead of to increase them. And we should act professionally at all times, including in those situations in which others might attempt to mock us, flee from us, lie to or about us, attack us, or even spit on us. As public and professional officers of trust, we have committed not to respond to such attacks because, when we took our oaths of office, we publicly committed ourselves to be better than that.

Wedding Ceremonies

One of the many things you as a judge can do outside the courtroom is to officiate at wedding ceremonies. Presiding over a wedding can be a fun experience, particularly if the wedding involves your own family members or friends. And sometimes it can bring lasting memories, like the time the bride in a first-class wedding chose Quaratotto and Santori's great song "Time to Say Goodbye" for the time she was walked down the aisle. I never asked, but I have always wondered if she meant to say good-bye to all of her old boyfriends or if she simply did not think about the lyrics. In addition, in most jurisdictions you can also use the weddings to augment your salary.

But be careful! When I presided over weddings, I used to shudder at the thought of mis-calendaring a wedding and not showing up. So I always double-checked my bookings. In fact, even if the wedding couple did not get back to me to finalize the plans for my involvement, I always tried to leave a message with them to verify that they did not need my services.

Another thing to be careful about with weddings is—again, depending upon the jurisdiction—whether there are any restrictions upon the days of the week that you may do weddings in return for payment. Some jurisdictions consider judges to be on "government time" twenty-four hours per day, except on the weekends. Thus, judges cannot receive any compensation for weddings during the workweek. And finally, in many states it is a violation of law to perform a wedding unless the person performing it ensures that the signed and completed wedding license is submitted to the proper governmental agency. I think you would agree that a newspaper article stating that a judge was being prosecuted or even investigated for abuse of established wedding procedures would not be a good thing to see.

If you are considering presiding over wedding ceremonies, decide in advance whether or not you want to perform weddings for people who have just been sentenced to a term in prison. I, myself, decline to do this for several reasons. One is that the party who is "left behind" might be making the decision to marry based upon emotion, or to show support for the one being incarcerated, and has not truly thought the decision out. Another is that the marriage could be done mainly for welfare or tax purposes, to show dependency. I basically see these latter cases as a fraud upon the taxpayers. So one way or the other, I simply decline to participate.

But weddings can be fun things to do, and as mentioned, in some jurisdictions they can provide a little extra revenue. If you are interested in performing weddings, you should contact your clerk's office, see if the office staff maintains a list of "Marry'n Judges," and get on that list. Also, you will want to develop a ceremony that you are comfortable with and confident in. I have included a sample wedding ceremony in Appendix 3 (see page 307) that has been well received at the weddings I have performed. Please feel free to use all or part of it as your own, and enjoy the experience.

Now you have plenty of ideas for involving yourself in your community and touching many lives. It is an incredible thing to do something for the sheer pleasure of helping a worthy cause. And in so doing, you will continually be reminded of the common truth that "giving is receiving."

THE MEDIA RELATIONS DILEMMA

If the first half of this chapter has convinced you that being in the public eye is the place to be, this next section might actually jar you a little. It is wonderful to seek connection with your local public and to produce fruits from that visibility. But it is not always so wonderful to be pursued and critiqued by the media, which can happen with high profile cases. So now let us discuss another side of small and large community involvement—media relations.

Most judges naturally shy away from all media contact, and in fact it is mostly the judicial "common wisdom" to do so. This point of view was further cemented after the 1995 incidents surrounding the infamous O. J. Simpson criminal trial. After that sensational murder trial many people came to the conclusion that television cameras should not be allowed in the courtrooms and that judges can only get hurt from contact with the media. But as I think you will see, for several reasons I think judges should reach different conclusions.

The big problem is that most judges find themselves in a constant dilemma in dealing with the media. On the one hand, the mandate is, "Judges are generally required to assist in the education of the public about the Third Branch of Government, and what better way than through the media?" Yet, on the other hand, "Judges are ethically prohibited from discussing any cases, whether they be their own or anyone else's, until all appeals are exhausted on them and a final judgment has been entered." Between these two mandates, the inherent conflict is obvious. In addition, many judges feel, with some justification, that most members of the media are out there looking for something sensational to exploit, and what could be a juicier target than a sitting judge?

As a result of these problems and perceptions, many judges have had a "closed door" policy on discussions with the media. (See "The Problem with 'No Comment'" on page 286 for further commentary on this issue.) Unfortunately, in many cases this policy has resulted in many judges' being wrongly and unfairly ridiculed in the media, and the judges' being forced to rely upon various bar associations or other knowledgeable people to step forward and set the record straight about what occurred. They can only hope the restrictions that they faced will become clear and understood. Fortunately, there is a better way, and that is to work with the media, but in a restricted fashion.

Healthy Communication Among Judges and Journalists

What the above paragraphs show is that the majority of judges have the opinion that "good news is no news," leave it at that, and hope for the best. Nevertheless, there are some things that judges can do both to avoid misunderstandings and to get truthful information out to the media—and thus to the public in general. One of those things is to refer the media representatives to pleadings from the parties or orders from the court that are already in the case files. Another is to make a statement on the record in open court before all of the parties and counsel, and then either to tell the media representatives that they are welcome to get a copy of the transcript or at least to talk to someone who was present in court in order to get the story. The judge can also have her staff hand out a copy of the statement that she read in open court. That does not at all mean that judges should make self-serving or irrelevant comments on the record, but there is nothing wrong with giving explanations about procedures and reasons for rulings while in open court and on the record.

In addition, if the court is utilizing a particular procedure, the judge or a court officer can call the attention of the media to the procedure that is being utilized and instruct them on how they can get a copy of it. Let us consider as an example a case of a high-profile defendant who is being offered a diversion program as a result of charges against him for the possession of illicit drugs. It is completely appropriate for the court to call the attention of the media to the fact that the diversion program is provided for by statute and is available to *all* defendants. That will rightfully show the public that the high-profile defendant is neither being provided special treatment by the courts nor being discriminated against because he is in the public eye.

Situations frequently arise in which neither the media nor the public is aware of the law that is being applied. As a result they do not understand the reasons behind a particular order that has been given. For example, for almost every offense except homicides there is an applicable statute of limitations. That means that, unless some exception applies, all non-homicide defendants must be indicted or formally charged with their offenses within a specified period of time. Otherwise, the charges cannot be pursued. In many jurisdictions, the charges must be filed within one year of a commission of a misdemeanor and within three years of a felony. Similar statutes actually require a defendant to be brought to trial within a specified period of time after the charges have been filed or else the charges will have to be dismissed. Bear in mind that it is not just criminal cases that are subject to statutes of limitations; civil cases also have periods of limitations.

The rationale for these statutes is that there should be some finality so that cases simply are not allowed to go on forever. But many people in the media and the public at large are neither aware of the statutes nor aware of the reasoning behind them. Accordingly, it is not at all unusual for a newspaper story to cry out, "Yesterday in Superior Court, Judge James P. Gray dismissed the charges of rape against a defendant on a technicality." Stories of this kind not only can be misleading for the public and unfair to the judge, but also they can be harmful to the entire administration of justice. Furthermore, as a practical matter, frequently the prosecutors know full well that the motions to dismiss the charges have merit under the law and the facts of the case, but they are silent about them, thus putting the impetus, spotlight, and the political "blame" upon the judicial officer.

This happened recently to a judicial colleague of mine who dismissed an emotional and highly watched civil case due to a failure by the plaintiff to comply with the applicable statute of limitations. The unhappy plaintiff was quoted in the local paper as saying, "I thought [the judge] had no conscience."[7] In other words, it was the "conscienceless judge" who was the reason for the dismissal, instead of the failure by that same plaintiff to file the case within the applicable period of the statute of limitations.

But these problems can be reduced if the judges and their staffs simply assist the media in becoming aware of the law that is being applied. Then, if the media and the public feel that the law is bringing an incorrect result, they can rightfully direct their attention to the legislature to change the law.

Other things to keep in mind are that if the media do not get their information from the judges or the court system on a particular matter, they will almost certainly get it from somewhere else. This is a highly competitive profession, and the people in it are under continual pressure due to their deadlines and their desire to "scoop" other reporters. So a judge on a high-profile case immediately should ask the media representatives when their deadline is. Then she will know how much time she has to get the appropriate information to them.

Establishment of Rules for the Media

When a judge is handed a case that has a high level of public interest, dense media coverage can be expected. Most states recognize that each case presents different and difficult problems, so they mostly leave the decision about how to deal with the media exclusively to the discretion of the trial judge. So what should the trial judge do other than what has already been mentioned above?

Well, the first thing I recommend is to keep the presiding judge informed about what is going on both for general media control and for security matters.

THE PROBLEM WITH "NO COMMENT"

Unfortunately, when many judges have cases or have made decisions that have drawn media attention, either they mistakenly fail to return telephone calls about them or they simply respond with the almost always misunderstood and vilified, "No comment." This "No comment" statement is, in turn, almost always passed along to the public, which almost always draws the inference that the judges had no reasonable explanation for their actions.

Instead, it is frequently better for judges to speak directly to the media representatives and explain to them the ethical prohibitions we have on discussions about open cases. In addition, they should explain that the cases will remain open until either an appeal is final or the time for an appeal to be filed has expired. That way both the media and the public will be much more likely to see the judges as professionals and understand the basic reasons for the further lack of judicial comment.

The second thing is for the trial judge to recognize the fact that, as some media representatives put it, "A gag order will not stop the locusts." If the judge prohibits the media from access to information through the front door, they will most likely get their information from some kind of substitutes or "leaks" in the system. As a result, the information that gets out to the public will probably be a lot less accurate and reliable than it would otherwise be. In addition, if a news reporter quotes a defense attorney or a prosecutor, the public is at least able to interpret the comment with the knowledge of who the source was. But if judges force the media to go underground for their information, the reporters will quote anonymous sources, or "a source close to the prosecution," with the results that the public will not be able to interpret it in the context of whose opinion or facts they are receiving. To put this differently, as one veteran news reporter once told me, "Civil cases run on papers, but criminal cases run on wind."

In my view, judges should cooperate with the media in high-profile cases and help them set up some guidelines for coverage. They also should—again, in my view—allow the presence of television cameras in the courtroom. I make this recommendation both for philosophical reasons and for practical ones. In the first place, with only a few exceptions, our trials are meant to be fully open to the public. That means to me that any member of the public who would like to see a hearing or a trial or an appellate argument in any of our courts should be able to do so. Since that is not always physically possible, that means anyone should be able to see it or read about it as comprehensively as possible through the media. If that is the case, it is much more advantageous for the public to see or hear the actual testimony of a witness, arguments of counsel, or explanations by a judge, than to have someone in the media simply describe what has occurred. On the other hand, judges should never lose sight of the fact that it is the job of the media to report on the trial, and not the job of the courts to be a "soundstage" whose job is to cater to the media. For judicial purposes, a high-profile case is no more or less important than any other case in the building.

But one problem in this area must be faced and discussed, and that is the increasingly popular attempt by counsel in both criminal and civil cases to prejudice or contaminate potential jurors with pre-trial publicity—in other words, to "try the case in the newspapers." This is a critical issue that plagues trial judges and the system of justice continually. Unfortunately, much of this prejudicial activity occurs before the case is even assigned to a judicial officer, so the judicial system is not in a position to regulate it. Think about all of the media's pre-trial activity: the press conference announcing an indictment, the photos of the arrest of the defendants, or the publicizing of the filing of the complaint in a large civil case. Then consider how the media runs and reruns the proclamations of the plaintiff's attorney, as he announces how justice will now be obtained for the victims of the fraud, or how the rightful redress of suffering brought about by the callous actions of such and such a defendant will now be realized. Then the defendants logically feel a need to respond in kind with attempts either to blunt this pre-trial publicity with attacks upon the motives of the prosecutors or plaintiffs, or with arguments attempting to deflect the possible blame to others.

There are no easy answers to these problems, other than encouraging the state's rules of professional conduct for attorneys to clamp down on this activity. But seeing the media as the "enemies of justice" is counterproductive. The more that the Judicial Branch of Government works with and helps to educate the representatives of the media, the more we will be able to balance the "public's right to know" with the right to a fair trial for all litigants in our courts before a fair, neutral, and uncontaminated jury.

Of course, there are some inherent media problems in cases even after they are assigned to a trial judge, such as the possibility that some of the participants in the trials might tend to "showboat" for the television cameras. But in my view, the answer to that problem, like so many others, is for the judges to take and maintain control from the outset over their courtrooms. Each case is different and has its own sensitivities, so most jurisdictions give a great deal of discretion to the trial judges on how to handle the media problems generated by those cases.[8] That is as it should be, but it calls for strong, experienced, and sensitive judges.

Once it has been decided that the trial judge will cooperate with the media in its coverage, what then should that judge do? According to some of its veteran members, the *responsible* news media actually appreciate rules, as long as they are consistently enforced for everyone, because rules that are uniformly enforced make their lives easier. For example, having some rules means that there will be an area in the courthouse for media interviews, so the reporters will not be required to chase the trial participants up and down the hallways or lie in wait for them as they get into their cars. It also means that they can obtain fresh footage to show as background while the television commentator describes what happened that day during the trial.

But as a practical matter, according to those veteran media members, the trial judge is well advised to "stay above the fray," and turn over the day-to-day enforcement of the rules to a committee of veteran media members. For example, the judge should decide how many seats in her courtroom will be available for the media but then allow the committee to allocate them. Obviously, if there are twenty cameras in the courtroom, that would be disruptive. But if there is a "camera pool" where only one or two cameras that are overseen by the committee are shared by all, everyone's interests will be well served. This procedure will also make it far easier to monitor the other rules set forth by the judge, such as the almost universal rule that the faces and identities of the jurors are never to be shown or disclosed.

If some member of the media does not follow the rules set out by the court, the veteran media members recommend that the judge pick up the telephone, call the offender's news editors, and tell them what happened. According to these people, this is an effective deterrent because that call will terrify the reporters. Having rules and enforcing them make life easier and more workable for everyone.

As an aside, it took me a long time to learn that almost never do the newspaper reporters actually write the headlines of their stories. The headlines are almost always written by the copy editors back at the office, with little or no input from the reporters. As a result, even though judges within their limitations try to provide pathways to the most accurate information and explanations to the media reporters and often are successful in those efforts, the headlines themselves will frequently give an entirely misleading representation of what occurred. This is a truly frustrating situation, but other than calling your attention to the problem, I do not have any remedies to suggest for it.

As another aside, I recommend that judges get to know reporters fairly well and have a long track record with them before they agree to provide any "off the record" background information. We know that newsgathering is a highly competitive business, and the news media are not necessarily the judges' friends. As a result, a judge should be prepared for anything and everything she says to a media representative to be reported in its entirety. Similarly, accuracy is her responsibility. Therefore, I suggest using simple and non-legal terminology. And after an interview, I recommend that the judge ask the reporters to read back her statements so that any errors can be corrected. In this as in virtually everything else, "That's not what I meant!" is not an effective defense. So if a statement is going to sound ambiguous or could be misinterpreted, the judge simply should not make it.

With regard to so-called "gag" orders, judges should bear in mind that because of some inherent difficulties there will probably be leaks. Judges have the task of deciding whether pursuing those leaks is in the best interest of society or not. If you are like me (and I know I am), you will usually decide that attempts to issue and enforce gag orders are not worth the effort.

Finally, on those rare occasions when a judge is placed in the position of ordering a member of the media to disclose her sources of information, the judge must simply assume that the reporter will not do so under any circumstances. This will make that reporter a hero in her profession for evermore, and make the judge the "goat." So stand advised.

Education of the Media

Another widely-held but erroneous view of the justice system in the mind of the general public is that statutes that judges like are constitutional, and those of which they disapprove are unconstitutional. And unfortunately these views have galvanized numbers of efforts to politicize the courts and otherwise generate attacks upon the judiciary. Retired U.S. Supreme Court Justice Sandra Day O'Connor has stated that she has been "saddened and disturbed" by verbal attacks by members of Congress upon state and federal judges when they disagree with their judicial decisions, which has resulted in threats of "mass impeachments" and cutting off court jurisdiction over certain types of cases in response to politically unpopular decisions. This attack upon the judiciary is actually an attack upon our way of life because, as Justice O'Connor says, "Without justices who could and would make decisions that they knew were unpopular, we would lose the protections of our Constitution."[9]

Accordingly, in my view we must seek out and deal with the media about those powers, protections, and limitations, and actually encourage thorough coverage of what we do. As I tell my jurors at the very conclusion of a case, I am proud of us, and believe that the more people are exposed to what we do and how we do it, the more they will be proud of us as well. That exposure will in turn build a confidence in the mind of the public about the Administration of Justice in our country.

Judges should be proactive in education and outreach to the public by trying to speak on radio and television talk shows and other areas of the media about our judicial system. They should explain, for example, the beauty of the "town hall justice" system in our Small Claims Courts; what to expect in a traffic trial, including the standard of "beyond a reasonable doubt"; the existence of calendars to issue restraining orders in matters of domestic violence, because all people in our society are entitled to live their lives free from being inappropriately hit or even touched; and the right of redress through the courts for everyone, regardless of their background or station in life.

Then people will be helped increasingly to understand that just because a statute is economically backward or a policy is unwise, this does not make that statute or policy unconstitutional. The role of judges in interpreting the Constitution and our statutes is not to do "justice" as they deem appropriate, but it is instead to do justice *under the law.* Under our system, redress from unwise public policies or laws must generally come from full and open debate and the ballot box, not through judicial action. In fact, on that point, I think most judges agree with what Ulysses S. Grant said in his first inaugural address: "I know no method to secure the repeal of bad or obnoxious laws so effective as their stringent execution."[10]

Judges have sworn by their oath of office to follow the law, even if they disagree with it, but they are not required to do so quietly. Similarly, the public should be assisted to understand that, as U.S. Supreme Court Justice John Paul Stevens stated, "It is not our job to apply laws that have not yet been written."[11] Our Founding Fathers bequeathed to us a magnificent system of checks and balances for the three separate but equal branches of government, and we judges must do our part to get out the word that one of them is under attack.

The Canons of Ethics for judges in most states not only allow but virtually require judges to help to educate the public about problems affecting the administration of justice. And there is little question that this community outreach education can most effectively be done through the media. To the extent that people in our society do not understand that judges do not make promises in exchange for public support, or do not "trade votes" on appellate cases or rig the system in order to favor one side or another, that is the fault of all of us, judicial officers, for not being more effective in educating the public. In point of fact, judges do not do anything except diligently attempt to follow and apply the rules of law. If judges allow the general public to believe that our judicial system simply responds and reacts to political stimuli and their own personal desires, our treasured system of justice will be irretrievably compromised—to the prejudice of us all.

So now that I have called your attention to these difficult areas, I can also say that, as a practical matter, most judges will go through a long career and never have a case with large media interest. And even if there is initial interest in a case, that attention often fades because court trials and proceedings in the real world are, for the most part, not all that interesting to the general public. For example, not long ago I received an ABC News petition for video coverage of a three-day felony preliminary hearing, and I granted their request. But apparently they were bored to death after the first afternoon, because after that they never returned. Perhaps we can consider that to be good news.

CONCLUSION

In this chapter we have focused upon the more public parts of being a judicial officer, including a few of the activities through which we can contribute to society during our "extra" time and our relationship with the media. With those thoughts we have now completed our analysis of many of the numerous arts and responsibilities of being a judge. What remains is to provide a few thoughts about how we can improve upon our System of Justice. And that is where we find ourselves in the Conclusion of this book.

Conclusion

Where the Judicial System Goes from Here

"Whatever degrades another degrades me,
And whatever is done or said returns at last to me."
—FROM *LEAVES OF GRASS*, WALT WHITMAN

I am deeply proud to be a part of the System of Justice in the United States of America. As I have commented several times, I believe that the more people see and understand what we do, the more they will be proud of us as well. But our system is constantly evolving. In most matters, I believe we are going in the right direction. But in some matters, I believe we are not.

Over the course of this book, we have already discussed some specific recommendations for changes. These included suggestions that states investigate and utilize some form of no-fault insurance program for routine automobile collisions (see page 93), adopt many of the provisions of Rule 26 of the Federal Rules of Civil Procedure for civil discovery matters (see page 91), and utilize a "Modified English Plan" to allow judges to have the *discretion* to award attorneys' fees in all civil cases (see page 92). But there remain some larger visions for improvement that require further discussion. And in the pages that remain, I will try to present those matters to you.

One of the areas of concern is that we continue to over-emphasize the false god of heavy punishment, particularly for non-violent offenders. And unless one is thinking of removing people from society for the rest of their lives, most of the time heavy punishment simply does not work. Therefore, I recommend that we, as a society, more fully rely upon the concept of Restorative Justice.

THE CONCEPT OF RESTORATIVE JUSTICE

Earlier in this book, I mentioned the purpose of the criminal justice system, which, in my view, is to reduce crime and all of the harm and misery that accompany it. I also mentioned a mandate that is important to enforce in order to meet that purpose, which is, "There must be negative consequences for criminal acts." But as a practical matter, it is not possible to accomplish these worthwhile goals through punishment alone. Many experienced judges understand that we must employ the concept of "Restorative Justice" for these goals to be maximized. And these judges understand the importance of rehabilitation, treatment, and community healing in that effort.

Looking at Prisons—The Costs and Effects

There is no doubt that we need to have prisons in our society. As stated earlier, there are some people who, for whatever reason, see the rest of us in society as their natural prey, and they present an unacceptable threat to public safety and well being. Accordingly, there is good cause to lock up people like that for the protection of the community. I have taken a tour of San Quentin State Prison in the San Francisco area, and I have never seen so many men who had "ball bearings for eyes." The bottom line is that I was very happy that they were where they were.

In my mind there is also no question that if people commit a grave offense, particularly one involving violence, they should be removed from society for a long time, if not for the rest of their lives. We, as members of a civilized society, have an obligation to treat the perpetrators humanely and to keep them safe while they are in our custody—no matter if they are Al Capone or Jack the Ripper. Why? Because as Fyodor Dostoyevsky put it, "The degree of civilization in a society is revealed by entering its prisons." But as long as we meet the threshold of providing the inmates with secure and humane treatment, society deserves to be protected from people who commit criminal violence, and the people who committed the violence deserve their fate.

On this subject, however, I think the comments of a man named Pat Nolan are instructive, and judges and everyone else should take note of them. Nolan was a former archconservative member of the California Legislature who always voted for longer and longer prison sentences for more and more offenders—until he himself was subsequently convicted of an election fraud offense and sentenced to two years in prison. He said upon his release that we have too many people in prison who simply should not be there. Then he went on to say, "We should reserve our prison space for people we are afraid of, not people we're mad at."

Unfortunately, for various reasons, people in our country—much more than those in most other countries in the world—have seized upon the idea that prisons are the answer to our criminal justice problems. In my view, we are attracted to that idea in a way that is similar to how the soldiers were attracted to the title character in Bizet's opera *Carmen*. When those admiring and enamored men ask Carmen when she will love them, she replies, "Maybe tomorrow, maybe never, but certainly not today." In a similar fashion, large-scale prisons provide an illusory hope that we have an answer to our problems for tomorrow, but that hope will *never* be realized today.

As we have all seen, laws increasing the length of prison sentences have become more prevalent. As a result, the United States broke a record at the end of 2005. That year, 2.2 million people were in prison or jail, which was an increase of a full 2.7 percent from the year before. An additional 4.1 million people were on probation, and more than 784,000 others were on parole. This means that 7 million people, or *one in every 32 adults in this country,* were afoul of the criminal justice system in 2005, and those numbers have only continued to grow.[1]

In this political climate, large numbers of inmates well into their elderly years routinely become eligible for parole but are turned down, even though many of them are actually taking dozens of medications and are shuffling around the prisons with walkers. Many of the facilities that hold them look like nursing homes surrounded by uniformed guards and concertina wire, with rooms instead of cells, beds instead of bunks, and ramps instead of steps. The showers have seats and the hallways have handrails. In fact, most of the inmates housed in facilities of this kind would not be *able* to hurt anyone else even if that was their desire! But the resultant cost to the taxpayers for the continued incarceration of elderly inmates like those described is generally about three times what it is for an inmate in good health.

For example, in Michigan the number of inmates above age sixty increased by 62 percent from 2000 to 2006. The result was that the cost of healthcare for Michigan's prison inmates went up by 50 percent during that period of time alone, from $120 million to $181 million per year.[2] In many ways this is an unnecessary expense, since numbers of studies show that the age of inmates is one of the best criteria to forecast whether they will return to crime. Consider that a U.S. Department of Justice study in 1990 found that only 2 percent of the men who were paroled after age fifty-five were returned to prison for violations; but for men between ages eighteen and twenty-four, the average figure was 22 percent.[3] Therefore, we must recognize that, although they certainly are necessary, prisons are also society's most expensive option for punishment in financial terms and often in human terms as well.

Finding Ways to Reduce Recidivism

Even considering the numbers offered above, the truth is that about 95 percent of the people who go to jail or prison will someday get out. And then what are those people going to be like? After their years of confinement in a prison, they are given a few items upon their release, such as a new pair of shoes, a new set of clothes, $200 in cash, and a bus ticket. Probably they will have gotten a tattoo while in prison that identifies them with whatever racial group they belong to. Probably they will still be vulnerable to the drug addictions that they had when they entered prison. And probably they will have been rendered functionally unemployable by their felony convictions. As such, the likelihood that they will become recidivists or re-offenders is painfully high. That also means, of course, that a large proportion of all prison admissions is for parole violators.

So if people are going to be confined but eventually released, we should assist in providing those people with the tools that will address the reasons why they were imprisoned in the first place. Then we should provide them some support once they are released. And we should do this if for no other reason than to protect our own safety, as well as our own pocketbooks!

Prison programs that teach and focus upon simple reading, writing, and mathematical skills are a great place to start. It is commonly known that a large majority of inmates in prison are functionally illiterate, and a basic education is *the* thing that will most probably keep them from re-offending. For example, about two-thirds of California's 173,000 prison inmates read below a ninth-grade level, and more than half of those fall below seventh-grade level! Even worse, a full 21 percent of California's inmates read below a third-grade level. What chance do they have, particularly when there is space for only 6 percent of the prison inmates in academic classes and only 5 percent in vocational classes?[4] Judges cannot control the prison system, but, if appropriate, we can keep some people from going there. As a result, experienced judges will, in the right cases, utilize sentences of strictly-applied probation instead of prison in order to encourage defendants in criminal cases, both adult and juvenile, to obtain their education, and will help to provide the tools to allow them to do so. Without those tools, people lose hope, and a person without hope is one of the most dangerous people in the world. But with those skills comes hope, and even some of the most hardened criminals can and will become responsible, productive citizens if educational tools and opportunities are made available to them.[5]

In addition to basic education, things we have discussed earlier such as anger management and other counseling, parenting skills, alcohol and other drug treatment, job skills training, and even meditation techniques will help to reduce the recidivism rate substantially. For example, a drug treatment program in Donovan State Prison in San Diego County that addresses these problems *and* has an aftercare support component has reduced the recidivism rate in that facility from 80 percent to 18 percent. But in California, about 56 percent of the inmates have a "high need" for treatment for their drug addictions, yet only about 9 percent receive *any* treatment at all. The same is true in California with regard to alcohol addictions, where about 42 percent of the inmates need treatment, but only 7.5 percent actually receive anything close to it.[6]

Private support groups such as Volunteers in Parole (VIP), which match recent parolees with a mentor and which we discussed in Chapter 10 (see page 280), are also enormously successful in reducing the recidivism rate. The state of Rhode Island has adopted this same far-seeing philosophy. There, political leaders, police officers, corrections officials, churches, and community groups have collaborated to establish "re-entry programs." The programs help people who have completed their time in custody successfully to adjust back into society and become productive members. Governor Donald L. Carcieri of Rhode Island summed up these efforts by saying, "The goal now is to see if you can rehabilitate lives instead of just locking them up."[7] Think of the people who will not be victimized, the police who will not have to investigate a crime, the prosecutors who will not have to prosecute, the jurors and judges who will not have to sit in judgment on the trials, and the tax money that will be saved by the reduced recidivism rate if we would all adopt this approach!

Making Distinctions Between Violent and Non-Violent Perpetrators

From my observations, and taking the advice of Pat Nolan to heart (see page 294), I recommend that we judges and legislators utilize much more of a distinction between violent as opposed to non-violent offenders. People convicted of violent offenses should be sent to prison as an appropriate sanction for their acts, and if they become repeat violent offenders, they should be removed from society for a long time. But similarly I believe we would be far better off by imposing much shorter sentences of incarceration on non-violent offenders convicted of property crimes. Then we should require those offenders to be on a meaningful and strictly-applied program of formal probation.

What would such a probation program involve? In addition to education, it would assist the offenders in addressing their fundamental problems of substance abuse, lack of job skills, anger and rage, and other similar concerns. It would also require them to obtain and hold full-time employment, which would allow them lawfully to support their families and keep their families together, and also require them to make monetary restitution to the victims of their offenses.

This approach in many ways parallels the traditions of Native American cultures and countries in East Asia and the Middle East. In response to criminal offenses, they incorporate elements of reconciliation and social balance for the victim, the offender, and the community. Such programs provide benefits to all of those parties.

In the first place, paying $150 per month or some reasonable amount to the victim would be a continual reminder to the perpetrators that there is a price for their misdeeds. Secondly, it would be therapeutic for the victims to receive this restitution from the perpetrators. Thirdly, the restitution would also help to reduce the victims' insurance rates because the insurance companies that paid the victims for their losses would be reimbursed. Finally, it would be beneficial to society not only to see that victims' losses were being addressed, but also, since incarceration is the most expensive option, it would reduce the overall cost of the system to the taxpayers.

Unfortunately, under today's system the victims of crime are actually punished three times: first by the offense itself; second when they are forced to come to court and testify on multiple occasions without compensation; and third when they are forced as taxpayers to reach into their pocketbooks and pay for the incarceration of the offenders. This program would begin to change that equation.

Of course, if those on formal probation fail to take the programs and their obligations seriously, they could always be sent back to jail for ever-increasing periods of time, until they decide to perform. That return to jail would serve as a "booster shot" to remind these offenders that the judicial system is serious about their obligation to make restitution. Or, if all else fails, they could at least serve as "a bad example" for other offenders by being forced to serve longer sentences in custody due to their irresponsibility.

I believe we are living in the Renaissance period of this insightful movement. It focuses upon restoring the losses suffered by victims, and it requires the offenders to take responsibility for their actions and for the harms they have caused by making restitution to the victims. The more that judges employ these concepts, the more we will reduce crime, insurance rates, victimization, the costs of the criminal justice system, and the number of people behind bars. I know this approach can be considered to be controversial, but what do you think?

DIGNITY FOR ALL

As I have stated several times on these pages, my father was one of the true heroes of my life for his outstanding qualities as both a judge and a human being. In that regard, one time he took my mother with him on a tour of Lompoc Federal Prison in Central California. At the end of the tour, it happened that the inmates were going to have a talent show, and the warden invited my parents to attend. On one side of my mother was seated my father, and next to him was the warden. On the other side of my mother was an inmate.

Before the show began, this inmate struck up a conversation with my mother and told her that he had been sentenced to the maximum sentence by my father. As the inmate said that, my mother tried to inch herself away from this fellow. But the man continued to elaborate on the way my father had talked to him as an individual and treated him with such respect that the inmate felt my father was the best judge he had ever been before—and, as he said, "that included quite a few judges."

I believe that criminal defendants know that the prosecutors, bailiffs, judges, and other legal officers are just doing their jobs. Moreover, they appreciate it when they are not treated like dirt, and most will respond appropriately when treated with dignity. This is yet another part of the vision I have for our justice system, as well as for every other part of our society. Firmness and fairness are certainly major goals, but so is dignity for all.

EARNED RESPECT FOR THE JUDICIARY

Unfortunately, when some people think of courts and the court process they identify with a most discouraging warning from Charles Dickens' *Bleak House* about having your fate decided by a court of law by saying, "Suffer any wrong that can be done you rather than come here."[8] Part of this feeling is based upon fact, part upon fiction, and part upon the "Fear of the Great Unknown." But we judges must continue to strive to change that viewpoint and those feelings. One of the big ways this will be changed is for each of us to work so that we can forever banish the slogan "Close enough for government work" from everyone's minds, with the result that people will appreciate and even admire the judicial system instead of resent it. Another way of phrasing this is to draw a distinction between the word "courtesy" and the word "respect." Judicial officers are entitled to be treated courteously because of their office, but respect cannot be commanded, it must be earned. Each day, in everything you do as a judge, try to earn the respect that should come with being known as "The Honorable."

It is fine and even expected for people to disagree with us, but when this happens, it should be a disagreement like people have with their family members or their business partners. Basically, we want them to think that we are the "good guys," and that we are pulling for them, but this time we concluded that the facts or the law did not support their position.

Similarly, we want to educate people about the justice system so that they will recognize us for what we are: an institution that protects all of us from harm and resolves disputes in our society. The courts should be viewed as a bastion that protects our cherished freedoms from the excesses of the majority. Then people will begin to see that if one looks back into history and thinks about it, if racial integration had been left up to the will of an opinion poll instead of an independent judiciary, we probably would still be operating with an officially segregated society.

There is an old Buddhist religious proverb that says, "To every man is given the key to the Gates of Heaven; but the same key also opens the Gates of Hell." Being a judge is a powerful position in society, and we can positively affect numbers of people's lives by "doing justice." In many ways, that gives us the key to Heaven. But for those who tend to feed off this power to attain some self-glamorization or ego aggrandizement—or just use their judicial position to take home an easy paycheck—the same key can open the Gates of Hell, and thereby perpetuate Dickens' advice to "suffer any wrong that can be done you" rather than come to a court presided over by this judge.

A FINAL NOTE

So there you have it. As a judge you will be exposed to factual situations that are challenging, pathetic, soap-operatic, tearful, mundane, energizing, and, on occasion, too strange to be fiction. You will also preside over the litigation of disputes that deeply affect the lives, family, and future of your fellow human beings in situations that are serious and demanding. Yet as long as you are diligent, conscientious, determined to develop your instincts, continually open to different approaches that work, and willing to accept some criticism from traditionalists, you can often resolve what appears to be unresolvable. And just like a man can spend an entire day weeding his garden only to look back at the end of his efforts and not see a single weed he has pulled—only the weeds that remain—often the efforts you have made and the problems you have addressed and resolved will not be seen by many people. But you will know you did the work and made our society a healthier and more just place. And that should be enough.

Appendix 1

Sample Trial Note-Taking Contractions and Symbols

¢	Complaint or disputed incident or injury	O/R	Overruled
2AX¢	Second Amended Cross-Complaint	O/C	Off Calendar
		Dec R	Declaratory Relief
c/a	cause of action	MO	Minute Order
TT	Plaintiff	SP	Specific Performance
TTT	Plaintiff Thompson	b/c	because
△	Defendant	w/	with
×TT Jones	Cross-Complainant Jones	w/in	within
×△ Wilson	Cross-Defendant Wilson	w/o	without
ⓦ	Witness	w/d	withdrawn
V	Victim	i/v	interview
p⁄	Police/Police officer	tx	transaction
Ⓓ	Deceased person, Death, Divorce	sh/	shareholder
		f/	function or fingerprints
⑦⑥	Age of a person, i.e. this person is 76 years old	pix	pictures or photos
		Ⓡ	Research or review this
Jd	Jurisdiction	⊖	Ask questions about this subject
HS	Hearsay		
RR	Refresh Recollection	⊘	Question answered
m/	motion	∴	Therefore
m/OST	motion for Order Shortening Time	±	More or less / About
		¢	Consider or Consideration
m/Cpl	motion to Compel	=	Equals/This is the same as that
m/SJ	motion for Summary Judgment		
		≠	This is not the same as that
m/stk	motion to strike	≃	This is similar to that
DMR	Demurrer	≄	This is not similar to that
G	Granted	/	In order to, e.g. "one must breathe/live"
D	Denied		
S	Sustained	⟶	This leads to that, e.g. "education⟶opportunities"

K	Contract or Child	⚡	Exhibit received by stipulation
P	Parent		
RP	Real Property	◿ₒ	Objection to exhibit
DoT	Deed of Trust	◿ₒ	Objection to exhibit sustained
S/L	Statute of Limitations or Strict Liability	◿ₒ	Objection to exhibit overruled and exhibit received into evidence
S/F	Statute of Frauds		
A/R	Assumption of the Risk	25/6-27/14	Read deposition from page 25 line 6 to page 27 line 14
AR	Accounts Receivable		
AP	Accounts Payable	✓	No objection to the reading of this deposition passage
B of L	Bill of Lading		
$	Money	◿ₒ	Objection to reading of the deposition passage overruled
C/R	Custodian of Records		
5X	Five times, e.g. "I told him five times."	◿ₒ	Objection to reading of the deposition passage sustained
NK	Not Know		
NR	Not Remember/Not Recall	<	This less than that
FTA	Fail to Appear	>	This more than that
FTP	Fail to Pay	↑	Large amount/Increased
NB	Northbound	↓	Small amount/Decreased
SB	Southbound	h/w	handwriting
i/s	intersection	h/c	handcuffs or handcuffed
✪	Traffic Signal	pt	patient
⊖	Stop Sign	e/ment	employment
d/w	driveway	e/er	employer
UI	Under the Influence	e/ee	employee
BR	Bedroom	LL	Landlord
BaR	Bathroom	T	Tenant/Trust
LR	Living Room	T/or	Trustor
D/W	Driveway	T/ee	Trustee
S&F	Slip and Fall	P of A	Power of Attorney
T&F	Trip and Fall	Gty	Guaranty
A&B	Assault and Battery	g/or	guarantor or grantor
LoE	Loss of Earnings	g/ee	guarantee or grantee
P&S	Pain and Suffering	A/ment	Assignment
Rx	Prescription, Medicine, Medication	A/or	Assignor
		A/ee	Assignee
✓	Exhibit identified and moved into evidence	f&c	fees and costs
		C̲	Computer
✓	Exhibit received into evidence	e̲	e-mail

Appendix 2

State Requirements
for Becoming a Judge

The following table offers information about the procedure under which a person in any of the fifty states or the District of Columbia can obtain a judicial position. As shown, a position can be obtained by election, appointment, or a combination of the two, and either with or without the recommendation of another person or organization, such as a nominating commission. The table also attempts to set forth the qualifications that a person seeking a judicial position must satisfy. Note that some of the boxes have been left blank. In these cases, to the best I can determine, the state has no specific requirement.

Some of the terms and abbreviations used in the chart on the following pages should be clarified. "Nom Comm" means nominating commission, underneath which "Mixed" means the state uses a nominating commission in combination with other organizations; "Vol" means voluntary, so the appointing authority can give weight to the commission's opinions or not; and "Some" means that a commission is used to fill some, but not all, of the state's judicial positions. Under "Retention," "Rtn Election" means retention election; "Comm Retains" means that the commission retains; "Non-Partisan" means that there is a non-partisan election; "Mixed" means that the state uses a combination of appointment and election and commission recommendations; and "Retention" means that there is an uncontested election—the incumbent, rather than being challenged by another person, is instead subjected to an up-or-down vote as to whether he ought to be retained for that particular office. Under "State Bar," "Yes" means that the state bar is involved in one's process of becoming a judge; and "Mixed" means that the state bar, along with some other entity, is involved in the process. Under "Years Residence In," "Yes" means that the candidate must at that time be a resident, but not for a specified length of time. "Lic'd in State" means licensed in state, and entries with numerals indicate the number of years a candidate must have been licensed in that state. Under "US Citizen," a numeral indicates the number of years a candidate, to be eligible for a judicial position, must have been a citizen.

If you are seriously interested in pursuing a judicial office, I strongly recommend that you contact the Secretary of State for your particular jurisdiction and request the current requirements directly. Obviously, some of the requirements are more complicated than can be presented in simple chart form. Moreover, requirements can and often do change.

State	Acquire Seat By: Election	Acquire Seat By: Appointment	Nom Comm	Years per Term	Retention	Vacancy Filled By:	Nom Comm
AL	Partisan			6	Reelection	Governor	Some
AK		Governor	Yes	6	Rtn Election	Governor	Yes
AZ	Mixed	Mixed	Yes	4*	Mixed	Governor	Yes
AR	Non-Partisan			6	Reelection	Governor	
CA	Non-Partisan			6	Reelection	Governor	Vol.
CO		Governor	Yes	6	Rtn Election	Governor	Yes
CT		Gov/Legis	Yes	8	Gov/Legis	Gov/Legis	Yes
DE		Gov/Senate	Yes	12	Gov/Senate	Gov/Senate	Yes
DC		Pres/Senate	Yes	15	Pres Re-Appt	Pres/Senate	Yes
FL	Non-Partisan			6	Reelection	Governor	Yes
GA	Non-Partisan			4	Reelection	Governor	Yes
HI		Gov/Senate	Yes	10	Comm Retains	Gov/Senate	Yes
ID	Non-Partisan			4	Reelection	Governor	Yes
IL	Partisan			6	Rtn Election	Supreme Ct.	
IN	Mixed			6	Mixed	Mixed	Mixed
IA		Governor	Yes	6	Rtn Election	Governor	Yes
KS	Mixed	Mixed	Mixed	4	Mixed	Governor	Mixed
KY	Non-Partisan			8	Reelection	Governor	Yes
LA	Partisan			6	Reelection	Spcl Election	
ME		Gov/Senate	Vol	7	Gov/Senate	Gov/Senate	Vol
MD	Mixed	Mixed	Mixed	15	Non-partisan	Governor	Yes
MA		Governor	Yes	Until 70	N/A	Governor	Yes
MI	Non-Partisan			6	Reelection	Governor	Vol.
MN	Non-Partisan			6	Reelection	Governor	Yes
MS	Non-Partisan			4	Reelection	Governor	
MO	Mixed	Mixed	Mixed	6	Mixed	Governor	Mixed
MT	Non-Partisan			6	Non-partisan	Gov/Senate	Yes
NE		Governor	Yes	6	Rtn Election	Governor	Yes
NV	Non-Partisan			6	Reelection	Governor	Yes
NH		Governor	Yes	Until 70	N/A	Governor	Yes
NJ		Gov/Senate		7	Gov/Senate	Gov/Senate	
NM	Partisan			6	Rtn Election	Governor	Yes
NY	Partisan			14	Reelection	Gov/Senate	Yes
NC	Non-Partisan			8	Reelection	Governor	
ND	Non-Partisan			6	Reelection	Governor	Yes
OH	Non-Partisan			6	Reelection	Governor	
OK	Non-Partisan			4	Reelection	Governor	Yes
OR	Non-Partisan			6	Reelection	Governor	
PA	Partisan			10	Retention	Gov/Senate	
RI		Gov/Senate	Yes	Life	N/A	Gov/Senate	Yes
SC	Legislature			6	Legislature	Legislature	
SD	Non-Partisan			8	Reelection	Governor	Yes
TN		Governor	Yes	8	Rtn Election	Governor	Yes
TX	Partisan			4	Reelection	Gov/Senate	
UT		Gov/Senate	Yes	6	Rtn Election	Gov/Senate	Yes
VT		Gov/Senate	Yes	6	Asmbly Election	Gov/Senate	Yes
VA	Legis Election			8	Legis Election	Legis Election	
WA	Non-Partisan			4	Reelection	Governor	
WV	Partisan			8	Reelection	Governor	
WI	Non-Partisan			6	Reelection	Governor	Yes
WY		Governor	Yes	6	Rtn Election	Governor	Yes

STATE POLICIES

* Different Requirements in Counties above 250,000

INDIVIDUAL QUALIFICATIONS

Age:		State Bar	Years Residence In:		Lic'd in State	Years of Practice	US Citizen
Min	Max		State	Local			
	70			1	Yes		
			5		Yes	5	Yes
30	70		5	1	Yes		
28			2			6	Yes
				Yes	10	10	
	72			Yes	5	5	
	70	Yes	Yes				
		Yes	Yes	Yes			
	74	5 Mixed**		90 Days		5**	Yes
	70			Yes		5**	
30			3	Yes		7	
	70		Yes	Yes		10**	Yes
30			2	1		10	Yes
	75		Yes	Yes	Yes		Yes
			Yes	Yes			
	72	Yes		Yes	Yes		
	70	5	Yes				
				2		8	Yes
	70			2	5	5**	
30	70	Yes	5	6 Mos		10	
		Yes	Yes		Yes	10	Yes
	70			Yes	Yes	5	
	70						
26			5	Yes		5	
30	70	Yes	3	1	Yes		Yes
18			2	Yes		5**	Yes
30		Yes		Yes	Yes	5**	Yes
25			2	Yes	Yes		
	70				10	10**	
35			3	Yes		6	
18	70		Yes	Yes	10	10**	
	72				Yes		
			Yes		Yes		Yes
	70			Yes		6	
				1		4	
	75		3	1	Yes	3**	Yes
21	70	Yes		1	Yes		
		Yes			Yes		
32	72		5			8	Yes
	70		Yes	Yes	Yes		Yes
30		Yes	5	1	Yes		
25		Yes	Yes	2	Yes	4	Yes
25		Yes	3		Yes		Yes
	70					5**	
	70	5	Yes	Yes		5	
	75				Yes		
30			5	Yes		5	
	70			Yes		5**	
28	70		2				Yes

** In that State

Appendix 3

Sample Wedding Ceremony

Marriage of _____

and _____

on _____

at _____

Family and friends, we are gathered here today to witness and to celebrate the coming together of two separate lives. We have come to join _____ and _____ in marriage, and to be with them and rejoice with them in the making of this commitment. The essence of the commitment of marriage is the taking of another person in his or her entirety, as a lover, as a companion, and most certainly as a friend. It is, therefore, a decision which is not to be entered into lightly, but rather undertaken with great consideration and respect for both the other person and for oneself.

Who is it that gives this woman to be married to this man?

It is love for one another that brings _____ and _____ here today. Love is life's highest destiny, its greatest purpose, and its finest work. It is love, of course, true love, unconditional love that shatters all limitations and dissolves all fears. This unconditional love is the true gift of marriage and is its greatest and most spirit-embracing work. It is love, kindled by romance and clasped by heartfelt marriage vows, that has the capacity to deliver marriage from being merely a domestic arrangement, or just a productive and supportive partnership, or even an emotional bonding, and elevate it into a spiritual enterprise.

Marriage symbolizes the intimate sharing of two lives. It is not just a ceremony, but is instead an ongoing commitment. Each day for the rest of their lives, _____ and _____ will make choices. They will choose whether to be faithful, whether to be kind and patient with each other. They will choose whether to find fault or whether to be forgiving. In the days and years ahead, they will have to choose, again and again, whether or not to keep their love as the most important part of their lives. They have chosen each other as life partners because they promise now to make their love for each other their ongoing choice. Although this will at times require sacrifice and attention, it will also give them the opportunity to experience the true joys of marriage, the comfort of a relationship built upon respect, trust, and a deep caring for each other.

Sometimes when we have finally arrived at a longed-for destination, there can be a temptation simply to be where we are, without discovering the possibilities of our new state. This marriage may feel like such a destination, a sweet and safe place in which _____ and _____ can finally rest; but it is also an opportunity for them to have an emotional and spiritual environment in which the two of them can both develop into their highest brilliance.

Here insert individualized comments about the bride, and then the groom, which you learned when you met with them in your chambers in order to introduce yourselves. I have found that most people witnessing a wedding seldom know both the bride and the groom, so they appreciate the opportunity to learn a little bit about them both. Keep it short. Depending upon the individuals, some of the following suggestions will work and some will not.

Start by saying where the bride was born and raised, where she went to school, and what she has done thereafter, but do not ever say anything that might even tend to embarrass either of them. Then use words to the effect that family is important to the bride, and take the opportunity to introduce the close family members who are present—particularly grandparents. You can group them together, such as, "We welcome the bride's aunts, uncles, and their families who came from Denver, Raleigh, and San Francisco." You can also introduce her longtime best friend since grammar school who came from Pittsburgh, etc. Most of the time, a fairly clear line of demarcation will develop, so that you do not upset some people by recognizing others but not them. Then you can sometimes relate something a little bit unusual about the bride—nothing embarrassing, but something that maybe even some of her close friends do not know. For example, someday the bride would like to travel to Tibet, or go river-rafting through the Grand Canyon, or write a musical. And finally, sometimes you can give a short sentence about what her life will look like ten years from now.

Then go through the same short recitation about "the man who has captured this beautiful young lady's eye and her heart." In these remarks, frequently it can be a nice touch to tell the story about how the bride and the groom met, and if some of the people who were instrumental in that meeting or their "romantic development" are present at the wedding, you can have some fun by introducing them. Finally, anywhere in your comments in which truthful flattery can be inserted, that is well received. For example, if the bride is or is studying to be a doctor, say that you would be happy to have her treat your children if they were sick. Or if the groom has just started a small business, compliment him by saying that people like that are the "backbone of America."

_____ and _____, this is the person with whom you can do all the precious things you have wanted all of your life to do. This is the time to fulfill not only the joys of your heart, but also the possibilities of your life. We know that sometimes there will be a temptation to think that "the grass is greener on the other side of the fence." But actually, the grass is greenest where it is watered and nourished. Water and nourish your priceless relationship with each other; always put each other first, and you will savor one of life's greatest treasures.

Weddings are often made special and memorable by having one or even two readings by just the right person. That can be a grandparent, the person who introduced them, or a mutual friend. The reading can be a religious passage, a poem, or even a letter of advice from the reader. But tell the bride and groom to be sure the readings are short, and to stay away from humor, because it often bombs.

In addition, if the bride or groom simply must have a particular person, such as a sister, sing at their wedding, recommend that it be done before the wedding ceremony begins, or later at the reception. If they still think it would be nice, ask them to practice standing together in front of a mirror for three minutes without doing anything. This is the length of most short songs, and the time almost always is interminable. That should convince them.

Finally, since the bride's mother has been dreaming about this day since before the bride was born, sometimes it is a nice gesture for the bride and groom to take the time during the ceremony to give each of their mothers a small gift, such as a rose or small engraved vase.

_____ and _____, on behalf of myself and all of the people who are so fortunate to be present here today, may I say that you are two truly special people. You are loved; we are happy for you; and we know that you will have a truly rewarding and satisfying life together. With that knowledge, and on behalf of all of those here assembled, I celebrate you by asking that your life's journey together be a full one, with many interesting detours along the way.

And now, with that spirit in your minds and in your hearts, will you prepare to take your vows of marriage to each other:

_____, do you take _____ to be your wife and your equal; do you promise to love her, comfort her, honor and cherish her, in sickness and in health, in richness or poverty, for better or worse, as long as you both shall live?

("I do.")

_____, do you take _____ to be your husband and your equal; do you promise to love him, comfort him, honor and cherish him, in sickness and in health, in richness or poverty, for better or worse, as long as you both shall live?

("I do.")

Here, if it is a second wedding and if one or both have children, insert comments about how the bride and/or groom are also marrying the children, and ask the children, by name, if they also consent. The parents will appreciate how you include their children, and the children will probably always remember it.

May I have the rings?

Your rings are symbols of your marriage—valuable and beautiful, like your love for each other. They are symbolic of the fact that you have, this day, pledged yourselves in marriage to one another, and of the fact that, as the encircling ring is unending, it the wish, hope, and expectation of us all that your marriage will also be unending.

_____, place the ring upon _____ 's finger, and as you do so, repeat after me: "With this ring I thee wed / and I give it to you / as a loving symbol of our marriage." (Husband repeats.)

_____, place the ring upon _____ 's finger, and as you do so, repeat after me: "With this ring I thee wed / and I give it to you / as a loving symbol of our marriage." (Wife repeats.)

And now, at the request of _____ and _____, I would like to read a passage from an Apache wedding ceremony:

Now you will feel no rain, for each of you will be shelter to the other.
Now you will feel no cold, for each of you will be warmth to the other.
Now there is no more loneliness, for each of you will be companion to the other.
Though you are two bodies, there is now only one life between you.
Go now to your dwelling place, to enter into the days of your togetherness,
And may your days be good and long upon the earth.
And now may the god of heaven always bless your lives together.

_____, there happens to be a tradition that at this point of the wedding ceremony, if you so choose, you may now kiss your beautiful bride.

Ladies and gentlemen, it gives me an extraordinary amount of pleasure to be able to be the first person in the world to present to you: Mr. and Mrs. _____.

Endnotes

Introduction

1. "Injustice anywhere is a threat to justice everywhere. We are caught in an inescapable network of mutuality, tied in a single garment of destiny. Whatever affects one directly affects all indirectly." Dr. Martin Luther King, Jr., "Letter from a Birmingham Jail," August, 1963, *The Atlantic Monthly*, March, 2006: 55.

2. *Newsweek*, August 15, 2005: 23.

3. For a well-written and similar book that provides insights for new attorneys, see Mark Hermann, *The Curmudgeon's Guide to Practicing Law* (ABA Publishing, 2006).

4. See Daniel M. Kolkey, "Lawyers Can Reap Results With Judge's Method," *Los Angeles Daily Journal*, March 22, 2006: 8.

5. George Washington, letter to Edmund Randolph, September 27, 1789.

Chapter 1

1. See *Trials of War Criminals Before the Nuremberg Military Tribunals Under Control Council Law* (Number 10, Vol. 3), United States Government Printing Office, Washington, D.C. (1951), case number three, the "Justice Case."

2. See E.P. Bruke, *Historical Essay on the Laws of and the Government of Rome*, Civil Law, Cambridge Press, London, 1827, Reprint, W.M.W. Gaunt and Sons, Inc. Florida 1994; William Burdick, *The Principle of Roman Law and their Relation to the Modern Law*, the Lawyers Co-Operative Publishing Co., Rochester, New York, 1938; and Amir Aaron Kakan, "Evolution of American Law, From its Roman Origin to the Present," *Orange County Lawyer*, February 2006: 31–47.

3. Justice Paul Boland, "In conversation with the Chief Justice," *California Courts Review*, Spring, 2006: 5.

4. Justice Robert H. Jackson, *Brown v. Allen*, (1953) 344 U.S. 443, 540, concurring opinion.

5. See Jean Guccione, "System Offers Justice Outside Spotlight," *Los Angeles Times*, May 7, 2006: B1, 7.

6. Alexis, Comte de Tocqueville, *Democracy in America*.

7. For more information, see National Center for State Courts at www.NCSConline.org/wc/Education/ProSeGuide.htm.

Chapter 2

1. Howard Zehr, *Changing Lenses: A New Focus for Crime and Justice*, Herald Press, Scottsdale, Pennsylvania (1990).

2. Benjamin Franklin, *Poor Richard's Almanac*, as quoted in *The Merriam-Webster Dictionary of Quotations*, Merriam-Webster, Inc., Springfield, Massachusetts (1992), 238.

3. Don J. DeBenedictis, "DUI Court Produces Proud Grads," *Los Angeles Daily Journal*, December 22, 2005: 1, 7.

4. Actually, we did not use the word "alcoholic" in our court because being called by that name often simply makes many people angry, and that is counterproductive. And besides, the word has many different meanings to different people. The functional definition of "alcoholic" or "drug addict" that we employed was "a person who drinks or uses other drugs in spite of the known adverse consequences." Nevertheless, in order not to alienate anyone unnecessarily, we simply referred to the perpetrators as "high risk problem drinkers" in the screening process.

5. For further information about our program, please refer to James P. Gray, "Non-Traditional Sanctions," *Drunk Driving Laws & Enforcement—An Assessment of Effectiveness,* American Bar Association, Criminal Justice Section, February 1986, 143–146.

6. Peggy O'Hare, "Bracelets Keep Alcohol Offenders Off the Bottle," *Los Angeles Daily Journal,* November 29, 2006: 8.

7. Melissa Healy, "Undoing Alcohol's Damage to the Mind," *Los Angeles Times,* December 25, 2006: F1, 6.

8. For a more complete discussion, see James E. Lessenger, MD, and Glade F. Roper, JD, editors, *Drug Courts: A New Approach to Treatment and Rehabilitation,* Springer (2007), and James L. Nolan, Jr., *Reinventing Justice, The American Drug Court Movement,* Princeton University Press (2001).

9. Judge Wendy Lindley, "The Collaborative Courts of Orange County," *Orange County Lawyer,* July 2006, 37–41.

10. Michael Craig Miller, M.D., "How to Break the Chain," *Newsweek,* December 12, 2005: 58.

11. Not only have I not been quiet about our failed and hopeless policy of Drug Prohibition, I have written a book about it. See Judge James P. Gray, *Why Our Drug Laws Have Failed and What We Can Do About It—A Judicial Indictment of the War on Drugs,* Temple University Press (2001).

12. Associated Press, "Experts: Drug Courts Working," *USA Today,* November 11, 1998: 21A. See also Staff Reports, "Study: Drug Courts Save State Millions," *Los Angeles Daily Journal,* August 23, 2006: 3.

13. See Michael Wilson, New York Times News Service, "One-of-a-Kind Court in N.Y. Dispenses Justice, Teaches Neighborliness," *Los Angeles Daily Journal,* August 23, 2006: 5; and Don J. DeBenedictis, "Distinguished Jurist of the Year Crusades for Special Courts," *Los Angeles Daily Journal,* May 19, 2006: 1, 5. For further information about Corroborative Courts in Orange County, California, see www.occourts.org/GenInfo/Collaborative/.

14. Michail J. Sniffen, Associated Press, "Half of Inmates Report Mental Health Problems," *Los Angeles Daily Journal,* September 8, 2006: 9.

15. Chris Tisch and Jacob H. Fries, "Disturbed Inmates Languish, Without Treatment," *Los Angeles Daily Journal,* January 11, 2007: 6.

16. Ibid.

17. Anne Marie Ruff, "Study Backs Mental-Health Courts," *Los Angeles Daily Journal,* March 5, 2007: 8.

18. Kristina Horton Flaherty, "Courts for the homeless offer help—and hope," *California Bar Journal,* December, 2006: 1

19. Erin Park, "Making Tough Calls Look Easy, in Court and on Bike," *Los Angeles Daily Journal,* March 29, 2006: 1, 5.

20. For a more detailed approach to the questions of criminal sentencing, see James Q. Wilson, *Thinking about Crime* (New York: Vintage Books, rev. ed., 1985), and Elliott Currie, *Crime and Pun-*

ishment in America: Why the Solutions to America's Most Stubborn Social Crisis Have Not Worked Out—and What Will (New York: Metropolitan Books, 1998).

21. Ron Word, "In Lieu of Jail, Some Offenders Ordered to Carry Signs, Wear Chicken Suits," *Los Angeles Daily Journal,* November 5, 2007: 4.

22. Craig Anderson, "Judge Accepts Job's Political Heat," *Los Angeles Daily Journal,* August 11, 2005: 3.

Inset: "Defining Alcoholism As a Disease"

1. Mark Pollman, editor, *Bottled Wisdom,* Wildstore Media (1998): 148.

Inset: "Judges Comment on the Power of Drug Court Programs"

1. Teresa Huggins, "Judge Says Presiding at Drug Court Transformed Her," *Los Angeles Daily Journal,* July 11, 2005: 1, 5.

2. "Drug Court Affords Second Chance," *Los Angeles Daily Journal,* February 14, 2006, A1, 5.

Inset: "An Opinion on Drug Control in Our Country"

1. Eric Bailey, "Marijuana is called nation's biggest cash crop in report," *Los Angeles Times,* December 18, 2006: B3.

2. Associated Press, "Advocates Say Shultz Conversion Will Add Fuel to Drug Legalization," *Wall Street Journal,* October 27, 1989.

3. Associated Press, "Dole Can Fight on Drug Issue," *San Antonio Express News,* September 13, 1996: B7.

Inset: "Should Some Defendants Get Celebrity Treatment When Being Sentenced?"

1. Plutarch, *Parallel Lives,* as quoted in *The Merriam-Webster Dictionary of Quotations,* Merriam-Webster, Inc. Springfield, Massachusetts (1992), 239.

2. Robert G. Ingersoll, *Prose-Poems and Selections* (1884).

Chapter 3

1. Archibald Cox, *The New York Times,* Dec. 30, 1973

2. Aesop, *Fables,* as quoted in *The Merriam-Webster Dictionary of Quotations,* Merriam-Webster, Inc., Springfield, Massachusetts (1992), 220.

3. *Texas v. Johnson* (Flag-burning case) (1989) 491 US 397, 420–421.

4. Justice Robert Jackson, *West Virginia Board of Education v. Barnette* (1943) 319 U.S. 624, 638.

5. Justice Antonin Scalia, *CTS Corp. v. Dynamics Corp. of America,* (1987) 481, U.S. 69, 96, concurring opinion.

6. Martin Luther King, Jr., *Strength to Love,* 1963.

7. Paul Kiesel and Bryan Borys, "The Cost $avings of the Complex Civil Litigation Program," *California Courts Review,* Summer 2007: 16–21.

8. Chief Justice Earl Warren, "Recalled on His Death," *Time Magazine,* July 22, 1974.

Chapter 4

1. Profile of Judge Brian J. Lamb, *Los Angeles Daily Journal,* July 20, 2005: 1.

2. Faust, F.L., and Brantingham, P.J., *Juvenile Justice Philosophy*, West Publishing, St. Paul, Minnesota (1974), 145.

3. Adam Liptak, "Lifers As Teenagers, Now Seeking Second Chance," *Los Angeles Daily Journal*, October 18, 2007: 8.

4. For example, see Jorge Ramos, "Gang Killer Dons Dispassion In Face of His Own Horrors," *Los Angeles Daily Journal*, April 19, 2006: 8.

5. Herbert Schreier, MD, "Learning Disability and Juvenile Crime," *San Francisco Medicine*, February 2000: 22–23.

6. Diane Curtis, "An alternative to juvenile detention—that works," *California State Bar Journal*, February, 2007: 1, 7.

7. Michael Schumacher and Gwen A. Kurz, *The 8% Solution, Preventing Serious, Repeat Juvenile Crime*, Sage Publications, Inc., Thousand Oaks, California (2000), or for further information, contact Program Planning and Research Division, 909 N. Main Street, Santa Ana, California 92701, or call (714) 569–2140.

8. See Katharine Webster, "When Nonlawyers Protect the Interests of Children in Court," *Los Angeles Daily Journal*, December 27, 2006: 2. For further information, contact the national CASA organization at www.nationalcasa.org; e-mail at staff@nationalcasa.org; or telephone at (800) 628–3233.

9. Susan McRae, "Becoming Better Dads: Single Fathers Learn in Groups," *Los Angeles Daily Journal*, October 30, 2006: 1, 10.

10. Susan McRae, "Friendly Persuader: From Cranky to Consensus Builder," *Los Angeles Daily Journal*, February 26, 2007: 1, 8.

11. Christopher Morley, as quoted in *The Portable Curmudgeon*, compiled and edited by Jon Winokur, Penguin Books, New York, NY (1987): 191.

12. Leonard P. Edwards, "The Mediation Miracle," *California Courts Review*, Spring 2006: 17–20.

Inset: "The Significant Work of Juvenile and Family Courts"

1. Leonard P. Edwards, Judge of the Superior Court, Santa Clara, California, "Remarks of Judge Leonard P. Edwards," *Journal of the Center for Families, Children & the Courts*, Judicial Council of California, Volume 5, 2004: 170.

Inset: "When Single Mothers Are Sent to Jail, What Happens to the Children?"

1. Jeffrey A. Lowe, "Women Are the Prison System's Hidden Victims," *Los Angeles Daily Journal*, December 22, 2006: 6.

Chapter 5

1. *Brown v. Walter*, 62 F.2d 798, 800 (2d Cir. 1933).

2. Leonard S. Karpman, M.D., "Decriminalizing Disease and Disability," *San Francisco Medicine, The Journal of the San Francisco Medical Society*, February, 2000: 11, 12.

3. Wernher von Braun, in *Chicago Sun Times*, as quoted in *Merriam-Webster Dictionary of Quotations*, Merriam-Webster, Inc., Springfield, Massachusetts (1992), 46.

4. National Center for State Courts' Center for Jury Studies: "The State of the States Survey of Jury Improvement Efforts" (2006). Telephone: (800) 616–6109.

5. *The Supreme Court of California* (2003 edition), published by the Supreme Court of California: 12.

Inset: "Promoting a Positive State of Mind"

1. K. Connie Kang, "Exploring the links between spirituality, mental health," *Los Angeles Times*, November 4, 2006: B2.

Chapter 6

1. Sir Francis Bacon, "Of Judicature" Essays (1625).

2. Aeschylus, *The Eumenides*, 458 BCE.

3. See *McCartney v. Commission on Judicial Qualifications* (1974) 12 Cal.3d 249, 256; *Estate of Dupont* (1943) 60 Cal.App.2d 276, 290; and *People v. Carlucci* (1979) 23 Cal.3d 249, 256, which said that if questions remained in the judge's mind after counsel had finished their questioning, the judge "should affirmatively clarify matters in order that he may render the best possible informed verdict."

4. Seneca, *De Ira*, as quoted in *Merriam-Webster Dictionary of Quotations*, Merriam-Webster, Inc., Springfield, Massachusetts (1992), 223.

5. See Henry N. Butler, *Economic Analysis for Lawyers*, Carolina Academic Press, Durham, NC (1998).

6. Cynthia Garber, "Interview With Justice David Sills," *Orange County Trial Lawyer's Association's The Gavel*, April, 2006: 16, 17.

Chapter 7

1. Gabe Friedman, "Finding Out What Matters—Besides Money," *Los Angeles Daily Journal*, May 19, 2006: 1, 2.

2. Roger Fisher, William Ury, and Bruce Patton, *Getting to Yes: Negotiating Agreement Without Giving In*, Penguin Books, Second Edition, 1991.

3. U. S. Grant, *Personal Memoirs of U.S. Grant*, Webster & Co., New York (1885) Vol. 1: 29–30.

4. Robert M. Bramson, PhD, *Coping With Different People: The Proven-Effective Battle Plan That Has Helped Millions Deal With the Troublemakers in Their Lives at Home and at Work*, Bantam Doubleday Dell Publishing Group, Inc., New York (1981).

Chapter 8

1. John Hanusz, "Boston-Area Native Is Noted for His Plain Talk," *Los Angeles Daily Journal*, March 30, 2006: 1, 7.

2. Actually, as a practical matter that is not quite true. For many years the President has by tradition given great weight to the thoughts and recommendations of the senior U.S. Senator in his own political party in the particular state on the subject of nominations to the federal district court, to the degree that it is virtually that senator alone who makes the appointment instead of the President.

3. Matthew 7:1

4. Roger K. Warren, "Politicizing America's State Courts: Critical Challenges Facing the Judiciary," *California Courts Review*, Winter 2007: 6, 9–12.

5. Roy A. Schotland, "The Crocodile in the Bathtub," *California Courts Review*, Fall 2005: 10, 11.

6. Justice James D. Ward, Ret., "Abiding Public Critics," *California Courts Review*, Summer, 2006: 36.

7.Stephanie Simon, "Call of the West: Rein In the Judges," *Los Angeles Times*, Oct. 15, 2006: A1, 20.

8. Donna Domino, "Judges Stand Up for Judicial Independence," *Los Angeles Daily Journal*, September 13, 2005: 1, 5.

9. Our county district attorney has a program called Trial Attorney Partnership (TAP) in which an attorney can receive an intensive training program for one week and then work full-time as a prosecutor for eight weeks. During that period the attorney can file and try misdemeanor and juvenile court cases, argue motions, and appear in various pre-trial conferences. There are similar programs all around the country. For further information, visit www.da.ocgov.com, or telephone (714) 347–8413.

10. Marc Humbert, Associated Press, "Panel Recommends N.Y. Judge's Removal," *Los Angeles Daily Journal*, April 3, 2006: 4.

11. David M. Rothman, *California Judicial Conduct Handbook*, California Judges Association, Second Edition (1999): 5.

12. Cynthia Gray (no relation), "12 Judges Removed in 2006," *Judicial Conduct Reporter*, Winter, 2007: 1

13. See, for example, David M. Rothman, ibid.

14. See Pennsylvania Informal Opinion 6/16a/05

15. See New York Opinion 05-107, Nevada Opinion JE04-004, or New York Opinion 03-47.

16. See Pennsylvania Informal Opinion 7/29/02.

17. For further examples and information about these matters, see the Center for Judicial Ethics web site at www.ajs.org/ethics/eth_advis_comm_links.asp.

18. Maryland Opinion 05-11; Colorado Opinion 05-3; New York Opinion 03-12; Arkansas Opinion 05-1; and Kansas Opinion JE-131 (2005).

19. I myself have used an advice hotline on two occasions. The first time was back in 1992, when I was considering speaking out publicly against our country's failed policy of Drug Prohibition. In that case, after spending an entire lunch hour on a conference call with five fellow judges, they split down the middle: Two thought I could comment about a subject like this that so directly affected the administration of justice, two felt that it was not a good idea, and one could not make up his mind. So I went forward, after telling my presiding judge and my fellow judges of my intentions. Thereafter, the story received a large amount of attention, and about three weeks later I received a letter from the California Judicial Performance Commission that said words to the following effect: "Dear Judge Gray, by now you have no doubt seen speculation in the media that we are investigating the ethics of your making public statements about our nation's drug policy. This letter is simply to inform you that we are not." As you can imagine, that was a most welcome letter for me and my family to have received.

The second occasion was recently, after I saw a justice of our court of appeal review a published book and recommend that "everyone get a copy." In response, I inquired if it would be ethically permissible for a judge to give a cover endorsement of this book, and I was told that it was not. As a result, I did not pursue any judicial endorsements for this book.

Chapter 9

1. David Frost and Anthony Jay. *The English* (1968).

2. William Shakespeare, *Hamlet, Prince of Denmark*, Act I, Scene 2.

Chapter 10

1. For further information, contact the American Inns of Court at 1229 King Street, 2nd Floor, Alexandria, Virginia 22314; telephone (703) 684–3590; and e-mail: info@innsof court.org.

2. For further information about mock trial programs, visit www.nationalmocktrial.org.

3. For further information about peer or teen court programs, I suggest you put those terms into a web research engine for your local area, or call the Orange County, California, Constitutional Rights Foundation at (714) 259–1521.

4. See Jeffrey A. Lowe, "Parole Reform Holds Key to Fixing California's Prison Problems," *Los Angeles Daily Journal*, June 8, 2005: 6; Robin Abcarian, "First, Tiny Steps on Path to a Saner World," *Los Angeles Times*, October 8, 1995; Eric Harrison, "Mentors Put Young Criminals on Right Path," *Los Angeles Times*, May 28, 1995; and David Borsari and Will Mittendorf, "VIP Orange County Celebrates 25 Years of Mentoring Success," *Orange County Lawyer*, April, 2007: 18–21.

5. For further information about Volunteers in Parole, visit www.VIPMentors.org; contact VIP-Statewide@VIPMentors.org; write to VIP Mentors, 180 Howard Street, 9th Floor, San Francisco, CA, 94105; or call (877) 484–7462.

6. See "Stay in School Program," Santa Ana, California, Unified School District, Support Services Division, or call the Nicholas Academic Center at (714) 834–0521, or write 412 W. 4th St., Santa Ana, CA 92701.

7. Associated Press, "Judge Tosses Fertility Suits Against UC Irvine," *Los Angeles Daily Journal*, July 25, 2006: 2.

8. See, for example, California Rule of Court, Rule 1.150, which says, "Photographing, recording and broadcasting of courtroom proceedings may be permitted as circumscribed in this rule if executed in a manner that ensures that the fairness and dignity of the proceedings are not adversely affected."

9. Eric Black, "O'Connor Decries Attacks by Lawmakers on the Judiciary," *Los Angeles Daily Journal*, May 25, 2006: 4.

10. Ulysses S. Grant, First Inaugural address, March 4, 1869.

11. Justice John Paul Stevens, *Sony v. Universal City Studios*, (1984) 404 US 417, 456.

CONCLUSION

1. Kasie Hunt of Associated Press, "Prison Population Swells to 1 in Every 32 American Adults," *Los Angeles Daily Journal*, December 1, 2006: 4.

2. Francis X. Donnelly of the *Detroit News*, "As Their Numbers Grow, Aging Inmates Crowd Prisons. Should They Be Freed? States Wonder," *Los Angeles Daily Journal*, January 3, 2006: 10.

3. Ibid.

4. James Sterngold, "Half of State's Inmates Are Illiterate, Department Says," *Los Angeles Daily Journal*, December 28, 2006: 10.

5. See Professor Lori B. Andrews, *Black Power, White Blood: The Life and Times of Johnny Spain*, Temple University Press (2000), and Lige Dailey, Jr., "Reentry: Prospects for Postrelease Success," *Prison Masculinities*, edited by Don Sabo, Terry A. Kupers and Willie London, Temple University Press (2001), 255.

6. Joe Domanick, "Prison of our Own Making," *Los Angeles Times*, December 10, 2006: M4.

7. Erik Eckholm of New York Times News Service, "Rhode Island Aims to Bridge Gap Between Prison and the Life Outside," *Los Angeles Daily Journal*, August 15, 2006: 10.

8. Charles Dickens, *Bleak House*, Signet Classic, New York (1964): 19.

About the Author

Judge James P. Gray was raised in the Los Angeles area by his parents Elizabeth Polin Gray and U.S. District Judge William P. Gray. He graduated from John Muir High School in Pasadena, California; received his undergraduate degree at the University of California, Los Angeles (UCLA) in 1966; and obtained his law degree from the University of Southern California (USC) in 1971. Judge Gray also served with the Peace Corps in Palmar Norte, Costa Rica, where he taught physical education, recreation, and health from 1966 to 1968.

From 1972 until 1975, Judge Gray was a Staff Judge Advocate and criminal defense attorney for the U.S. Navy JAG Corps at U.S. Naval Air Station in Guam and the Naval Air station in Lemoore, California. While in the service, he was awarded National Defense, Vietnam Service, and Combat Action Ribbons.

For over three years, Judge Gray was a federal prosecutor with the United States Attorney's Office in Los Angeles, where he eventually headed a unit that prosecuted various frauds against the Federal Housing Administration (FHA), Veterans Administration (VA), and other agencies of the federal government.

At the end of 1978, Judge Gray began working in civil litigation in Century City and Newport Beach, California, with the law firm of Wyman, Bautzer, Rothman & Kuchel. Then he was appointed by Governor George Deukmejian to the Santa Ana Municipal Court in December of 1983. His efforts in trying to combat the major problem of the drinking driver and other alcohol-related offenses earned a commendation from the Orange County Board of Supervisors in 1990.

Judge Gray was elevated by Governor Deukmejian to the Orange County Superior Court in July of 1989. While serving with that court he received such awards as the 1992 "Judge of the Year" by the Business Litigation Section of the Orange County Bar Association; the 1995 "Judge of the Year" by the Orange County Constitutional Rights Foundation; and the Justice Gerald Le Dain Award for Jurisprudence from the Drug Policy Foundation. Judge Gray has also been a member of the California Judicial Council; the Alcohol Advisory Board to the Orange County Board of Supervisors; the Advisory Board to the California Department of Alcohol & Drug Programs; the Board of Directors of the Volunteer Center of Orange County, the Orange County Law Library, and the Orange County YMCA. And he has served as an instructor for the Orange County Bar Association's College of Trial Advocacy and as an elected member of the Executive Committee of the Orange County Superior Court.

In addition to the above listed positions and commitments, Judge Gray also has been the founding president of the William P. Gray Chapter of the American Inns of Court; a founder of the Former Assistant U.S. Attorney's Association in Los Angeles; a member of the Board of Councilors of the USC Law School; a member of the Committee on Juvenile Justice for the California Judicial Council; and a founder of Peer Court, which adjudicates real juvenile cases in numbers of Orange County's high schools using students as jurors. He has been awarded Honorary Doctorate of Law degrees from Western State University College of Law in 1994, and from Chapman University School of Law in 2007. Finally, Judge Gray took an unpaid leave of absence from the bench for a year on two occasions—one as a Republican candidate for U.S. Congress in 1998, and one as the Libertarian Party candidate for the U.S. Senate in 2004.

Outside of the courtroom and his role as judge, James P. Gray is married to Grace Walker Gray and has four children, including an adopted Vietnamese son. He is a member of the Methodist Church and lives in Newport Beach, California. Judge Gray is the author of *Why Our Drug Laws Have Failed and What We Can Do About It—A Judicial Indictment of the War on Drugs* (Temple University Press, 2001) and the composer of the musical *Americans All*, which is distributed by Heuer Publishing, LLC. He can be reached at JimPGray@sbcglobal.net, or at his blog at JudgeJimGray.JudgeJimGray.com.

Index